LIVING RELIGIONS
WESTERN TRADITIONS

LIVING RELIGIONS

WESTERN TRADITIONS

MARY PAT FISHER

SPECIALIST CONSULTANTS

Dr. Martin Forward, Aurora University Center for Faith and Action

Dr. Dvora Weisberg, Hebrew Union College

Dr. Amir Hussain, California State University at Northridge

Dr. Eugene Gallagher, Connecticut College

PRENTICE-HALL

Upper Saddle River, N.J. 07458

Published 2003 by Prentice-Hall Inc.
A Division of Pearson Education
Upper Saddle River, N.J. 07458

10 9 8 7 6 5 4 3 2 1

ISBN 0-13-182929-7

This book was designed and produced by
Laurence King Publishing Ltd, London
www.laurenceking.co.uk

The material in this volume is taken from *Living Religions* (5th edition),
copyright © Mary Pat Fisher, 2002
Acquisitions editors: Ross Miller (Prentice Hall) and
Melanie White (Laurence King Publishing)
Marketing manager: Clare Bitting
Project manager (5th edition): Jessica Spencer
Designer (5th edition): Richard Foenander
Picture researcher (5th edition): Bridget Tily
Maps: Andrea Fairbrass, Advanced Illustration Ltd, Cheshire
Typeset by Fakenham Photosetting, Norfolk

Printed in Hong Kong

Cover: *Sunset in Paradise* (detail), Philip Sutton (contemporary artist),
Private Collection/Bridgeman Art Library, London
Half title: Choir of the Bethel AME Church of Eastville, Virginia
Frontispiece: Sukkot celebrated at Western Wall, Jerusalem

CONTENTS

Unique FREE online resource for world religion!

www.prenhall.com/fisher

Prentice Hall's exclusive Companion Website™ that accompanies *Living Religion,* offers tools and support for teachers and students alike to learn more about world religion. Tied directly to the text, the Companion Website™ is a comprehensive online resource that features a variety of learning and teaching activities, including:

For Students:

- **Chapter learning objectives** that help students organize key concepts
- **Online quizzes** which include instant scoring and coaching
- **Writing activities** that foster critical thinking
- **Essay questions** that test students' critical thinking skills
- **Video essays** for many chapters, based on Quicktime™
- **Video clips** of important elements of that faith
- **Dynamic web links** that provide a valuable source of supplemental information
- **Communication tools** such as chat rooms and message boards to facilitate online collaboration and communication
- **Key word searches** that are easy to use and feature built-in search engines
- **Built-in routing** that offers students the ability to forward essay responses and graded quizzes to their instructors

For Instructors:

- **Syllabus Manager™** tool provides an easy-to-follow process for creating, posting, and revising a syllabus online that is accessible from any point within the companion website.
  Faculty resources: Located by chapter, instructors have access to the Instructor's manual which contains lecture outlines and material. Plus, most chapters have Powerpoint™ slides with maps and images for use in classroom presentations.

- **Faculty Resources** for each chapter offers lectures, detailed overviews, activities, and other resources for instructors. Also included are maps and images in Powerpoint™ format for use in classroom presentations.

Also new and available free on the Companion Website is eThemes of the New York Times! This up-to-date archive from the world's leading newspaper on current topics in religion will help students witness first-hand the relevance of religion in the 21st Century.

The Companion Website makes integrating online resources into your course exciting and easy! Join us online and enter a new world of teaching and learning.

PREFACE

Religion is not a museum piece. As the twenty-first century unfolds, religion is a vibrant force in the lives of many people around the world, and many religions are presently experiencing a renaissance.

Living Religions: Western Traditions is a sympathetic approach to what is living and significant in the world's major religious traditions that have originated in the West as well as in local indigenous religions and new religious movements. This book provides a clear and straightforward account of the development, doctrines, and practices of these faiths. The emphasis throughout is on the personal consciousness of believers and their own accounts of their religion and its relevance in contemporary life.

Special features

One of the unique features of this text is personal interviews with followers of each faith. This material provides interesting and informative first-person accounts of each religion as perceived from within the tradition. This volume includes special boxes featuring interviews with a Jewish holocaust survivor, a Southern Baptist Christian, who is now manager of a wilderness camp for inner-city youth, an Egyptian pharmacist, who returned to Islam because he learned to appreciate it from a scientific point of view, and a German follower of the Unification Movement. In addition, first-person accounts have been interwoven throughout the text.

Living Religions: Western Traditions also includes feature boxes on "Religion in Public Life." These portray the spiritual roots of selected followers of Western religions each of whom is making a significant contribution to modern society—Senator Joseph Lieberman, Archbishop Desmond M. Tutu, and Muslim scholar Farid Esack. In their stories, one recognizes that deep religiosity can go hand-in-hand with deep social commitment.

There are also feature boxes on "Religion in Practice," such as Mother Teresa's Missionaries of Charity, and "Teaching Stories," which can serve as take-off points for discussions about core values imbedded in each faith.

Violence perpetrated in the name of religion is often in the news these days. *Living Religions: Western*

Traditions includes probing discussions of this disturbing factor in the major Western religions and also in new religious movements. Distinctions are made between the basic teachings of religions, none of which condones wanton violence, and the ways in which religions have been politicized. There is extensive coverage of the socio-political context of the contemporary practice of religions, especially the changes that have come in the wake of the September 11, 2001 attacks in the United States.

Throughout the book, women's contributions and women's issues are carefully considered. Women's voices are woven into the discussions throughout, including those of female theologians who are bringing vital new perspectives to religious scholarship. African and African–American religious experiences are also of increasing interest, and these are extensively covered in this volume. There are poignant descriptions, for instance, of the lives of American Muslim converts who are trying to maintain traditional piety in the midst of modern materialistic society.

The opening chapter, "The Religious Response," brings critical scholarship to bear on underlying issues in the study of religion. Throughout the book the latest scholarship has been applied. The book incorporates extensive quotations from primary sources to give a direct perception of the thinking and flavor of each tradition. Particularly memorable brief quotations are set off in boxes.

One of the most engaging features of *Living Religions: Western Traditions* is its illustrations. I have been glad to have the chance to use 120 illustrations, 64 of them in color, to help bring religions to life. Narrative captions accompanying the illustrations offer additional insights into the characteristics and orientation of each tradition and the people who practice it.

Learning aids

I have tried to present each tradition clearly and without the clutter of less important names and dates. Key terms, defined and highlighted in boldface when they first appear, can also be found in an extensive glossary. Because students are often unfamiliar with terms from other cultures, useful guides to the pronunciation of words that may be unfamiliar are included in the glossary.

Maps are used throughout the text to give a sense of geographical reality to the historical discussions as well as to illustrate the present distribution of the religions. There is also a map of the missionary journeys undertaken by the apostle Paul in the chapter on Christianity. Timelines are used to recapitulate the historical development of the major religions up to the present.

I assume that readers will want to delve further into the literature. At the end of each chapter, therefore, I offer an annotated list of books that might be particularly interesting and useful in a deeper study of that religion.

Acknowledgments

The material in this volume is based on my well-received textbook on the religions of the world *Living Religions*, which has now gone through five editions. In order to try to understand each religion from the inside, I have traveled for many years to study and worship with devotees and teachers of all faiths and to interview them about their experience of their tradition. People of all religions also come to the Gobind Sadan Institute for Advanced Studies in Comparative Religions, where it is my good fortune to meet and speak with them about their spiritual experiences and beliefs.

In preparing the previous editions of *Living Religions*, I worked directly with consultants who are authorities in specific traditions and who offered detailed suggestions and resources. To prepare the material involved in the fifth edition, I was blessed with extraordinarily capable and helpful consultants: Dr. Dvora Weisberg of Hebrew Union College; Dr. Martin Forward, formerly of Cambridge University and now directing the Aurora University Center for Faith and Action; Dr. Amir Hussain of California State University at Northridge and Dr. Eugene Gallagher of Connecticut College. I am extremely grateful for their generous and enthusiastic help and for the assistance of the many scholars who served as consultants to the earlier editions of *Living Religions* and are specially acknowledged therein.

Living Religions has been extensively reviewed by professors who are teaching courses in world religions. Reviewers of the first edition included George Braswell, Southeastern Baptist Theological Seminary; Howard R. Burkle, Grinnell College; James Carse, New York University; Frances Cook, University of California; Ronald Flowers, Texas Christian University; Rita Gross, University of Wisconsin; Willard Johnson, San Diego State University; Anjum Khilji, Institute of Parapsychology at Durham Technical Community College; Dennis Klass, Webster University; Robert Minor, University of Kansas; Kusumita P. Pederson, New York University; Lynda Sexson, Montana State University; Paul Schwartz, San Francisco State University; Herb Smith, McPherson College. In addition, Reverend Stan Possell, Rabbi Steven Razin, Mohammad T. Mehdi, and Prajapati O'Neill read and commented on specific chapters.

Reviewers of the second edition included: Gary Alexander, University of Wisconsin; Howard R. Burkle, Grinnell College; Francis H. Cook, University of California (retired); Ronald B. Flowers, Texas Christian University; Eugene V. Gallagher, Connecticut College; John A. Grim, Bucknell University; Marcia K. Hermansen, San Diego State University; Wayne R. Husted, Penn State University; John P. Keenan, University of Pennsylvania; Lynn Ross-Bryant, University of Colorado; Larry D. Shinn, Bucknell University; H. Michael Simmons, Center for Zoroastrian Research; Maurine Stein, Prairie State College; James D. Tabor, University of North Carolina. In addition, Robert Carter of Trent University and Balkar Singh of Punjabi University at Patiala offered suggestions on the chapters on Shinto and Sikhism, respectively, and S. A. Ali of Hamdard University and R. P. Jain of Delhi were very helpful in guiding me to literature on Islam and Jainism.

Reviewers of the third edition included: William R. Goodman, Jr., Lynchburg College; Robert Imperato, Saint Leo College; Barbara Ring Kotowski, University of Texas at El Paso and El Paso Community College; Scott Lowe, University of North Dakota; Elizabeth Neumeyer, Kellogg Community College; Maurine Stein, Prairie State College. Lee Bailey of Ithaca College was also generous in his help. Many Russian scholars reviewed the text, and their comments were very helpful in preparing additions, particularly with concern to the contemporary and historical situations in the former Soviet Union.

Reviewers of the fourth edition included: Professor Philip C. Schmitz, Eastern Michigan University; Dr. Christopher S. Queen, Harvard University; Dr. Ted J. Solomon, Drake University; Dr. Nancy A. Hardesty, Clemson University; Dr. Krishna Mallik, Bentley College; Dr. Guy L. Beck,

College of Charleston; Dr. David Chappell, University of Hawaii at Manoa.

Reviewers for the fifth edition offered extremely detailed constructive suggestions. They include: Robert Imperato, Saint Leo University; Sallie King, James Madison University; Jonathan Brumberg-Kraus, Wheaton College; George Mummert, Moberly Area Community College; Bob Badra, Kalamazoo Valley Community College; Hugh Urban, Ohio State University; John Gilman, San Diego State University; David Suter, St. Martin's College; Jeffrey Brodd, California State University, Sacramento; Mark MacWilliams, St. Lawrence University; Mark Webb, Texas Technical University. Other people who have generously helped with source material for this edition include Rev. Marcus Braybrooke, Shivaprakash, Dr. M. A. Pradhani, Marianne Vandiver, Michelle Brand, Galina Ermolina, Edward Fisher, Vladimir Sova, William Beeman, Yale Partlow, Alexandra Engel, Jean Armour Polly, Wolfgang Hecker, G. Gispert-Sauch, S.J., Mohammed Rafiq Shariq Warsi, and Swami Dharmanand.

As always, Laurence King Publishing has provided me with excellent editorial help. Melanie White and Jessica Spencer have guided this edition through its development and production with loving and patient skill, and Bridget Tily has worked very hard to track down the many new illustrations I requested.

Finally, I cannot adequately express my gratitude to my own revered teacher, Baba Virsa Singh of Gobind Sadan. People of all faiths from all over the world come to him for his spiritual blessings and guidance. In the midst of sectarian conflicts, his place is an oasis of peace and harmony. Now more than ever, we are learning from Babaji to regard each other as members of one human family. May God bless us all to move in this direction.

Mary Pat Fisher
Gobind Sadan Institute for Advanced Studies
in Comparative Religion, New Delhi

CHAPTER 1

THE RELIGIOUS RESPONSE

Before sunrise, members of a Muslim family rise in Malaysia, perform their purifying ablutions, spread their prayer rugs facing Mecca, and begin their prostrations and prayers to Allah. In a French cathedral, worshippers line up for their turn to have a priest place a wafer on their tongue, murmuring, "This is the body of Christ." In a South Indian village, a group of women reverently anoint a cylindrical stone with milk and fragrant sandalwood paste and place around it offerings of flowers. The monks of a Japanese Zen Buddhist monastery sit cross-legged and upright in utter silence, broken occasionally by the noise of the *kyosaku* bat falling on their shoulders. On a mountain in Mexico, men, women, and children who have been dancing without food or water for days greet an eagle flying overhead with a burst of whistling from the small wooden flutes they wear around their necks. After the terrorist attacks on the World Trade Center in New York, there is a common response everywhere: People gather for prayer.

These and countless other moments in the lives of people around the world are threads of the tapestry we call "religion." The word is probably derived from the Latin, meaning "to tie back," "to tie again." All of religion shares the goal of tying people back to something behind the surface of life—a greater reality, which lies beyond, or invisibly infuses, the world that we can perceive with our five senses.

Attempts to connect with this greater reality have taken many forms. Many of them are organized institutions, such as Buddhism or Christianity, with leaders, sacred scriptures, beliefs, rituals, ethics, spiritual practices, cultural components, and historical traditions. Others are private personal experiences of individuals who belong to no institutionalized religion but nonetheless have an inner life of prayer, meditation, or direct experience of an inexplicable presence.

In this introductory chapter, we will try to develop some understanding of religion in a generic sense—why it exists, its encounters with modern science, and what general forms it takes—before studying the characteristics of the particular group religions that are practiced today.

Why are there religions?

In many cultures and times, religion has been the basic foundation of life, permeating all aspects of human existence. But from the time of the European Enlightenment, there has been a Western tendency to regard religion as a separate compartment of human life. Travelers brought the news that religious

behaviors of various sorts could be found everywhere that there are people, trig-
gering attempts to explain their origin. Religion has become an object to be
studied, rather than an unquestioned basic fact of life. Cultural anthropologists,
sociologists, philosophers, psychologists, and even biologists have peered at
religion through their own particular lenses, trying to explain what religion is and
why it exists, to those who no longer take it for granted. In the following pages
we will briefly examine some of the major theories that have evolved.

From candles and oil lamps to sacred fires, light is universally used to remind worshippers of an invisible reality. At Gobind Sadan, outside New Delhi, worship at a sacred fire continues twenty-four hours a day.

Materialistic perspective: humans invented religion

During the past two centuries, scientific **materialism** gained considerable prominence as a theory to explain the fact that religion can be found in some form in
every culture around the world. The materialistic point of view is that the supernatural is imaginary; only the material world exists. From this point of view, religions have been invented by humans.

An influential example of this perspective can be found in the work of the
nineteenth-century philosopher Ludwig Feuerbach (1804–1872). He reasoned
that there are no supernatural entities; deities are simply projections, objectifica-
tions of people's fears and desires. What we can neither understand nor control,
we fear; thus, according to Feuerbach, people living close to the land made gods
of the most fearsome aspects of nature, such as lightning and death.

Following this line of reasoning, twentieth-century psychoanalyst Sigmund
Freud described religion as a collective fantasy, a "universal obsessional neurosis"—a cosmic projection and replaying of the loving and fearful relationships
that we had (and have) with our parents. Religious belief gives us an external
God who is so powerful that He or She can protect us from the terrors of life, and
will reward or punish us for obedience or nonobedience to social norms. From

Some religions try to transcend the mundane, glimpsing what lies beyond. Others, such as the Zen Buddhism that influenced this 18th-century drawing of The Meditating Frog, *find ultimate reality in the here and now, intensely experienced.*

Freud's extremely sceptical point of view, religious belief is an illusion springing from people's infantile insecurity and neurotic guilt; as such it closely resembles mental illness.

Others believe that religions have been created or at least used to manipulate people. Historically, religions have often supported and served centers of secular power. The nineteenth-century socialist philosopher Karl Marx argued that a culture's religion—as well as all other aspects of its social structure—springs from its economic framework. In Marx's view, religion's origins lie in the longings of those who suffer from oppression. It may have developed from the desire to revolutionize society and combat exploitation, but in failing to do so, it became otherworldly, an expression of unfilled desires for a better, more satisfying life:

> *Man makes religion: religion does not make man. . . . The religious world is but the reflex of the real world. . . . Religion is the sigh of the oppressed creature, the sentiment of a heartless world, and the soul of soulless conditions. It is the opium of the people. . . .*[1]

According to Marx, not only do religions pacify people falsely; they may themselves become tools of oppression. He observed that religious authorities claim to possess absolute truth and then permit that claim to be wielded as a weapon by social and political forces. For instance, he charged Christian authorities of his times with supporting "vile acts of the oppressors" by explaining them as due punishment of sinners by God. Other critics have made similar complaints against Eastern religions that blame the sufferings of the poor on their own misdeeds in their previous lives. Such interpretations and uses of religious teachings lessen the perceived need for society to help those who are oppressed and suffering. Marx's ideas thus led toward atheistic communism, for he had asserted, "The abolition of religion as the *illusory* happiness of the people is required for their real happiness."[2]

Functional perspective: religion is useful

Another line of reasoning has emerged in the search for a theory explaining the universal existence of religions: They are found everywhere because they are useful.

Pioneering work in this area was done by French sociologist Emile Durkheim (1858–1917). He proposed that humans cannot live without organized social structures, and that religion is a glue that holds a society together. He attempted to analyze Australian tribal religions, assuming them to be as simple as the material culture of their practitioners, to show the relationship between beliefs and group life. From this effort, he deduced a definition of religion, as "a unified system of beliefs and practices relative to sacred things, that is to say, things set apart and forbidden—beliefs and practices which unite into one single moral community called a church, all those who adhere to them."[3] To Durkheim, religious phenomena were symbols and reinforcers of the social order.

This kind of thinking about religion as functional system persists to today. John Bowker, author of the 1995 book *Is God a Virus?*, asserts that religions are organized systems that serve the essential biological purpose of bringing people together for their common survival, as well as giving their lives a sense of meaning. To Bowker, religion is universal because it protects gene replication and the nurturing of children. He proposes that because of its survival value, the potential for religiosity may even be genetically inherent in human brains.

The twentieth-century psychoanalyst Erich Fromm (1900–1980) looked at the usefulness of religion for individuals and concluded that humans have a need for a stable frame of reference, and that religion fulfills this need. As Mata Amritanandamayi, a contemporary Indian spiritual teacher, explains:

> *Faith in God gives one the mental strength needed to confront the problems of life. Faith in the existence of God is a protective force. It makes one feel safe and protected from all the evil influences of the world. To have faith in the existence of a Supreme Power and to live accordingly is a religion. When we become religious, morality arises, which, in turn, will help to keep us away from malevolent influences. We won't drink, we won't smoke, and we will stop wasting our energy through unnecessary gossip and talk. . . . We will also develop qualities like love, compassion, patience, mental equipoise, and other positive traits. These will help us to love and serve everyone equally. . . . Where there is faith, there is harmony, unity and love. A nonbeliever always doubts. . . . He cannot be at peace; he's restless. . . . The foundation of his entire life is unstable and scattered due to his lack of faith in a higher principle.*[4]

Research conducted by the Center for the Study of Religion/Spirituality and Health at Duke University indicates that religious faith is also beneficial for our physical health. They have found that those who attend religious services or read scriptures frequently are significantly longer lived, less likely to be depressed, less likely to have high blood pressure, and nearly ninety percent less likely to smoke.

Many of our psychological needs are not met by the material aspects of our life on earth. For example, we have difficulty accepting the commonsense notion that this life is all there is. We are born, we struggle to support ourselves, we age, and we die. If we believe that there is nothing more, fear of death may inhibit enjoyment of life and make all human actions seem pointless. Confronting mortality is so basic to the spiritual life that, as the Christian monk Brother David Steindl-Rast observes, whenever monks from any spiritual tradition meet, within five minutes they are talking about death.

> *It appears that throughout the world man has always been seeking something beyond his own death, beyond his own problems, something that will be enduring, true and timeless. He has called it God, he has given it many names; and most of us believe in something of that kind, without ever actually experiencing it.*
>
> *Jiddu Krishnamurti[5]*

Many of us seek an assurance that life continues in some form beyond the grave. But we may also want this present life to have some meaning. For many, the desire for material achievement offers a temporary sense of

The Golden Temple in Amritsar, India. Religious edifices attempt to reflect the sacred realm.

purposefulness. But once achieved, these material goals may seem hollow. The Buddha said:

> *Look!*
> *The world is a royal chariot, glittering with paint.*
> *No better.*
> *   Fools are deceived, but the wise know better.*[6]

All religions help to uncover meaning in the midst of the mundane. The influential twentieth-century scholar of comparative religion, Mircea Eliade (1907–1986), wrote of the distinction between the **profane**—the everyday world of seemingly random, ordinary, and unimportant occurrences—and the **sacred**—the realm of the extraordinary and supernatural, the source of the universe and its values, which is charged with significance. Religions open pathways to the sacred by exploring the **transpersonal** dimension of life—the eternal and infinite, beyond limited personal or communal concerns.

Religions propose ideals that can radically transform people. Mahatma Gandhi was an extremely shy, fearful, self-conscious child. His transformation into one of the great political figures of our time occurred as he meditated single-mindedly on the great Hindu scripture, the ***Bhagavad-Gita***. Gandhi was particularly impressed by the second chapter, which he says was "inscribed on the tablet of my heart."[7] It reads, in part:

> *He is forever free who has broken*
> *Out of the ego-cage of* I *and* mine
> *To be united with the Lord of Love.*
> *This is the supreme state. Attain thou this*
> *And pass from death to immortality.*[8]

People long to gain strength for dealing with personal problems. Those who are suffering severe physical illness, privation, terror, or grief often turn to the divine for help. Agnes Collard, a Christian woman near death from four painful years of cancer, reported that her impending death was bringing her closer to God:

> *I don't know what or who He is, but I am almost sure He is there. I feel His*
> *presence, feel that He is close to me during the awful moments. And I feel love.*
> *I sometimes feel wrapped, cocooned in love.*[9]

Religious literature is full of stories of miraculous aid that has come to those who have cried out in their need. Rather than what is construed as divine intervention, sometimes help comes as the strength and philosophy to accept burdens. The eighteenth-century Hasidic Jewish master known as the Baal Shem Tov (c. 1700–1760) taught that the vicissitudes of life are ways of climbing toward the divine. Islam teaches patience, faithful waiting for the unfailing grace of Allah. Despite his own trials, the Christian apostle Paul wrote of "the peace of God, which passeth all understanding."[10] Gandhi was blissful in prison, for no human could bar his relationship with the Lord of Love.

Rather than seeking help from without, an alternative approach is to gain freedom from problems by changing our ways of thinking. According to some Eastern religions, the concept that we are distinct, autonomous individuals is an illusion;

what we think of as "our" consciousnesses and "our" bodies are in perpetual flux. From this point of view, freedom from problems lies in recognizing and accepting the reality of temporal change and devaluing the "small self" in favor of the eternal self. The ancient sages of India referred to it as "This eternal being that can never be proved, . . . spotless, beyond the ether, the unborn Self, great and eternal, . . . the creator, the maker of everything."[11]

Many contemplative spiritual traditions teach methods of turning within to discover and eradicate all attachments, desires, and resentments associated with the small earthly self, revealing the purity of the eternal self. Once we have found it within, we begin to see it wherever we look. This realization brings a sense of acceptance in which, as philosopher William James observed:

> *Dull submission is left far behind, and a mood of welcome, which may fill any place on the scale between cheerful serenity and enthusiastic gladness, has taken its place.[12]*

Kabir, a fifteenth-century Indian weaver who was inspired alike by Islam and Hinduism and whose words are included in Sikh scripture, described this state of spiritual bliss:

> *The blue sky opens out farther and farther,*
> *the daily sense of failure goes away,*
> *the damage I have done to myself fades,*
> *a million suns come forward with light,*
> *when I sit firmly in that world.[13]*

Some people feel that their true selves are part of that world of light, dimly remembered, and long to return to it. The nineteenth-century Romantic poet William Wordsworth wrote:

> *Our birth is but a sleep and a forgetting;*
> *The Soul that rises with us, our life's Star*
> *   Hath had elsewhere its setting*
> *   And cometh from afar;*
> *   Not in entire forgetfulness,*
> *   And not in utter nakedness,*
> *But trailing clouds of glory do we come*
> *   From God, who is our home.[14]*

We look to religions for understanding, for answers to our many questions about life. Who are we? Why are we here? What happens after we die? Why is there suffering? Why is there evil? Is anybody up there listening? For those who find security in specific answers, some religions offer **dogma**—systems of doctrines proclaimed as absolutely true and accepted as such, even if they lie beyond the domain of one's personal experiences. Absolute faith provides some people with a sense of relief from anxieties, a secure feeling of rootedness, meaning, and orderliness in the midst of rapid social change. Religions may also provide rules for living, governing everything from diet to personal relationships. Such prescriptions are seen as earthly reflections of the order that prevails in the cosmos. Some religions, however, encourage people to explore the perennial questions by themselves, and to live in the uncertainties of not knowing intellectually, breaking through old concepts until nothing remains but truth itself.

A final need that draws some people to religion is the discomforting sense of being alone in the universe. This isolation can be painful, even terrifying. The divine may be sought as a loving father or mother, or as a friend. Alternatively, some paths offer the way of self-transcendence. Through them, the sense of isolation is lost in mystical merger with the One Being, with Reality itself.

Faith perspective: Ultimate Reality exists

From the point of view of religious faith, there truly is an underlying reality that cannot readily be perceived but that some people in all cultures have experienced. Human responses to this Supreme Reality have been expressed and institutionalized as the structures of religions.

Religious belief often springs from mystical experience—the overwhelming awareness that one has been touched by a reality that far transcends ordinary life. Those who have had such experiences find it hard to describe them, for what has touched them lies beyond the world of time and space to which our languages refer. These people usually know instantly and beyond a shadow of doubt that they have had a brush with spiritual reality. Pierre Teilhard de Chardin (1881–1955), a highly respected French paleontologist and Jesuit priest, became convinced that God is "the heart of All" because of his fiery personal encounters with "the unique Life of all things."[15] George William Russell (1867–1935), an Irish writer who described his mystical experiences under the pen name "AE," was lying on a hillside:

> not then thinking of anything but the sunlight, and how sweet it was to drowse there, when, suddenly, I felt a fiery heart throb, and knew it was personal and intimate, and started with every sense dilated and intent, and turned inwards, and I heard first a music as of bells going away ... and then the heart of the hills was opened to me, and I knew there was no hill for those who were there, and they were unconscious of the ponderous mountain piled above the palaces of light, and the winds were sparkling and diamond clear, yet full of colour as an opal, as they glittered through the valley, and I knew the Golden Age was all about me, and it was we who had been blind to it but that it had never passed away from the world.[16]

Encounters with a **transcendent** reality are given various names in spiritual traditions: enlightenment, God-realization, illumination, **kensho**, awakening, self-knowledge, **gnosis**, ecstatic communion, coming home. They may arise spontaneously, as in near-death experiences in which people seem to find themselves in a world of unearthly radiance, or may be induced by meditation, fasting, prayer, chanting, drugs, or dancing. To the frustration of many who now try these techniques in search of enlightenment without seeing immediate results, it seems that we cannot grasp the Ultimate Reality solely by our own efforts. Rather, it grasps us.

This spontaneous experience of being grasped by Reality is the essential basis of religion, according to the influential German professor of theology, Rudolf Otto (1869–1937). The experience is ineffable, "*sui generis* and irreducible to any other;

The existential loneliness some feel is hauntingly depicted by the sculptures of Alberto Giacometti, such as his Walking Man, c. 1947–48.

and therefore, like every absolutely primary and elementary dictum, while it admits of being discussed, it cannot be strictly defined."[17] This experience of the Holy, asserts Otto, brings forth two general responses in a person: a feeling of great awe or even dread, and a feeling of great attraction. These responses, in turn, have given rise to the whole gamut of religious beliefs and behaviors.

Though ineffable, the nature of genuine religious experience is not unpredictable, according to the research of Joachim Wach (1898–1955), a German scholar of comparative religion. In every religion, it seems to follow a certain pattern: (1) It is an experience of what is considered Ultimate Reality; (2) It involves the person's whole being; (3) It is the most shattering and intense of all human experiences; and (4) It motivates the person to action, through worship, ethical behavior, service, and sharing with others in a religious grouping.

These predictable, if dramatic and transformative, results cannot be rigidly schematized, however, according to the Canadian scholar, Wilfred Cantwell Smith (1917–2000). He asserted that what are commonly called "religions" are themselves elusive, complex systems that do not fit neatly into labeled, reified categories such as "Hinduism" and "Christianity." And the experiential basis of religion means that it cannot be fully described and analyzed as an object. Smith proposed: "Fundamentally it is the outsider who names a religious system. . . . The participant is concerned with God; the observer has been concerned with 'religion.' "[18]

A sense of the presence of the Great Unnamable may burst through the seeming ordinariness of life. (Samuel Palmer, The Waterfalls, Pistyll Mawddach, North Wales, 1835–36.)

> *[The "flash of illumination" brings] a state of glorious inspiration, exaltation, intense joy, a piercingly sweet realization that the whole of life is fundamentally right and that it knows what it's doing.*
>
> *Nona Coxhead*[19]

Modes of encountering Ultimate Reality

We have two basic ways of apprehending reality: rational thought and non-rational modes of knowing. To reason is to establish abstract general categories from the data we have gathered with our senses, and then to organize these abstractions to formulate seemingly logical ideas about reality. Reason may lead different people to different conclusions, however. The seventeenth-century English rationalist philosopher Thomas Hobbes (1588–1679) reasoned that God is simply an idea constructed by the human imagination from ideas of the visible world. His contemporary, the rationalist French philosopher René Descartes (1596–1650), asserted that his awareness of his own existence and his internal reasoning were indications of the existence of God.

Some people come to religious convictions indirectly, through belief in what has been uttered by great religious figures or what has been established as doctrine by religious tradition. Other people develop faith only after their own questions have been answered. Martin Luther, father of the Protestant branches of Christianity, recounted how he searched for faith in God through storms of doubt, "raged with a fierce and agitated conscience."[20]

The human mind does not function in the rational mode alone; there are differing modes of consciousness. In his classic study, *The Varieties of Religious Experience*, William James concluded:

> *Our normal waking consciousness, rational consciousness as we call it, is but one special type of consciousness, whilst all about it, parted from it by the flimsiest of screens, there lie potential forms of consciousness entirely different . . .*
>
> *No account of the universe in its totality can be final which leaves these other forms of consciousness quite disregarded.*[21]

In some religions, people are encouraged to develop their own intuitive abilities to perceive spiritual truths directly, beyond the senses, beyond the limits of human reason, beyond blind belief. This way is often called **mysticism**. In the ancient *Upanishads* (teachings given by great Indian masters of meditation to their students), the pupils are urged to sit in deep meditation and, with their minds fully absorbed in love, direct their consciousness toward the eternal One. In indigenous traditions, people may be taught to undergo austerities and then cry out for a sacred vision from the unseen to help guide their actions.

Many religions have developed meditation techniques that encourage intuitive wisdom to rise from the depths—or the voice of the divine to descend into individual consciousness. Whether this wisdom is perceived as a natural faculty within or an external voice, the process is similar. The consciousness is initially turned away from the world and even from one's own feelings and thoughts, letting them all go. Often a concentration practice, such as watching the breath or

staring at a candle flame, is used to collect the awareness into a single, unfragmented focus. Once the mind is quiet, distinctions between inside and outside drop away. The seer becomes one with the seen, in a fusion of subject and object through which the inner nature of things often seems to reveal itself.

Our ordinary experience of the world is that our self is separate from the world of objects that we perceive. But this dualistic understanding may be transcended in a moment of enlightenment in which the Real and our awareness of it become one. The *Mundaka Upanishad* says, "Lose thyself in the Eternal, even as the arrow is lost in the target." For the Hindu, this is the prized attainment of *moksha*, or liberation, in which one enters into awareness of the eternal reality known as **Brahman**. This reality is then known with the same direct apprehension with which one knows oneself. The Sufi Muslim mystic Abu Yazid said, "I sloughed off my self as a snake sloughs off its skin, and I looked into my essence and saw that 'I am He.' "[22]

This enlightened awareness cannot be communicated to those who have not had a similar experience, although our sacred literature is full of attempts to do so. Neither human language nor human logic, both of which deal with the experience of a world of separate forms, is adequate to describe the unitary experience of Ultimate Reality.

Understandings of Ultimate Reality

Approached by different ways of knowing, by different people, from different times and different cultures, the sacred has many faces. The Ultimate Reality may be conceived as **immanent** (present in the world) or transcendent (existing above and outside of the material universe). Many people perceive the sacred as a personal being, as Father, Mother, Teacher, Friend, Beloved, or as a specific deity. Religions based on one's relationship to the Divine Being are called **theistic**. If the being is worshipped as a singular form, the religion is **monotheistic**. If many attributes and forms of the divine are emphasized, the religion may be labeled **polytheistic**. Religions that hold that beneath the multiplicity of apparent forms there is one underlying substance are called **monistic**.

Ultimate Reality may also be conceived in **nontheistic** terms. It may be experienced as a "changeless Unity," as "Suchness," or simply as "the Way." There may be no sense of a personal Creator God in such understandings.

Some people believe that the sacred reality is usually invisible but occasionally appears visibly in human **incarnations**, such as Christ or Krishna, or in special manifestations, such as the flame Moses reportedly saw coming from the center of a bush but not consuming it. Or the deity that cannot be seen is described in human terms. Theologian Sallie McFague thus writes of God as "lover" by imputing human feelings to God:

God as lover is the one who loves the world not with the fingertips but totally and passionately, taking pleasure in its variety and richness, finding it attractive and valuable, delighting in its fulfilment. God as lover is the moving power of love in the universe, the desire for unity with all the beloved.[23]

Opposite *Many religions use ritual cleansing with water to help remove inner filth that obscures awareness of Ultimate Reality.*

Throughout history, there have been religious authorities who have claimed that the deity they worship is the true one and that all others are worshipping false gods. They have labeled others as "pagans" or "nonbelievers." For their part, the others apply similar negative epithets to them. When these rigid positions are taken, often to the point of violent conflicts or forced conversions, there is no room to consider the possibility that all may be talking about the same indescribable thing in different languages or referring to different aspects of the same unknowable Whole.

Atheism is the belief that there is no deity. Following Karl Marx, many communist countries in the twentieth century discouraged or suppressed religious beliefs, attempting to replace them with secular faith in supposedly altruistic government. The distinguished Protestant theologian Reinhold Niebuhr (1892–1971) described atheistic communism as "an irreligion transmuted into a new political religion, canonized precisely in the writings of Marx (and the later Lenin) as sacred scripture" with Marx cast as "the revered prophet of a new world religion."[24] It was not uncommon for people of all faiths in all continents of the world to embrace as a new religion of sorts Marx's message of collectivism in contrast to the dehumanizing effects of modern industry and capitalism, and with it, his stinging criticism of oppression of the people in the name of religion.

Atheism may also arise from within, in those whose experiences give them no reason to believe that there is anything more to life than the mundane. One American college student articulates a common modern form of unwilling atheism:

> To be a citizen of the modern, industrialized world with its scientific worldview is to be, to a certain extent, an atheist. I myself do not want to be an atheist; the cold mechanical worldview is repugnant to my need for the warmth and meaning that comes from God. But as I have been educated in the secular, scientistic educational system—where God is absent but atoms and molecules and genes and cells and presidents and kings are the factors to be reckoned with, the powers of this world, not a divine plan or a divine force as my ancestors must have believed—I cannot wholly believe in God.[25]

Agnosticism is not the denial of the divine but the feeling, "I don't know whether it exists or not," or the belief that if it exists it is impossible for humans to know it. Religious scepticism has been a current in Western thought since classical times; it was given the name "agnosticism" in the nineteenth century by T. H. Huxley, who stated its basic principles as a denial of metaphysical beliefs and of most (in his case) Christian beliefs since they are unproven or unprovable, and their replacement with scientific method for examining facts and experiences.

These categories are not mutually exclusive, so attempts to apply the labels can sometimes confuse us rather than help us understand religions. In some polytheistic traditions there is a hierarchy of gods and goddesses with one highest being at the top. In Hinduism, each individual deity is understood as an embodiment of all aspects of the divine. In the paradoxes that occur when we try to apply human logic and language to that which transcends rational thought, a person may believe that God is both a highly personal being and also present in all things. An agnostic may be deeply committed to moral principles. Or mystics may have personal encounters with the divine and yet find it so unspeakable that they say it is beyond human knowing. The Jewish scholar Maimonides (1135–1204) asserted that:

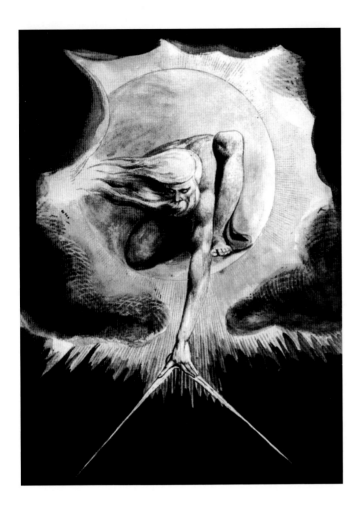

The concept of God as an old man with a beard who rules the world from the sky has been supported by the art of patriarchal monotheistic traditions, such as William Blake's frontispiece to "Europe," The Act of Creation, *1794.*

the human mind cannot comprehend God. Only God can know Himself. The only form of comprehension of God we can have is to realize how futile it is to try to comprehend Him.[26]

Jaap Sahib, the great hymn of praises of God by the Tenth Sikh Guru, Guru Gobind Singh, consists largely of the negative attributes of God, such as these:

Salutations to the One without colour or hue,
Salutations to the One who hath no beginning.
Salutations to the Impenetrable,
Salutations to the Unfathomable ...
O Lord, Thou art Formless and Peerless
Beyond birth and physical elements. ...
Salutations to the One beyond confines of religion. ...
Beyond description and Garbless
Thou art Nameless and Desireless.
Thou art beyond thought and ever Mysterious.[27]

Some people believe that the aspect of the divine that has revealed itself to them is the only one. Others feel that there is one being with many faces, that all religions come from one source. Father Bede Griffiths, a Catholic monk who lived in a community in India, attempting to unite Eastern and Western traditions, was among those who feel that if we engage in a deep study of all religions we will find their common ground:

> *In each tradition the one divine Reality, the one eternal Truth, is present, but it is hidden under symbols. . . . Always the divine Mystery is hidden under a veil, but each revelation (or "unveiling") unveils some aspect of the one Truth, or, if you like, the veil becomes thinner at a certain point. The Semitic religions, Judaism and Islam, reveal the transcendent aspect of the divine Mystery with incomparable power. The oriental religions reveal the divine Immanence with immeasurable depth. Yet in each the opposite aspect is contained, though in a more hidden way.*[28]

Worship, symbol, and myth

No matter how believers conceive of the Ultimate Reality, it inspires their reverence. The outer forms of religions consist in large part of human attempts to express this reverence and perhaps enter the sacred state of communion with that which is worshipped. Around the world, rituals, sacraments, prayers, and spiritual practices are used to create a sacred atmosphere or state of consciousness in which people hope to touch or be touched by whispers of the eternal.

> *Our religious ceremonies are but the shadows of that great universal worship celebrated in the heavens by the legions of heavenly beings on all planes, and our prayers drill a channel across this mist separating our earthbound plane from the celestial ones through which a communication may be established with the powers that be.*
>
> Pir Vilayat Inayat Khan[29]

Group ceremonies often include sharing of food, fire or candles, purification with water, flowers, fragrances, and offerings of some sort. When such worshipful actions are predictable and repeated rather than spontaneous, they are known as **rituals**. Religious rituals usually involve repetition, specific intentions, patterned performance, traditional meanings, and purposefulness. In reference to offerings, Professor Antony Fernando of Sri Lanka explains:

> *Even the most illiterate person knows that in actual fact no god really picks up those offerings or is actually in need of them. What people offer is what they own. Whatever is owned becomes so close to the heart of the owner as to become an almost integral part of his or her life. Therefore, when people offer something, it is, as it were, themselves they offer. . . . Sacrifices and offerings are a dramatic way of proclaiming that they are not the ultimate possessors of their life and also of articulating their determination to live duty-oriented lives and not desire-oriented lives.*[30]

What religions attempt to approach is beyond human utterance. Believers build statues and buildings through which to worship the divine, but these forms are not the divine itself. Because people are addressing the invisible, it can be suggested only through metaphor. Deepest consciousness cannot speak the language of everyday life; what it knows can be suggested only in **symbols**—images borrowed from the material world that are similar to ineffable spiritual experiences. They appeal to the emotions and imagination rather than to the rational mind.

Many peoples have used similar images to represent similar sacred meanings. The sun, for example, is frequently honored as a symbol of the divine because of its radiance; the sky is the abode of many gods, for it is elevated above the earth. A vertical symbol placed at the center of the world—such as a pillar, tree, or mountain—appears in many cultures as a symbol of a basic holy connection between the earthly plane and the unseen heavenly planes.

Myths are stories based on symbols. Religious myths attempt to express ultimate divine reality, basic truths, or the inner meaning of life for believers. A primary function of religious myth is to establish models for human behavior. Stories about the heroic lives of the great founders and saints are held up as examples for molding one's own life. They also establish belief in a superhuman

This symbolic representation of a World Tree comes from 18th-century Iran. It is conceived as a tree in Paradise, about which the Prophet Muhammad reportedly said, "God planted it with His own hand and breathed His spirit into it."

dimension to these lives. Great holy figures are often said to have been born of virgin mothers, for instance, for their seminal source is not human but rather the Invisible One. There are also myths of **cosmogony** (sacred accounts of the creation of the world) and of **eschatology** (beliefs concerning the purported end of the world). These myths form a sacred belief structure that supports the laws, rituals, and institutions of the religion, as well as explaining the cosmic situation and the ways of the community.

While believers may perceive myths and invisible beings as real facts, it is now common for scholars to interpret them metaphorically rather than literally and to see them as serving functions for the society or the individual. For example, the American mythologist Joseph Campbell (1904–1987) speculated that the sacred myths of a group serve basic social purposes: awakening a sense of wonder at creation, incorporating the group's ethical codes, and helping individuals pass harmoniously through life-cycle changes. Following psychoanalyst Carl Jung's lead, Campbell interpreted legends of the hero's journey (stories of separation, initiation, and return bearing truth to the people) as a form of psychological instruction for individuals:

> It is the business of mythology to reveal the specific dangers and techniques of the dark interior way from tragedy to comedy. Hence the incidents are fantastic and "unreal": they represent psychological, not physical, triumphs. The passage of the mythological hero may be overground, [but] fundamentally it is inward—into depths where obscure resistances are overcome, and long lost, forgotten powers are revivified, to be made available for the transfiguration of the world.[31]

Absolutist and liberal interpretations

Within each faith people often have different ways of interpreting their traditions. The **orthodox** stand by an historical form of their religion. They try to be strict followers of its established practices, laws, and creeds. Those who try to resist contemporary influences and affirm what they perceive as the historical core of their religion could be called **absolutists**. In our times, many people feel that their distinctive identity as individuals or as members of an established group is threatened by the sweeping social changes brought by modern industrial culture. The breakup of family relationships, loss of geographic rootedness, decay of clear behavioral codes, and loss of local control may be very unsettling. To find stable footing, some people may try to stand on selected religious doctrines or practices from the past. Religious leaders may encourage this trend toward rigidity by declaring themselves absolute authorities or by telling the people that their scriptures are literally and exclusively true. They may encourage antipathy or even violence against people of other religious traditions.

The term **fundamentalism** is often applied to this selective insistence on parts of a religious tradition and to violence against people of other religions. This use of the term is misleading, for no religion is based on hatred of other people and because those who are labeled "fundamentalists" may not be engaged in a return to the true basics of their religion. A Muslim "fundamentalist" who insists on the veiling of women, for instance, does not draw this doctrine from the foundation of Islam, the Holy Qur'an, but rather from historical cultural practice in some Muslim countries. A Sikh "fundamentalist" who concentrates on externals, such as wearing a turban, sword, and steel bracelet, overlooks the central insistence of the Sikh Gurus on the inner rather than outer practice of religion. A Hindu "fundamentalist" who objects to the presence of Christian missionaries working among the poor ignores one of the basic principles of ancient Indian religion, which is the tolerant assertion that there are many paths to the same universal truth. Rev. Valson Thampu, editor of the Indian journal *Traci*, writes that this selective type of religious extremism "absolutises what is spiritually or ethically superfluous in a religious tradition. True spiritual enthusiasm or zeal, on the other hand, stakes everything on being faithful to the spiritual essence."[32]

A further problem with the use of the term "fundamentalism" is that it has a specifically Protestant Christian connotation. The Christian fundamentalist movement originated in the late nineteenth century as a reaction to liberal trends, such as historical-critical study of the Bible. Other labels may, therefore, be more cross-culturally appropriate, such as "absolutist," "extremist," or "reactionary," depending on the particular situation.

Those who are called religious **liberals** take a more flexible approach to religious tradition. They may see scriptures as products of a specific culture and time rather than the eternal voice of truth, and may interpret passages metaphorically rather than literally. If activists, they may advocate reforms in the ways their religion is officially understood and practiced. Those who are labeled **heretics** publicly assert controversial positions that are unacceptable to the orthodox establishment. **Mystics** are guided by their own spiritual experiences, which may coincide with any of the above positions.

The encounter between science and religion

Divisions among absolutist, liberal, and sceptical interpretations of religion are related to the development of modern science. Like religion, science is also engaged in searching for universal principles that explain the facts of nature. The two approaches have influenced each other since ancient times, when they were not seen as separate endeavors. In both East and West, there were continual attempts to understand reality as a whole.

In ancient Greece, source of many "Western" ideas, a group of thinkers who are sometimes called "nature philosophers" tried to understand the world through their own perceptions of it. By contrast, Plato distrusted the testimony of the human senses. He thus made a series of distinctions: between what is perceived by the senses and what is accessible through reason, between body and soul, appearance and reality, objects and ideas. In Plato's thought, the soul was superior to the body, and the activity of reason preferable to the distraction of the senses. This value judgment dominated Western thought through the Middle Ages, with its underlying belief that all of nature had been created by God for the sake of humanity.

In the seventeenth century, knowledge of nature became more secularized (that is, divorced from the sacred) as scientists developed models of the universe

The Hubble space telescope is revealing an unimaginably vast cosmos, with billions of galaxies in continual flux. The Eagle Nebula shown here is giving birth to new stars in "pillars of creation" which are 6 trillion miles high.

as a giant machine. Its ways, like the running of a clock, could be discovered by human reason, by skillful attempts to study its component parts and mathematically quantify its characteristics and activities. However, even in discovering such features, many scientists regarded them as the work of a divine Creator or Ruler. Isaac Newton, whose gravitational theory shaped modern physics, speculated that space is eternal because it is the emanation of "eternal and immutable being." Drawing on biblical quotations, Newton argued that God exists everywhere, containing, discerning, and ruling all things.

During the eighteenth-century Enlightenment, rational ways of knowing were increasingly respected, with a concurrent growing scepticism toward claims of knowledge derived from such sources as divine revelation or illuminated inner wisdom. The sciences were viewed as progressive; some thinkers attacked institutionalized religions and dogma as superstitions. Scepticism was applied even to science itself, as early modern scientists gave up trying to find absolute certainties. Rather, they developed hypotheses that were seen as only provisionally true, subject to further investigation and revision.

Unitary concepts of science and religion faced their most serious challenge in

1859, when the naturalist Charles Darwin published *The Origin of Species*, a work that propounded the theory of evolution by natural selection. Darwin demonstrated that certain genetic mutations give an organism a competitive advantage over others of its species, and thus its lineage is naturally more likely to survive. According to Darwin's theory, over great lengths of time this process has directed the development of all forms of life. The theory of natural selection directly contradicted a literal understanding of the biblical Book of Genesis, in which God is said to have created all life in only six days. By the end of the nineteenth century, all such beliefs of the Judeo-Christian tradition were being questioned. The German philosopher Nietzsche proclaimed, "God is dead!"

From twentieth-century scientific research, it is clear that the cosmos is mind-boggling in its complexity and that what we perceive with our five senses is not Ultimate Reality. For instance, the inertness and solidity of matter are only illusions. Each atom consists mostly of empty space with tiny particles whirling around in it. These subatomic particles—such as neutrons, protons, and electrons—cannot even be described as "things." Twentieth-century theories of quantum mechanics, which tried to account for the tiniest particles of matter, uncovered the Uncertainty Principle—the demonstration that the position and velocity of a subatomic particle cannot be simultaneously determined. Subatomic particles behave like energy as well as like matter, like waves as well as like particles. Their position can be determined only statistically. Their behaviors can best be described in terms of a dynamic, interdependent system which includes the observer. Human consciousness is inextricably involved in what it thinks it is "objectively" studying. As physicist David Bohm puts it, "Everything interpenetrates everything."[33]

Our own bodies appear relatively solid, but they are in a constant state of flux and interchange with the environment. Our eyes, ears, noses, tongues, and skin do not reveal absolute truths. Rather, our sensory organs may operate as filters, selecting from a multi-dimensional universe only those characteristics that we need to perceive in order to survive. Imagine how difficult it would be simply to walk across a street if we could see all the electromagnetic energy in the atmosphere, such as x-rays, radio waves, gamma rays, and infrared and ultraviolet light, rather than only the small band of colors we see as the visible spectrum. Though the sky of a starry night appears vast to the naked eye, the giant Hubble telescope placed in space is revealing an incomprehensibly immense cosmos whose limits have not been found. It contains matter-gobbling black holes, vast starmaking clusters, inter-galactic collisions, and cosmic events that happened billions of years ago, so far away that their light is just now being captured by our most powerful instruments for examining what lies far beyond our small place in this galaxy. We know that more lies beyond what we have yet been able to measure. And even our ability to conceive of what we cannot sense may perhaps be limited by the way our brain is organized.

As science continues to question its own assumptions and theories, various new hypotheses are being suggested about the nature of the universe. "Superstring theory" proposes that the universe may not be made of particles at all, but rather of tiny vibrating strings and loops of strings. According to Superstring theory, whereas we think we are living in four observable dimensions of space and time, there may be ten dimensions, with the unperceived six dimensions "curled up" or "compactified" within the four dimensions that we can perceive. According to "M theory," there may be a total of eleven dimensions, including one called "supergravity."

New branches of science are finding that the universe is not always predictable, nor does it always operate according to human notions of cause and effect. And whereas scientific models of the universe were until recently based on the assumption of stability and equilibrium, physicist Ilya Prigogine observes that "today we see instability, fluctuations, irreversibility at every level."[34]

Science cannot accurately predict even the future orbits of planets within this solar system, for all the relevant factors will never be known to human researchers. Physicist Murray Gell-Mann says that we are "a small speck of creation believing it is capable of comprehending the whole."[35]

Contemporary physics approaches metaphysics in the work of physicists such as David Bohm. He describes the dimensions we see and think of as "real" as the *explicate* order. Behind it lies the *implicate* order, in which separateness resolves into unbroken wholeness. Beyond may lie other subtle dimensions, all merging into an infinite ground that unfolds itself as light. This scientific theory is very similar to descriptions by mystics from all cultures about their intuitive experiences of the cosmos. Indeed, realization of the inadequacy of empirical inquiry came long ago in Eastern religious traditions. They recognized the value of perception and reason for the acquisition of ordinary, utilitarian knowledge, but discounted their use for the acquisition of transcendent knowledge of the mystery of being. This mystery, they hold, can be apprehended only through spiritual experience.

> *The most beautiful and profound emotion that we can experience is the sensation of the mystical. It is the sower of all true science. He to whom this emotion is a stranger, who can no longer wonder and stand rapt in awe, is as good as dead. To know that what is impenetrable to us really exists, manifesting itself as the highest wisdom and the most radiant beauty which our dull faculties can comprehend only in their most primitive forms—this knowledge, this feeling is at the center of true religiousness. . . . A human being is part of the whole. . . . He experiences himself, his thoughts and feelings as something separated from the rest—a kind of optical delusion of his consciousness. . . . Our task must be to free ourselves from this prison by widening our circle of compassion to embrace all living creatures, and the whole [of] nature in its beauty.*
>
> *Albert Einstein*[36]

One of the major controversies between science and religion is the conflict between religious concepts of intentional divine creation and the scientific concept of a universe that has evolved mechanistically by processes such as genetic mutations and random combinations of elements. Scientific research is continually revealing a universe whose perfections are suggestive of purposefulness. They have found, for instance, that stars could never have formed if the force of gravity were ever so slightly stronger or weaker. Biologists find that the natural world is an intricate harmony of beautifully elaborated, interrelated parts. Even to produce the miniature propeller that allows a tiny bacterium to swim, some forty different proteins are required. The huge multinational Human Genome Project has discovered that the basic genetic units that are found in all life forms are repeated 3.1 billion times in complex combinations to create human beings.

The question arises: Can the complex maps that produce life be the consequences of chance arrangements of atoms, or are they the result of deliberate design by some First Cause? Current research has demonstrated that the development of certain complex biochemical systems, such as the Krebs citric acid cycle, which unleashes the chemical energy stored in food and makes it available to support life, can be explained by Darwinian mechanics. Some feel that evolution theory presupposes blind, uncaring mechanics, since so many species that have arisen have become extinct. The feeling is that if there were a Creator God, how could that God be so wasteful or cruel? However, the theory of evolution does not necessarily conflict with religious beliefs, if both are examined carefully. Biology professor Kenneth Miller proposes that:

Evolution is certainly not so "cruel" that it cannot be compatible with the notion of a loving God. All that evolution points out is that every organism that has ever lived will eventually die. This is not a special feature of Darwinian theory, but an observable, verifiable fact. The driving force behind evolutionary charge is differential reproductive success, the fact that some organisms leave more offspring than others. Yes, the struggle for existence sometimes involves competition and predation, but just as often it involves cooperation, care, and extraordinary beauty.[37]

Geneticist Francis Collins, Director of the United States' National Human Genome Research Institute at the National Institutes of Health, is both a serious scientist and a "serious" Christian. He does not find the two facets to his life incompatible. Rather, he says:

When something new is revealed about the human genome, I experience a feeling of awe at the realization that humanity now knows something only God knew before. It is a deeply moving sensation that helps me appreciate the spiritual side of life, and also makes the practice of science more rewarding.[38]

According to contemporary "Big Bang" theory, the entire cosmos originated from one point in an explosion whose force is still expanding. Astronomer Fred Hoyle (1915–2001), who originated the term "Big Bang," cautioned that it may not have been a chance happening:

The universe has to know in advance what it is going to be before it knows how to start itself. For in accordance with the Big Bang Theory, for instance, at a time of 10

Some contemporary scientists feel that the perfect details of the natural world cannot have arisen without some kind of guiding intelligence in the cosmos.

[to the minus 43] seconds the universe has to know how many types of neutrino there are going to be at a time of 1 second. This is so in order that it starts off expanding at the right rate to fit the eventual number of neutrino types. . . . An explosion in a junkyard does not lead to sundry bits of metal being assembled into a working machine.[39]

Religious beliefs that, if interpreted literally, seem to be contradicted by scientific fact can instead be interpreted as belonging to the realm of myth. Myths give us symbolic answers to ultimate questions that cannot be answered by empirical experience or rational thought, such as "What are we here for?"

At the cutting edge of research, scientists themselves find they have no ultimate answers that can be expressed in scientific terms. The renowned theoretical physicist Stephen Hawking asks, "What is it that breathes fire into the equations and makes a universe for them to describe?"[40]

Women and the feminine in religions

Another long-standing dichotomy in the sphere of religion is the exclusion of women and the feminine in favor of male-dominated systems. According to some current though controversial theories, many of the myths surviving in today's religions may be related to the suppression of early female-oriented religions by later male-oriented religious systems. Archaeological evidence from many cultures was re-interpreted during the twentieth century as suggesting that worship of a female high goddess was originally widespread. Although there were, and are now, cultures that did not ascribe gender or hierarchy or personality to the divine, some that did may have seen the highest deity as a female.

Just as today's male high deity goes by different names in different religions (God, Allah), the Great Goddess had many names. Among her many identities, she was Danu or Diti in ancient India, the Great Mother Nu Kwa of China, the Egyptian cobra goddess Ua Zit, the Greek earth goddess Gaia, the sun goddess Arinna of Turkey, Coatlique the Mother of Aztec deities, Queen Mother Freyja of the Scandinavians, Great Spider Woman of the Pueblo peoples of North America, and Mawu, omnipotent creator of the Dahomey. A reverent address to Ishtar, an important Mesopotamian goddess, dating from some time between the eighteenth and seventh centuries BCE suggests some of the powers ascribed to her:

An early image of what appears to be the Great Mother, creator and sustainer of the universe. (Tel Halaf, 5th millennium BCE.)

Unto Her who renders decision, Goddess of all things. Unto the Lady of Heaven and Earth who receives supplication; Unto Her who hears petition, who entertains prayer; Unto the compassionate Goddess who loves righteousness; Ishtar the Queen, who suppresses all that is confused. To the Queen of Heaven, the Goddess of the Universe, the One who walked in terrible Chaos and brought life by the Law of Love; And out of Chaos brought us harmony.[41]

Temples and images that seem to have been devoted to worship of the goddess have been found in almost every Neolithic and early historic archaeological site in Europe and West Asia. She was often symbolically linked with water, serpents, birds, eggs, spirals, the moon, the womb, the vulva, the magnetic currents of the earth, psychic powers, and the eternal creation and renewal of life.

In Hindu tradition, the great goddess Durga (left) is understood as the active principle that can vanquish the demonic forces. She carries symbols of the cosmic energies of other aspects of the divine. (Durga slaying the Buffalo Demon, India, c. 1760.)

In the agricultural cultures that may have worshipped the goddess, women frequently held strong social positions. Hereditary lineages were often traced through the mother, and women were honored as priestesses, healers, agricultural inventors, counselors, prophetesses, and sometimes warriors.

What happened to these apparently goddess-oriented religions? Scholars are now trying to piece together not only the reality, extent, and characteristics of Goddess worship, but also the circumstances of its demise. A cross-cultural survey by Eli Sagan (*The Dawn of Tyranny*) indicates that male-dominant social and religious structures accompanied the often violent shift from communal kinship groups and tribal confederations to centralized monarchies. In these kingdoms, social order was based on loyalty to the king and fear of his power. In Europe and West Asia, worship of the goddess was suppressed throughout the third and second millennia BCE by invading Indo-European groups (most probably from the steppes of southern Russia) in which males were dominant and championed worship of a supreme male deity. The Indo-Europeans' major deity was often described as a storm god residing on a mountain and bringing light (seen as the good) into the darkness (portrayed as bad and associated with the female).

In some cases, worship of the goddess co-existed with or later surfaced within male deity worship. In India, the new gods often had powerful female consorts or counterparts or were androgynous (that is, both male and female). The Hindu Durga, represented as a beautiful woman riding a lion, is worshipped as the blazing splendor and power of the Godhead. In Christianity, some scholars feel that devotion to Mary, Mother of Jesus, is in some ways a substitute for earlier worship of the goddess.

Nevertheless, as worship of the goddess was suppressed, so was ritual participation of women. In patriarchal societies, women often became property and were expected to be obedient to the rule of men. Although Christ had honored and worked with women, his later male followers limited the position of women within the Christian Church. Not only was women's spiritual contribution cast aside; in replacing the goddess, patriarchal groups may also have devalued the "feminine" aspect of religion—the receptive, intuitive, ecstatic mystical communion that was perhaps allowed freer expression in the goddess traditions. Women have been the major victims of this devaluation of the feminine, but there has also been distrust of mystics of both sexes who dared to reveal their ecstatic and personal relationship with the divine.

Although women are still barred from equal spiritual footing with men in many religions, this situation is now being widely challenged. The contemporary feminist movement includes strong efforts to make women's voices heard in the sphere of religion. Women are trying to discover their own identity, rather than having their identities defined by others. They are challenging patriarchal religious institutions that have excluded women from active participation. They are also challenging gender-exclusive language in holy texts and authoritarian masculine images of the divine. Their protests also go beyond gender issues to question the narrow and confining ways in which religious inspiration has been institutionalized. At prestigious Christian seminaries in the United States, women preparing for the ministry now outnumber men and are radically transforming views of religion and religious practice. Many feminists are deeply concerned about social ills of our times—violence, poverty, ecological disaster—and are insisting that religions be actively engaged in insuring human survival, and that they be life-affirming rather than punitive in approach. Feminist Christian theologian Rosemary Ruether feels that the movement toward greater religious participation by women may help to heal other fragmentations in our spiritual lives:

> *The feminist religious revolution ... reaches forward to an alternative that can heal the splits between "masculine" and "feminine," between mind and body, between males and females as gender groups, between society and nature, and between races and classes.*[42]

The negative side of organized religion

Tragically, religions have often split rather than unified humanity, have oppressed rather than freed, have terrified rather than inspired.

Since the human needs that religions answer are so strong, those who hold religious power are in a position to dominate and control their followers. In fact, in many religions leaders are given this authority to guide people's spiritual lives, for their wisdom and special access to the sacred is valued. Because religions involve the unseen, the mysterious, these leaders' teachings may not be verifiable by everyday physical experience. They must more often be accepted on faith. While faith is one of the cornerstones of spirituality, it is possible to surrender to spiritual leaders who are misguided or unethical. Religious leaders, like secular leaders, may not be honest with themselves and others about their inner motives. They may mistake their own thoughts and desires for the voice and will of God. Some people believe, however, that the most important thing for the disciple is to surrender the ego; even an unworthy leader can help in this goal simply by playing the role of one to whom one must surrender personal control.

Because religions paint pictures of life after death, they may play on people's fear of death or punishment, both here and hereafter. This excerpt from a famous sermon by the New England Calvinist minister Jonathan Edwards illustrates the terrifying images that can be conjured up:

> *You are thus [sinners] in the hands of an angry God; 'tis nothing but his mere*
> *pleasure that keeps you from being this moment swallowed up in everlasting*
> *destruction. The God that holds you over the pit of hell, much as one holds a spider*
> *or some loathsome insect over the fire, abhors you, and is dreadfully provoked; his*
> *wrath towards you burns like fire; he looks upon you as worthy of nothing else,*
> *but to be cast into the fire.[43]*

Religions try to help us make ethical choices in our lives, to develop a moral conscience. But in people who already have perfectionist or paranoid tendencies, the fear of sinning and being punished can be exaggerated to the point of neurosis or even psychosis by blaming, punishment-oriented religious teachings. If they try to leave their religion for the sake of their mental health, they may be haunted with guilt that they have done a terribly wrong thing. Religions thus have the potential for wreaking psychological havoc on their followers.

Because some religions, particularly those that developed in the East, offer a state of blissful contemplation as the reward for spiritual practice, the faithful may use religion to escape from their everyday problems. Psychologist John Welwood observes that Westerners sometimes embrace Eastern religions with the unconscious motive of avoiding their unsatisfactory lives. He calls this attempt "spiritual bypassing":

> *Spiritual bypassing may be particularly tempting for individuals who are having*
> *difficulty making their way through life's basic developmental stages, especially*
> *at a time when what were once ordinary developmental landmarks—earning*
> *a livelihood through dignified work, raising a family, keeping a marriage together—*
> *have become increasingly difficult and elusive for large segments of the population.*
> *While struggling with becoming autonomous individuals, many people are*
> *introduced to spiritual teachings and practices which come from cultures that assume*
> *a person having already passed through the basic developmental stages.[44]*

Because religions may have such a strong hold on their followers—by their fears, their desires, their deep beliefs—they are potential centers for political power. When church and state are one, the belief that the dominant national religion is the only true religion may be used to oppress those of other beliefs within the country. As the 1991 World Conference of Religions in Kochi, India, concluded:

> *We found that interpretation of religious teachings has often been used to support social*
> *injustices, such as the oppression of women, racial oppression, human rights abuses,*
> *genocide, and marginalization of the poor. Religion has been misused to manipulate,*
> *exploit and divide people, rather than to draw us into compassionate unity.[45]*

Religion may also be used as a rallying point for wars against other nations, casting the desire for control as a holy motive. Throughout history, huge numbers of people have been killed in the name of eradicating "false" religions and replacing them with the "true" religion. Our spirituality has the potential for uniting us

Angels Weep

Wherever there is slaughter of innocent men, women, and children for the mere reason that they belong to another race, color, or nationality, or were born into a faith which the majority of them could never quite comprehend and hardly ever practice in its true spirit; wherever the fair name of religion is used as a veneer to hide overweening political ambition and bottomless greed, wherever the glory of Allah is sought to be proclaimed through the barrel of a gun; wherever piety becomes synonymous with rapacity, and morality cowers under the blight of expediency and compromise, wherever it be—in Yugoslavia or Algeria, in Liberia, Chad, or the beautiful land of the Sudan, in Los Angeles or Abuija, in Kashmir or Conakry, in Colombo or Cotabato—there God is banished and Satan is triumphant, there the angels weep and the soul of man cringes; there in the name of God humans are dehumanized; and there the grace and beauty of life lie ravished and undone.

Dr. Syed Z. Abedin, Director of the Institute
for Muslim Minority Affairs[46]

all in bonds of love, harmony, and mutual respect. But often it has served instead to divide us by creating barriers of hatred and intolerance.

As institutionalized religions attempt to spread the teachings of their founders, there is also the danger that more energy will go into preserving the outer form of the tradition than into maintaining its inner spirit. Max Weber (1864–1920), an influential early twentieth-century scholar of the sociology of religion, referred to this process as the "routinization of charisma." **Charisma** is the rare quality of personal magnetism often ascribed to founders of religion. Their followers feel that these teachers have extraordinary or supernatural powers. When the founder dies, the center of the movement may shift to people with managerial prowess and those who turn the original inspirations into routine rituals and dogma.

No religion is free from these historical shifts. To keep religion alive, true, and vibrant requires a genuine connection with the unseen, scrupulous honesty, and pure-heartedness. As we survey the various contemporary manifestations of the religious impulse, we will find people and groups—in all traditions—who are keeping the spark of the divine alive today. To find them, we will attempt to drop the lens of seeing from the point of view of our own culture, and try instead to see religions as they see themselves. To use Mircea Eliade's term, we will be delving into the **phenomenology** of religion—its specifically sacred aspects—rather than trying to explain religions only in terms of other disciplines such as history, politics, economics, sociology, or psychology. The phenomenology of religion involves an appreciative—even loving—investigation of religious phenomena in order to comprehend their spiritual intention and meaning. We will also be striving for "thick description," a term used by the cultural anthropologist Clifford Geertz, not only reporting outward behaviors but also attempting to explain their meaning for believers within the faith. To take such a journey through many religions does not presuppose that we must forsake our own religious beliefs or our scepticism. But the journey is likely to broaden our perspective and thus bring us closer to understanding other members of our human family. Perhaps it will bring us closer to Ultimate Reality itself.

Suggested reading

Campbell, Joseph, *The Hero with a Thousand Faces,* second edition, Princeton, New Jersey: Princeton University Press, 1968. Brilliant leaps across time and space to trace the hero's journey—seen as a spiritual quest—in all the world's mythologies and religions.

Campbell, Joseph with Bill Moyers, *The Power of Myth*, New York: Doubleday, 1988. More brilliant comparisons of the world's mythologies, with deep insights into their common psychological and spiritual truths.

Capra, Fritjof, *The Tao of Physics*, third edition, Boston: Shambhala, 1991. A fascinating comparison of the insights of Eastern religions and contemporary physics.

Carter, Robert E., ed., *God, The Self, and Nothingness—Reflections: Eastern and Western*, New York: Paragon House, 1990. Essays from major Eastern and Western scholars of religion on variant ways of experiencing and describing Ultimate Reality.

Eliade, Mircea, *The Sacred and the Profane*, translated by William R. Trask, New York: Harper and Row, 1959. Encompassing all religions, a study of religious myth, symbolism, and ritual as ways of creating a place for the sacred within a secular environment.

Ferguson, Kitty, *The Fire in the Equations: Science, Religion and the Search for God*, New York/London: Bantam Books, 1994. A wide-ranging, perceptive analysis of the implications of scientific research for religious beliefs.

Hick, John, *An Interpretation of Religion*, New Haven: Yale University Press, 1992. A leading philosopher of religion offers a rational justification for seeing the major world religions as culturally conditioned forms of response to the great mystery of Being.

King, Ursula, *Women and Spirituality: Voices of Protest and Promise*, second edition, University Park, Pennsylvania: Pennsylvania State University Press, 1993. Excellent cross-cultural survey of feminist theology and spiritual activism.

Marty, Martin E. and R. Scott Appleby, *The Fundamentalism Project*, 5 volumes, Chicago: University of Chicago Press, 1991. Scholarly analyses of fundamentalist phenomena in all religions and around the globe.

Otto, Rudolf, *The Idea of the Holy*, second edition, London: Oxford University Press, 1950. An important exploration of "nonrational" experiences of the divine.

Paden, William E., *Interpreting the Sacred: Ways of Viewing Religion*, Boston: Beacon Press, 1992. A gentle, readable introduction to the complexities of theoretical perspectives on religion.

Sharma, Arvind, ed., *Women in World Religions*, Albany, New York: State University of New York Press, 1987. Analyses of the historic and contemporary place of women in each of the major religions.

Shinn, Larry D., ed., *In Search of the Divine: Some Unexpected Consequences of Interfaith Dialogue*, New York: Paragon House Publishers, 1987. Scholars from various religions present a tapestry of understandings of the Sacred Reality.

Stone, Merlin, *When God was a Woman*, San Diego, California: Harcourt Brace Jovanovich, 1976. Pioneering survey of archaeological evidence of the early religion of the Goddess.

Ward, Keith, *God, Chance and Necessity*, Oxford: Oneworld Publications, 1997. A leading Christian theologian critiques scientific theories that deny the existence of God.

CHAPTER 2

INDIGENOUS SACRED WAYS

"Everything is alive"

Here and there around the globe, pockets of people still follow local sacred ways handed down from their remote ancestors and adapted to contemporary circumstances. These are the traditional **indigenous** people—descendants of the original inhabitants of lands now controlled by larger political systems in which they may have little influence.

Indigenous people comprise at least four percent of the world population. Some who follow the ancient spiritual traditions still live close to the earth in non-industrial, small-scale cultures; many do not. But despite the disruption of their traditional lifestyles, many indigenous people maintain a sacred way of life that is distinctively different from all other religions. These enduring ways, which indigenous people may refer to as their "original instructions" on how to live, were almost lost under the onslaught of genocidal colonization, conversion pressures from global religions, mechanistic materialism, and the destruction of their natural environments by the global economy of limitless consumption.

Much of the ancient visionary wisdom has disappeared. There are few traditionally trained elders left and few young people willing to undergo the lengthy and rigorous training necessary for spiritual leadership in these sacred ways. Nevertheless, in our time there is a renewal of interest in these traditions, fanning hope that what they offer will not be lost.

> *To what extent can [indigenous groups] reinstitute traditional religious values in a world gone mad with development, electronics, almost instantaneous transportation facilities, and intellectually grounded in a rejection of spiritual and mysterious events?*
>
> *Vine Deloria, Jr.*[1]

Understanding indigenous sacred ways

Indigenous spirituality is a lifeway, a particular approach to all of life. It is not a separate experience, like meditating in the morning or going to church on Sunday. Rather, spirituality ideally pervades all moments, from reverence in gathering clay to make a pot, to respect within tribal council meetings. As an elder of the Huichol in Mexico puts it:

Everything we do in life is for the glory of God. We praise him in the well-swept floor, the well-weeded field, the polished machete, the brilliant colors of the picture and embroidery. In these ways we prepare for a long life and pray for a good one.[2]

In most native cultures, spiritual lifeways are shared orally. Teachings are experienced rather than read from books. There are therefore no scriptures of the sort that other religions are built around (although there once existed some texts, such as the Mayan codices, which were destroyed by conquering groups). This characteristic helps to keep the indigenous sacred ways dynamic and flexible rather than fossilized. It also keeps the sacred experience fresh in the present. However, not until the latter part of the twentieth century did outside investigators begin to study the oral narratives as clues to the historical experiences of the individuals or groups.

The lifeways of many small-scale cultures are tied to the land on which they live and their entire way of life; they are meaningful only within this context. The people generally respect the rights of others to their own ways and make no attempt to convert outsiders to theirs.

Despite the hindrances to understanding of indigenous forms of spirituality, the doors to understanding are opening somewhat in our times. Firstly, the traditional elders are very concerned about the growing potential for planetary disaster. Some are beginning to share their basic values, if not their esoteric practices, in hopes of preventing industrial societies from destroying the earth. Secondly, those of other faiths are beginning to recognize the value and profundity of indigenous ways, which were in the past viewed as abhorrent and suppressed by organized religions. Thirdly, many people who have not grown up in native cultures are attempting to embrace indigenous spiritual ways, finding their own traditions lacking in certain qualities for which they long, such as love for the earth.

Cultural diversity

In this chapter we are considering the faith-ways of indigenous peoples as a whole. However, behind these generalizations lie many differences in social contexts, as well as in religious beliefs and practices. There are hundreds of different tribal traditions in North America alone. Indigenous traditions have evolved within materially as well as religiously diverse cultures. Some are descendants of civilizations with advanced urban technologies that were needed to support concentrated populations. When the Spanish conqueror Cortés took over Tenochtitlán (which now lies beneath Mexico City) in 1519, he found it a beautiful clean city with elaborate architecture, indoor plumbing, a highly accurate calendar, and advanced systems of mathematics and astronomy.

At the other extreme are those few cultures that still maintain a survival strategy of hunting and gathering. For example, some Australian aborigines continue to live as mobile foragers, though restricted to government-owned stations. A nomadic survival strategy necessitates simplicity in material goods; whatever can be gathered or built rather easily at the next camp need not be dragged along. But material simplicity is not a sign of spiritual poverty. The Australian aborigines have a complex **cosmogony**, or model of the origins of the universe and their purpose within it, as well as a working knowledge of their own bioregion.

Some traditional people live in their ancestral enclaves, somewhat sheltered

The indigenous community of Acoma Pueblo—built on a high plateau in New Mexico—may be the oldest continuously occupied city in the United States.

from the pressures of modern industrial life, though not untouched by the outer world. The Hopi people have continuously occupied a high plateau area of the southwestern United States for between eight hundred and one thousand years; their sacred ritual calendar is tied to the yearly farming cycle.

Other indigenous people visit their sacred sites and ancestral shrines but live in more urban settings because of job opportunities. The people who participate in ceremonies in the Mexican countryside include subway personnel, journalists, and artists of native blood who live in Mexico City.

In addition to variations in lifestyles, indigenous traditions vary in their adaptations to dominant religions. Often native practices have become interwoven with those of global religions, such as Buddhism, Islam, and Christianity. In Southeast Asia, household Buddhist shrines are almost identical to the spirit houses in which the people still make offerings to honor the local spirits. The Dahomey tradition from West Africa was carried to Haiti by thousands of African slaves and called **Voodoo**, from *vodu*, one of the names for the chief non-human spirits. Forced by the European colonialists to adopt Christianity, worshippers of Voodoo secretly fused their old gods with their images of Catholic saints.

Despite their different histories and economic patterns, indigenous sacred ways do tend to have some characteristics in common. Perhaps from ancient contact across land-bridges that no longer exist, there are linguistic similarities between the languages of the Tsalagi in the Americas, Tibetans, and the aboriginal Ainu of Japan. Striking similarities found among the myths of geographically separate peoples can be accounted for both by global diffusion by trade, travel, and other kinds of contact, and by parallel origin because of basic similarities in human experience, such as birth and death, pleasure and pain, day and night, and wonderment about the cosmos and our place in it.

The circle of right relationships

For many indigenous peoples, everything in the cosmos is intimately interrelated. A symbol of unity among the parts of this sacred reality is a circle. This symbol is not used by all indigenous people; the Navajo, for instance, regard a completed circle as stifling and restrictive. However, many other indigenous people hold the circle sacred because it is infinite—it has no beginning, no end. Time is circular rather than linear, for it keeps coming back to the same place. Life revolves around the generational cycles of birth, youth, maturity, and physical death, the return of the seasons, the cyclical movements of the moon, sun, stars, and planets.

This understanding of life as a complex of circles is thought to be the perfect framework for harmony. As Lame Deer, a Lakota Sioux holy man, explained:

Nature wants things to be round. The bodies of human beings and animals have no corners. With us the circle stands for the togetherness of people who sit with one another around the campfire, relatives and friends united in peace while the pipe passes from hand to hand. The camp in which every tipi *had its place was also a ring. The* tipi *was a ring in which people sat in a circle and all the families in the village were in turn circles within a larger circle, part of the larger hoop which was the seven campfires of the Sioux, representing one nation. The nation was only a part of the universe, in itself circular and made of the earth, which is round, of the sun, which is round, of the stars, which are round. The moon, the horizon, the rainbow—circles within circles within circles, with no beginning and no end.[3]*

To maintain the natural balance of the circles of existence, most indigenous peoples have traditionally been taught that they must develop right relationships with everything that is. Their relatives include the unseen world of spirits, the land and weather, the people and creatures, and the power within.

Relationships with spirit

Many indigenous traditions worship a Supreme Being who they believe created the cosmos. This being is known by the Sioux as "Wakan Tanka" or "Great Mysterious" or "Great Spirit."

African names for this being are attributes, such as "All-powerful," "Creator," "the one who is met everywhere," "the one who exists by himself," or "the one who began the forest." The Supreme Being is often referred to by male pronouns, but in some groups the Supreme Being is a female, such as Ala, earth mother goddess of the Ibo. Some tribes of the southwestern United States call her "Changing Woman"—sometimes young, sometimes old, the mother of the earth, associated with women's reproductive cycles and the mystery of birth, the creatrix. Many traditional languages make no distinction between male and female pronouns, and some see the divine as androgynous, a force arising from the interaction of male and female aspects of the universe.

Awareness of one's relationship to the Great Power is thought to be essential, but the power itself remains unseen and mysterious. An Inuit **shaman** described his people's experience of:

a power that we call Sila, which is not to be explained in simple words. A great spirit, supporting the world and the weather and all life on earth, a spirit so mighty

Deity may be conceived as either male or female in indigenous religions. In Navajo belief, divinity is personified as both Father Sky and Mother Earth. In this traditional sand-painting, Father Sky is on the left, with constellations and the Milky Way forming his "body." Mother Earth is on the right, with her body bearing the four sacred plants: squash, beans, tobacco, and corn.

that [what it says] to mankind is not through common words, but by storm and snow and rain and the fury of the sea; all the forces of nature that men fear. But Sila has also another way of [communicating]; by sunlight and calm of the sea, and little children innocently at play, themselves understanding nothing. . . . When all is well, Sila sends no message to mankind, but withdraws into endless nothingness, apart.[4]

To traditional Buryats of Russia, the chief power in the world is the eternally blue sky, Tengry. In many cultures, the Great Mysterious is thought to have been less distant at one time. African myths suggest that the High God was originally so close to humans that they became disrespectful. The All-powerful was like the sky, they say, which was once so close that children wiped their dirty hands on it, and women (blamed by men for the withdrawal) broke off pieces for soup and bumped it with their sticks when pounding grain. Although southern and central Africans believe in a high being who presides over the universe, including less powerful spirits, they consider this being either too distant, too powerful, or too dangerous to worship or call on for help.

Many unseen powers are perceived to be at work in the material world. In various traditions, some of these are perceived without form, as mysterious and sacred presences. Others are perceived as having more definite, albeit invisible, forms and personalities. These may include deities with human-like personalities, the nature spirits of special local places, such as venerable trees and mountains, animal spirit helpers, personified elemental forces, ancestors who still take an interest in their living relatives, special beings such as the spirit keepers of the four directions recognized by some Native Americans.

Ancestors may be extremely important. Traditional Africans understand that even the person is not an individual, but a composite of many souls—the spirits of one's parents and ancestors—resonating to their feelings. Continued communication with the "living dead" is extremely important to traditional Africans. These are ancestors who have died recently enough for some people still to remember them personally. Food and drink are set out or poured for them, acknowledging that they are still in a sense living and engaged with the people's lives. Failure to keep in touch with the ancestors is a dangerous oversight, which may bring misfortunes to the family.

West African groups, descendants of hierarchical ancient civilizations, recognize a great pantheon of deities, the **orisa** or *vodu*, each the object of special cult worship. This worship is most highly elaborated among the Yoruba, who honor 1,700 divinities. The *orisa* are embodiments of the dynamic forces in life, such as Oya, goddess of death and change, experienced in tornadoes, lightning, winds, and fire. At the beginning of time, in Yoruba cosmology, there was only one godhead, described by Clyde Ford as "a beingless being, a dimensionless point, an infinite container of everything, including itself."[5] The ultimate purpose of the *orisa*—and that of those who pay attention to them as inner forces—is to return to that original state of wholeness.

The spirits are available to reverent seekers as helpers, as intermediaries between the people and the power, and as teachers. Their teachings may come in frightening forms, such as thunder and lightning, which test one's faith and courage. But a right relationship with these spirit beings can be a sacred partnership. Seekers respect, silently listen for, and learn from them; they also purify themselves in order to engage their services for the good of the people. As we will later see, those who are best able to call on the spirits for help are the shamans who have dedicated their lives to this service.

Teachings about the spirits also help the people to understand how they should live together in society. Professor Deidre Badejo observes that in Yoruba tradition there is an ideal of social balance between the awesome potential and creativity of women who give and sustain life, and the power of men who protect life. Under various internal and external pressures, this balance has swung toward male dominance, but the stories of feminine power and the necessity for men to recognize it remain in the culture, teaching an ideal symmetry between female and male roles.

Kinship with all creation

Within the spiritually charged, visible world, all things may be understood as spiritually interconnected. Everything is therefore experienced as family. The community is paramount, and it may extend beyond the living humans in the area. Many traditional peoples know the earth as their mother. The land one lives on is part of her body, loved, respected, and well known. Oren Lyons, an elder of the Onondaga Nation Wolf Clan, speaks of this intimate relationship:

> [The indigenous people's] knowledge is profound and comes from living in one
> place for untold generations. It comes from watching the sun rise in the east and set
> in the west from the same place over great sections of time. We are as familiar with
> the lands, rivers and great seas that surround us as we are with the faces of our
> mothers. Indeed we call the earth Etenoha, our mother, from whence all life
> springs. . . . We do not perceive our habitat as wild but as a place of great security
> and peace, full of life.[6]

An indigenous earthwork in Ohio, representing a snake and an egg, symbols of fertility and transformation. The spiral in the snake's tail may be an appreciative symbol of the life force and wisdom inherent in the earth.

Some striking feature of the natural environment of the area—such as a great mountain or canyon—may be perceived as the center from which the whole world was created. Such myths heighten the perceived sacredness of the land.

In contrast to the industrial world's attempts to use and dominate the earth, native people say they consider themselves caretakers of their mother, the earth. They are now raising their voices against the destruction of the environment. Their prophecies warn of the potential for global disaster. Some indigenous visionaries say they hear the earth crying.

The earth abounds with living presences, in traditional worldviews. Rocks, bodies of water, and mountains—considered inanimate by other peoples—are personified as living beings by indigenous peoples. Before one can successfully climb a mountain, one must ask its permission. Visionaries can see the spirits of a body of water, and many traditional cultures have recognized certain groves of trees as places where spirits live, and where specially trained priests and priestesses can communicate with them. As a Pit River Indian explained, "Everything is alive. That's what we Indians believe."[7]

All creatures may be perceived as kin, endowed with consciousness and the power of the Great Spirit. Many native peoples have been raised with an "ecological" perspective: they know that all things depend on each other. They are taught that they have a reciprocal, rather than dominating, relationship with all beings. Hawaiian *kahuna* (shaman-priest) Kahu Kawai'i explains:

How you might feel toward a human being that you love is how you might feel toward a dry leaf on the ground and how you might feel toward the rain in the

*forest and the wind. There is such intimacy that goes on that everything speaks to
you and everything responds to how you are in being—almost like a mirror
reflecting your feelings.*[8]

Trees, animals, insects, and plants are all to be approached with caution and
consideration. If one must cut down a tree or kill an animal, one must first
explain one's intentions and ask forgiveness of the being. Indigenous people feel
that those who harm nature may themselves be harmed in return.

There are many stories of indigenous people's relationships with non-human
creatures. Certain trees tell the healing specialists which herbs to use in curing the
people. Australian aboriginal women are adept at forming hunting partnerships
with dogs. Birds are thought to bring messages to the people from the spirit world.
A Hopi elder said he spent three days and nights praying with a rattle-snake. "Of
course he was nervous at first, but when I sang to him he recognized the warmth of my body and calmed down. We made good prayer together."[9]

Relationships with power

A second common theme is developing an appropriate relationship with spiritual
energy.

> *All animals have power, because the Great Spirit dwells in all of them, even a tiny
> ant, a butterfly, a tree, a flower, a rock. The modern, white man's way keeps that
> power from us, dilutes it. To come to nature, feel its power, let it help you, one needs
> time and patience for that. . . . You have so little time for contemplation. . . . It
> lessens a person's life, all that grind, that hurrying and scurrying about.*
> *Lame Deer, Lakota nation*[10]

In certain places and beings, the power of spirit is believed to be highly concentrated. It is referred to as *mana* by the people of the Pacific islands. This is the vital
force that makes it possible to act with unusual strength, insight, and effectiveness.

Tlakaelel, a contemporary spiritual leader of the descendants of the Toltecs of
Mexico, describes how a person might experience this power when looking into
an obsidian mirror traditionally made to concentrate power:

> *When you reach the point that you can concentrate with all your will, inside there,
> you reach a point where you feel ecstasy. It's a very beautiful thing, and everything
> is light. Everything is vibrating with very small signals, like waves of music, very
> smooth. Everything shines with a blue light. And you feel a sweetness. Everything
> is covered with the sweetness, and there is peace. It's a sensation like an orgasm, but
> it can last a long time.*[11]

Sacred sites may be recognized by the power that believers feel there.
Concentrated power spots were known to ancient as well as contemporary peoples
of the earth. Some sacred sites have been used again and again by successive religions, either to capitalize on the energy or to co-opt the preceding religion. Chartres
Cathedral in France, for instance, was built on an ancient ritual site.

Because power can be built up through sacred practices, the ritual objects of
spiritually developed persons may have concentrated power. Special stones and

At a remote shrine used by indigenous people in New Mexico, a ring of stones protects the sacred area where sun-bleached antlers and offerings have been placed around two stones naturally shaped like mountain lions.

animal artifacts may also carry power. A person might be strengthened by the spiritual energy of the bear or the wolf by wearing sacred clothing made from its fur. Power can also come to one through visions or by being given a sacred pipe or the privilege of collecting objects into a personal sacred bundle.

In some cultures—such as that of the traditional peoples of the North American plains—women are thought to have a certain natural power; men have to work harder for it. Women's power is considered mysterious, dangerous, uncontrolled. It is said to be strongest during their menstrual period. In certain rituals in which both men and women participate, women's menstrual blood is often thought to diminish or weaken the ritual or the men's spiritual power. In most Native American nations that have sweat lodge ceremonies for ritual purification, menstruating women are not allowed to enter the lodge. Nevertheless, a few cultures, such as the Ainu of Japan, have prized menstrual blood as a potent offering returned to the earth.

Gaining power is both desirable and dangerous. If misused for personal ends, it becomes destructive and may turn against the person. To channel spiritual power properly, native people are taught that they must live within certain strict limits. Those who seek power or receive it unbidden are supposed to continually purify themselves of any selfish motives and dedicate their actions to the good of the whole. A pipe carrier must be ethically impeccable and must never turn away anyone who asks for help.

Spiritual specialists

In a few of the remaining hunting and gathering tribes, religion is a relatively private matter. Each individual has direct access to the unseen. Although spirit is invisible, it is considered a part of the natural world. Anyone can interact with it spontaneously, without complex ceremony and without anyone else's aid.

More commonly, however, the world of spirit is thought to be dangerous, like a fire that can burn those who are unprepared for its power. Although everyone is expected to observe certain personal ways of worship, such as offering prayers before taking plant or animal life, many ways of interacting with spirit are thought to be best left to those who are specially trained for the roles. These specialists are gradually initiated into the secret knowledge that allows them to act as intermediaries between the seen and the unseen.

Storytellers and other sacred roles

Specialists' roles vary from one group to another, and the same person may play several of these roles. One common role is that of storyteller. Because the traditions are oral rather than written, these people must memorize long and complex stories and songs so that the group's sacred traditions can be remembered and taught, generation after generation.

Such stories are important clues to understanding the universe and one's place in it. What is held only in memory cannot be physically destroyed, but if a tribe is small and all its storytellers die, the knowledge is lost. This happened on a large scale during contacts with colonial powers, as native people were killed by war and imported diseases.

There are also bards who carry the energy of ancient traditions into new forms. Rather than memory, they cultivate the muse. In Africa, poets are considered "technicians of the sacred," conversing with a dangerous world of spirits. They are associated with the flow and rhythms of water.

Players of the "talking drums" are highly valued as communicators with the spirits, ancestors, and Supreme Being. Drumming creates a rhythmic environment in which the people can draw close to the unseen powers. By counterposing basic and complex cross-rhythmic patterns with a "return beat," Yoruba drummers create a tension that draws listeners into the unfilled spaces between the beats.

"Tricksters" such as foxes often appear in the stories of indigenous traditions. They are paradoxical, transformative beings. Similarly, sacred clowns may endure the shame of behaving as fools during public rituals in order to teach the people through humor. Often they poke fun at the most sacred of rituals, keeping the people from taking themselves too seriously. A sacred fool, called **heyoka** by the Lakota, must be both innocent and very wise about human nature, and must have a visionary relationship with spirit as well.

> *Life is holiness and everyday humdrum, sadness and laughter, the mind and the belly all mixed together. The Great Spirit doesn't want us to sort them out neatly.*
> *Leonard Crow Dog, Lakota medicine man[12]*

A more coveted role is that of being a member of a secret society in which one can participate by initiation or invitation only, whether to enhance one's prestige or to draw closer to the spirit world. When serving in ceremonial capacities, members often wear special costumes to hide their human identities and help them take on the personas of spirits they are representing. In African religions, some members of secret societies periodically appear as impersonators of animal spirits or of dead ancestors, helping to demonstrate that the dead are still watching the living and are available as awe-inspiring protectors of villages.

Sacred dancers likewise make the unseen powers visible. Body movements are a language in themselves expressing the nature of the cosmos, a language that is understood through the stories and experiences of the community. Such actions keep the world of the ancestors alive for succeeding generations.

In some socially stratified societies there are also priests and priestesses. These are specially trained and dedicated people who carry out the rituals that ensure proper functioning of the natural world, and perhaps also communicate with particular spirits or deities. Though West African priests or priestesses may have part-time earthly occupations, they are expected to stay in a state of ritual purity and spend much of their time in communication with the spirit being to whom they are devoted, paying homage and asking the being what he or she wants the people to do.

Shamans

The most distinctive spiritual specialists among indigenous peoples are the shamans. They are called by many names, but the Siberian word "shaman" is used as a generic term by scholars for those who offer themselves as mystical intermediaries between the physical and the non-physical world for specific purposes, such as healing. Archaeological research has confirmed that shamanic methods are extremely ancient—at least 20,000 to 30,000 years old. Ways of becoming a shaman and practicing shamanic arts are remarkably similar around the globe.

Shamans may be helpers to society, using their skills to benefit others. They are not to be confused with sorcerers, who practice black magic to harm others or promote their own selfish ends, interfering with the cosmic order. Spiritual power is neutral; its use depends on the practitioner. What Native Americans call "**medicine** power" does not originate in the medicine person. Black Elk explains:

> Of course it was not I who cured. It was the power from the outer world, and the visions and ceremonies had only made me like a hole through which the power could come to the two-leggeds. If I thought that I was doing it myself, the hole would close up and no power could come through.[13]

There are many kinds of medicine. One is the ability to heal physical, psychological, and spiritual problems. Techniques used include physical approaches to illness, such as therapeutic herbs, dietary recommendations, sweatbathing, massage, cauterization, and sucking out of toxins. But the treatments are given to the whole person—body, mind, and spirit, with special emphasis on healing relationships within the group—so there may also be metaphysical divination, prayer, chanting, and ceremonies in which group power is built up and spirit helpers are called in. These shamanic healing methods, once dismissed as quackery, are now beginning to earn respect from the scientific medical establishment.

Black Elk, visionary and healer.

Mexican curandera *(healer) Maria Sabina has eaten hallucinogenic mushrooms to enter an ecstatic state. She chants, "I am a doctor woman . . . I am the morning star woman . . . I am the moon woman . . . I am the heaven woman . . . they say it is like softness there."*

Shamans are contemplatives, Lame Deer explains:

The wicasa wakan *[holy man] wants to be by himself. He wants to be away from the crowd, from everyday matters. He likes to meditate, leaning against a tree or rock, feeling the earth move beneath him, feeling the weight of that big flaming sky upon him. That way he can figure things out. Closing his eyes, he sees many things clearly. What you see with your eyes shut is what counts. . . . He listens to the voices of the* wama kaskan—*all those who move upon the earth, the animals. He is as one with them. From all living beings something flows into him all the time, and something flows from him.[14]*

The role of shaman may be hereditary or it may be recognized as a special gift. Either way, training is rigorous. In order to work in a mystical state of ecstasy, moving between ordinary and non-ordinary realities, shamans must experience physical death and rebirth. Some have spontaneous near-death experiences. Uvavnuk, an Inuit shaman, was spiritually initiated when she was struck by a lightning ball. After she revived, she had great power, which she dedicated to serving her people. Other potential shamans undergo rituals of purification, isolation, and bodily torment until they make contact with the spirit world.

In addition to becoming familiar with death, a potential shaman must undergo lengthy training in shamanic techniques, the names and roles of the spirits, and secrets and myths of the tribe. Novices are taught both by older shamans and reportedly by the spirits themselves. If the spirits do not accept and teach the shaman, he or she is unable to carry the role.

The helping spirits that contact would-be shamans during the death-and-rebirth crisis become essential partners in the shaman's sacred work. Often it is a spirit animal who becomes the shaman's guardian spirit, giving him or her special powers. The shaman may even take on the persona of the animal while working.

Many tribes feel that healing shamans need the powers of the bear; Lapp shamans metamorphosed into wolves, reindeer, bears, or fish.

Not only do shamans possess a power animal as an alter-ego, they also have the ability to enter parallel, spiritual realities at will in order to bring back knowledge, power, or help for those who need it. An altered state of consciousness is needed. Techniques for entering this state are the same around the world: drumming, rattling, singing, dancing, and in some cases hallucinogenic drugs. The effect of these influences is to open what the Huichol shamans of Mexico call the *narieka*—the doorway of the heart, the channel for divine power, the point where human and spirit worlds meet. It is often experienced and represented artistically as a pattern of concentric circles.

Group observances

Indigenous ways are community-centered. Through group rituals, traditional people not only honor the sacred but also affirm their bonds with each other and all of creation. Humans can help to maintain the harmony of the universe by their ritual observances.

Each group has its own ways of ritual dedication to the spirits of life, but they tend to follow certain patterns everywhere. Some honor major points in the human life cycle, such as birth, naming, puberty, marriage, and death. These rites of passage assist people in the transition from one state to another and help them become aware of their meaningful contribution to life. When a Hopi baby is twenty days old, it is presented at dawn to the rays of Father Sun for the first time and officially given a name. Its face is ritually cleansed with sacred cornmeal, a ceremony that will be repeated at death for the journey to the Underworld.

There are also collective rituals to support the group's survival strategies. In farming communities these include ways of asking for rain, of insuring the growth of crops, and of giving thanks for the harvest. In the Great Drought of 1988, Sioux holy man Leonard Crow Dog was asked by three non-native Midwestern communities to perform rainmaking ceremonies for them, thus honoring the power of the traditional medicine ways. Dhyani Ywahoo explains, "When Native American people sing for the rain, the rain comes—because those singers have made a decision that they and the water and the air and the Earth are one."[15]

Ritual dramas about the beginnings and sacred history of the people engage performers and spectators on an emotional level through the use of special costumes, body paint, music, masks, and perhaps sacred locations. These dramas provide a sense of orderly interface among humans, the land, and the spiritual world. They also dramatize mysticism, drawing the people toward direct contact with the spirit world. Those who have sacred visions and dreams are supposed to share them with others, and often this is done through dramatization.

According to legend, the Plains Indians were given the sacred pipe by White Buffalo Calf Woman as a tool for communicating with the mysteries and understanding the ways of life. The bowl of the pipe represents the female aspect of the Great Spirit, the stem the male aspect. When they are ritually joined, the power of the spirit is thought to be present as the pipe is passed around the circle for collective communion with each other and with the divine.

This altar in the home of a Mexican healer illustrates the blending of indigenous ways with those of later religions. The serpent, masks, vegetables, eggs, and "bird's nest" derive from indigenous sacred ways, but are juxtaposed with Christian symbols.

Groups also gather for ritual purification and spiritual renewal of individuals. Indigenous peoples of the Americas "smudge" sites and possessions, cleansing them with smoke from special herbs, such as sage and sweetgrass. Many groups make an igloo-shaped "sweat lodge" into which hot stones are carried. People huddle together in the dark around the stone pit. When water is poured on the stones, intensely hot steam sears bodies and lungs. Everyone prays earnestly.

Pilgrimages to sacred sites are often communal. The Huichol Indians of the mountains of western Mexico make a yearly journey to a desert they call Wirikuta, the Sacred Land of the Sun. They feel that creation began in this place. And like their ancestors, they gather their yearly supply of peyote cactus at this sacred site. Peyote has the power to alter consciousness: it is their "little deer," a spirit who helps them to communicate with the spirit world.

When indigenous groups are broken up by external forces, they lose the cohesive power of these group rituals. Africans taken to the New World as slaves lost not only their own individual identity but also their membership in tight-knit groups. In an attempt to re-establish a communal sense of shared spiritual traditions among African-Americans, Professor Maulana Ron Karenga created a contemporary celebration, Kwanzaa, based on indigenous African "first fruits" harvest festivals.

Individual observances

In indigenous sacred ways, it is considered important for each person to experience a personal connection with the spirits. The people acknowledge and work with the spirits in many everyday ways. For instance, when searching for herbs, a person is not to take the first plant found; an offering is made to it, with the prayer that its relatives will understand one's needs. Guardian spirits and visions are sought by all the people, not just specialists such as shamans. The shaman may have more spirit helpers and more power, but visionary experiences and opportunities for worship are available to all. Indigenous traditions have therefore been called "democratized shamanism."

To open themselves for contact with the spirit world, individuals in many indigenous cultures undergo a **vision quest**. After ritual purification, they are sent alone to a sacred spot to cry to the spirits to reveal something of their purpose in life and help them in their journey. This may also be done before undertaking a sacred mission, such as the sun dance. Indigenous Mexican leader Tlakaelel describes the vision quest as he observes it:

> *You stay on a mountain, desert, or in a cave, isolated, naked, with only your sacred things, the things that you have gained, in the years of preparation—your eagle feathers, your pipe, your* copal *[tree bark used as incense]. You are left alone four days and four nights without food and water. During this time when you are looking for your vision, many things happen. You see things move. You see animals that come close to you. Sometimes you might see someone that you care about a lot, and they're bringing water. You feel like you're dying of thirst, but there are limits around you, protection with hundreds of tobacco ties. You do not leave this circle, and this vision will disappear when they come to offer the water or sometimes they will just drop it on the ground. Or someone comes and helps you with their strength and gives you messages.*[16]

In the traditional sacred ways, one is not supposed to ask for a vision for selfish personal reasons. The point of this individual ordeal, which is designed to be physically and emotionally stressful, is to ask how one can help the people and the planet.

Contemporary issues

Sadly, traditional spiritual wisdom has been largely obliterated in many parts of the world by those who wanted to take the people's lands or save their souls with some other path to the divine. Under the slogan "Kill the Indian and save the man," the American founder of the boarding school system for native children took them away from their families at a young age and transformed their cultural identity, presenting the native ways as inferior and distancing them from normal participation in the traditional sacred life.

In contemporary urban African areas, the traditional interest in the flow of the past into the present, with value placed on the intensity of present experience, has been rapidly replaced by a Westernized view of time, in which one is perpetually anxious about the future. This shift has led to severe psychological disorientation and social and political instability.

Some indigenous people feel that their traditional sacred ways are not only valid, but actually essential for the future of the world. They see these understandings as antidotes to mechanistic, dehumanizing, environmentally destructive

Winona LaDuke

As the narrator of Winona LaDuke's semi-fictional novel, *Last Standing Woman*, puts it, her clanspeople have a special destiny:

> *In times past, they were warriors, the* ogichidaa, *those who defended the people. Sometimes we still are. We are what we are intended to be when we have those three things that guide our direction—our name, our clan, and our religion.*[17]

Winona herself is a prime example. She is continually in the news as a fighter on behalf of the future of the earth and its disadvantaged peoples. When in 1996 she ran as the Green Party candidate for Vice-President of the United States, she campaigned for reforms oriented toward long-term survival:

> *I am interested in reframing the debate on the issues of this society, the distribution of power and wealth, abuse of power, the rights of the natural world, the environment, and the need to consider an amendment to the U.S. Constitution in which all decisions made today would be considered in light of the impact on the seventh generation from now.*[18]

Winona now lives on her father's traditional tribal lands in northern Minnesota in the White Earth Reservation. Her father, like many, had left the reservation in search of economic opportunity and as a consequence of internal political oppression, but now Winona is trying to re-establish an economic base that will allow her Anishinaabe people to return to their land and to have the legal right to control its use. The land is of spiritual as well as economic importance to her people.

Part of the land on which Winona's Mississippi band of the Anishinaabe had long lived was formally granted to them by an 1867 treaty establishing a reservation of 837,000 acres, in exchange for their giving up their rights to most of Minnesota and Wisconsin. But over time, land slipped away through foreclosures, illegal land transfers, and a 1986 settlement in which Anishinaabe were forced to accept, under pressure from large government agencies and timber companies, sale of remaining lands for only pennies an acre. Now the White Earth Reservation occupies only about one-sixth of the original area. Using part of a $20,000 Reebok company award for her human rights work, Winona established the White Earth Land Recovery Project to begin to repurchase the land. She says, "We are going to recover our land acre by acre, inch by inch. Our burial grounds must be ours forever, even if we have to buy them back."[19]

The project she initiated has already repurchased over 1,300 acres of former tribal lands, and is trying to add more through further purchases, bequests, and legislation. The lands include burial grounds with undisturbed birch and sugar maple forests, and a 715-acre area encompassing two lakes, nesting sites for waterfowl, wild rice, and many medicinal plants. The latter area is earmarked to teach Anishinaabe children their own traditional cultural practices, and also to demonstrate to the world their value for planetary survival.

Winona, a Harvard-educated journalist, lives in a lakeside log cabin on the reservation with her two children, Ajuawak and Wasey, trying to teach them traditional beliefs. She has no fear of fighting against large-scale vested interests. In 1994, for instance, she chained herself to a paper company's gates to protest their clearance of forests including thousand-year-old trees to make phone books. As a result, she was put in jail for five hours but the publicity led other companies to cancel their contracts with that paper company.

She is now trying to help develop long-range plans for sustainable management of White Earth lands as ecosystems that, if restored, can provide medicines and materials for Anishinaabe traditional culture. The goal is to make it possible for people to return to the land. A tribal prophecy indicates that the people of the seventh fire—the current period—will look around and discover the things they had lost. With loss of the land had come loss of traditional spiritual principles. At the end of *Last Standing Woman*, the narrator speaks in the year 2018, describing her culture, which has rediscovered its spiritual traditions:

> *To understand our relationship to the whole and our role on the path of life. We also understand our responsibility. We only take what we need, and we leave the rest. We always give thanks for what we are given. What carries us through is the relationship we have to the Creation and the courage we are able to gather from the experience of our* aanikoobijigan, *our ancestors, and our* oshkaabewisag, *our helpers.*[20]

ways of life. Rather than regarding their ancient way as inferior, intact groups such as the Kogi of the high Colombian rainforest feel they are the elder brothers of all humanity, responsible for keeping the balance of the universe and re-educating their younger brothers who have become distracted by desire for material gain.

Personal visions and ancient prophecies about the dangers of a lifestyle that ignores the earth and the spiritual dimensions of life are leading native elders around the world to gather internationally and raise their voices together. They assert indigenous spiritual insights and observations about the state of the planet, political matters, and contemporary lifestyle issues. Award-winning author Rigoberta Menchú of the K'iché Maya writes,

> *Many people have said that indigenous peoples are myths of the past, ruins that have died. But the indigenous community is not a vestige of the past, nor is it a myth. It is full of vitality and has a course and a future. It has much wisdom and richness to contribute. They have not killed us and they will not kill us now. We are stepping forth to say, "No, we are here. We live."* [21]

Suggested reading

Beck, Peggy V. and Walters, Anna L., *The Sacred: Ways of Knowledge, Sources of Life*, Tsaile (Navajo Nation), Arizona: Navajo Community College Press, 1977. A fine and genuine survey of indigenous sacred ways, particularly those of North America.

Berger, Julian, *The Gaia Atlas of First Peoples: A Future for the Indigenous World*, New York: Anchor Books, 1990. An illustrated survey of contemporary survival issues facing the original inhabitants of many lands, with particular reference to threats to their environment from invading cultures.

Brown, Joseph Epes, *The Sacred Pipe*, 1953, New York: Penguin Books, 1971. Detailed accounts of the sacred rites of the Oglala Sioux by Black Elk, a respected holy man.

Eliade, Mircea, *Shamanism: Archaic Techniques of Ecstasy*, translated from the French by Willard Trask, London: Routledge & Kegan Paul, 1964. The first scholarly book to examine shamanism as an authentic religious form rather than as an anthropological oddity.

Ewen, Alexander, *Voice of Indigenous Peoples*, Santa Fe, New Mexico: Clear Light Publishers, 1994. Speeches and writings from indigenous speakers at the 1992 United Nations Human Rights Day, analyzing the political conditions facing indigenous peoples.

Gill, Sam D., *Native American Religions*, Belmont, California: Wadsworth, 1982. A sensitive academic survey of indigenous sacred ways in the United States.

Halifax, Joan, *Shamanic Voices: A Survey of Visionary Narratives*, New York: E. P. Dutton, 1979, and Harmondsworth, London: Penguin, 1980. First-hand accounts of shamanistic visionary experiences.

Harvey, Graham, *Indigenous Religions: A Companion*, London and New York: 2000. Scholarly articles about specific cultures, attempting to transcend the tendency to understand indigenous religions in terms of concepts taken from other religions.

Lame Deer, John and Richard Erdoes, *Lame Deer: Seeker of Visions*, New York: Pocket Books, 1976. Fascinating first-hand accounts of the life of a rebel visionary who tried to maintain the old ways.

CHAPTER 3
JUDAISM

A covenant with God

Judaism, which has no single founder and no central leader or group making theological decisions, is the diverse tradition associated with the Jewish people, who may be defined either as a religious group or as an ethnic group.

In religious terms, Jews are those who experience their long and often difficult history as a continuing dialogue with God. According to one tradition, God offered to share the divine law with seventy nations, but the semi-nomadic tribes of Israel were the only people in the world to answer God's call and to enter into a living covenant with their creator. Jews feel that this call is still available to all peoples. In a religious sense, "Israel" refers to all those who answer the call and who acknowledge and strive to obey the one God, through the **Torah**, or "teaching," given to the patriarchs, Moses, and the prophets.

As a nation, "Israel" is a people who have been repeatedly dispersed and oppressed. After the horrors of the Holocaust, some Jews founded a homeland in the land of Israel, the former center of their ancestors' faith. Other Jews live in communities around the world. Many who consider themselves Jews have been born into a Jewish ethnic identity but do not feel or practice a strong connection to Jewish religious traditions.

In this chapter we will focus on Judaism as that which Mordecai Kaplan (1881–1983) called "an evolving religious civilization," first by taking an overview of the history of the Jewish people and then by examining the religious concepts and practices that generally characterize the followers of the Torah today.

A history of the Jewish people

The Jewish sense of history begins with the stories recounted in the Hebrew Bible or **Tanakh** (which Christians call "the Old Testament"). Biblical history begins with the creation of the world by a supreme deity, or God, and progresses through the patriarchs, matriarchs, and Moses who spoke with God and led the people according to God's commandments, and the prophets who heard God's warnings to those who strayed from the commandments. But Jewish history does not end where the stories of the Tanakh end, about the second century BCE. After the holy center of Judaism, the Temple of Jerusalem, was captured and destroyed by the Romans in 70 CE, Jewish history is that of a dispersed people, finding unity in their evolving teachings and traditional practices, which were eventually codified in the great compendium of Jewish law and lore, the **Talmud**.

TORAH	The Five Books of Moses	NEVI'IM	The Prophets
בראשית	GENESIS	יהושע	JOSHUA
שמות	EXODUS	שופטים	JUDGES
ויקרא	LEVITICUS	שמואל א	I SAMUEL
במדבר	NUMBERS	שמואל ב	II SAMUEL
דברים	DEUTERONOMY	מלכים א	I KINGS
		מלכים ב	II KINGS
		ישעיה	ISAIAH
		ירמיה	JEREMIAH
		יחזקאל	EZEKIEL

KETHUVIM	The Writings		The Twelve Minor Prophets
תהילים	PSALMS	הושע	HOSEA
משלי	PROVERBS	יואל	JOEL
איוב	JOB	עמוס	AMOS
שיר השירים	THE SONG OF SONGS	עבדיה	OBADIAH
רות	RUTH	יונה	JONAH
איכה	LAMENTATIONS	מיכה	MICAH
קהלת	ECCLESIASTES	נחום	NAHUM
אסתר	ESTHER	חבקוק	HABAKKUK
דניאל	DANIEL	צפניה	ZEPHANIAH
עזרא	EZRA	חגי	HAGGAI
נחמיה	NEHEMIAH	זכריה	ZECHARIAH
דברי הימים א	I CHRONICLES	מלאכי	MALACHI
דברי הימים ב	II CHRONICLES		

The Jewish scriptures consist of the Torah (or Pentateuch), the Prophets, and the Writings. These books date roughly from the 10th to 2nd century BCE, and were written mostly in classical Hebrew. They are often referred to as Tanakh, an acronym from the first syllables of each division—Torah, Nev'im, Kethuvim.

Biblical stories

Although knowledge of the early history of the Children of Israel is based largely on the narratives of the Tanakh, scholars are uncertain of the historical accuracy of the accounts. Some of the people, events, and genealogies set forth cannot be verified by other evidence, such as archaeological findings or references to the Israelites in the writings of neighboring peoples. It may be that the Israelites were too small and loosely organized a group to be noted by historians of other cultures. No mention of Israel appears in other sources until about 1230 BCE, but biblical narratives and genealogies place Abraham, said to be the first patriarch of the Israelites, at about 1700 to 1900 BCE.

Jews hold the **Pentateuch**, the "five books of Moses" that appear at the beginning of the Tanakh, as the most sacred part of the scriptures. Traditionalists believe that these books were divinely revealed to Moses and written down by him as a single document. Some contemporary biblical researchers disagree. On the basis of clues, such as the use of variant names for God, they speculate that these books were oral traditions reworked and set down later by several different sources with the intent of interpreting the formation of Israel from a religious point of view, as

JUDAISM

BCE	
BCE 1900	c.1900–1700 Abraham, the first patriarch
1500	c.13th or 12th century Moses leads the Israelites out of bondage in Egypt
1000	c.1010–970 David, king of Judah and Israel 961–931 King Solomon builds the first Temple in Jerusalem
600	586 First Temple destroyed; Jews exiled to Babylon
500	515 Second Temple built c.430 Torah established: Ezra the Scribe
100	30 BCE–10 CE Hillel the Elder
CE	
100	70 Jerusalem falls to the Romans c.90 Jewish Canon fixed c.200 Mishnah compiled
500	
600	c.600 Babylonian Talmud completed
1000	
	1135–1204 Life of Maimonides 1480 The Inquisition begins 1492 Mass expulsion of Jews from Spain
1500	1555 onward Ghettos of Italy and Germany
1700	1700–1760 The Baal Shem Tov c.1720–1780 The Enlightenment in Europe
1900	
	1940–1945 The Holocaust 1947 Discovery of the Dead Sea Scrolls 1948 Israel declared an independent state 1967 The Six-Day War 1990 onward Israeli–Palestinian conflicts and peace initiatives
2000	

the results of God's actions in human history. The Pentateuch seems to have assumed its final form in the days of Ezra the Scribe (fifth century BCE).

Some of the stories in the Pentateuch, such as the Creation, the Garden of Eden, the Great Flood, and the Tower of Babel, are similar to earlier Mesopotamian legends. In the narratives of the continuing history of the Israelites, only the last four books (I and II Samuel and I and II Kings) are thought to be edited directly from contemporary sources. Although the accuracy of many of the stories has not yet been independently documented, they are of great spiritual significance in Christianity and Islam as well as in Judaism. They are also politically important, for along with the Talmud they later gave a scattered people a special sense of group identity.

FROM CREATION TO THE GOD OF ABRAHAM   The Hebrew scriptures begin with a sweeping poetic account of the creation of heaven and earth by God in six days, from the time of "the earth being unformed and void, with darkness over the surface of the deep and a wind from (or: the spirit of) God sweeping over the water."[1] After creating the material universe, God created man and woman in the divine "image" or "likeness," placing them as masters of the earth, rulers of "the fish of the sea, the birds of the sky, and all the living things that creep on the earth."[2] In this account, God is portrayed as a transcendent Creator, without origins, gender, or form, a being utterly different from what has been created. Since Hebrew has no gender-neutral pronouns, God is generally—though not always—described in male singular terms. This creation story (in Genesis 1 and 2:1–4) is attributed by scholars to the "priestly source," thought to be editors writing immediately before or after the exile of the Jews to Babylon in 586 BCE.

A second, probably earlier, version of the creation story follows, beginning in Genesis 2:4. It is thought to be a contribution to the scriptures from the "Yahwist source," which used the word transliterated as "Yahweh" for the supreme male deity. Instead of presenting woman as the equal of man, it portrays her as an offshoot of Adam, the first man, formed to keep him company. This version has commonly been interpreted as blaming woman for the troubles of humanity, although this reading is not supported in the Hebrew manuscripts. According to the legend of Adam and Eve, originally God placed the first two humans in a garden paradise. The woman Eve ("mother of all the living") was promised wisdom by a serpent (later often interpreted as a symbol of Satan) to tempt her to taste the fruit of the tree of knowledge of good and evil, against God's command. She gave some to Adam as well. According to the legend, this ended their innocence. God cursed the serpent and the land, and banished Adam and Eve from their garden; their lives were no longer paradisical nor were they immortal, for they no longer had access to the "tree of life."

The theme of exile reappears continually in the Hebrew Bible, and in later Jewish history the people are rendered homeless again and again. The biblical narratives emphasize that the people risk God's displeasure every time they stray from God's commands. They are repeatedly exiled from their spiritual home and continually seek to return to it.

A more optimistic interpretation developed later, however. This was the feeling that the Jewish people were spread throughout the world by God's will, for a sacred purpose: to be good citizens of whatever land they reside in, and to help

The Adam and Eve account in Genesis, as portrayed by Lucas Cranach the Elder (1472–1553).

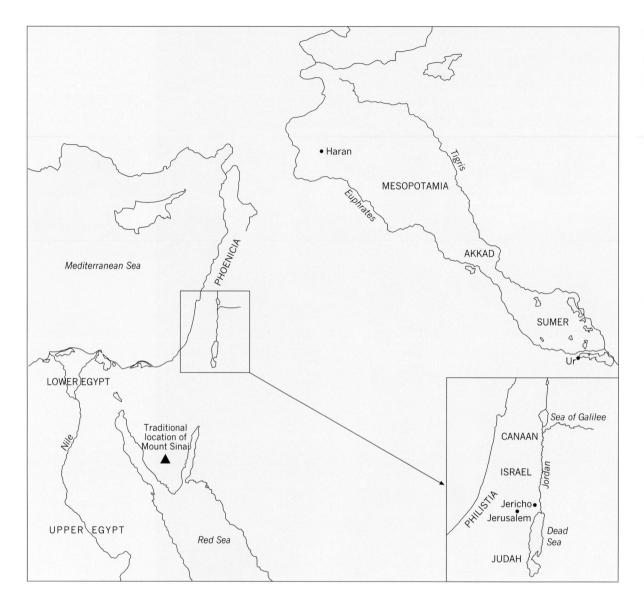

The Israelites identified themselves as a people whose ancestors, Abraham and Sarah, moved from Ur and Haran in Mesopotamia to Canaan; Abraham's grandson, Jacob, called "Israel," resettled his large family in Egypt, where the Israelites were eventually treated as slaves.

raise the imperfect world back up to the condition of perfection in which God had created it. Israel would find its way home only when all of creation was lifted up. The rabbinic tradition, which began in the first century CE and has shaped Jewish theology into the modern period, emphasized that the way out of exile was through study and righteous living. Commandments have their origin in God and, if followed, will lead humanity back to a life in harmony with God.

Again and again, however, according to the scriptural stories, the people disobey God's will. One of the legends recounted concerns Noah, the sole righteous man of his generation. According to the narrator, who attributes thoughts and emotions to God, God despairs of the general wickedness of humans, regrets having created them, and sends a great flood "to destroy all flesh under the sky."[3]

But with Noah, God establishes a covenant and gives directions for the building of an ark, which saves Noah's family and two of each of God's creatures. God promises never again to destroy the created world or to interfere with the established natural order, with the rainbow as a sign of this covenant "between me and all flesh that is on earth."[4]

God does, however, continue to intervene in history, according to the narrators. Ten generations after the legend of Noah, the narrative focuses on Abraham, Isaac, and Jacob (the "patriarchs"), and their wives, Sarah, Rebecca, Leah, and Rachel (the "matriarchs"). According to the biblical narratives, Abraham was born in Ur (now in Iraq), migrated to Haran (now in Turkey), and then was called by God to journey to Canaan. With his wife Sarah and his household, he left the land of his father and also the religion of his father, a worshipper of the old gods.

Abraham is held up as an example of obedience to God's commands. Without hesitation, he is said to undergo circumcision (cutting away of the foreskin of the penis) as an initiatory rite, a sign of the covenant in which God agrees to be the divine protector of Abraham and his descendants, with all males to be likewise circumcised on the eighth day after birth.

After Abraham has a son, Ishmael, by the Egyptian slave woman Hagar, God blesses the one-hundred-year-old Abraham's ninety-year-old wife Sarah, saying that she will become the "mother of nations: the kings of many people shall spring from her" (Genesis 17:16). According to the biblical account, Sarah does indeed give birth to a son, Isaac, and then insists that Ishmael and Hagar be banished to the wilderness. God supports this demand, assuring Abraham that he will be father of two nations—one line through Isaac (to become the Israelites) and one through Ishmael (whom Arabs consider their ancestor).

God then tests Abraham by asking him to sacrifice his son Isaac. When the patriarch prepares to comply, the Lord stops him, satisfied that "now I know that you fear God."[5] The Hebrew word *yirah*, usually translated as "fear" of God, also implies "awe of God's greatness," or what Rabbi Lawrence Kushner calls "trembling in the presence of ultimate holiness."[6]

Scholars disagree on whether pure monotheism—the worship of a single God of the universe, exclusive of any other divine beings—was practiced by the early patriarchs. Many names for divinity are used in the early scriptures, and some researchers consider them names of separate gods. It is known that the religion of the Canaanites had some influence on that of the Israelites. The Canaanites were polytheistic, with highly developed mythology and ritual directed largely to agricultural fertility.

As is common in the growth of any new religion, elements of the older faiths of the area were incorporated into or adapted to the new one. However, the ultimate thrust of Judaism was the rejection of the gods of surrounding peoples. The Israelites came to see themselves as having been chosen by a single divine patron. In their patriarchal culture, this God was perceived as a ruler in a close relationship to the people, like a parent to children, or a sovereign to vassals. At first Israel's God may have

The settled agricultural peoples of Canaan paid homage to a high male god, called El, and an earlier Great Mother Goddess (Ishtar, disguised as his consort). The goddess (shown here), associated with vegetation, agricultural knowledge, and abundance, was worshipped as asherahs, sacred tree-symbol altar poles, which the Israelites destroyed.

Abraham's descendants are said to have given birth to the twelve tribes of Israel. They are symbolically depicted here as sitting in the patriach's lap. (Souvigny Bible, 12th century, France.)

been perceived as a private tribal god, later known as the supreme and only deity of the universe.

ISRAEL'S BIRTH IN STRUGGLE   It is also unclear who the people of the biblical narratives were. Some scholars think the word "Hebrew" is derived from the generic term *habiru*, used for the low-class, landless people who lived as outlaws and were often hired as mercenaries. Others point to *'ibri* as the biblical word for Hebrew, meaning "children of Eber," an ethnic term. But because of frequent moving and intermarrying, the Israelites were actually of mixed ethnic stock, including Hebrew, Aramaean, and Canaanite. The word **Semite** is a modern linguistic term applied to Jews, Arabs, and others of eastern Mediterranean origin whose languages are classified as Semitic; it is often inaccurately used as an ethnic designation.

According to the genealogies set forth in the Pentateuch, the people who became known as Israelites were the offspring of Israel (first called Jacob), grandson of Abraham. Jacob received the new name after wrestling all night with a being who turned out to be an angel of God. "Israel" means "the one who struggled with God."

This story in which a human being struggles and finally is reborn at a higher level of spirituality has been taken as a metaphor for the spiritual evolution of the people of Israel. As a result of the struggle, Israel the patriarch receives not only a new name but also the promise that many nations will be born from him. The nation Israel—"the smallest of peoples"[7]—is perceived as the spiritual center for the world to grow toward God. This is its destiny, though Jews do not feel that it has yet been fulfilled.

EGYPT: BONDAGE AND EXODUS   Jacob/Israel is said to have had one daughter and twelve sons by his two wives and their two maidservants. The twelve sons became the heads of the twelve tribes of Israel. The whole group left Canaan for Goshen in Egypt during a famine. Exodus, the second book of the Tanakh, opens about four centuries later with a statement that the descendants of Israel had become numerous. To keep them from becoming too powerful, the reigning pharaoh ordered that they be turned into slaves for massive construction projects. To further curb the population, the pharaoh ordered midwives to kill all boy babies born to the Israelite women.

One who escaped this fate was Moses, an Israelite of the tribe of Levi, who was raised in the palace by the pharaoh's own daughter. He is said to have fled the country after killing an Egyptian overseer who was beating an Israelite worker. While he lived in exile in Midian, the oppression of the Israelites in Egypt grew worse and worse.

According to the scriptural Book of Exodus, Moses was chosen by God to defy the pharaoh and lead the people out of bondage, out of Egypt. On Mount Sinai, an angel

God speaks to Moses from a burning bush, as depicted by Marc Chagall (1887–1985). (Stained-glass window, detail, Cathedral of St. Etienne, Metz, France.)

According to the legend of Exodus, God empowered Moses to hold back the waters of the Red Sea to let the children of Israel pass through, and then drown the pursuing Egyptians in the returning waters. (Hebrew MS 6 Haggadah.)

of God appeared to him from within a bush blazing with fire but not consumed by it. God called to him out of the bush and yet cautioned, "Do not come closer. Remove your sandals from your feet, for the place on which you stand is holy ground."[8] When God told Moses to go rescue "My people, the Israelites, from Egypt,"[9] Moses demurred, but God insisted:

I will be with you ... Thus you shall say to the Israelites, "Ehyeh [I Am] sent me to you. ... The LORD, the God of your fathers, the God of Abraham, the God of Isaac, and the God of Jacob, has sent me to you."[10]

The word given in this biblical translation as "LORD" is considered too sacred to be pronounced. In the Hebrew scriptures it is rendered only in consonants as YHWH or YHVH; the pronunciation of the vowels is not known.

With his brother Aaron to act as spokesperson, Moses did indeed return to Egypt. Many chapters of Exodus recount miracles used to convince the pharaoh to let the people go into the wilderness to worship their God. These signs included a rod that turned into a serpent, plagues of locusts, flies, and frogs, animal diseases, a terrible storm, lasting darkness, and finally the killing by the Lord of all firstborn children and creatures. The Israelites were spared this fate, marking their doors with the blood of a slaughtered lamb so that the Lord would pass over them. (The holiday Passover commemorates this story.) At this, the pharaoh at last let the Israelites go. The redemption from bondage by the special protection of the Lord has served ever since as a central theme in Judaism.

According to the scriptural account, the Lord's presence led the Israelites, manifesting as a pillar of cloud by day and a pillar of fire by night. The armies of the deceitful pharaoh pursued them until the famous scene in which Moses stretched his staff toward the sea and God caused an east wind to blow all night, dividing the waters so that the Israelites could pass through safely on a dry seabed. As the Egyptians tried to follow, God told Moses again to hold out his arm over the sea, and the walls of water came crashing down on them, drowning every one.

FROM THE WILDERNESS TO CANAAN   According to the Pentateuch, God told Moses that he would lead the people back to Canaan. First, however, it was necessary to travel to the holy Mount Sinai to re-establish the covenant between God and the people. The Lord is said to have descended to its summit in a terrifying show of lightning, thunder, fire, smoke, and trumpeting. God is said to have then given the people through Moses a set of rules for righteous living, later called the Torah. Among them are the Ten Commandments. God also gave a set of social norms, prescribed religious feasts, and detailed instructions for the construction of a portable tabernacle with a holy ark, the **Ark of the Covenant**, in which to keep the stone tablets on which God inscribed the commandments.

THE TEN COMMANDMENTS

"I am the Lord your God who brought you out of Egypt, out of the land of slavery. You shall have no other god to set against me.

You shall not make a carved image for yourself nor the likeness of anything in the heavens above, or on the earth below, or in the waters under the earth.

You shall not bow down to them or worship them; for I, the Lord your God, am a jealous god. I punish the children for the sins of the fathers to the third and fourth generations of those who hate me. But I keep faith with thousands, with those who love me and keep my commandments.

You shall not make wrong use of the name of the Lord your God; the Lord will not leave unpunished the man who misuses his name.

Remember to keep the sabbath day holy. You have six days to labor and do all your work. But the seventh day is a sabbath of the Lord your God; that day you shall not do any work, . . . for in six days the Lord made heaven and earth, the sea, and all that is in them, and on the seventh day he rested. Therefore the Lord blessed the sabbath day and declared it holy.

Honor your father and your mother, that you may live long in the land which the Lord your God is giving you.

You shall not commit murder.

You shall not commit adultery.

You shall not steal.

You shall not give false evidence against your neighbor.

You shall not covet your neighbor's house; you shall not covet your neighbor's wife, his slave, his slave-girl, his ox, his ass, or anything that belongs to him."

Exodus 20:2–17

God's presence abided with the Israelites, wandering or stationary, in the portable Ark of the Covenant, which was said to house the tablets of Moses. This third-century CE painting from the Dura Europos Synagogue shows the Ark leaving the land of the Philistines. They had captured the Ark but sent it back after being cursed by bubonic plague.

During the forty days that Moses was on the mountain receiving these instructions, the people who had just agreed to a holy covenant with God became disturbed and impatient. The biblical account says that under Aaron's reluctant supervision, they melted down their gold jewelry and cast it into the form of a golden calf, practicing what the authors of the biblical narratives considered idol-worship, which had been explicitly forbidden by God. Moses is said to have been so outraged by their idolatry that he smashed the stone tablets and destroyed the idol. He ordered the only people still siding with YHWH, the Levites, to slay 3,000 of those who had strayed.

After another forty-day meeting with God on the summit of Mount Sinai, Moses again returned with stone tablets on which God had inscribed the commandments. Moses' face was said to be so radiant from his encounter with God that he had to veil it. Aaron and his sons were invested as priests, the tabernacle was constructed as directed, and the people set off for the land of Canaan, with the Presence of the Lord filling the tabernacle.

Even with the powerful presence of the Ark they carried, the Israelites had to wander for forty years through the desert before they could re-enter the promised land, fertile Canaan, which at that time belonged to other peoples. The long sojourn in the wilderness is a familiar metaphor in the spiritual search. Faith is continually tested by difficulties. But even in the wilderness, the Israelites' God did not forsake them. Every day they found their daily bread scattered on the ground, in the form of an unknown food, which they named manna.

A stone inscription, the Merneptah Stele, written for the Egyptian Pharaoh

From the Hebrew Bible—David and Goliath

David, the youngest son of Jesse of Bethlehem, was a bright-eyed, ruddy-cheeked shepherd, but from the time he was secretly anointed by the prophet Samuel as the future king of Israel, the power of the living God was with him. His father had become feeble, so David was tending Jesse's flocks while his three elder brothers were doing battle with the Philistines in King Saul's Israelite army.

One day Jesse asked David to carry some food to his brothers and their commanding officer and to bring back news from the front. When David arrived at the battlefield, he learned that every day, Goliath, the champion of the Philistines, came out of the Philistine encampment to challenge the Israelites to send one man to do battle with him. Goliath's challenge: If any Israelite could kill him in a fair one-to-one fight, the Philistines would surrender to the Israelites and become their slaves. If the Israelite lost, the Israelites would become slaves of the Philistines.

No Israelite had dared to take up this challenge, for Goliath was a giant of a man. He stood over nine feet tall, wore heavy bronze armor, and carried a massive spear. David alone was undismayed. He presented himself to King Saul and said, according to the biblical account,

"Do not lose heart, sir, I will go and fight this Philistine." Saul answered, "You cannot go and fight with this Philistine; you are only a lad, and he has been a fighting man all his life." David said to Saul, "Sir, I am my father's shepherd; when a lion or bear comes and carries off a sheep from the flock, I go after it and attack it and rescue the victim from its jaws. Then if it turns on me, I seize it by the beard and batter it to death. Lions I have killed and bears, and this uncircumcised Philistine will fare no better than they; he has defied the army of the living God. The Lord who saved me from the lion and the bear will save me from this Philistine." "Go then," said Saul, "and the Lord will be with you." He put his own tunic on David, placed a bronze helmet on his head and gave him a coat of mail to wear; he then fastened his sword on David

over his tunic. But David hesitated, because he had not tried them, and said to Saul, "I cannot go with these, because I have not tried them." So he took them off. Then he picked up his stick, chose five smooth stones from the brook and put them in a shepherd's bag which served as his pouch. He walked out to meet the Philistine with his sling in his hand.

The Philistine came on towards David, with his shield-bearer marching ahead; and he looked David up and down and had nothing but contempt for this handsome lad with his ruddy cheeks and bright eyes. He said to David, "Am I a dog that you come out against me with sticks?" And he swore at him in the name of his god. "Come on," he said, "and I will give your flesh to the birds and the beasts." David answered, "You have come against me with sword and spear and dagger, but I have come against you in the name of the Lord of Hosts, the God of the army of Israel which you have defied. The Lord will put you into my power this day; I will kill you and cut your head off and leave your carcass and the carcasses of the Philistines to the birds and the wild beasts; all the world shall know that there is a God in Israel. All those who are gathered here shall see that the Lord saves neither by sword nor spear; the battle is the Lord's, and he will put you all into our power."

When the Philistine began moving towards him again, David ran quickly to engage him. He put his hand into his bag, took out a stone, slung it, and struck the Philistine on the forehead. The stone sank into his forehead, and he fell flat on his face on the ground. So David proved the victor with his sling and stone; he struck Goliath down and gave him a mortal wound, though he had no sword. Then he ran to the Philistine and stood over him, and grasping his sword, he drew it out of the scabbard, dispatched him and cut off his head. The Philistines, when they saw that their hero was dead, turned and ran [but were killed by the pursuing Israelites]. ... David took Goliath's head and carried it to Jerusalem.[11]

Merneptah, places the Hebrews as being in Canaan about 1207 BCE. Through what was described as the miraculous help of God, they fought many battles against the kings and tribes of Canaan. Archaeological evidence indicates that every Canaanite town was destroyed from one to four times between the thirteenth and eleventh centuries BCE, though the identity of the conquerors is not known. At Sinai, God had vowed to oust the inhabitants of the lands into which the Israelites advanced, warning them against adopting the local spiritual practices: "No, you must tear down their altars, smash their pillars, and cut down their sacred posts."[12] The editors of the scriptures clearly considered the Canaanite religion spiritually invalid and morally inferior to their own. But the Israelites' attention to their God was not absolute. According to the scriptures, whenever they turned away from YHWH, forgetting or worshipping other gods, surrounding peoples found them easy prey.

THE FIRST TEMPLE OF JERUSALEM   David, the second king of Israel, is remembered as Israel's greatest king. An obscure shepherd, David was chosen by the prophet Samuel to be anointed on the head with oil, for thus were future kings found and divinely acknowledged in those times. Composer and singer of psalms, David was summoned to the court of the first Israelite king, Saul, to play soothing music whenever an evil spirit seized the king. When Saul and his son were killed in battle, David was made king. By defeating or making allegiances with surrounding nations, David created the beginnings of a secure, prosperous Israelite empire. He made the captured city of Jerusalem its capital and brought the Ark of the Covenant there.

Under the reign of King Solomon (son of David), a great Temple was built in Jerusalem. It was to be a permanent home for the Ark of the Covenant, which was housed in the innermost sanctum, and a place for making the burned offerings of animals, grain, and oil to the divine. There already existed an ancient practice among pre-Israelite peoples of using high places for altars where sacrifices were made to the gods. After centuries of wandering worship, the Israelites now had a central, stationary place where God would be most present to them. God is said to have appeared to Solomon after the fourteen-day Temple dedication ceremony and pledged: "I consecrate this House which you have built and I set My name there forever. My eyes and My heart shall ever be there."[13]

The Temple became the central place for sacrifice in Judaism. But its builder, Solomon, also accumulated great personal wealth, at the expense of the people, and built altars to the gods of his wives, who came from other nations. This so angered the Lord, according to the scriptures, that he divided the kingdom after Solomon's death. An internal revolt of the ten northern tribes established a new kingdom of Israel, which was independent of Jerusalem and the dynasty of David. The southern kingdom, continuing in its allegiance to the house of David and retaining Jerusalem as its capital, renamed itself Judah, after David's tribe.

Prophets such as Elijah warned the people against worshipping gods other than the Lord, and exhorted them to end their evil ways. Over the centuries, these prophets were men and women who had undergone transformational ordeals that made them instruments for the word of God. The "early prophets," such as Elijah, focused on the sin of idolatry; the "later prophets" warned that social injustice and moral corruption would be the ruin of the Jewish state.

By the reign of King Hoshea of Israel, the kingdom was so corrupt and idolatrous that, in the scriptural interpretation, God permitted the strong kingdom of
Assyria to overtake what was left of the small country. To sustain the population
needed for its empire-building and to keep Israel from rising again as a nation,
Assyria carried off most of the Israelites to exile among the **Gentiles** (non-Jewish
people). Most of the Israelites became dispersed within Assyria; these people who
thenceforth lost a distinct ethnic identity are known as the "Ten Lost Tribes of
Israel." This destruction of the northern kingdom took place in 722 BCE and is
attested in Assyrian annals.

Judah maintained its independence, declining and continually warned of
impending doom by its prophets, until King Nebuchadnezzar of Babylonia
(which by 605 BCE had taken over the Assyrian Empire) captured Jerusalem. In
586 BCE the great walls of Jerusalem were battered down and its buildings put to
the torch by the Babylonians. The great Temple was emptied of its sacred treasures, the altar dismantled, and the building destroyed. Many Judaeans were
taken to exile in Babylonia, where they were thenceforth known as "Jews," since
they were from Judah.

The prophets interpreted these events as reasonable punishment by God for
Judah's idolatry. Nevertheless, Isaiah and a later anonymous prophet prophesied
that God would soon usher in a new era of peace and justice among all peoples,
from his holy Temple in Jerusalem.

I never could forget you.
See, I have engraved you
On the palms of My hands . . .

Isaiah 49:15–16

Return to Jerusalem

After fifty years of exile in Babylon, a small group of devoted Jews, probably
fewer than 50,000, returned to their holy city. They were allowed to do so by the
Persian king, Cyrus. He authorized the rebuilding of the Temple in Jerusalem,
which was completed in 515 BCE.

The second Temple became the central symbol to a scattered Jewish nation,
most of whom did not return to Jerusalem from Babylon, which was now their
home (and were thenceforth said to be living in the **Diaspora**, from the Greek
word for "disperse"). A new emphasis on Temple rites developed, with an hereditary priesthood tracing its ancestry to Aaron.

The priestly class, under the leadership of Ezra, a priest and a scribe, also
undertook to revise, or redact, the stories of the people, editing the Pentateuch to
reveal the hand of God. Some scholars think that it was these priestly editors who
wrote the creation account in Genesis 1, glorifying the greatness and omnipotence of their God as creator of the universe.

The Torah was now established as the spiritual and secular foundation of the
dispersed nation. In approximately 430 BCE, Ezra the scribe set the precedent of
reading for hours from the Torah scrolls in a public square. These "five books of
Moses" were accepted as a sacred covenant.

As the Jews lived under foreign rule—Persian, Greek, Parthian, and then Roman—Judaism became somewhat open to cross-cultural religious borrowings. Concepts of Satan, the hierarchy of angels, reward or punishment in an afterlife, and the final resurrection of the body on the Day of Judgment are thought by some scholars to have made their way into Jewish belief from the Zoroastrianism of the Persian Empire, for these beliefs were absent from earlier Judaic religion. However, they were not uniformly accepted. Greek lifestyle and thought were introduced into the Middle East by Alexander the Great in the fourth century BCE. The rationalistic, humanistic influences of Hellenism led many wealthy and intellectual Jews, including the priests in Jerusalem, to adopt a Hellenistic attitude of scepticism rather than unquestioning belief.

Tension between traditionalists and those embracing Greek ways came to a head during the reign of Antiochus IV Epiphanes, a Hellenistic ruler of Syria (175–164 BCE), the nation that then held political sovereignty over the land of Israel. Antiochus seems to have tried to achieve political unity by forcing a single Hellenistic culture on all his subjects, abolishing the Torah as the Jewish constitution, burning copies of the Torah, killing families who circumcised their sons, building an altar to Zeus in the Temple in Jerusalem, and sacrificing a hog on it (in defiance of the Mosaic law against eating or touching dead pigs as unclean). The Maccabean rebellion, a revolt led by the Hasmon family of priests, called in Hebrew the Maccabees ("Hammers"), won a degree of independence for Judaea in 164 BCE. The successful rebellion established a new and independent kingdom, once again called Israel, once again centered around Jerusalem, and ruled by the Hasmonean family. This kingdom lasted only until its conquest by the Roman general Pompey in 63 BCE, and was the last independent Jewish nation until the twentieth century.

Under the Hasmonean kings, three **sects** of Jews formed in Judaea. One was the **Sadducees**, priests and wealthy businesspeople, conservatives intent on preserving the letter of the law. The **Pharisees** were more liberal citizens from all classes who sought to study the applications of Torah to everyday life. A third group was uncompromising in their piety and their disgust with what they considered a corrupted priesthood. Some of them retreated to a fortified compound at Qumran, near the Dead Sea, where they joined or formed the **Essenes**. Their leader was the "Teacher of Righteousness," a priest, reformer, and mystic whose name was not uttered. The library of this Essene community, now known as the Dead Sea Scrolls, was discovered near Qumran at the northwest end of the Dead Sea in 1947. From these 2,000-year-old texts, we now know that the Essenes emphasized discipline, communal living, obedience, study, and spiritual preparation for the Day of Judgment they anticipated, the New Age when the "sons of light" would be victorious over the "sons of darkness."

Eventually the conflicts among the Hasmoneans erupted into civil war. The Roman general Pompey was called in from Syria in 63 BCE to choose between contenders to the Hasmonean throne, but he took over the country instead. There followed four centuries of oppressive Roman rule of Judaea.

Under Roman rule, a popular belief grew among Jews that a **Messiah** would come at last to rescue the people from their sufferings. For example, a vision had reportedly been given to Daniel when the Jews were in exile in Babylon. Daniel foresaw that one "like a human being" (or "son of man") would come on heavenly

Zoroastrianism, a Bridge between East and West

One of the religions thought to have contributed to the development of Jewish thought is still surviving today, though just barely. This is Zoroastrianism, a religion from ancient Iran. At present, it has perhaps only 130,000 remaining practitioners. But for more than a thousand years, it may have been the official religion of the vast Iranian Empire, which extended from Iraq or Turkey to India. It is in some ways a bridge between Eastern and Western religions. Its origins are synchronous with, and similar to, Hinduism; it is thought to have influenced Buddhism; and it introduced beliefs that were later integrated into Jewish, Christian, and Muslim religions. These include a belief in heaven and hell, an evil force, judgment of the individual and resurrection of the body after death, and a dramatic apocalyptic end of the world with the final resurrection of the dead.

The theology of ancient Zoroastrianism itself is subject to debate, for over the centuries a large portion of its sacred scriptures was destroyed or forgotten and the meanings of the old language were lost. Early elements of the faith are thought to have come from the Indo-Iranians, a branch of the same Aryan tribes who have traditionally been thought to have made their way down from the steppes of southern Russia into the Indian subcontinent. Like the Vedic Indians, they honored the divinities of nature in daily priestly rituals called *yasna* with libations to the god of fire and the goddesses of water, which are similar to Brahmanic rituals known as *yagna* in India. They worshipped a pantheon of gods representing the elements, aspects of nature, and abstract principles. These gods often corresponded with those worshipped by the Vedic Indians and were similarly named *daevas*, like the Indian *devas*. The ritual worship conducted by the priest was designed, as in India, to maintain the natural order, truth, and righteousness of the universe by re-enacting the original sacrifice that led to its creation.

Whereas the faith is known in Iran as Mazdayasna—"the worship of the Wise Lord, Ahura Mazda"—Western scholars refer to the tradition by the name of one of its great reformers, the prophet Zarathushtra (Greek: Zoroaster). He may have lived about 1100 to 550 BCE or even earlier. It is thought that he was trained as a priest in the Indo-Iranian tradition. He was also apparently a mystical seeker who spent many years in spiritual retreat. At the age of thirty, he is said to have had a stunning vision of a great shining being, Vohu Manah, the embodiment of the loving mind. Vohu Manah led him into the presence of Ahura Mazda, the creator God. From repeated contacts with Ahura Mazda and his angels, Zarathushtra reportedly determined that in contrast to the multiplicity of gods worshipped by the Indo-Iranians, Ahura Mazda was the Supreme Lord, from whom all good things flowed.

Zarathushtra is thought to have been troubled by violent aspects of the old religion. He is also said to have disapproved of the worship of the nature spirits through fear, accompanied by requests for personal benefits. Zarathushtra denounced all cruelty, selfishness, distortion, and hypocrisy in the name of religion. He insisted that Ahura Mazda creates only goodness and should be worshipped by good thoughts, words, and deeds. There is a cosmic battle between sustaining and destroying forces, and to assure the victory of good over evil, humans must dedicate themselves as spiritual warriors for goodness.

It is very difficult to trace the later spread of Zarathushtra's teachings. The Magi—a tribe of priestly specialists in western Iran—seem to have become involved with the transmission of Zoroastrianism some time after Zarathushtra died, but they may have altered it significantly. Ahura Mazda was apparently revered by the Achaemenid kings of the great Persian Empire, the largest the world had known, which was created in the mid-sixth century BCE by King Cyrus. Cyrus seems to have been a follower of Ahura Mazda, but he and the succeeding Achaemenid kings left no written mention of Zarathushtra. However, there are remnants of Zoroastrian-like fire holders and some references in inscriptions to Ahura Mazda.

The empire Cyrus had created by far-reaching conquests stretched from the Indus Valley to what is now Greece. The Jews within this territory were allowed to practice their own religion, but some seem to have adopted certain Zoroastrian beliefs, such as the belief that there is an evil aspect in life, an angelic hierarchy, an immortal soul, reward or punishment in an afterlife, and the final resurrection of the body on the Day of Judgment. From Judaism, these beliefs may have passed indirectly into Christianity and Islam.

The Essenes seem to have lived communally and ascetically, awaiting the final judgment in settlements such as this one excavated at Qumran, where ancient biblical scrolls were found hidden in caves.

clouds, and on him the white-haired, fiery-throned "Ancient of Days" would confer "everlasting dominion" over all people, a kingship "that shall not be destroyed."[14] By the first century CE, expectations had developed that through this Messiah, God would gather the chosen people and not only free them from oppression but also reinstate Jewish political sovereignty in the land of Israel. Then all nations would recognize that Israel's God is the God of all the world. The messianic end of the age, or end of the world, would be heralded by a period of great oppression and wickedness. Many felt that this time was surely at hand. There were some who felt that Jesus was the long-awaited Messiah.

Spurred by anti-Roman militias called **Zealots**, the Jews rose up in armed rebellion against Rome in 66 CE. The rebellion was suppressed, and after heroic resistance, the Jewish defenders were slaughtered in the holy walled city of Jerusalem in 70 CE. The Roman legions destroyed the Jewish Temple in Jerusalem, leaving only a course of foundation stones still standing. This Temple has never been rebuilt; the foundation stones, called the Western Wall, have been a place of Jewish pilgrimage and prayer for twenty centuries. The Essene movement was apparently annihilated in this uprising.

A second disastrous revolt followed in 132–135 CE. Ultimately, Jerusalem was reduced to ruins, along with all Judaean towns. Those remaining Jews who had not been executed were forbidden to read the Torah, observe the Sabbath, or circumcise their sons. None was allowed to enter Jerusalem when it was rebuilt as the Roman city Aelia Capitolina, except on the anniversary of the destruction of the Temple, when they could pay to lean against all that remained of it—the Western Wall—and lament the loss of their sacred home. Judaea was renamed Palestine after the ancient Philistines. Judaism no longer had a physical heart or a geographic center.

Rabbinic Judaism

Judaism could have died then, as its people scattered throughout the Mediterranean countries and western Asia. One of the groups who survived the destruction of Judaea were the **rabbis**, inheritors of the Pharisee tradition. They are the founders of rabbinic Judaism, which has defined the major forms of Jewish practice over the last two thousand years. Another was the messianic movement that had formed up around Jesus of Nazareth, later known as Christianity. Between them they have kept the teachings of the Tanakh vibrantly alive. Both Christianity and rabbinic Judaism used the Hebrew Bible as a foundation document, but from it they have developed in their own ways.

The rabbis were teachers, religious decision-makers, and creators of liturgical prayer. No longer were there priests or Temple for offering sacrifices. The substitute for animal sacrifice was liturgical prayer and ethical behavior. Without the Jerusalem Temple, the community itself gained new importance. The people met in **synagogues**, which simply means "meeting places," to read the Torah and to worship communally, praying simply and directly to God. Synagogue services did not involve animal sacrifices, but rather prayer, song, and readings from the Torah. A *minyan*—a quorum of ten adult males—had to be present for community worship.

Everyone was taught the basics of the Torah as a matter of course, but, from the age of five or six, many men also occupied themselves with deep study of the scriptures. Women were excluded or exempted from formal Torah study. Women's family responsibilities at home were considered primary for them; else-

A rabbi reading the Talmud.

where they were to be subordinate to men. Literacy was highly valued for men, and this characteristic persisted through the centuries even in the midst of largely illiterate societies. It is said that in the afterlife one can see the Jewish sages still bent over their books studying. This is Paradise.

The revealed scriptures were closed; what remained was to interpret them as indications of God's word and will in history. This process continues to the present, giving Judaism a continually evolving quality in tandem with unalterable roots in the ancient books of Moses. Centering the religion in books and teachings rather than in a geographical location or a politically vulnerable priesthood has enabled the dispersed community to retain a sense of unity across time and space, as well as a common heritage of law, language, and practice.

The rabbis set themselves the task of thoroughly interpreting the Hebrew scriptures. Their process of study, called **Midrash**, yielded two types of interpretation: legal decisions, called *halakhah* ("proper conduct"), and non-legal teachings, called *haggadah* (folklore, sociological and historical knowledge, theological arguments, ritual traditions, sermons, and mystical teachings).

In addition to delving into the meanings of the written Torah, the rabbis undertook to apply the biblical teachings to their contemporary lives, in very different cultural circumstances from those of the ancients, and to interpret scripture in ways acceptable to contemporary values. The model for this delicate task of living interpretation had been set by Hillel the Elder, who taught from about 30 BCE to 10 CE, probably overlapping with the life of Jesus. He was known as a humble and pious scholar, who stressed loving relationships, good deeds, and charity toward the less-advantaged. He also established a valuable set of rules for flexible interpretation of Torah.

> *What is hateful to you, do not do to your neighbor:*
> *that is the entire Torah;*
> *the rest is commentary;*
> *go and learn it.*
>
> *Hillel the Elder[15]*

This process of Midrash yielded a vast body of legal and spiritual literature, known in Jewish tradition as the oral Torah. According to rabbinical tradition, God gave Moses two versions of the Torah at Sinai: the written Torah, which appears in the five books of Moses, and the oral Torah, a larger set of teachings, which was memorized and passed down through the generations all the way to the early rabbis. After the fixing of the Jewish canon—the scriptures admitted to the Tanakh in about 90 CE—the rabbinical schools set out to systematize all the commentaries and the oral tradition, which was continually evolving on the basis of expanded and updated understandings of the original oral Torah. In about 200 CE, Judah the Prince completed a terse edition of legal teachings of the oral Torah, which was thenceforth known as the **Mishnah**.

The Mishnah's method of deriving legal principles for social order is based on logical analysis of how things are and why they are so. It systematically sets up hierarchical classifications, such as this example, illustrating levels of women's status:

4.5   A. *For all purposes is she in the domain of the father, until she enters the domain of the husband through marriage.*
      B. *(1) [If] the father handed her over to the agents of the husband, lo, she [from that point on] is in the domain of the husband. . . .*

5.5   A. *These are the kinds of labor which a woman performs for her husband:*
      B. *She (1) grinds flour, (2) bakes bread, (3) does laundry, (4) prepares meals, (5) feeds her child, (6) makes the bed, (7) works in wool.*
      C. *[If] she brought with her a single slave girl, she does not (1) grind, (2) bake bread, or (3) do laundry.*

D. [If she brought] two, she does not (4) prepare meals and does not (5) feed her child.

E. [If she brought] three, she does not (6) make the bed for him and does not (7) work in wool.

F. If she brought four, she sits on a throne.

G. Rabbi Eliezer says, "Even if she brought him a hundred slave girls, he forces her to work in wool.

H. ". . . for idleness leads to unchastity."[16]

The ultimate point in the hierarchy is God, but God's role is often implicit rather than explicit in the Mishnah. Professor Jacob Neusner explains:

The cases are particular, the principles universal. . . . God in the form, God in the order, God in the structure, God in the heights, God at the head of the great chain of hierarchical being. True, God is premise, scarcely mentioned. But it is because God's name does not have to be mentioned when the whole of the order of being says that name, and only that name, and always that name, the name unspoken because it is always in the echo, the silent, thin voice, the numinous in all phenomena.[17]

The Mishnah became the basic study text for rabbinic academies in Judaea and Babylonia, and after several centuries, the Mishnah and the rabbis' commentaries on it were organized into the Talmud. This is a vast compendium of law, Midrash, and argument. It does not have a beginning, middle, and end in any traditional sense. It records disagreements among rabbis and sometimes leaves them standing. Drawing on "prooftexts" from the Torah, the rabbis came to different and often inventive conclusions.

There are actually two authorized Talmuds. The Jerusalem Talmud is the earlier one, written down about 400 CE. It emphasizes continual study of the Torah as a spiritual practice, a primary way of coming to know the will and ways of God. Studying the Torah is said to increase one's holiness and spiritual power. In the Jerusalem Talmud it is written, for instance, that a river parted at the word of a rabbi who was intent on studying the Torah:

Once Rabbi Phinehas was going to the house of study, and the river Ginai which he had to pass was so swollen that he could not cross it. He said, "O river, why do you prevent me from getting to the house of study?" Then it divided its waters, and he passed over. And his disciples said, "Can we too pass over?" He said, "He who knows that he has never insulted an Israelite can pass over unharmed."[18]

The Babylonian Talmud grew out of the other major center of rabbinical study: Babylonia. Completed about 500 CE, it is more developed as an encyclopedia of the Torah, for Jewish life in Babylonia was less precarious. The Babylonian Talmud was also better preserved than the Jerusalem Talmud, and it has thus become the dominant version in Jewish theology and law. It, too, describes study of the Torah as essential to Israel's special destiny as a nation upholding God's laws.

Midrash is still open-ended, for significant commentaries and commentaries on commentaries have continued to arise over the centuries. No single voice has dominated this continual study of the Torah and its interpretations. Rabbis have often disagreed in their interpretations, and these disagreements, sometimes between rabbis from different centuries, are presented together. This continual

A father teaches his son the Talmud and Bible.

interweaving of historical commentaries, as if all Jewry were present at a single marathon Torah-study event, has been a significant unifying factor for the far-flung, often persecuted Jewish population of the world.

In the process of **exegesis**, the rabbis have actually introduced new ideas into Judaism, while claiming that they were merely revealing what already existed in the scriptures. Notions of the soul are not found in the Tanakh, but they do appear in the Talmud and Midrash. The ways in which God is referred to and perceived also change. In the early biblical narratives, the Lord appears to the patriarchs and Moses in dramatic forms, such as the burning bush and the smoking mountain. Later, the prophets are visited by angelic messengers, and they sometimes hear a divine inner voice speaking to them. In the rabbinical tradition, God is presented in even more transcendent, less anthropomorphic ways. God's presence in the world, in relationship to the people, is called the **Shekhinah**, a feminine noun that often represents the nurturing aspect of God.

According to Midrash, the Shekhinah came to the earth at creation, but as a result of human wickedness she withdrew to the heavens, to be brought down by human acts of faithfulness, charity, and loving-kindness. God spoke to Moses from a burning thorn-bush, rather than some more lofty object, to demonstrate that there is no place where the Shekhinah cannot dwell. Sometimes the loving protection of the Shekhinah is depicted as a radiant, winged presence.

It is noteworthy that despite the subordination of women to men in traditional Jewish legal codes, there are also directives regarding men's responsibility to women and, in general, the responsibility of rulers and privileged members of society to insure legal justice for people of all classes and to provide for the material well-being of the lower classes, widows, orphans, and resident aliens. Accordingly, Jews have often been prominent in movements for social justice.

*The Throne of the
Shekhinah, as depicted
by contemporary artist
Hannah Omer and
cyber-architect Yitzhak
Hayut-Man.*

Judaism in the Middle Ages

In the early centuries of the Common Era, the Jewish population of the land of Israel declined. Some Jews settled in other regions of the Roman Empire, and larger numbers established themselves beyond the boundaries of Rome among the Zoroastrian Persians in Mesopotamia. The city of Babylon, which already had a sizable Jewish population dating back to the biblical exile, became the major center of Jewish intellectual activity, a position it would hold well into the tenth century. Religious leadership was held by the **Geonim**, the administrators of the two great Babylonian rabbinic academies, or *yeshivas*. Under the leadership of the Geonim, the authoritative Babylonian Talmud received its final editing in the middle of the sixth century CE.

Even when the Talmud was complete, the rabbinic enterprise continued. Seen as the pre-eminent legal authorities, the Geonim were often appealed to with difficult questions from far-flung Jewish communities. Their answers, which were considered binding on all Jews, and the questions themselves, became a new and enduring form of legal writing, *Responsa* literature, which continues to the present.

When Baghdad became the capital city of the great Abassid Empire in the eighth century, Jewish life concentrated around that city as well. Jews were treated relatively well under Islamic rule. Like Christians, they were recognized as a "People of the Book," and were allowed to maintain their religious traditions and run their communities autonomously as long as they paid a substantial head tax in acknowledgment of their subordinate status. In Baghdad, as throughout the Islamic Middle East, many Jews were prosperous merchants, professionals, and craftsmen. In the early Middle Ages, in fact, Jews tended to dominate international trade between Muslim and Christian realms because of their facility with languages and their ability to find supportive co-religionists in virtually any community.

Life under Islamic rule was also intellectually exciting for the Jewish community, which had rapidly adopted Arabic as its spoken language. During its early centuries, Islam was far advanced beyond Christian Europe in its explorations of science, medicine, philosophy, poetry, and the fine arts. Jews living in Muslim countries benefited from an atmosphere of cultural creativity and tolerance, and themselves developed Jewish religious philosophy and Hebrew secular poetry. Many Jews were well-known physicians. Muslim Spain, in particular, where some Jews rose to high political position in Muslim courts, is renowned for its outstanding Hebrew poets and major philosophical and scientific Jewish writers.

From time to time, however, Jews were threatened by intolerant Muslim rulers and were forced to flee to other territories. The great scholar and physician Maimonides (1135–1204) was forced to leave his ancestral home of Cordoba, Spain, in the mid-twelfth century; he and his family eventually settled in Egypt. Considered one of the greatest of all Jewish intellectuals, Maimonides is particularly famous for his synthesis between reason and faith. In writings such as *The Guide of the Perplexed* he spoke on behalf of the rationality that had characterized Judaism since the dawning of the rabbinic age:

> *What is man's singular function here on earth? It is, simply, to contemplate abstract intellectual matters and to discover truth ... And the highest intellectual contemplation that man can develop is the knowledge of God and his unity.*[19]

Jews who lived in Christian countries were less exposed to the vibrant intellectual energy of the Islamic world between the seventh and twelfth centuries. Christian Europe in those centuries was primarily a feudal agricultural society in which literacy mainly belonged to the Church. Jews, who were primarily merchants, were among the few town dwellers, and generally lived under charters of protection from the ruler of the area. In France and Germany, Jewish intellectual life flourished, but Christians assumed the financial functions. Jews became expendable, and throughout the later Middle Ages there was a steady pattern of expulsions of Jews from countries in which they had long lived.

The ultimate event of this kind was the expulsion of the Jews from Spain in 1492, when tens of thousands of Jews were forced to leave a country in which they had lived for over a thousand years. Some Jews fled to safety in Portugal or Italy, or the Muslim realms of North Africa and the Ottoman Empire of Turkey. Others chose to convert to Christianity rather than to leave their homeland even though staying in Spain as *conversos* (converted Jews) would expose them to the dreaded Inquisitions, which had been established in Spain in 1483. The Inquisition represented the Roman Catholic Church, and its mission was to

According to the Spanish inquisitors, the murder of hundreds of thousands of people — many of them marranos, or secret Jews—was an auto da fe, *an "act of faith" to rid the church of heretics.*

discover perceived heretics within the Christian community. It had no power over Jews, but it did have jurisdiction over the large numbers of Jews who had converted to Christianity, whether voluntarily or by force, and who might be practicing their religion in secret. The Inquisition, which had the power to torture the accused and to execute the convicted, continued to function in Spain and in Spanish territories well into the eighteenth century.

There was further deterioration of Jewish life in western Europe in the sixteenth and seventeenth centuries. After 1555, those Jews who remained in some cities of Italy and Germany were forced to live in **ghettos**, special Jewish-only quarters, which were often walled in and locked at night and during Christian holy days, to limit mixing between Christians and Jews. Despite the constriction and crowding, Jewish leaders ran the ghettos according to talmudic law, providing for the needs of the poor, and fostering Jewish study and scholarship.

During the later Middle Ages, Poland had become a haven for the expelled Jews of western Europe. Jews were welcomed by Poland's feudal leaders who needed a middle class for the economic development of their agricultural country. Jews were allowed freedom of residence and occupation in Poland, and they rapidly grew in numbers, finding in their new home an enclave of peace and prosperity. By the sixteenth and early seventeenth centuries eastern Europe had become the major European center of Jewish life and scholarship. Jews lived an intensely religious life in villages and towns that were almost completely Jewish, speaking Yiddish, a distinctive Jewish language that was based on the medieval German they had spoken in western Europe. In 1648, the situation changed drastically with the revolt against Polish rule by the Cossack peasants of the Ukraine. Associating Jewry with their Roman Catholic Polish oppressors, the Russian Orthodox Cossacks led terrible massacres against the Jews, which were followed by even more killing as Poland collapsed.

In this time of despair in both eastern and western Europe, Jews were heavily taxed and ill-treated. Their longing for deliverance from danger, poverty, and oppression fueled the old messianic dream. Among the "pseudo-Messiahs" who rose to the occasion, the most famous was Shabbatai Tzevi (1626–1676) of Smyrna, a Turkish port. A rather unstable personality, he became convinced that it was his calling to be the Messiah. A young man named Nathan, who became his enthusiastic prophet, sent letters to Jews throughout Europe, Asia, and Africa announcing that the Messiah had at last appeared in his master. Many believed him and prepared for their return to the Holy Land. However, when Tzevi entered the Ottoman Empire, he was arrested and put in jail. Given the choice of converting to Islam or being executed, he chose conversion and was given a government position. The shock to his supporters was terrible.

Enlightenment

The eighteenth-century European movement called the Enlightenment brought better conditions for the Jews in western Europe. It played down tradition and authority in favor of tolerance, reason, and material progress. In such a rational atmosphere, restrictions on Jews began to decrease. The French Revolution (1789–1792) brought equality for the masses, including Jews living in France, and in the course of the nineteenth century this trend slowly spread to other European nations. Ghettos were torn down, and some Jews even ascended to positions of prominence in western European society. The Rothschild family, for instance, became international financiers, benefactors, and patrons of the arts. Moses Mendelssohn (1729–1786), a German Jew, founded a movement known as the Jewish Enlightenment, whose goal was to integrate Jews more fully into European culture. Mendelssohn urged his fellow Jews to learn German and to dress and comport themselves as non-Jews, at the same time as he urged the governments of his time to separate Church and State, and to tolerate differences in beliefs among their citizens.

In the midst of such modernizing influences, some Jews began to revise Jewish worship to remove what were seen as antiquated and "oriental" practices. Hymns and sermons in the vernacular language instead of Hebrew began to replace the traditional liturgy, while references to a return to the land of Israel and the rebuilding of the Temple were removed from the service. Leaders of this new Reform Judaism saw their religion as continually evolving and harmonizing with the times; they believed that Jews could best accomplish "the mission of Israel" as loyal citizens of the countries in which they lived.

Kabbalah and Hasidism

Mystical yearning has always been a part of Jewish tradition. The fervent experience of and love for God is an undercurrent in several writings of the biblical prophets, and is incorporated into the Talmud as well. Some mystical writings are found outside the biblical canon, in the extra-biblical collections of texts known as the Apocrypha and the Pseudepigrapha. The apocryphal Book of Enoch describes the ascent to God as a journey through seven heavenly spheres to an audience with the King of the celestial court. The core mystical encounter with

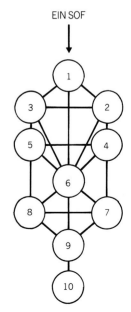

A central Kabbalistic image is the Tree of God, a representation of the emanation of the qualities of the infinite Ein Sof into revealed aspects, the sephiroth.

indescribable sanctity is based on the vision of the prophet Isaiah (Isaiah 6), and includes the chant of the heavenly court, "*Kadosh, Kadosh, Kadosh*" ("Holy, Holy, Holy"), which is included in all Jewish communal prayer.

In the Middle Ages, Jewish mystical traditions, known as **Kabbalah**, began to be put into writing. The most important of these books is the Zohar ("Way of Splendor"). The Zohar is a massive and complex offering of stories, explanations of the esoteric levels of the Torah, and descriptions of visionary practice and experiences. It depicts the world we perceive with our senses as but a lower reflection of a splendid higher world. Mystics held the Hebrew Bible in great esteem but felt that it was not to be interpreted literally. During the sixteenth century Kabbalah's most influential leader was Isaac Luria (1534–1572). He explained creation as the beaming of the divine light into ten special vessels, some of which were shattered by the impact because they contained lower forces that could not bear the intensity of the light. The breaking of the vessels spewed forth

In a Hasidic school, preservation of traditional ways is maintained in the teacher's dark dress, beard, and side curls.

particles of evil as well as fragments of light into the world. According to Lurianic teachings, only the coming of the Messiah will bring *tikkun* ("correction" or "repair" of this situation), ending chaos and evil in the world. Humans have a great responsibility to prepare by regathering the "sparks of holiness" in the unclean realms to repair the holy vessels. To this end, Luria asked his followers to follow strict ascetic purification practices, prayer, and observance of the commandments of the Torah, and to chant sacred formulas.

Lurianic Kabbalism resurfaced in a very different form in the eighteenth century as **Hasidism**, the path of ecstatic piety. It developed in Ukraine and Poland, where Jews were subject to legal limitations, poverty-stricken, and fearful for their lives from riots and murders. The rabbis had little to offer them, retreating into academic debates about legal aspects of the Torah.

Into this grim setting came the Baal Shem Tov (1700–1760), a beloved healer and Hasidic teacher, who offered a joyful version of Jewish holiness. He believed that Torah study and obedience to the letter of the law were not superior to deep-felt, pure-hearted prayer; everyone is capable of the highest enlightenment. He asserted that the divine could be found everywhere, in the present, thereby de-emphasizing the perennial waiting for a future Messiah. "Leave sorrow and sadness," he cried; "man must live in joy and contentment, always rejoicing in his lot."[20] Followers of the Baal Shem Tov worshipped through joyous songs and ecstatic, swaying prayer, and found God in the midst of the ghetto.

God can be found everywhere, emphasized the Baal Shem Tov, but can be seen only by those who are not taken in by surface appearances and who really want to find him. God is here in the midst of even the most mundane everyday activities; if carried out in remembrance of God, even eating, drinking, and working become holy acts. It is through the ups and downs of everyday life that the soul advances toward God. The highest goal is *devekut*, "cleaving" to God, free of the egotism and vanity that separate humans from the Holy One.

> *As the hand held before the eye conceals the greatest mountain, so the little earthly life hides from the glance the enormous lights and mysteries of which the world is full, and he who can draw it away from before his eyes, as one draws away a hand, beholds the great shining of the inner worlds.*
> *Attributed to Reb Nachman of Bratzlav*

Soon an estimated half of all eastern European Jews were followers of the Hasidic path. Spread of the teachings is credited to Dov Ber, who emphasized the importance of the **tzaddik**, or enlightened saint and teacher, called *rebbe* (or Reb) when ordained as a Hasidic spiritual guide. Dov Ber urged Hasidim to take spiritual shelter with a *tzaddik*, whose prayers and wisdom would be more powerful than their own because of the *tzaddik*'s personal relationship with God. This idea stirred enormous opposition from non-Hasidic leaders, who believed that each Jew should be his or her own *tzaddik*. While the position of *tzaddik* became hereditary and was sometimes subject to exploitation by less-than-holy lineage carriers, such charismatic leadership remains a central element and perhaps one of the enduring attractions of modern Hasidism. The religious fervor associated with Hasidism clearly continues as an influence within Judaism.

American Judaism

Substantial Jewish immigration to the United States began in the mid-nineteenth century. By 1880, there were 250,000 Jews in the United States, mostly of German origin, and middle class in occupations and attitudes.

Between 1881 and the early 1920s, Jewish immigration to the United States totalled two million, mainly Jews from eastern Europe. This exodus was prompted by virulent anti-semitism in Czarist Russia and endemic Jewish poverty in both Russia and eastern provinces of Austria–Hungary. If these new immigrants were religious, they tended to be extremely Orthodox; if they were political, their politics were far to the left; socially, they tended to be craftsmen and laborers.

Today, the United States, with approximately six million Jews, has the largest Jewish population in the world. It continues to be a highly diverse population, consisting of both Jews who are religiously affiliated and those who are not.

The Holocaust

For many Jews the defining event of the twentieth century was the **Holocaust**, the murder of almost six million European Jews by the Nazi leadership of Germany during World War II. These Jews constituted over a third of the Jewish people in the world and half of all Jews in Europe. The Holocaust is the overwhelmingly tragic event of Jewish history, and an indelible marker for all time of the depths of twentieth-century inhumanity and evil.

Anti-semitism, or prejudice against Jews, was part of Greco–Roman culture and had been present in Europe since the Roman Empire first adopted Christianity as its state religion in the fourth century CE. New and virulent strains of this disease appeared in western Europe at the end of the nineteenth century. Racist theories spread that those of "pure" Nordic blood were genetically ideal, while Jews were a dangerous "mongrel" race.

Reactionary anti-Jewish feelings also resurfaced late in the nineteenth century in Russia and in eastern Europe, where Jews formed a sizable minority of the population and where they were accumulating wealth and establishing a presence in higher educational circles. Jews were increasingly associated with left-wing movements pushing for social change, even though many Jewish socialists were non-observant Jews. Leon Trotsky, for example, was religiously indifferent but of Jewish

A young Jewish man is forced to wear a Star of David armband for identification in Nazi Germany. The Star of David had begun to be widely used by Jews themselves as a symbol of Judaism in the 19th century.

ancestry. His leadership in the violent Bolshevik Revolution and the Red Army brought terrible reprisals, called **pogroms**, against Jewish communities by the White Russians in the civil war. In a thousand separate incidents, up to 70,000 Jews were killed by unrestrained rioting mobs. Even after the Bolshevik Revolution, continuing social chaos in Russia led to massacres of an estimated quarter of a million Jews.

In the aftermath of Germany's defeat in World War I and the desperate economic conditions that followed, Adolf Hitler's Nazi Party bolstered its popular support by blaming the Jews for all of Germany's problems. Germany, the Nazis claimed, could not regain its health until all Jews were stripped of their positions in German life or driven out of the country. Demands to eliminate the Jews for the sake of "racial hygiene" were openly circulated. Seeing the writing on the wall, many Jews, including eminent professionals, managed to emigrate, leaving their homes, their livelihoods, and most of their possessions behind. Others stayed, hoping that the terrifying signs would be short-lived.

Beginning in 1935, German Jews were deprived of their legal and economic rights by the Nuremberg Laws, and when Hitler annexed Austria in 1938, Austrian Jews fell under the same laws. Jewish businesses were forcibly taken over by "Aryans." Polish Jews living in Germany were rounded up into trucks and conveyed to the Polish border, where Polish officials refused to take them in.

By 1939, 300,000 of Germany's 500,000 Jews, together with another 150,000

Hitler's Final Solution was to herd Jews into concentration camps throughout Nazi-occupied Europe and then ship the survivors east into extermination camps in Poland. The pie charts show the number of Jews in each country who were left after the Holocaust, relative to their previous populations.

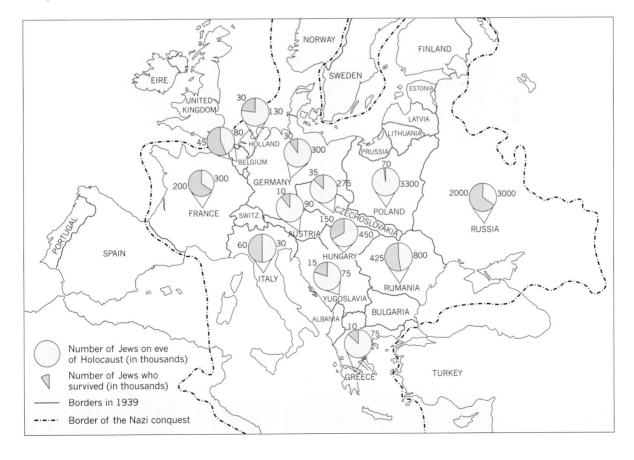

from Austria, had fled. Few countries, however, would allow them to enter. The United States government's attempts to arrange for systematic emigration were abandoned when Germany invaded Poland and then in rapid succession Denmark, Norway, Belgium, Holland, and France, thereby placing several million more Jews under Nazi control.

World War II began with the German invasion of Poland in 1939. Immediately, systematic oppression began, with orders to all Polish Jews to move into the towns, where walled ghettos were created to confine them. Jews were made to wear a yellow or white badge with the Star of David on it to reveal their stigmatized status, and since all other jobs were taken away from them, they could do only menial labor.

Along the Russian front, special "Action Groups" were assigned to slaughter Jews, gypsies, and commissars (heads of government departments) as the German troops advanced, and to incite the local militia to do the same. One cannot comprehend the numbers of men, women, and children killed in these mass murders—34,000 at Babi Yar, 26,000 at Odessa, 32,000 at Vilna—probably totalling hundreds of thousands.

By 1942, large-scale death camps had been set up by the Nazis to facilitate the "Final Solution"—the total extermination of all Jews in Europe, a population the Nazis estimated at 11 million. From the ghettos Jews were transported by cattle cars (in which many suffocated to death) from all over Europe to concentration camps. There they were starved, worked to death as slaves, tortured, "experimented" on, and/or shipped to extermination camps. Industrial-scale gas chambers were found to be the most efficient means of killing and also an impersonal way to get around the increasing unwillingness of German military personnel, as well as Polish and Russian prisoners of war, to kill so many Jewish men, women, and children.

Hitler was the architect and the motivating force behind the genocide, but he was not the only one responsible. There were tremendous numbers of people throughout western and eastern Europe whose active or passive participation was needed to carry out the killings.

The governments of some countries, to a greater or lesser extent, tried to protect their Jews; also some individuals, at great personal risk, in every part of Europe, hid Jews or tried to help them escape. But there was little outcry from the outside world. In hindsight, many historians have concluded that Hitler's hideous policy could have been slowed by determined resistance from free Allied countries.

No modern Jewish thinker can ignore the challenge that the Holocaust poses to traditional Jewish beliefs of an omnipotent and caring God. Elie Wiesel (b. 1928), who as a boy survived a Nazi death camp in Poland, but lost all his other family members and was witness to and sufferer of great atrocities, had been a very religious child. But his experiences in the holocaust so embittered him against God that he could not bring himself to utter the traditional prayers:

Why should I bless Him? In every fiber I rebelled. Because He had had thousands of children burned in His pits? Because He kept six crematoria working night and day, on Sundays and feast days? Because in His great might He had created Auschwitz, Birkenau, Buna, and so many factories of death? How could I say to Him: "Blessed art Thou, Eternal, Master of the Universe, Who chose us from among the races to be tortured day and night, to see our fathers, our mothers, our brothers, end in the crematory? Praised be Thy Holy Name, Thou Who has chosen us to be butchered on Thine altar?"[21]

Wiesel feels that the painful memories must be continually rekindled. He says that we cannot turn away from the questions about how it could happen, for genocidal actions are being undertaken against other minority groups in our times as well. As Wiesel points out:

According to Jewish tradition, the death of one innocent person tarnishes the cosmos. Other people's tragedies are our tragedies. We must study the past, the horrors of the past and the melancholy of the past, if we are to be sensitive in the present. [In this] there are eternities of distress—the terrifying power of evil over innocence—but also some strength in the resolve of the victim never to become a killer.[22]

The Jewish philosopher Emil Fackenheim insists that the "Voice of Auschwitz" commands Jewish commitment to faith:

Jews are forbidden to hand Hitler posthumous victories. They are commanded to survive as Jews, lest the Jewish people perish. They are commanded to remember the victims of Auschwitz, lest their memory perish. They are forbidden to despair of man and his world, and to escape into either cynicism or otherworldliness, lest they cooperate in delivering the world over to the forces of Auschwitz. Finally, they are forbidden to despair of the God of Israel, lest Judaism perish.[23]

Zionism

Zionism is the Jewish movement dedicated to the establishment of a politically viable, internationally recognized Jewish state in the biblical land of Israel. While political Zionism was a reaction to increasing anti-semitism in Europe in the late nineteenth century, it is a movement with deep roots in Judaism and Jewish culture. The desire to end the centuries-long exile from Zion (the site of the Jerusalem Temples) was a central theme in all Jewish prayer and in many religious customs. Jewish messianism is focused around a descendant of King David who will return his united people to the land of Israel, where Jewish sovereignty will be eternally re-established in an atmosphere of universal peace. Professor Aviezer Ravitzky describes the Zionist ideal:

It was a dream of utter perfection: the day would come when the entire Jewish people, the whole Congregation of Israel, would reassemble as one in an undivided Land of Israel, reconstituting its life there according to the Torah in all its aspects. The Jewish people would free itself completely from its subjugation to the great powers. It would then be a source of blessing for all nations, for its redemption would bring about the redemption of the world as a whole, "For the land shall be filled with devotion to the Lord as water covers the sea" (Isaiah 11:9).[24]

Zionism became an organized international political movement under the leadership of the Viennese journalist Theodor Herzl (1860–1904), who believed that the Jews could never defend themselves against anti-semitism until they had their own nation. Herzl worked to provide political guarantees for Jewish settlement and to offer institutional support through the formation of various Zionist organizations. Simultaneously, pioneers, mainly secular Jews from eastern Europe, began establishing a Jewish presence on the land. The 1917 Balfour Declaration stated Britain's support for limited Jewish settlement in Palestine following World War I and the defeat of Turkey, when Britain expected to take over control of the region. While most Jews worldwide also applauded this Zionist victory, not all supported the movement. Most Reform Jews of that time believed the destiny of Jews was to be lived out among the Gentiles, where the Enlightenment had fueled hopes of a freer future and where Jews hoped they could be recognized as legitimate citizens of the countries in which they lived. Some support for Zionism came from traditional Orthodox Jews, but not all of the traditional community embraced the idea. Many felt it was God who had punished the people for their unfaithfulness by sending them away from the promised land and that only God would end the exile. They rejected active political initiative in favor of passive waiting for miraculous divine intervention, citing an oath from the Midrash and Talmud "not to force the End." Exile is not only a geographical matter; it is an internal absence of redemption, which will not be hastened by settling for partial, secular solutions.

Nonetheless, by a United Nations decision in 1947, Palestine was partitioned into two areas, one to be governed by Jews and the other by Arabs. Political tensions between the two groups have been violently expressed again and again in the area. Israel declared the Law of Return, which welcomed all Jews who chose to resettle in their homeland, and continues to resettle Jews to this day. Israel established itself as a sovereign state in 1948, yet it still faces the hostility of many of its Arab neighbors and of the large Palestinian population of the territories occupied in 1967. Many Jews are unhappy with the bitterness of the relations between peoples who have so much in common. Some feel that Israel's Jews must not forget their own history of oppression and must maintain their compassion for the oppressed people among them. Rabbi Michael Lerner, editor of *Tikkun* magazine, writes,

Much of the Promised Land to which the Jews wanted to return was a desert. This group is celebrating the founding of Tel Aviv, now a modern city, on sand dunes in 1909.

A peach orchard in Kibbutz Sede Boquer, Israel, 1994. Kibbutzes, or collective farming communities of volunteers, were established with high social idealism and have developed successful methods of dry-land agriculture.

Yes, we need to fight anti-Semitism. . . . But no, you are not automatically anti-Semitic if you fight for social justice for Palestinians. . . . Let us all remember the spirit of generosity that God communicated to Isaiah: "My House shall be a House for all peoples." Unless it is for all peoples, it is not God's house. May it happen speedily in our days.[25]

In addition to pressures from neighbors, tensions exist within Israel. Jewish settlers have come to Israel from many divergent backgrounds. Those who are of eastern European origin—the Ashkenazi who founded the state—tend to regard themselves as superior to Jewish settlers from other areas. Ultra-Orthodox religious authorities insist on strict observance of religious rituals, assert considerable control over education and politics in the nation, and claim that converts consecrated by Reform and Conservative rabbis in the United States are not really Jews at all. The Orthodox rabbis generally favor hardline political policies in Israel. However, they do not represent the majority of Israeli citizens in religious terms, for only an estimated fifteen percent of Israelis claim to live completely according to religious laws. The majority are non-Orthodox or secular, not religiously observant at all. There is also internal dissension over relationships with the Palestinian minority within Israel. By contrast with those who sympathize with the Palestinians' situation, some Jewish factions believe that the land has been promised to them by God and should never be given into Arab hands. Thus the ancient Zionist vision remains unfulfilled, and the area is fraught with strife. Aviezer Ravitzky comments, "As the rabbis said, the End of Days continues to 'tarry.'"[26]

Torah

It is difficult to outline the tenets of the Jewish faith. As we have seen, Jewish spiritual understanding has changed repeatedly through history. Rationalists and mystics have often differed. Since the nineteenth century, there has been disagreement between liberal and traditional Jews, to be discussed at the end of the chapter.

Nevertheless, there are certain major themes that can be extricated from the vast history and literature of Judaism. Jewish teachings are known as Torah. In its narrowest sense, Torah refers to the Five Books of Moses. On the next level, it means the entire Hebrew Bible and the Talmud, the written and the oral law. For some, "Torah" can refer to all sacred Jewish literature and observance. At the highest level, Torah is God's will, God's wisdom.

The one God

The central Jewish belief is monotheism. It has been stated in different ways in response to different cultural settings (emphasizing the divine unity when Christians developed the concept of the Holy Trinity, for instance, and emphasizing that God is formless and ultimate holiness in opposition to the earthly local gods). But the central theme is that there is one Creator God, the "cause of all existent things."[27]

God is everywhere, even in the darkness, as David sings in Psalms:

Where can I escape from Your spirit?
Where can I flee from Your presence?
If I ascend to Heaven, You are there:
if I descend to Sheol [the underworld],
You are there too.

If I take wing with the dawn
to come to rest on the western horizon,
even there Your hand will be guiding me,
Your right hand will be holding me fast.
                                    Psalm 139:7–14

This metaphysical understanding of God's oneness is difficult to explain in linear language, which refers to the individual objects perceived by the senses. As the eleventh-century Spanish poet and mystical philosopher Ibn Gabirol put it, "None can penetrate ... the mystery of Thy unfathomable unity."[28]

One of the most elegant attempts to "explain" God's oneness has been offered by the great twentieth-century thinker Abraham Joshua Heschel (1907–1972). He linked the idea of unity to eternity, explaining that in eternity, "past and future are not apart; here is everywhere, and now goes on forever." Time as we know it is only a fragment, "eternity broken in space." According to Heschel:

The craving for unity and coherence is the predominant feature of a mature mind.
All science, all philosophy, all art are a search after it. But unity is a task, not a
condition. The world lies in strife, in discord, in divergence. Unity is beyond, not

*within, reality. . . . The world is not one with God, and this is why his power does
not surge unhampered throughout all stages of being. Creature is detached from the
Creator, and the universe is in a state of spiritual disorder. Yet God has not
withdrawn entirely from this world. The spirit of this unity hovers over the face of
all plurality, and the major trend of all our thinking and striving is its mighty
intimation. The goal of all efforts is to bring about the restitution of the unity of
God and world.[29]*

> *Plurality is incompatible with the sense of the ineffable. You cannot ask in regard to
> the divine: Which one? There is only one synonym for God: One.*
> *Abraham Joshua Heschel*[30]

In traditional Judaism, God is often perceived as a loving Father who is
nonetheless infinitely majestic, sometimes revealing divine power when the
children need chastising.

Love for God

The essential commandment to humans is to love God. The central prayer in any
Jewish religious service and the inscription on the *mezuza* at the doorpost of every
traditional Jewish home is the *Shema Israel*:

> *Hear, O Israel! The Lord is our God, the Lord alone. You shall love the Lord your
> God with all your heart and with all your soul and with all your might. Take to
> heart these instructions with which I charge you this day. Impress them upon your
> children. Recite them when you stay at home and when you are away, when you lie
> down and when you get up. Bind them as a sign on your hand and let them serve
> as a symbol on your forehead; inscribe them on the doorposts of your house and on
> your gates.*
>
> *Deuteronomy 6:4–9*

Even Maimonides, the great proponent of reason and study, asserted the primacy of love for God. He emphasized that one should not love God from selfish
or fearful motivations, such as receiving earthly blessings or avoiding problems in
the life after death. One should study Torah and fulfill the commandments out of
sheer love of God.

The sacredness of human life

Humans are the pinnacle of creation, created in the "image" of God, according to
the account of Creation in Genesis 1. Jews do not take this passage to mean that
God literally looks like a human. It is often interpreted in an ethical sense: that
humans are so wonderfully endowed that they can mirror God's qualities, such
as justice, wisdom, righteousness, and love.

All people are potentially equal; they are said to be common descendants of
the first man and woman. But they are also potentially perfectible, and in raising
themselves they uplift the world. God limited the divine power by giving humans

*Jewish theology has
been shaped by the
most compelling thinkers
of each era. In the
20th century, Martin
Buber described the
cherished human–divine
encounter as an I–Thou
relationship, in which
the self experiences its
wholeness.*

free will, involving them in the responsibility for the world's condition, and their own. If we are suffering, according to the Talmud, we should examine our own deeds.

The German scholar Martin Buber (1878–1965) described the relationship between God and humans as reciprocal:

> *You know always in your heart that you need God more than everything; but do you not know too that God needs you—in the fulness of His eternity needs you? How would man exist, how would you exist, if God did not need him, did not need you? You need God, in order to be—and God needs you, for the very meaning of your life. . . . There is divine meaning in the life of the world . . . of human persons, of you and of me. . . . We take part in creation, meet the Creator, reach out to him, helpers and companions.*[31]

Human life is sacred, rather than lowly and loathsome; Judaism celebrates the body. Sexuality within marriage is holy, and the body is honored as the instrument through which the soul is manifested on earth. Indeed, according to some thinkers, body and soul are an inseparable totality.

I praise You, for I am awesomely, wondrously made.   *Psalm 139:14*

Law

Because of the great responsibility of humankind, traditional Jews give thanks that God has revealed in the written and oral Torah the laws by which they can be faithful to the divine will and fulfill the purposes of Creation by establishing a Kingdom of God here on earth, in which all creatures can live in peace and fellowship. In the words of the biblical prophet Isaiah, speaking for God,

> *The wolf and the lamb shall graze together,*
> *And the lion shall eat straw like the ox,*
> *And the serpent's food shall be earth.*
> *In all my sacred mount*
> *Nothing evil or vile shall be done.*[32]

To the extent that traditional Jews act according to the Torah, they feel they are upholding their part of the ancient covenant with God.

The Torah, as indicated through rabbinic literature, is said to contain 613 commandments, or **mitzvot** (singular: mitzvah). Jewish law does not differentiate between sacred and secular life, so these include general ethical guidelines such as the Ten Commandments and the famous saying in Leviticus 19:18—"Love your fellow as yourself"—plus detailed laws concerning all aspects of life, such as land ownership, civil and criminal procedure, family law, sacred observances, diet, and ritual slaughter. The biblical Book of Genesis also sets forth what is called the Noahide Code of seven universal principles for a moral and spiritual life: idolatry (worshipping many gods or images of God), blasphemy against God, murder, theft, sexual behaviors outside of marriage, and cruelty to animals are all prohibited, and the rule of law and justice in society is affirmed as a positive value.

From the time of its final editing in Babylonia in the mid-sixth century CE, the Talmud, together with its later commentaries, has served as a blueprint for Jewish social, communal, and religious life. Through the rabbinic tradition, law became the main category of Orthodox Jewish thought and practice, and learned study of God's commandments one of the central expressions of faith.

From a contemporary point of view, Ismar Schorsch notes that many of the ancient commandments are ecologically useful, for they restrain humanity's ways of using the natural environment. They are addressed to humans not as wise masters of the earth, as envisioned in the first account of Creation in Genesis, but as the Adam and Eve of the second Creation story, who are disobedient and must be saved from themselves lest they destroy the planet, "for as the Bible so often avers: the land ultimately belongs to its Creator and we mortals are but His tenants."[33]

A Sabbath prayer, *Ahavat Olam*, expresses Jews' profound gratitude for God's laws:

> *With everlasting love You have loved Your people Israel. You have taught us the Torah and its* Mitzvot. *You have instructed us in its laws and judgments.*
>
> *Therefore, O Lord our God, when we lie down and when we rise up we shall speak of Your commandments and rejoice in Your Torah and* Mitzvot.
>
> *For they are our life and the length of our days; on them we will meditate day and night.*[34]

Suffering and faith

Jewish tradition depicts the universe as being governed by an all-powerful, personal God who intervenes in history to reward the righteous and punish the unjust. Within this context, Jews have had considerable difficulty in answering the eternal question: Why must the innocent suffer? This question has been particularly poignant since the Holocaust.

The Hebrew Bible itself brings up the issue with the challenging parable of Job, a blameless, God-fearing, and wealthy man. The story involves Satan, depicted as an angel beneath God, who, in a conversation with God, predicts that Job will surely drop his faith and blaspheme the Lord if he is stripped of all his possessions. With God's assent, Satan tests Job by destroying all that Job has, including his children and his health. On hearing the news of his children's deaths

> *Job arose, tore his robe, cut off his hair, and threw himself on the ground and worshipped. He said, "Naked came I out of my mother's womb, and naked shall I return there; the Lord has given, and the Lord has taken away, blessed be the name of the Lord."*[35]

With an itchy inflammation covering him from head to foot, Job begins to curse his life and to question God's justice. In the end, Job acknowledges not only God's power to control the world but also his inscrutable wisdom, which is beyond human understanding. God then rewards him with long life and even greater riches than he had before the test.

Debate over the meanings of this ancient story has continued over the centuries. One rabbinical interpretation is that Satan was cooperating with God in helping Job grow from fear of God to love of God. Another is that faith in God will finally be rewarded in this life, no matter how severe the temporary trials. Another is that those who truly desire to grow toward God will be asked to suffer more, that their sins will be expiated in this life so that they can enjoy the divine bliss in the life to come. Such interpretations assume a personal, all-powerful, loving God doing what is best for the people, even when they cannot understand God's ways. In such belief, God is seen as always available, like a shepherd caring for his sheep, no matter how dark the outer circumstances.

> *Though I walk through a valley of deepest darkness,*
> *I fear no harm, for You are with me;*
> *Your rod and Your staff—they comfort me.*
>
> *Psalm 23:4*

On the other hand, oppression and then the Holocaust have led some Jews to complain to God in anguish. They, too, feel close to God, but in a way that allows them to scream at God, as it were. In questioning the justice of history, they hold God responsible for what is inexplicably monstrous. But even in the Holocaust, there were those who held fast to hope for better times. As they walked to their death in Nazi gas chambers, some were reciting the hymn *Ani maamin*: "I believe with complete faith in the coming of the Messiah, and even though he may delay, nevertheless I anticipate every day that he will come."[36]

Sacred practices

Since the rabbinic period began, a major Jewish spiritual practice has been daily scriptural study. Boys were traditionally taught how to read and write ancient Hebrew and how to interpret scripture through the process of exegesis, by means of the oral Torah. This required extensive knowledge of the scriptures and concentrated intellectual effort. This classical pattern continues today even in the Diaspora, where some children continue to be trained in special schools to carry on the study of the Torah, thus encouraging them not only to learn and obey the commandments but also through rational analysis to delve into deeper understanding of truth.

In addition to study, a Jew is urged to remember God in all aspects of life, through prayer and observance of the commandments. These commandments are not otherworldly. Many are rooted in the body, and spiritual practices often engage all the senses in awareness of God.

Boys are ritually circumcised when they are eight days old, to honor the seal of God's commandment to Abraham. Orthodox Jews consider women ritually unclean during their menstrual periods and for seven days afterwards, during which time they are not to have sexual intercourse with their husbands. At the end of this forbidden period Othodox Jewish women undertake complete immersion in a **mikva**, a special deep bath structure, symbolizing their altered state. Marital sex is sacred, with the **Sabbath** night the holiest time for making love.

By contrast, adultery is strictly forbidden as one of the worst sins against God, for Jewish tradition is extremely concerned with maintaining pure lines of descent.

What one eats is also of cosmic significance, for according to the Torah some foods are definitely unclean. For example, the only ritually acceptable, or **kosher**, meats, are those from warmblooded animals with cloven hoofs which chew their cuds, such as cows, goats, and sheep. Poultry is kosher, except for birds of prey, but shellfish is not. Meat is also kosher only if it has been butchered in the traditional way with an extremely sharp, smooth knife by an authorized Jewish slaughterer. Great pains are taken to avoid eating blood; meat must be soaked in water and then drained on a salted board before cooking. Meat and milk cannot be eaten together, and separate dishes are maintained for their preparation and serving.

These dietary instructions are laid out in the biblical Book of Leviticus, which quotes God as saying to Moses and Aaron, "For I the Lord am He who brought you up from the land of Egypt to be your God: you shall be holy, for I am holy."[37] The rules of diet, if strictly followed, give Jews a feeling of special sacred identity and link them to the eternal authority of the Torah.

Some contemporary Jews feel that consciousness about what they eat should be extended to environmental considerations. To them, the styrofoam box in which a cheeseburger is sold at fast-food places is as much a problem as the mixing of meat and milk. Nuclear power-generated electricity used for cooking might itself be non-kosher, as long as there is no safe provision for disposing of nuclear waste.

For traditional Jews, the morning begins with a prayer before they open their eyes to thank God for restoring the soul. The hands must then be washed before

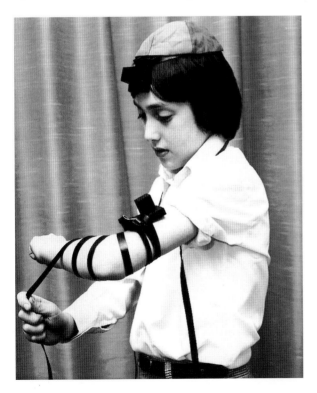

Before praying, traditional Jewish men bind t'fillin to their arms and foreheads in remembrance of their covenant with God.

reciting blessings and, for all traditional male Jews, putting a special fringed rectangle of cloth around the neck. It is usually worn under the clothes as a reminder of the privilege of being given divine commandments. For weekday morning prayers men also put **t'fillin**, or phylacteries, small leather boxes containing biblical verses about the covenant with God, on the forehead and the upper arm, held against the heart, in fulfillment of the Shema commandment, as literally understood: "Bind them [the Shema's words about the primacy of love for God] as a sign on your hand and let them serve as a symbol on your forehead." Traditional Jewish men also wear a fringed prayer shawl, or **talit**, whose fringes act as reminders of God's commandments, and keep their heads covered at all times, if possible.

Traditionally, prayers are recited on waking and at bedtime. In addition, three prayer services are chanted daily in a synagogue by men if there is a *minyan* (quorum of ten). Women can say them also, but they are excused from rigid schedules because their household responsibilities are considered important.

Jews are also expected to give thanks continually. One should recite a hundred benedictions to God every day. To this end, there is a blessing to be said every time one takes a drink of water. There is even a blessing to be recited after using the toilet:

> *Blessed art thou, our God, Ruler of the universe, who hast formed (human) beings in wisdom, and created in them a system of ducts and tubes. It is well known before thy glorious throne that if but one of these be opened, or if one of those be closed, it would be impossible to exist in thy presence. Blessed art thou, O God, who healest all creatures and doest wonders.*[38]

The Jewish Sabbath runs from sunset Friday night to sunset Saturday night, because the Jewish "day" begins with nightfall. The Friday night service welcomes the Sabbath as a bride and is often considered an opportunity to drop away the cares of the previous week so as to be in a peaceful state for the day of rest. Just as God is said to have created the world in six days and then rested on the seventh, all work is to cease when the Sabbath begins. Ruth Gan Kagan describes the experience:

> *I am aware of a wave of peace flooding my heart and that transparent veils of tranquility are covering the World around me. A moment before I would probably be rushing around trying to finish all the preparations, ... but all this tension and rush vanishes when the fixed moment arrives; not a second earlier nor a second later. The moment I light the Sabbath candles and usher in the Sabbath spirit everything undergoes a magical transformation.*
>
> *The Queen has arrived. In Her presence there are not even talks of weekday matters. The mind quiets down leaving business, plans and worries behind as one quietly walks to the synagogue for services; the sky is aglow with the colours of sunset; the bird-song is suddenly more present; the people of the congregation gather to welcome in the Sabbath in song, prayer and silence.*
>
> *Coming home, the stars are out; in a religious neighborhood, no travelling cars break the descended peace; children are holding their parents' hands, walking in the middle of the road without fear of death.*[39]

The Saturday morning service incorporates public and private prayers, singing, and the reading of passages from the Pentateuch and Prophets sections of the

Living Judaism

Herman Taube is a poet, Professor Emeritus of Jewish Studies and Yiddish Literature, and volunteer chaplain to nursing home patients. He emigrated to the United States in 1947 from Poland with his wife, who had earlier been sent to a concentration camp where her younger sister and mother died. During World War II, Herman was a medic working side by side with Russian Orthodox and Muslim doctors in Uzbekhistan to aid people in a refugee camp. He says,

"If you do charitable work—if you help in clinics, if you help unfortunate children, if you go into the jails to help inmates— this is God's work. It is not the responsibility of the rich only to help the poor. Even the poorest man has to give charity. This is the law in Jewish religion.

"Maimonides says, and Jews are saying every morning in their prayers, that a human being has to believe every day in the coming of the Messiah. Messiah does not come with a long beard and a donkey. Messiah can be you. Messiah can be a man on the street who helps a fellow human being. In the Hebrew Bible, in the Talmud, there are quotations indicating that the Messiah will come in a generation which is full of innocence or full of guilt—one of the two. And he will spiritually lead the people away from evil. I think this will become a messianic era.

"Look at the fall of communism, the fall of fascism in our generation. Something is changing. You don't have to go far—look at Washington. You see good people living in the streets, with no roof over their head. They cannot make a meal. On the other side, you see those big parties where people spend millions. There is a need for a messianic age, a need for a better world.

"A reporter asked me, 'Can you believe in God after the Holocaust?' Belief is not something static. My wife and I sometimes ask, 'Where was God?' A million and a half Jewish children were killed. Little boys and girls who were just learning how to say, 'Mama,' and the grandmother said, 'How big is the baby?' and tried to pick up their hands. And this child was taken and thrown into a lamppost. So yes, there are questions. We have no answers.

"Why did Polish people, nuns and plain peasants risk their lives to save Jewish people, when they knew that for saving a Jew's life their house would be burned down? And their children were taken into forced labor. Why did the people of Assisi save sixty Jewish people under the noses of the Nazis? The Vatican wasn't too helpful, didn't speak up, but they, the simple people, risked their lives. So there is goodness in the world, too. There is goodness and Godness in the hearts of those people.

"The Talmud says God said, 'You don't believe in me? So you don't believe in me. But keep my commandments. Care for the poor and for the widows.' This is exactly what a lot of those Messiahs are doing.

"About chosenness: My grandfather was a really Orthodox Jew. He prayed three times a day, studied, studied the Bible, was always praying, always reciting Psalms, a really generous man. He found time to give charity. He did the same thing that I do now: He volunteered to go to the hospitals. Some of the people couldn't afford to go to the hospital, so he went to their homes, on the fifth floors in Poland, with no elevators, sitting with somebody sick all night. On the way home he would go to services. Then at home, something to eat—dry bread, a piece of herring, imitation coffee. This is the way he lived. This man, this chosen man, was one of the first Jews of the Lodz ghetto to be taken to the concentration camp. The Nazis used gas to kill them, and then disposed of them. If this is the chosenness that God wants us for—thank you, choose another people.

"My wife doesn't like to be interviewed. It's like pulling off a bandage from an open wound. Even after forty-five years, it comes to the holidays and she's missing her mother and her sister. That unbelievable guilt feeling: Why did we survive and they die?

"I believe in God. There is a Power above us that rules our life. We do not see it, we cannot comprehend it. But there is something. I do not deny Him—or Her; maybe it's a Her. And I don't deny my roots."

Celebration of the Sabbath meal at a kibbutz in Erez, Israel.

Hebrew Bible. Torah scrolls are kept in a curtained ark on the wall facing Jerusalem. They are hand-lettered in Hebrew and are treated with great reverence. It is a great honor to be "called up" to read from the Torah.

More liberal congregations may place emphasis on an in-depth discussion of the passage read. Often it is examined not only from an abstract philosophical perspective but also from the point of its relevance to political events and everyday attempts to live a just and humane life. Torah study, and study of all Jewish literature, is highly valued as a form of prayer in itself, and synagogues usually have libraries for this purpose, sometimes in the same space that is used for worship.

In Hasidic congregations, the emphasis falls on the intensity of praying, or **davening**, even in saying fixed prayers from the prayer book. Some sway their bodies to induce the self-forgetful state of ecstatic communion with the Loved One. Others quietly shift their attention from earthly concerns to "cleave to God." The rabbinical tradition states the ideal in prayer: "A person should always see himself as if the Shekhinah is confronting him."[40]

In addition to, or instead of, going to a service welcoming the Sabbath, observant families usually begin the Sabbath eve with a special Friday night dinner. The mother lights candles to bring in the Sabbath light; the father recites a blessing over the wine. Special braided bread, *challah*, is shared as a symbol of the double portions of manna in the desert. The rituals help to set a different tone for the day of rest, as do commandments against working, handling money, traveling except by foot, lighting a fire, cooking, and the like. The Sabbath day is set aside for public prayer, study, thought, friendship, and family closeness, with the hope that this renewed life of the spirit will then carry through the week to come.

It is customary to recognize coming of age, at thirteen, in Jewish boys by the **Bar Mitzvah** ("son of the commandment") ceremony. The boy has presumably undertaken some religious instruction, including learning to pronounce Hebrew, if not always to understand it. He is called up to read a portion from the Torah scroll and recite a passage from one of the books of the prophets, in Hebrew, and then perhaps to give a short teaching about a topic from the reading. Afterwards there may be a simple *kiddush*, a celebration with blessing of wine and sweet bread or cake, but a big party is more likely. This custom of welcoming the boy to adult responsibilities has been extended to girls in non-Orthodox congregations in the **Bat Mitzvah**. As in the Bar Mitzvah, this means "one obligated to observe the commandments."

Holy days

Judaism follows an ancient lunar calendar of annual holidays and memorials linked to special events in history.

The spiritual year begins with the High Holy Days of Rosh Hashanah and Yom Kippur. Rosh Hashanah (New Year's Day), a time of spiritual renewal, is celebrated on the first two days of the seventh month (around the fall equinox). For thirty days prior to Rosh Hashanah, each morning synagogue service brings the blowing of the *shofar* (a ram's horn that produces an eery, unearthly blast) to remind the people that they stand before God. At the service on the eve of Rosh Hashanah, a prayer is recited asking that all humanity will remember what God has done, that there will be honor and joy for God's people, and that righteousness will triumph while "all wickedness vanishes like smoke."[41]

The ten Days of Awe follow Rosh Hashanah. People are encouraged to change inwardly, by looking at their mistakes of the past year. It is said that during this

Rosh Hashanah includes the blowing of the shofar *in three ways: a note of alarm, three wails, and nine sobbing blasts of contrition.*

Repentance and inner renewal are central themes of the High Holy Days. (Rothschild MS, c. 1470.)

period, God makes it easier for a person to be repentant and is also more likely to accept repentance. A biblical passage from the prophet Isaiah is cited: "Seek ye the Lord while He may be found, Call ye upon Him while He is near."[42]

Yom Kippur completes the High Holy Days, renewing the sacred covenant with God in a spirit of atonement and cleansing. Historically, this was the only time when the high priest entered the Holy of Holies in the Temple of Jerusalem, and the only time that he would pronounce the sacred name of the Lord, YHWH, in order to ask for forgiveness of the people's sins. Today, there is an attempt at personal inner cleansing, and individuals must ask pardon from everyone they may have wronged during the past year. If necessary, restitution for damages should be made. Congregations also confess their sins communally, ask that their negligence be forgiven, and pray for their reconciliation to God in a new year of divine pardon and grace.

Sukkot is a fall harvest festival. A simple outdoor booth (a *sukkah*) is built and decorated as a dwelling place of sorts for seven days. Usually this is done as a ritual act, but seeking a deeper experience of the meaning of Sukkot, some contemporary Jews are actually attempting to live in the *sukkah* they construct. Michael Lerner relates:

The idea of moving out of my apartment or house to live in a sukkah *always seemed impractical to me until I tried it. Living in a temporary shelter— particularly one with a water-permeable roof made of twigs, reeds, vines, tree*

*branches, and other forms of vegetation arranged in such a way that one can see
through them to the stars—has a special effect of reconnecting urban and suburban
dwellers to the natural order, and to the transitory nature of our carefully
constructed forms of material security.*[43]

The fragile home reminds the faithful that their real home is in God, who sheltered their ancestors on the way from Egypt to the promised land of Canaan. Some contemporary groups also pray for peace amid our vulnerability to nuclear war. Participants hold the *lulav* (a bundle made of a palm branch, myrtle twigs, and willow twigs) in one hand and the *etrog* (a citrus fruit) in the other and wave them together toward the four compass directions and to earth and sky, praising God and acknowledging him as the unmoving center of creation. Traditionally there was an offering of water, precious in the desert lands of the patriarchs, and great merrymaking. During the second Temple days, the ecstatic celebration even included burning of the priests' old underclothes. The day after the seven-day Sukkot festival is Simhat Torah ("Joy in Torah"), ending the yearly cycle of Torah readings, from Creation to the death of Moses, and beginning again.

Near the winter solstice, the darkest time of the year, comes Hanukkah, the Feast of Dedication. Each night for eight nights, another candle is lit on a special candle holder. The amount of light gradually increases like the lengthening of sunlight. Historically, Hanukkah was a celebration of the victory of the Maccabean Rebellion against the attempt by Antiochus to force non-Jewish practices on the Jewish people. According to legend, when the Jews regained access to the Temple, they found only one jar of oil left undefiled, still sealed by the high priest. It was enough to stay alight for only one day, but by a miracle, the oil stayed burning for eight days. Many Jewish families also observe the time by nightly gift-giving. The children have their own special Hanukkah pastimes, such

Simhat Torah is a joyous celebration of the Torah, with everyone joining in the dancing and singing. This one is taking place at the western "Wailing Wall," where for nearly two thousand years Jews have made pilgrimages to pray.

For children of all ages, the lighting of Hannukah candles is a special event in the darkness of winter.

as "gambling" for nuts with the *dreidel*, a spinning top with four letters on its sides as an abbreviation of the sentence "A great miracle happened there."

As the winter rainy season begins to diminish in Israel, Jews everywhere celebrate the reawakening of nature on Tu B'shvat. Observances lavish appreciation on a variety of fruits and plants. In Israel, the time is now marked by the planting of trees to help restore life to the desert.

On the full moon of the month before spring comes Purim. It theoretically commemorates the legend of Esther, queen of Persia, and Mordecai, who saved their fellow Jews from destruction by the evil viceroy Haman. It has been linked to Mesopotamian mythology about the goddess Ishtar, whose spring return brings joy and fertility. Purim is a bawdy time of dressing in costumes and mocking life's seriousness, and the jokes frequently poke fun at sacred Jewish practices. As the story of Esther is read from an ornate scroll, the congregation responds with noisy stomping, rattles, horns, and whistles whenever Haman's name is read.

The next major festival is Pesach, or Passover, which celebrates the liberation from bondage in Egypt and the spring-time advent of new life. It was the tenth plague, death to all first-born sons of the Egyptians, that finally brought the pharaoh to relent. The Israelites were warned to slaughter a lamb for each family and mark their doors with its blood so that the angel of death would pass over them. They were to roast the lamb and eat it with unleavened bread and bitter herbs. So quickly did they depart that they didn't even have time to bake the bread, which is said to have baked in the sun as they carried it on their heads. The beginning of Pesach is still marked by a **Seder** dinner, with the eating of unleavened bread (*matzah*) to remember the urgency of the departure, and bitter herbs as a reminder of slavery, so that they would never impose it on other peoples. Also on the table are *charoset* (a sweet fruit and nut mixture, a reminder of the mortar that the enslaved Israelites molded into bricks) and salt water (a reminder of the tears of the slaves) into which parsley or some other plant (a reminder of spring life) is dipped and eaten. Children ask ritual questions about why these things are done, as basic religious instruction. A movement for contemporary **liturgical** renewal has yielded many new scripts for the Seder—such as special liturgies for feminists, for secular Zionists, and for co-celebration of Pesach with Muslims.

A new holy day may be celebrated in April or May: Holocaust Memorial Day. Observances often include the singing in Yiddish of a song from the Jewish Resistance Movement. In part:

> *Never say that you are*
> *going your last way,*
> *though leaden skies*
> *blot out the blue of day.*
> *The hour for which we*
> *long will certainly appear.*[44]

Early summer brings Shavuot, traditionally identified with the giving of the Torah to Moses at Mount Sinai and the people's hearing of the voice of God. It is likely that Shavuot was initially a summer harvest festival that later was linked with the revelation of the Torah. In Israeli kibbutzim, the old practice of bringing the first fruits to God has been revived. Elsewhere, the focus is on reading the Ten Commandments and on presenting the Torah as a marriage contract between God and Israel. In some congregations, Shavuot is a time to celebrate children's graduation from religious school.

Then come three weeks of mourning for the Temples, both of which were destroyed on the ninth day of the month of Av (July or August), Tisha Be-av. This is traditionally a time of fasting and avoidance of joyous activities. Some feel that there is no longer cause for mourning because even though the Temple has not been rebuilt, the old city of Jerusalem has been recaptured. Others feel that we are all still in exile from the state of perfection.

Contemporary Judaism

Within the extended family of Judaism, there are many groups, many different focuses, and many areas of disagreement. Currently disputed issues include the degree of adherence to the Torah and Talmud, requirements for conversion to Judaism, the extent of the use of Hebrew in prayer, and the full participation of women.

Major branches today

Judaism, like all modern religions, has struggled to meet the challenge of secularization: the idealization of science, rationalism, industrialization, and materialism. The response of the Orthodox has been to stand by the Hebrew Bible as the revealed word of God and the Talmud as the legitimate oral law. Orthodox Jews feel that they are bound by the traditional rabbinical *halakhah*, as a way of achieving closeness to God. But within this framework there are great individual differences, with no central authority figure or governing body. Orthodoxy includes mystics and rationalists, Zionists and anti-Zionists. The Orthodox also differ greatly in their tolerance for other Jewish groups and in their degree of accommodation of the surrounding secular environment. Thus, while some Hasidic groups practice complete withdrawal from the secular world and the rest of the Jewish community, others, such as the Lubavich Hasidim (originally from Lithuania, with strong communities in many countries), are devoted to extending their message to as many Jews as possible, using all the tools of modern technology for their sacred purpose. The Lubavich, who offer highly structured and nurturing communities in which male–female roles are strictly defined and an all-embracing piety and devotion to a charismatic leader are universally shared, have had considerable success in attracting young Jews to their way of life. They are seen as strong role models and present themselves as true Jews. This return to a structured practice of Judaism has surprised many observers. When the seventh Lubavich rabbi came to the United States, he was discouraged by other Jewish rabbis from trying to interest people in the Torah in a country where so many had abandoned their tradition and were living secular lives. To the contrary, the emphasis on the Torah proved to have great appeal and encouraged many to return to their Jewish roots.

The Reform movement, at the other end of the religious spectrum from Orthodoxy, began in nineteenth-century Germany as an attempt to help modern Jews appreciate their religion rather than regarding it as antiquated, meaningless, or even repugnant. In imitation of Christian churches, synagogues were redefined as places for spiritual elevation, with choirs added for effect, and the Sabbath service was shortened and translated into the vernacular. The liturgy was also changed to eliminate references to the hope of return to Zion and animal sacrifices in the Temple. Halakhic observances were re-evaluated for their relevance to modern needs, and Judaism was understood as an evolving, open-ended religion rather than one fixed forever by the revealed Torah. Reform congregations are numerous in North America, where they are continually engaged in a "creative confrontation with modernity." Rather than exclusivism, Reform rabbis cultivate a sense of the universalism of Jewish values. It is felt that only by making Judaism meaningful to modern tastes and modern minds can it survive.

Given this approach, it is not surprising that Reform Judaism, particularly in North America, has been at the forefront in the establishment of interfaith dialogue and civic cooperation with non-Jewish groups. Reform Judaism is not fully accepted in Israel, where the Israeli Rabbinate, which has considerable civil and political power, does not recognize the authority of non-Orthodox rabbis. For example, Israeli religious officials are reluctant to acknowledge Reform converts as true Jews who can be Israeli citizens.

The liberalization process has also given birth to other groups with intermediate positions. Conservative Judaism is the largest Jewish movement in the United States. While Conservative Jews feel they are totally dedicated to traditional rabbinical Judaism, at the same time they are restating and restructuring it in modern terms so that it is not perceived as a dead historical religion. To appeal to intelligent would-be believers, Conservative Judaism has sponsored critical studies of

Jewish texts from all periods in history. They believe that Jews have always searched and added to their laws, liturgy, Midrash, and beliefs to keep them relevant and meaningful in changing times. Some of the recent changes introduced are acceptance of riding to a synagogue for Sabbath services and acceptance of women into rabbinical schools as candidates for ordination as rabbis.

Rabbi Mordecai Kaplan, a highly influential American thinker who died in 1983, branched off from Conservatism (which initially rejected his ideas as too radical), and founded a movement called Reconstructionism. Kaplan held that the Enlightenment had changed everything and that strong measures were needed to preserve Judaism in the face of rationalism. Kaplan asserted that "as long as Jews adhered to the traditional conception of the Torah as supernaturally revealed, they would not be amenable to any constructive adjustment of Judaism that was needed to render it viable in a non-Jewish environment."[45] He defined Judaism as an "evolving religious civilization," both cultural and spiritual, and asserted that the Jewish people are the heart of Judaism. The traditions exist for

Rabbi Pauline Bebe
with the Torah scroll.

the people, and not vice versa, he said. Kaplan denied that the Jewish people were specially chosen by God, an exclusivist idea. Rather, they had chosen to try to become a people of God. Kaplan created a new prayer book, deleting traditional portions he and others found offensive, such as derogatory references to women and Gentiles, references to physical resurrection of the body, and passages describing God as rewarding or punishing Israel by manipulating natural phenomena such as rain. Women were accepted fully into synagogue participation.

In addition to those who affiliate with a religious movement, there are many Jews who identify themselves as secular Jews, affirming their Jewish origins and maintaining various Jewish cultural traditions while eschewing religious practice. There are also significant numbers of people of Jewish birth, particularly in North America and western Europe, whose Jewish identity is vestigial at best, and unlikely to survive in future generations. The possibilities for total assimilation into Western culture are evident in statistics indicating that over fifty percent of Western Jews marry non-Jews. In most cases, neither spouse in such a marriage converts, and research indicates that it is highly unlikely that their children will identify as Jews. Thus, one of the great ironies of the liberty offered to the Jewish people by democratic secular societies is the freedom to leave Judaism as well as to affirm it.

Jewish feminism

In contrast to the option of leaving Judaism, some feminists are coming back to religious observance, but not in the traditional mold, which they regard as patriarchal and sexist. Women have begun to take an active role in claiming their rights to full religious participation—to be counted as part of a *minyan*, for instance, to sit with the men rather than behind a curtain in the synagogue, or to be ordained as rabbis. They are also redefining Judaism from a feminist perspective. Part of this effort involves trying to reconstruct the history of significant Jewish women, for the Torah was written down by men who devoted far more space to the doings of men than of women. There are hints, for instance, that there were powerful prophetesses, such as Miriam and Huldah, but very little information is given about them.

Among those who champion the rights of women to participate equally with men in ritual and prayer, there are also some who are making an ongoing effort to revise liturgical language in gender-neutral and gender-inclusive ways, both in reference to worshippers, and in reference to God. The Hebrew scriptures describe God as both female and male, validating new translations from the Hebrew that use gender-neutral language. As an example of the shift from male-centered to gender-neutral language, the biblical passage: "And God created man in his own image, in the image of God created He them; male and female created He them"[50] has been re-translated thus: "Thus God created us in the divine image, creating us in the image of God, creating us male and female."[51]

Feminist Susannah Heschel explains that changing God-language has profound implications for one's spirituality:

Whereas God may be neither male nor female, our language for God is overwhelmingly and decidedly male. The consequences of that exclusivity are

Senator Joseph Lieberman

Joseph Lieberman has long been active in American public life, including several terms as a U.S. Senator from Connecticut. In 2000, he almost became the Vice President of the United States as Albert Gore's running mate in an extraordinarily tight race. He maintains that despite scandals and abuses of power, public service deserves more positive attention if a democracy is to succeed. Senator Lieberman is himself an observant Jew, and Jewish observances and principles form the background for his public service. He explains:

I got into politics through the surprising portal of my faith because it has so much to do with the way I navigate each day, personally and professionally. It has provided a foundation, order, and purpose to my life.

I was raised in a religiously observant family, which gave me the clear answers of faith to life's most difficult questions. My parents and my rabbi, Joseph Ehrenkranz, taught me that our lives were a gift from God, the Creator, and with it came a covenantal obligation to serve God with gladness by living as best we could, according to the law and values that God gave Moses on Mount Sinai. The summary of our aspirations was in the Hebrew phrase tikkun olam, *which is translated "to improve the world," or "to repair the world," or, more boldly, "to complete the Creation which God began." In any translation, this concept of tikkun olam presumes the inherent but unfulfilled goodness of people and requires action for the benefit of the community. It accepts our imperfections and concludes that we, as individuals and as a society, are constantly in the process of improving and becoming complete. Each of us has the opportunity and responsibility to advance that process both within ourselves and the wider world around us. As Rabbi Tarfon says in the Talmud, "The day is short and there is much work to be done. You are not required to complete the work yourself, but you cannot withdraw from it either."*[46]

As is so often the case, Senator Lieberman credits his grandmother as being one of the major spiritual influences in his life. He relates:

Born and raised in Central Europe, widowed with five children while she was in her thirties, Baba was a deeply religious women and very resilient. . . . [Before coming to America] she spent her life in a European village where Jews were not, to say the least, always treated kindly. To move from such a place to a small American city where, as she walked to synagogue on a Saturday, her Christian neighbors would pass and say respectfully, "Good Sabbath, Mrs. Manger!" was an endless source of delight and gratitude for her. . . . She never took her freedom and opportunity here for granted, and she made sure I didn't either. Baba also set a standard for service in our family, as one of the founders of the Hebrew Ladies Educational League in Stamford, a classic immigrant, self-help, pre-welfare organization which raised money and gave it quietly to those who needed it for food or clothing or birth or burial.[47]

Though a committed Jew, Lieberman revels in the pluralism of American society. He cites his participation in Martin Luther King's 1963 March on Washington as a major formative experience in his life. The march, he relates,

culminated at the Lincoln Memorial in [King's] soaring "I Have a Dream" speech. For me, this was America at its best. . . . Hundreds of thousands of us, of all religions, races, and nationalities, joined together peacefully but powerfully to petition our government to right the wrong of racial bigotry.[48]

Despite his deep commitment to public service, Senator Lieberman insists on setting aside time for the Sabbath except in cases of extreme emergency sessions of the Senate. He explains:

In the helter-skelter push and pull of Senate life, Hadassah [his wife] and I have found that our religious observances provide very welcome relief, particularly the Sabbath, that weekly sanctuary between sunset on Friday and sundown on Saturday. This is the time when the worldly concerns of the rest of the week are put on hold so that we can focus on appreciating all that God has given us. It is a day apart, when my family and I are able to reconnect with one another and with our spiritual selves, to pray, to talk, to read, to rest, or to just plain enjoy ourselves. It is a "time beyond time," as one rabbi called it. In fact, I usually don't wear a watch on the Sabbath. I treasure that time, twenty-four hours with no meetings, no telephone calls, no television, no radio, no traveling, no business of any sort.[49]

theological and practical. For instance, we might assume that if God were imaged as female, it might be difficult to justify women's relegation behind the mehitza *[partition separating men and women in a synagogue] as preventing men from being distracted during their prayers. ... We might also speculate about the impact on our experience at prayer if God were imaged as Mother as well as Father. How would the experience of Yom Kippur be different if we asked forgiveness from "Our Mother, Our Queen," rather than "Our Father, Our King"?*[52]

There is also a feminist critique of women's position in the state of Israel. Women among the early Zionist settlers envisioned a society in which men and women would work side by side and each apply their full capabilities to the creation of a new society. Even though laws were created that supported gender equality, traditional sexual divisions of labor were perpetuated, especially once the Orthodox parties took a major role in the formation and governance of the state. Judith Plaskow links the discrimination against women in Israel to the disempowerment of other minorities, including Palestinians and non-Ashkenazi Jews. She argues passionately,

The recognition of diverse constituencies as parts of larger communities involves an obligation to redefine communal life as the sum of all pieces. When one part has been accustomed to speaking for the whole—male Ashkenazi Jewish Israelis for Israelis, elite male Jews for Jews, middle-class white feminists for women—this definition may mean dislodging long-fixed patterns of dominance with difficult and dramatic results.[53]

Jewish renewal

Both men and women from varied backgrounds are being attracted to newly revitalized expressions of Jewish spirituality. After the Holocaust, many Jews had retreated from religious observance to avoid being conspicuous. Now, not only are some Jews becoming comfortable with being openly religious, but also conversions to Judaism seem to be increasing.

Although anti-semitism continues to flare up here and there, many non-Jews are developing sensitivity against negative stereotyping of Jews. The Evangelical Lutheran Church in America has issued an historic public apology for the anti-Jewish writings of Martin Luther, the father of Protestant Christianity. In part, they declared:

As did many of Luther's own companions in the sixteenth century, we reject this violent invective, and yet more do we express our deep and abiding sorrow over its tragic effects on subsequent generations. In concert with the Lutheran World Federation, we particularly deplore the appropriation of Luther's words by modern anti-Semites for the teaching of hatred toward Judaism or toward the Jewish people in our day. ... We recognize in anti-Semitism a contradiction and an affront to the Gospel, a violation of our hope and calling, and we pledge this church to oppose the deadly working of such bigotry.[54]

In post-Soviet Russia, where under Stalin Jews had been so persecuted that only a few rabbis remained in all of Russia, there are now Jewish seminaries and universities, schools, and kindergartens. Rabbi Dovid Karpov, whose congregation

Jane and Chris King and friends stage a Millennium Epiphany Renewal in Jerusalem, reading from their poetry. Jane pronounces, "I have come here to remind you./You are Him, and I am She,/and we/the ark of the world. . . . For the Renewal of all life/lies in this sacred realm,/and that rare stranger in the garden,/ the immortal Beloved,/ is also Yourself." (Genesis of Eden website: www.dhushara.com)

serves one hundred and fifty free hot meals a day in Moscow, says that Judaism has begun to flourish again after years of secrecy and danger:

> *Now we can celebrate holidays such as Hanukkah openly. It is not yet a mass movement, but there are more people than you can count on your fingers. We feel that soon we will see the fruit of our work. Judaism survives despite all the persecutions. The new world is coming very soon and it will have a very different form. The Messiah is coming. The time will soon come when we will have the peace that everyone is waiting for. It will happen sooner than anyone can imagine.*[55]

Contemporary Jewish renewal is not just an absence of fear. It is an active search for personal meaning in the ancient rituals and scriptures, and the creation of new rituals for our times. There are now numerous small *havurot*, or communities of Jews, who are not affiliated with any formal group but get together on a regular basis to worship and celebrate the traditions. They favor a democratic organization and personal experience, and are often engaged in trying to determine what parts of the traditions to use and how. Some incorporate study groups, continuing the ancient intellectual tradition of grappling with the ethical, philosophical, and spiritual meanings of the texts. Some are bringing fresh ideas to traditional celebrations, so that they are actively transformational rather than simply matters of empty habit.

From highly conservative to highly liberal quarters, there are now attempts to renew the ancient messianic ideal of Judaism, that by its practice the world might be healed. Michael Lerner, whose magazine title, *Tikkun*, is a Hebrew word that refers to the healing and transformation of the world, explains:

*A new generation of teachers, rabbis, community activists, and thinkers has begun
to reclaim the central insights of Judaism. It is no wonder that after having faced
massive and staggering destruction and dislocations, many Jews feel spiritually and
emotionally dead. We sought refuge from pogroms and genocide in societies that
were themselves spiritually and emotionally dead, and we did our best to assimilate
our Judaism to these societies because we hoped that inconspicuousness would
keep us from becoming targets. It has taken many decades for Jews to feel secure
enough to begin to renew the spiritual tradition. We are witnessing today the
miraculous regeneration of the primary ideals of Judaism that have been part of
our tradition since Abraham and Moses. . . . In every historical period, there has
been a recreation of the tradition through commentary, Midrash, and creative
reinterpretation. . . .*

*After reading the Torah on Shabbat morning, Jews return the Torah to its ark
or resting point, and in fervent devotion sing a moving prayer: "It is a tree of life
to those who hold fast to it, and its precepts are right. Its paths are paths of
pleasantness, and all its paths are peace. Return us to thee, Lord, and we shall
return."*[56]

Suggested reading

Ariel, David S., *The Mystic Quest: An Introduction to Jewish Mysticism*, Northvale, New Jersey:
Jason Aronson, 1988. An accessible introduction to mystical Jewish thinking.

Baskin, Judith R., ed., *Jewish Women in Historical Perspective*, Detroit: Wayne State
University Press, 1991. Twelve pioneering essays by modern scholars explore Jewish
women and their activities in a variety of times and places.

Ben-Sasson, H. H., ed., *A History of the Jewish People*, Cambridge, Massachusetts: Harvard
University Press, 1976. Leading scholars of the Hebrew University in Jerusalem offer a
comprehensive, scholarly analysis of Jewish history, which assumes some knowledge of
the tradition.

Berger, Alan L., ed., *Judaism in the Modern World*, New York: New York University Press,
1994. Articles by leading contemporary Jewish scholars on facets of the changing
identities and paradoxes of modern Jewry.

Cohen, Arthur A. and Mendes-Flohr, Paul, eds., *Contemporary Jewish Religious Thought*,
New York: Charles Scribner's Sons, 1987. Brief essays on all aspects of Jewish belief,
from aesthetics to Zionism, by writers from all Jewish schools.

Encyclopedia Judaica, Jerusalem: Keter Publishing House Jerusalem Ltd., 1972. The
authoritative, multi-volume reference on all aspects of Judaism, as seen from a broad
spectrum of points of view.

Glatzer, Nahum N., ed., *The Judaic Tradition*, Boston: Beacon Press, 1969. A useful
compilation of writings from all periods of Jewish history.

Grossman, Susan and Haut, Rivka, eds., *Daughters of the King: Women and the Synagogue*,
Philadelphia: Jewish Publication Society, 1992. An excellent anthology of history,
halakhah, and contemporary testimonies concerning women and synagogue
participation.

Heschel, Abraham J., *Between God and Man: An Interpretation of Judaism*, ed., Fritz A. Rothschild, New York: The Free Press, 1959. An intimate exploration of the relevance of traditional Judaism for today's world, by a great twentieth-century theologian.

Holtz, Barry, *Back to the Sources*, New York: Schocken Books, 1984. Excellent introduction to classical Jewish religious texts. Each chapter takes the reader through a step-by-step approach on how to read representative selections of the Bible, Talmud, Midrash, the Zohar, liturgical texts, and others.

Jacobs, Louis, *Principles of the Jewish Faith*, Northvale, New Jersey: Jason Aronson, 1964, 1988. Many commentaries spanning the centuries are brought to bear on thirteen central principles of Judaism as set forth by Maimonides.

Lerner, Michael, *Jewish Renewal: A Path to Healing and Transformation*, New York: Harper-Collins, 1994. Profound and moving analyses of why Jews left Judaism and the revitalization that is drawing them back to faith.

Plaskow, Judith, *Standing Again at Sinai: Judaism from a Feminist Perspective*, San Francisco: Harper San Francisco, 1991. Studies of all aspects of Jewish feminism, including the reconstruction of women's history, women in Israel, gender-equal God-language, sexuality in feminist religious context, and women's role in the repair of the world.

Ravitzky, Aviezer, *Messianism, Zionism, and Jewish Religious Radicalism*, Chicago: University of Chicago Press, 1996. Extensive analysis of varying Orthodox religious responses to Jewish statehood in Israel.

Schachter-Shalomi, Zalman, with Donald Gropman, *The First Step: A Guide for the New Jewish Spirit*, New York: Bantam Books, 1983. A modern explanation of the essence of Judaism, of special interest to non-observant Jews who want to find their way back into the faith.

Scholem, Gershom G., *Major Trends in Jewish Mysticism*, New York: Schocken Books, 1974. The classic scholarly work on the development of mystical Judaism.

Seltzer, Robert, *Jewish People, Jewish Thought: The Jewish Experience in History*, New York: Macmillan, 1980. An excellent, comprehensive, one-volume history of the Jewish people, with a particular emphasis on philosophy, mysticism, and religious thought.

Tanakh: The Holy Scriptures, The New JPS Translation according to the Traditional Hebrew Text, Philadelphia: The Jewish Publication Society, 1988. The preferred translation of the Hebrew scriptures, in graceful and spiritually sensitive modern English.

Wiesel, Elie, *Night*, New York: Bantam, 1960. Short, searing memoir of a teenage boy's Holocaust experience.

Wouk, Herman, *This is my God*, Boston: Little, Brown, 1959, 1988. A very readable personal description of a lived faith.

CHRISTIANITY

"Jesus Christ is Lord"

Christianity is a faith based on the life, teachings, death, and resurrection of Jesus. He was born as a Jew about two thousand years ago in Roman-occupied Palestine. He taught for fewer than three years and was executed by the Roman government on charges of sedition. Nothing was written about him at the time, although some years after his death, attempts were made to record what he had said and done. Yet his birth is now celebrated around the world and since the sixth century has been used as the major point from which public time is measured, even by non-Christians. The religion centered around him has more followers than any other.

In studying Christianity we will first examine what can be said about the life and teachings of Jesus, based on accounts in the Bible and on historians' knowledge of the period. We will then follow the evolution of the religion as it spread to all continents and became theologically and liturgically more complex. This process continues in the present, in which there are not one but many different versions of Christianity.

The Christian Bible

The Bibles used by various Christian churches consist of the Hebrew Bible (called the "Old Testament"), and in some cases non-canonical Jewish texts called the Apocrypha, plus the twenty-seven books of the "New Testament" written after Jesus's earthly mission. What we know about Jesus's life and teachings is derived largely from the first four books of the New Testament, which are called the **gospels** (good news). On the whole, they seem to have been originally written about forty to sixty years after Jesus's death. They are based on the oral transmission of the stories and discourses, which may have been influenced by the growing split between Christians and Jews. The documents, thought to be pseudonymous, are given the names of Jesus's followers Matthew and John, and of the apostle Paul's companions Mark and Luke. The gospels were first written down in Greek and perhaps Aramaic, the everyday language that Jesus spoke, and then copied and translated in many different ways over the centuries. They offer a composite picture of Jesus as seen through the eyes of the Christian community.

How do Christians approach the gospels? Traditionally, the holy scriptures have been reverently regarded as the divinely inspired Word of God. Furthermore, in Eastern Orthodox Christianity, "the Gospel is not just Holy Scripture but also a symbol of Divine Wisdom and an image of Christ Himself."[1]

Nonetheless, some Christians have attempted to clarify what Jesus taught and how he lived, so that people might truly follow him. In general, interpretations of the stories and sayings of Jesus may be literal, allegorical, mystical, or moral. During the eighteenth century, critical study of the Bible from a strictly historical point of view began in western Europe. This approach, now accepted by many Roman Catholics and Protestants, is based on the literary method of interpreting ancient writings in their historical context, with their intended audience and desired effect taken into account.

We do not know what Jesus, the founder of the world's largest religion, looked like. Rembrandt used a young European Jewish man as his model for this sensitive "portrait" of Jesus.

Three of the gospels, Matthew, Mark, and Luke, are so similar that they are called the **synoptic** gospels, referring to the fact that they can be "seen together" as presenting rather similar views of Jesus's career, though they are organized somewhat differently. Most historians think that Matthew and Luke are largely based on Mark and another source called "Q." This hypothesized source would probably be a compilation of oral and written traditions. It is now thought that the author of Mark put together many fragments of oral tradition in order to develop a connected narrative about Jesus's life and ministry, for the sake of propagating the faith.

The other two synoptic gospels often parallel Mark quite closely but include additional material. The gospel according to Matthew (named after one of Jesus's original disciples, a tax collector) is sometimes called a Jewish Christian gospel. It represents Jesus as a second Moses as well as the Messiah ushering in the Kingdom of Heaven, with frequent references to the Old Testament. Matthew's stories emphasize that the Gentiles (non-Jews) accept Jesus, whereas the Jews reject him as savior.

Luke, to whom the third gospel is attributed, is traditionally thought to have been a physician who sometimes accompanied Paul the apostle. The gospel seems to have been written with a **Gentile** Christian audience in mind. Luke presents Jesus's mission in universal rather than exclusively Jewish terms and accentuates the importance of his ministry to the underprivileged and lower classes.

The Gospel of John, traditionally attributed to "the disciple Jesus loved," is of a very different nature from the other three. It concerns itself less with following the life of Jesus than with seeing Jesus as the eternal Son of God, the word of God made flesh.

Other gospels circulating in the early Christian church were not included in the canon of the New Testament. They include magical stories of Jesus's infancy, such as an account of his making clay birds and then bringing them to life. The Gospel of Thomas, one of the long-hidden manuscripts discovered in 1945 by a peasant in a cave near Nag Hammadi, Egypt, is of particular interest. Some scholars feel that its core may have been written even earlier than the canonical gospels. It contains many sayings in common with the other gospels but places the accent on mystical concepts of Jesus:

Jesus said: I am the Light that is above them all. I am the All,
the All came forth from me and the All
attained to me. Cleave a (piece of) wood,
I am there; lift up the stone and you will
find Me there.[2]

The life and teachings of Jesus

It is not possible to reconstruct from the gospels a single chronology of Jesus's life nor to account for much of what happened before he began his ministry. Nevertheless, the stories of the New Testament are important to Christians as the foundation of their faith. And after extensive analysis most scholars have concluded on grounds of linguistics and regional history that many of the sayings attributed to Jesus by the gospels may be authentic.

Birth

Most historians think Jesus was probably born a few years before the first year of what is now called the **Common Era**. When sixth-century Christian monks began figuring time in relationship to the life of Jesus, they may have miscalculated slightly. Traditionally, Christians have believed that Jesus was born in Bethlehem. This detail fulfills the rabbinic interpretation of the Old Testament prophecies that the Messiah would be born in Bethlehem, the home of David the great king, and in the lineage of David. The gospel of Matthew offers a genealogy tracing Jesus through David back to Abraham; the gospel of Luke traces his lineage all the way back to Adam, the son of God. Some scholars suggest that Jesus was actually born in or near Nazareth, his own home town in Galilee. This region, whose name meant "Ring of the Gentiles" (non-Jews), was not fully Jewish; it

Jesus is often pictured as a divine child, born in a humble stable, and forced to flee on a donkey with his parents. (Monastère Bénédictin de Keur Moussa, Senegal, Fuite en Egypte.)

"The Nativity," Jesus's humble birth depicted in a 14th-century fresco by Giotto. (Scrovegni Chapel, Padua, Italy.)

John the Baptist is said to have baptized Jesus only reluctantly, saying that he was unworthy even to fasten Jesus's shoes. When he did so, the Spirit allegedly descended upon Jesus as a dove. (Painting by Esperanza Guevara, Solentiname, Nicaragua.)

was also scorned as somewhat countrified by the rabbinic orthodoxy of Judaea. Both Judaea and Galilee were ruled by Rome at the time.

According to the gospels, Jesus's mother was Mary, who was a virgin when she conceived him by the Holy Spirit; her husband was Joseph, a carpenter from Bethlehem. Luke states that they had to go to Bethlehem to satisfy a Roman ruling that everyone should travel to their ancestral cities for a census. When they had made the difficult journey, there was no room for them in the inn, so the baby was born in a stable among the animals. He was named Jesus, which means "God saves." This well-loved birth legend exemplifies the humility that Jesus taught. According to Luke, those who came to pay their respects were poor shepherds to whom angels had appeared with the glad tidings that a Savior had been born to the people. Matthew tells instead of Magi, sages from "the east", who may have been Zoroastrians and who brought the Christ child symbolic gifts of gold and frankincense and myrrh, confirming his kingship and his adoration by Gentiles.

Preparation

No other stories are told about Jesus's childhood in Nazareth until he was twelve years old, when he accompanied his parents on their yearly trip to Jerusalem for Passover. Left behind by mistake, he was said to have been discovered by his parents in the Temple discussing the Torah with the rabbis; "all who heard him were amazed at his understanding and his answers." When scolded, he reportedly replied, "Did you not know that I must be in my Father's house?"[3] This story is used to demonstrate his sense of mission even as a boy, his knowledge of Jewish tradition, and the close personal connection between Jesus and God. In later accounts of his prayers, he spoke to God as "Abba," a very familiar word for father.

The New Testament is also silent about the years of Jesus's young manhood. What is described, however, is the ministry of John the Baptist, a prophet citing Isaiah's prophecies of the coming Kingdom of God. He was conducting baptism in the Jordan River in preparation for the Kingdom of God. **Apocalyptic** expectations were running high at the time, with Israel chafing under Roman taxation and rule.

According to all four gospels, at the age of about thirty Jesus appeared before John to be baptized. John was calling people to repent of their sins and then be spiritually purified and sanctified by immersion in the river. He felt it improper to perform this ceremony for Jesus, whom Christians consider sinless, but Jesus insisted. How can this be interpreted? One explanation is that, for Jesus, this became a ceremony of his consecration to God as the Messiah. The gospel writer reports,

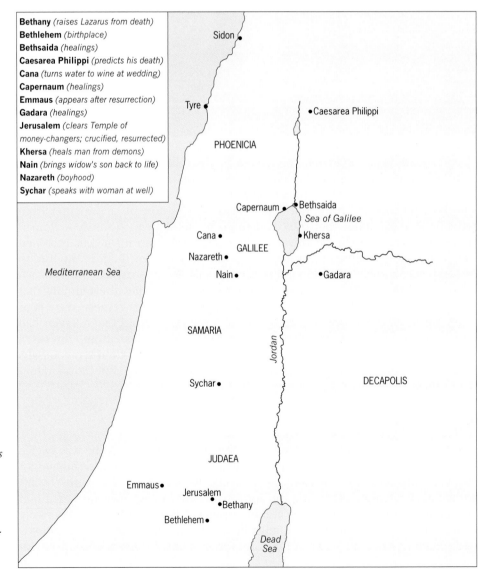

Bethany (raises Lazarus from death)
Bethlehem (birthplace)
Bethsaida (healings)
Caesarea Philippi (predicts his death)
Cana (turns water to wine at wedding)
Capernaum (healings)
Emmaus (appears after resurrection)
Gadara (healings)
Jerusalem (clears Temple of money-changers; crucified, resurrected)
Khersa (heals man from demons)
Nain (brings widow's son back to life)
Nazareth (boyhood)
Sychar (speaks with woman at well)

Sidon

Tyre

Caesarea Philippi

PHOENICIA

Capernaum • Bethsaida
Sea of Galilee
Cana • Khersa
GALILEE
Nazareth •
Nain • • Gadara

Mediterranean Sea

SAMARIA

Jordan

DECAPOLIS

Sychar •

JUDAEA

Emmaus •
Jerusalem
• Bethany
Bethlehem •

Dead Sea

From north to south, the area covered by Jesus during his ministry was no more than 100 miles (161 km). Yet his mission is now worldwide, with more followers than any other religion.

*When he came up out of the water, immediately he saw the heavens opened and the
Spirit descending upon him like a dove; and a voice came from heaven. "Thou art
my beloved Son; with thee I am well pleased."[4]*

Another interpretation is that Jesus's baptism was the occasion for John's publicly
announcing that the Messiah had arrived, beginning his ministry. A third
interpretation is that by requesting baptism, Jesus identified himself with sinful
humanity. Even though he had no need for repentance and purification, he
accepted baptism on behalf of all humans.

After being baptized, Jesus reportedly undertook a forty-day retreat in the
desert wilderness, fasting. During his retreat, the gospel writers say he was
tempted by Satan to use his spiritual power for secular ends, but he refused.

Ministry

In John's gospel, Jesus's baptism and wilderness sojourn were followed by his
gathering of the first disciples, the fisherman Simon (called Peter), Andrew
(Peter's brother), James, and John (brother of James), who recognized him as the
Messiah. First of all Jesus warned his disciples that they would have to leave all
their possessions and human attachments to follow him—to pay more attention
to the life of the spirit than to physical comfort and wealth. This call to discipleship continues to be experienced by Christians today, and a person's response
makes all the difference. The great German theologian Dietrich Bonhoeffer
(1906–1945), who ultimately gave his life for his beliefs, wrote that to follow
Jesus one must immediately leave worldly ties and self-centered ways of thinking behind: "Only the man who is dead to his own will can follow Christ."[5]

Jesus said that it was extremely difficult for the wealthy to enter the kingdom
of heaven. God, the Protector, takes care of physical needs, which are relatively
unimportant anyway:

*Is not life more than food, and the body more than clothing? Look at the birds of
the air; they neither sow nor reap nor gather into barns, and yet your heavenly
Father feeds them. Are you not of more value than they? And which of you by
being anxious can add one cubit to his span of life?[6]*

Jesus taught that his followers should concentrate on laying up spiritual treasures in heaven, rather than material treasures on earth, which are short-lived.
Because God is a generous parent, those who love God and want to follow the
path of righteousness should pray for help, in private: "Ask, and it will be given
you; seek, and you will find; knock, and it will be opened to you."[7]

As Jesus traveled, speaking, he is said to have performed many miracles, such
as turning water into wine, healing the sick, restoring the dead to life, walking on
water, casting devils out of the possessed, and turning a few loaves and fish into
enough food to feed a crowd of thousands, with copious leftovers. Jesus reportedly performed these miracles quietly and compassionately; the gospels interpreted them as signs of the coming Kingdom of God.

The stories of the miracles performed by Jesus have symbolic meanings taken
from the entire Jewish and early Christian traditions. In the sharing of the loaves
and fishes, for instance, it may have been more than physical bread that Luke was

Jesus is said to have brought Lazarus back to life four days after he died and was laid in a tomb. (Fresco by Giotto, Scrovegni Chapel, Padua, Italy.)

talking about when he said, "and all ate and were satisfied."[8] The people came to Jesus out of spiritual hunger, and he fed them all, profligate with his love. Bread often signified life-giving sustenance. Jesus was later to offer himself as "the bread of life."[9]

On another level of interpretation, the story may prefigure the Last Supper of Jesus with his disciples, with both stories alluding to the Jewish tradition of the Great Banquet, the heavenly feast of God, as a symbol of the messianic age. The fish were a symbol of Christ to the early Christians; what he fed them was the indiscriminate gift of himself.

Theological interpretations of the biblical stories are based on the evidence of the Bible itself, but people also bring their own experiences to them. To William, a twentieth-century Nicaraguan peasant, the miracle was not the multiplication of the loaves but the sharing: "The miracle was to persuade the owners of the bread to share it, that it was absurd for them to keep it all while the people were going hungry."[10]

Jesus preached and lived by truly radical ethics. In contrast to the prevailing patriarchal society and extensive proscriptions against impurity, he touched lepers and a bleeding woman to heal them; in his "table fellowship," he ate with

Living Christianity

Born into a devout small-town Southern Baptist family, David Vandiver is now the manager of a wilderness camp in the Appalachian Mountains near Washington, D.C., for inner-city African-American children whose backgrounds are very different from his own. Here he describes the evolution of his understanding and practice of Christianity.

"Becoming a Christian and a Baptist came as naturally as learning to walk and talk. The primary values as I grew up were ones of honesty, fairness, and caring for others. The great sins were the ones most affecting families—divorce, adultery, and irresponsible parenting. It was not until much later in my life that the vast scope of values held by Christians in differing places in the world came to my attention. I was not aware, for example, that there were Christians who believed God wanted them to influence politics for justice, work for equal rights for all people, protect the natural environment, or make peace with other nations and peoples of differing faiths. Our form of faith did a good job of supporting what was valuable in society, but did little to tear down what was destructive. We had no cause to practice tolerance because we were all so similar, except for the African-Americans in our town—about twenty per-cent of the population—who were already Christian and from whom we, as Anglo-Americans, wished to stay separated. I grew up with racism all around me.

"Nonetheless, as a high school youth in the early 1970s, I joined my friends in dragging my church into the foray of the U.S. Civil Rights Movement because I couldn't see Jesus as one who would keep any group of people powerless and poor. Christianity was a voice for the downtrodden and oppressed of the world, and if I was to follow Jesus, I would have to take up their cause for justice in some way.

"The most accessible way for me to take up this cause was to enter a path that would lead to a paid vocation as a Christian minister. It guided me to a Religion/Psychology major in college and later to a Masters of Divinity in Pastoral Counseling at a Baptist seminary. It was here that I began to consider the teachings of Jesus the Christ more deeply. What did it mean to 'love my neighbor as myself'? In practical terms, it came to mean that I could not simply spend the rest of my life pursuing a comfortable living while ignoring the fact that millions are living in poverty and oppression.

"Early in my seminary days, I was married to a wonderful woman, who lost her life in an automobile accident four months after our wedding. I found myself doubting the existence of a caring God. I was plunged into a dark night of the soul and feared I would never escape it. Slowly, as I re-emerged, it began to dawn on me that my plight was not mine alone; that millions had suffered and were suffering similar losses; that in fact, to love anyone was to risk such loss, and that the deeper the love the greater the loss. My understanding of God was transformed. It became clear to me that anything good and loving in life was a gift, sent as a precious favor.

"When I left seminary, on the one hand, I saw that following Jesus would take me out of the mainstream of the world in order to love it fully. On the other hand, I was painfully aware of the impossibility of loving others unconditionally. What as a child was an inherent identity that I learned as easily as learning to walk became a life-long journey that I would never fully complete.

"Vocationally and geographically, I have found a home as the manager of a wilderness camp for inner-city children from Washington. It is the perfect melding of my rural, small-town roots and the passion to serve the poor and oppressed. Many of the children who come to our camp have never been out of the city. As I watch and listen to them entering this environment that is foreign to them, they become my teachers, helping me to understand the fears with which they face the wilderness, and the fears they confront at home in the city. Each time I am with them, I am reminded of how I grew up, unaware of the larger world around me. I work to help them find the tools that will assist them in loving those they find difficult to love: their enemies, abusers, oppressors, and those who ignore them. The memories of all those who have given me those tools, and have held up the imperatives of Jesus to love the world, even those whom I find difficult to love, inspire me to carry on here in this wilderness of familiar and unfamiliar experiences and people."

people of all classes. In a culture in which the woman's role was strictly circumscribed, he welcomed women as his disciples. Mary Magdalene, Mary the mother of James the younger and Joses, Salome the mother of the disciples James and John, Mary of Bethany, Martha, Susanna, and Joanna are among those mentioned in the gospels. Some of them traveled with Jesus and even helped to support him and his disciples financially, a great departure from orthodox Jewish tradition. His was a radically egalitarian vision. He also extended the application of Jewish laws: "You have heard that it was said to the men of old," Jesus began, "You shall not kill; and whoever kills shall be liable to judgment. But I say to you that every one who is angry with his brother shall be liable to judgment."[11] Not only should a man not commit adultery; it is wrong even to look at a woman lustfully. Rather than taking revenge with an eye for an eye, a tooth for a tooth, respond with love. If a person strikes you on one cheek, turn the other cheek to be struck also. If anyone tries to rob you of your coat, give him your cloak as well. And not only should you love your neighbor, Jesus says:

> *Love your enemies and pray for those who persecute you, so that you may be sons of your Father who is in heaven; for he makes his sun rise on the evil and on the good, and sends rain on the just and on the unjust.*[12]

The extremely high ethical standards of the Sermon on the Mount (Matthew 5–7) may seem impossibly challenging. Who can fully follow them? And Jesus said these things to people who had been brought up with the understanding that to fulfill incompletely even one divine commandment is a violation of the Law. But when people recognize their helplessness to fulfill such commandments, they are ready to turn to the divine for help. Jesus pointed out, "With man this is impossible, but not with God; all things are possible with God."[13]

The main thing Jesus taught was love. He stated that to love God and to "love your neighbor as yourself"[14] were the two great commandments in Judaism, upon which everything else rested. To love God means placing God first in one's life, rather than concentrating on the things of the earth. To love one's neighbor means selfless service to everyone, even to those despised by the rest of society. Jesus often horrified the religious authorities by talking to prostitutes, tax-collectors, and the poorest and lowliest of people. He set an example of loving service by washing his disciples' feet. This kind of love, he said, should be the mark of his followers, and at the Last Judgment, when the Son of Man judges the people of all time, he will grant eternal life in the kingdom to the humble "sheep" who loved and served him in all:

> *Then the righteous will answer him, "Lord, when did we see thee hungry and feed thee, or thirsty and give thee drink? And when did we see thee a stranger and welcome thee, or naked and clothe thee? And when did we see thee sick or in prison and visit thee?" And the King will answer them, "Truly, I say to you, as you did it to one of the least of these my brethren, you did it to me."*[15]

Jesus preached that God is forgiving to those who repent. He told a story likening God to the father who welcomed with gifts and celebration his "prodigal son" who had squandered his inheritance and then humbly returned home. He told story after story suggesting that those who considered themselves superior were more at odds with God than those who were aware of their sins. Those who

TEACHING STORY

The Good Samaritan

On one occasion a lawyer came forward to put this test question to Jesus: "Master, what must I do to inherit eternal life?" Jesus said, "What is written in the Law? What is your reading of it?" He replied, "Love the Lord your God with all your heart, with all your soul, with all your strength, and with all your mind; and your neighbor as yourself." "That is the right answer," said Jesus; "do that and you will live."

But he wanted to vindicate himself, so he said to Jesus, "And who is my neighbor?" Jesus replied, "A man was on his way from Jerusalem down to Jericho when he fell in with robbers, who stripped him, beat him, and went off leaving him half dead. It so happened that a priest was going down by the same road; but when he saw him, he went past on the other side. So too a Levite came to the place, and when he saw him went past on the other side. But a Samaritan [a person from a region against whom the Jews of Judaea had developed religious and racial prejudice] who was making the journey came upon him, and when he saw him was moved to pity. He went up and bandaged his wounds, bathing them with oil and wine. Then he lifted him on to his own beast, brought him to an inn, and looked after him there. Next day he produced two silver pieces and gave them to the innkeeper, and said, 'Look after him; and if you spend any more, I will repay you on my way back.' Which of these three do you think was neighbor to the man who fell into the hands of the robbers?" He answered, "The one who showed him kindness." Jesus said, "Go and do as he did."[16]

sincerely repent—even if they are the hated toll-collectors, prostitutes, or ignorant common people—are more likely to receive God's merciful forgiveness than are the learned and hypocritically self-righteous. Indeed, Jesus said, it was only in childlikeness that people could enter the kingdom of heaven. In a famous series of statements about supreme happiness called the **Beatitudes**, Jesus is quoted as having promised blessings for the "poor in spirit,"[17] the mourners, the meek, the seekers of righteousness, the pure in heart, the merciful, the peacemakers, and those who are persecuted for the sake of righteousness and of spreading the gospel.

Jesus's stories were typically presented as **parables**, in which earthly situations familiar to people of his time and place were used to make a spiritual point. He spoke of parents and children, of masters and servants, of sowing seeds, of fishing. For example,

The kingdom of heaven is like a dragnet cast into the sea that brings in a haul of all kinds. When it is full, the fishermen haul it ashore; then, sitting down, they collect the good ones in a basket and throw away those that are no use. This is how it will be at the end of time: the angels will appear and separate the wicked from the just to throw them into the blazing furnace where there will be weeping and grinding of teeth.[18]

As we have seen, messianic expectations were running very high among Jews of that time, oppressed as they were by Roman rule. They looked to a time when the people of Israel would be freed and the authority of Israel's God would be

CHRISTIANITY

CE	c.4 BCE–30 CE Life of Jesus
50	c.50–60 St. Paul organizes early Christians
	c.70–95 Gospels written down
100	
300	
	306–337 Constantine emperor of Roman Empire
	354–430 Life of St. Augustine
400	379–395 Christianity becomes state religion under rule of Emperor Theodosius
500	c.480–542 Life of St. Benedict and creation of his monastic rule
800	800–1300 Middle Ages in Europe; centralization of papal power
1000	
	1054 Split between Western and Eastern Orthodox Church
	1095–1300 The Crusades
1100	
	1182–1226 Life of St. Francis of Assisi
1200	
1300	1300s Proliferation of monastic orders
1400	
1500	
	1509–1564 Life of John Calvin
	1517 Martin Luther posts 95 Theses
	1534 Church of England separates from Rome
	1545–1563 The Council of Trent; Roman Catholic Reformation
1700	1703–1791 Life of John Wesley
	c.1720–1780 The Enlightenment in Europe
1800	
1900	
	1945 Discovery of the Nag Hammadi manuscripts
	1948 World Council of Churches formed
	1962–1965 The Second Vatican Council
	1988 Churches reopened in USSR
2000	2000 Pope John Paul II asks forgiveness for sins of the Roman Catholic Church

recognized throughout the world. Jesus reportedly spoke to them again and again about the fulfillment of these expectations: "The time is fulfilled, and the kingdom of God is at hand; repent, and believe in the gospel"[19]; "I must preach the good news of the kingdom of God . . . for I was sent for this purpose."[20] He taught them to pray for the advent of this kingdom: "Thy kingdom come, Thy will be done on earth as it is in heaven."[21] However, in contrast to expectations of secular deliverance from the Romans, Jesus seems to refer to the kingdom as manifestation of God's full glory, the consummation of the world.

> *Every one who drinks of this water will thirst again, but whoever drinks of the water that I shall give him will never thirst; the water that I shall give him will become in him a spring of water welling up to eternal life.*
> *Jesus, as quoted in the Gospel of John, 4:13–14*

Jesus's references to the kingdom, as reported in the gospels, indicate two seemingly different emphases: one that the kingdom is expected in the future, and the other that the kingdom is already here. In his future references, as in the apocalyptic Jewish writings of the time, Jesus said that things would get much worse right before the end. He seemed to foretell the destruction of Jerusalem by the Romans that began in 70 CE. But:

> *then will appear the sign of the Son of man in heaven, and then all the tribes of the earth will mourn, and they will see the Son of man coming on the clouds of heaven with power and great glory; and he will send out his angels with a loud trumpet call, and they will gather his elect from the four winds, from one end of heaven to the other.*[22]

It was his mission, he said, to gather together everyone who could be saved.

Challenges to the authorities

As Jesus traveled through Galilee, many people gathered around him to be healed. Herod Antipas, a Jew who had been appointed by the Romans as ruler of Galilee, had already executed John the Baptist and may have been concerned that Jesus might be a trouble-maker, perhaps one of the **Zealots** of Galilee who were stirring up support for a political uprising against the Romans. Jesus therefore moved outside Herod's jurisdiction for a while, to carry on his work in Tyre and Sidon (now in Lebanon).

According to the gospels, Jesus was also regarded with suspicion by prominent Jewish groups of his time—the emerging **Pharisees** (the shapers of rabbinic Judaism), **Sadducees** (the priests and upper class), and the scribes (specially trained laymen who copied the written law and formulated the oral law of Judaism). Jesus seems not to have challenged Mosaic law, but rather, its interpretations in the evolving rabbinic traditions and the hypocrisy of some of those who claim to be living by the law. It is written in the Gospel of Matthew that the Pharisees and scribes challenged Jesus's disciples for not washing their hands before eating. Jesus responded:

Hypocrites! It was you Isaiah meant when he so rightly prophesied: "This people honors me only with lip service / while their hearts are far from me. / The worship they offer me is worthless; / the doctrines they teach are only human regulations."[23]

He called the people to him and said, "Listen, and understand. What goes into the mouth does not make a man unclean; it is what comes out of the mouth that makes him unclean. . . . For things that come out of the mouth come from the heart, and it is these that make a man unclean. For from the heart come evil intentions. . . . But to eat with unwashed hands does not make a man unclean."[24] . . .

"Alas for you, scribes and Pharisees, you hypocrites! You who are like whitewashed tombs that look handsome on the outside, but inside are full of dead men's bones and every kind of corruption. In the same way you appear to people from the outside like good honest men, but inside you are full of hypocrisy and lawlessness."[25]

Many seemingly anti-Jewish statements in the New Testament are suspected by some modern scholars as additions or interpretations dating from the period after Jesus's death, when rabbinic Judaism and early Christianity were competing for followers. Nevertheless, more universal teachings are apparent in such stories attributed to Jesus. For instance, in all times and all religions there have been those who do not practice what they preach when claiming to speak with spiritual authority.

Jesus is said to have also confronted the commercial interests in the Temple of Jerusalem, those who were making a living by charging a profit when exchanging money for Temple currency and selling animals for sacrificial offerings:

So they reached Jerusalem and he went into the Temple and began driving out those who were selling and buying there; he upset the tables of the money changers and the chairs of those who were selling pigeons. Nor would he allow anyone to carry anything through the Temple. And he taught them and said, "Does not scripture say; 'My house will be called a house of prayer for all the peoples?'[26] But you have turned it into a robbers' den."[27] This came to the ears of the chief priests and the scribes, and they tried to find some way of doing away with him; they were afraid of him because the people were carried away by his teaching.[28]

According to the gospel accounts, Jesus appropriated to himself the messianic prophecies of Second Isaiah. It is written that he privately asked his disciples, "Who do you say that I am?" Peter answered, "You are the Christ."[29] "Christ" is Greek for "anointed one," a translation of the Aramaic word *M'shekha* or **Messiah**, which also means "perfected" or "enlightened one." His disciples later spoke of him as the Messiah after he died and was resurrected. And his follower Martha, sister of Lazarus whom Jesus reportedly raised from the dead, is quoted as having said to Jesus, "I now believe that you are the Messiah, the Son of God who was to come into the world."[30] Some contemporary biblical scholars have concluded, however, that Jesus rejected the title of Messiah, for it might have been misunderstood.

A spectacular event, the "Transfiguration," was witnessed by three disciples. Jesus had climbed a mountain to pray, and as he did:

He was transfigured before them, and his face shone like the sun, and his garments became white as light. And behold, there appeared to them Moses and Elijah,

At the Last Supper, Jesus foretold his death and instructed his disciples to maintain mystic communion with him through a ceremony with bread and wine. (The Last Supper, attributed to Francisco Henriques, fl. 1500–18.)

talking with him. . . . When lo, a bright cloud overshadowed them, and a voice from the cloud said, "This is my beloved Son, with whom I am well pleased; listen to him."[31]

The presence of Moses and Elijah (who in Jewish apocalyptic tradition were expected to return at the end of the world) placed Jewish law and prophecy behind the claim that Jesus is the Christ. They were representatives of the old covenant with God; Jesus brought a new dispensation of grace.

Jesus claimed that John the Baptist was Elijah come again. The authorities had killed John the Baptist, and, Jesus prophesied, they would attack him, too, not recognizing who he was. John quotes Jesus as saying things like "My teaching is not mine, but his who sent me"; "I am the light of the world"; "You are from below, I am from above; you are of this world, I am not of this world"; and "Before Abraham was, I am."[32]

Jesus characterized himself as a good shepherd who is willing to lay down his life for his sheep. Foreshadowing the Crucifixion, he said he would offer his own flesh and blood as a sacrifice for the sake of humanity. His coming death would mark a "new covenant" in which his blood would be "poured out for many for the forgiveness of sins."[33]

It is possible that such passages defining Jesus's role were later interpolations by the early Christians as they tried to explain the meaning of their Master's life and death in new terms during the decades when the New Testament was in the process of formation.

Crucifixion

The anti-institutional tenor of Jesus's teachings did not endear him to those in power. Jesus knew that to return to Jerusalem would be politically dangerous. But eventually he did so, at Passover. He entered the town in a humble way, riding on a donkey and accompanied by supporters who waved palm branches and announced him as the Messiah, crying,

> "Hosanna! Blessed be he who comes in the name of the Lord! Blessed be the kingdom of our father David that is coming! Hosanna in the highest!"[34]

However, Jesus warned his disciples that his end was near. At the Last Supper, a meal during the Passover season, he is said to have given them instructions for a ceremony with bread and wine to be performed thenceforth to maintain an ongoing communion with him. However, one of the disciples would betray him, he said. This one, Judas, had already done so, selling information leading to Jesus's arrest for thirty pieces of silver.

Jesus took three of his followers to a garden called Gethsemane, on the Mount of Olives, where he is said to have prayed intensely that the cup of suffering would pass away from him, if it be God's will, "yet not what I will, but what thou wilt."[35] The gospels often speak of Jesus's spending long periods in spontaneous prayer to God, whom he addressed very personally as "Abba." It is possible to interpret Jesus's prayer at Gethsemane as a confirmation of his great faith in God's mercy and power. In the words of New Testament theologian Joachim Jeremias:

> Jesus takes into account the possibility that God may rescind his own holy will ... The Father of Jesus is not the immovable, unchangeable God who in the end can only be described in negations. He is not a God to whom it is pointless to pray. He is a gracious God, who hears prayers and intercessions, and is capable in his mercy of rescinding his own holy will.[36]

Nevertheless, after this period of prayer Jesus said, according to Mark's gospel, "It is all over. The hour has come."[37] A crowd including Judas approached with swords and clubs; they led Jesus away to be questioned by the chief priest, elders, and scribes.

Jesus's Crucifixion was interpreted by many later Christians as the sacrifice of an innocent lamb as atonement for the sins of humanity. Another interpretation was that God gave "himself or herself" in love, drawing the world into a loving relationship with the divine. (Rembrandt, The Three Crosses, 1653.)

All four gospels report a hearing before the high priest, Joseph Caiaphas. The high priest asked Jesus, "Are you the Christ?" Jesus answered:

You have said so. But I tell you, hereafter you will see the Son of man seated at the right hand of Power, and coming on the clouds of heaven.[38]

Caiaphas pronounced this statement blasphemy, punishable by death. They took him to Pontius Pilate, the Roman governor, for sentencing. To Pilate's leading question, "Are you King of the Jews?" Jesus is said to have replied, "You have said so."[39]

To quell the cries of the crowd calling for Jesus to be crucified, Pilate released Jesus to his Roman military guard. They took Jesus to a hill called Golgotha and nailed him to a cross, as was the Roman executionary custom. The accusation— "This is Jesus, King of the Jews"—was set over his head, and two robbers were crucified alongside him. The authorities, the people, and even the robbers mocked him for saying that he could save others when he could not even save himself.

Jesus hung there for hours until, according to the gospels, he cried out, "My God, my God, why hast thou forsaken me?"[40] This is the first line of Psalm 22, which is actually a great proclamation of the faith in God of one who is persecuted. Then Jesus died. This event is thought to have happened on a Friday some time between 27 and 33 CE. A wealthy Jewish disciple named Joseph of Arimathea asked Pilate for Jesus's body, which Joseph wrapped in a linen shroud and placed in his own tomb, with a large stone against the door. A guard was placed at the tomb to make sure that no followers would steal the body and claim that Jesus had risen from the dead.

Resurrection

That seemed to be the end of it. Jesus's disciples were terrified, so some of them hid, mourning and disheartened. The whole religious movement could have died out, as did other messianic cults. However, what happened next, according to varying gospel accounts, seemed to change everything. Some of the women who had been close to Jesus and had traveled with him from Galilee visited the tomb on Sunday to prepare the body for a proper burial, a rite that had been postponed because of the Sabbath. Instead, they found the tomb empty, with the stone rolled away. Angels then appeared and told them that Jesus had risen from death. The women ran and brought two of the male disciples, who witnessed the empty tomb with the shroud folded.

Then followed numerous reports of appearances of the risen Christ to various disciples. He dispelled their doubts about his resurrection, having them touch his wounds and even eating a fish with them. He said to them, as recounted in the gospel of Matthew:

> All authority in heaven and on earth has been given to me. Go therefore and make disciples of all nations, baptizing them in the name of the Father and of the Son and of the Holy Spirit, teaching them to observe all that I have commanded you; and lo, I am with you always, to the close of the age.[41]

The details of the appearances of the resurrected Jesus differ considerably from gospel to gospel, and the Gospel of Mark does not mention any resurrection appearances. However, some scholars think that to have women as the first witnesses to the empty tomb suggests that there must be some historical truth in the claims of Jesus's resurrection, for no one trying to build a case would have rested it on the testimony of women, who had little status in a patriarchal society. Feminist scholar Elisabeth Schüssler Fiorenza finds deep meaning in the presence of women disciples at the time of Jesus's death and resurrection. The gospels mention a woman who anoints Jesus, a sign that she recognizes him as the Messiah. (According to the gospel of John, this was Jesus's close follower, Mary of Bethany, sister of Lazarus.) The reports that it is women who faithfully visit the tomb suggest that, as Schüssler Fiorenza puts it,

> Whereas according to Mark the leading male disciples do not understand this suffering messiahship of Jesus, reject it, and finally abandon him, the women disciples who have followed Jesus from Galilee to Jerusalem suddenly emerge as the true disciples in the passion narrative. They are Jesus' true followers who have understood that his ministry was not rule and kingly glory but diakonia, "service" (Mark 15:41). Thus the women emerge as the true Christian ministers and witnesses. The unnamed woman who names Jesus with a prophetic sign-action in Mark's Gospel is the paradigm for the true disciple. While Peter had confessed, without truly understanding it, "you are the anointed one," the woman anointing Jesus recognizes clearly that Jesus' messiahship means suffering and death.[42]

It was the resurrection that turned defeat into victory for Jesus, and discouragement into powerful action for his followers. As the impact of all they had seen set in, the followers came to believe that Jesus had been God present in a human life, walking among them.

The Early Church

Persecution became the lot of Jesus's followers. But by 380 CE, despite strong opposition, Christianity became the official religion of the vast Roman Empire. As it became the establishment, rather than a tiny, scattered band of dissidents within Judaism, Christianity continued to define and organize itself.

From persecution to empire

The earliest years of what became the mainstream of Christianity are described in the New Testament books that follow the gospel accounts of the life of Jesus. "The Acts of the Apostles" was presumably written by the same person who wrote the Gospel of Luke, for the style is the same, both books are addressed to the same person named Theophilus, and Acts refers back to the Gospel of Luke as an earlier part of a single history of the rise of Christianity. Acts is followed by letters to some of the early groups of Christians, most of them apparently written by Paul, a major organizer and apostle (missionary), in about 50 to 60 CE.

Like the gospel accounts, the stories in these biblical books are examined by many contemporary scholars as possibly romanticized, idealized documents, used to convert, to increase faith, to teach principles, and to establish Christian theology, rather than to accurately record historical facts.

According to Acts, an event called **Pentecost** galvanized the early Christians into action. At a meeting of the disciples, something that sounded like a great wind came down from the sky, and what looked like tongues of fire swirled around to touch each one's head. The narrative states that they all began speaking in different languages, so that all who listened could understand in their own language. Some mocked them, saying they were drunk, but Peter declared that they had been filled with the Spirit of God, as the Old Testament prophet Joel had prophesied would happen in the last days before the onset of the kingdom of God. He testified that the Jesus whom the people had crucified had been raised up by God, who had made him "both Lord and Christ."[43] Reportedly, 3,000 people were so convinced that they were baptized that day.

One of the persecutors of Christians was Saul. He was a Pharisee tentmaker who lived during the time of Jesus but never met him. Instead, after Jesus died, he helped to throw many of his followers into prison and sentence them to death. Acts relates that on the way to Damascus in search of more heretics, he saw a light brighter than the sun and heard the voice of Jesus asking why Saul was persecuting him. This resistance was useless, said the vision of Jesus, who then appointed him to do the opposite—to go to both Jews and Gentiles:

to open their eyes, that they may turn from darkness to light and from the power of Satan to God, that they may receive forgiveness of sins and a place among those who are sanctified by faith in me.[44]

BOOKS OF THE NEW TESTAMENT

Gospels
Matthew
Mark
Luke
John

The Acts of the Apostles

The Letters of Paul
Romans
1 and 2 Corinthians
Galatians
Ephesians*
Philippians
Colossians*
1 and 2* Thessalonians
1 and 2 Timothy*
Titus*
Philemon

The General Epistles
Hebrew
James
1 and 2 Peter
1, 2, and 3 John
Jude

Revelation

*Scholars question whether these letters were written by Paul or by others using his name as a pseudonym, in the custom of the times.

This meeting with the risen Christ, and through him, God, was an utterly transformational experience for Paul. He wrote about his previous life,

> *I count everything sheer loss, because all is so far outweighed by the gain of knowing Christ Jesus my Lord, for whose sake I did in fact lose everything. I count it so much garbage, for the sake of gaining Christ and finding myself incorporate in him, with no righteousness of my own, no legal rectitude, but the righteousness which comes from faith in Christ, given by God in response to faith. All I care for is to know Christ.*[45]

Saul was baptized and immediately began promoting the Christian message under his new name, Paul. His indefatigable work in traveling around the Mediterranean was of great importance in shaping and expanding the early Christian church. He was shipwrecked, stoned, imprisoned, and beaten, and probably died as a martyr in Rome, but nothing short of death deterred him from his new mission.

Paul tried to convince Jews that Jesus's birth, death, and resurrection had been predicted by the Old Testament prophets. This was the Messiah they had been waiting for, and now, risen from death, he presided as the cosmic Christ, offering God's forgiveness and grace to those who repented and trusted in God rather than in themselves. Some Jews were converted to this belief, and the Jewish authorities repeatedly accused Paul of leading people away from Jewish law and tradition. There was not only one Jewish tradition, however. The Pharisees, for instance, did not see God as belonging only to Israel, but rather as the parent watching over and taking care of every individual. They addressed God by new names, such as *Abinu she-Bashamayim* ("Our Father Who art in Heaven"), the same form of address by which Jesus reportedly taught his followers to pray to God (Matthew 6:9). However, a major difference remained between Jews and Christians over the central importance given to Jesus. It is possible that Jesus himself may not have claimed that he was the Messiah, and that it was Paul who developed this claim. To this day, Jews tend to feel that to put heavy emphasis on the person of Jesus takes attention away from Jesus's message and from God.

In Paul's time, those Jews who emphasized that Jews had been especially chosen by God were offended by interpretations of Jesus's life and teachings that saw Christianity as a universal mission of salvation for all peoples. These interpretations made the new sect, Christianity, seem irreconcilable with exclusive versions of Judaism, and the gap between the two became deep and bitter. The New Testament writings reflect the criticisms of the early Christians against the large Jewish majority who did not accept Jesus as their Messiah. These polemics have been echoed through the centuries as anti-semitism.

Paul also tried to sway Gentiles: worshippers of the old gods whose religion was in decline, supporters of the emperor as deity, ecstatic initiates of mystery cults, and followers of dualistic Greco-Roman philosophers who regarded matter as evil and tried to emancipate the soul from its corrupting influence. He taught them that God did not reside in any idol but yet was not far from them, "For in him we live and move and have our being."[46] For Gentiles embracing Christianity, Paul and others argued that the Jewish tradition of circumcision should not be required of them. As Paul interpreted the gospel, salvation came by repentant faith in the grace of Christ, rather than by observance of a traditional law. In

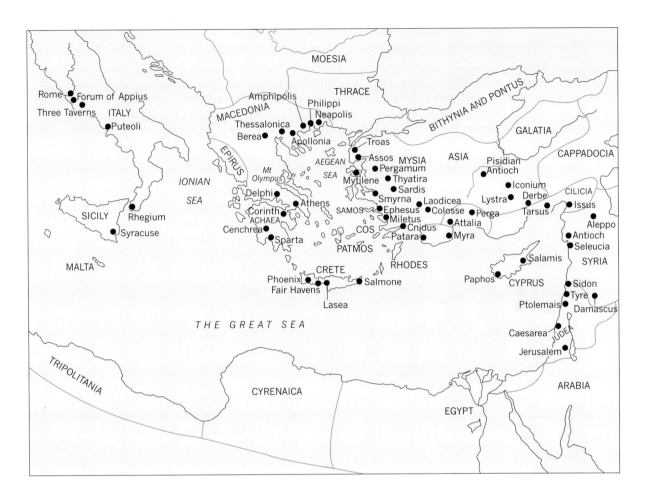

Paul's letter to the church in Rome, he argues that even Abraham was **justified**, or accepted by God in spite of sin, because of his great faith in God rather than by his circumcision.

Places visited by the apostle Paul during his far-reaching missionary journeys, 46–60 CE.

Christianity spread rapidly and soon became largely non-Jewish in membership. By 200 CE, it had spread throughout the Roman Empire and into Mesopotamia, despite fierce opposition. Many Christians were subjected to imprisonment, torture, and confiscation of property, because they rejected polytheistic beliefs, idols, and emperor worship in the Roman Empire. They were suspected of being revolutionaries, with their talk of a Messiah, and of strange cultic behaviors, such as their secret rituals of symbolically drinking Jesus's blood and eating his flesh. Persecution did not deter the most ardent of Christians; it united them intimately to the passion and death of Christ.

With the rise of Constantine to imperial rule early in the fourth century CE, opposition turned to the official embracing of Christianity. Constantine said that God showed him a vision of a cross to be used as a standard in battle. After he used it and won, he instituted tolerance of Christianity alongside the state cult, of which he was the chief priest. Just before his death, Constantine was baptized as a Christian.

By the end of the fourth century CE, people of other religions were stripped of all rights, and ordered into Christian churches to be baptized. Some paid outward service to Christianity but remained inwardly faithful to their old traditions. As Christianity became the favored religion, many converted for secular reasons.

By the end of the fifth century CE, Christianity was the faith claimed by the majority of people in the vast Roman Empire. It also spread beyond the empire, from Ireland in the west to India and Ceylon in the east.

Evolving organization and theology

During its phenomenal growth from persecuted sect to state religion throughout much of the ancient world, Christianity was developing organizationally and theologically. By the end of the first century CE, it had a bureaucratic structure that carried on the rites of the Church and attempted to define true Christianity.

One form that was judged to be outside the mainstream was Gnostic Christianity, which appeared as a movement in the second century CE. **Gnosticism** means mystical perception of knowledge. The Nag Hammadi library found in Egypt presents Jesus as a great Gnostic teacher. His words are interpreted as the secret teachings given only to initiates. "He who is near to me is near to the fire," he says in the Gospel of Thomas.[47] The Gnostics held that only spiritually mature individuals could apprehend Jesus's real teaching: that the Kingdom of Heaven is a present reality experienced through personal realization of the Light.

When the New Testament canon of twenty-seven officially sanctioned texts was set and translated into Latin in the fourth century, the Gnostic gospels were not included. Instead, the Church treated possession of Gnostic texts as a crime against church law because the Christian faith community felt that Jesus had not taught an elitist view of salvation and had not discriminated against the material aspect of creation.

The Nag Hammadi manuscripts found in Egypt were buried about 400 CE. They contain copies and translations of early Christian texts condemned as heretical by the Church.

What became mainstream Christianity is based not only on the life and teachings of Jesus, as set forth in the gospels selected for the New Testament, but also on the ways that they have been interpreted over the centuries. One of the first and most important interpreters was Paul. His central contribution—which was as influential as the four gospels in shaping Christianity—was his interpretation of Jesus's death and resurrection.

Paul spoke of *agape*—altruistic, self-giving love—as the center of Christian concern. He placed it above spiritual wisdom, asceticism, faith, and supernatural "gifts of the Spirit," such as the ability to heal, prophesy, or spontaneously speak in unknown tongues. Love was applied not only to one's neighbors but also to one's relationship with the divine. It was love plus gnosis—knowledge of God, permeated with love—that became the basis of contemplative Christianity, as it was shaped by the "Fathers" of the first centuries.

Let all that you do be done in love.

1 Corinthians 16:14

The cross, with or without an image of Jesus crucified on it, became a central symbol of Christianity. It marked the path of suffering service, rather than political domination, as the way of conquering evil and experiencing union with a compassionate God. To participate in Jesus's sacrifice, people could repent of their sins, be baptized, and be reborn to new life in Christ. In the early fifth century CE the bishop Augustine, one of the most influential theologians in the history of western Christianity, described this spiritual rebirth thus:

Where I was angry within myself in my chamber, where I was inwardly pricked, where I had sacrificed, slaying my old man and commencing the purpose of a new life, putting my trust in Thee—there hadst Thou begun to grow sweet unto me and "hadst put gladness in my heart."[48]

Theologian and Archbishop of Canterbury Rowan Williams explains this repentance and spiritual resurrection as:

the refusal to accept that lostness is the final human truth. Like a growing thing beneath the earth, we protest at the darkness and push blindly up in search of light, truth, home—the place, the relation where we are not lost, where we can live from deep roots in assurance. "Because I live, you will live also."[49]

The feeling of expectation of the coming of God's kingdom, so fervent in the earliest Christianity, began to wane as time went by. The notion of the Kingdom of God began to shift to the indefinite future, with emphasis placed on a preliminary judgment at one's death. There was nevertheless the continuing expectation that Christ would return in glory to judge the living and the dead and bring to fulfillment the "new creation." This belief in the "Second Coming" of Christ is still an article of faith today for some Christians; others regard it symbolically, pointing to the certainty of God's coming rule of love and peace.

Another early doctrinal development was the doctrine of the Holy **Trinity**. Christians believed that the transcendent, invisible God—the Father—had become immanent in the person of Jesus, God the Son. Furthermore, after his physical death Jesus promised to send the Holy Spirit to his followers. This makes three aspects of God, or three "persons" within the one divine being: Father, Son, and Holy Spirit. Christian theologians believed that the mystery of God was one, expressed in three ways. The Father is envisioned as the almighty transcendent creator of heaven and earth. The Son is the incarnation of the Father, the divine in human form, who returned at the ascension to live with the Father in glory, though he remains fully present in and to his "mystical body" on earth—the community of believers. The Holy Spirit or Holy Ghost is the power and presence of God, actively guiding and sustaining the faithful.

Although Jesus had spoken in parables with several levels of meaning, the evolving Church found it necessary to articulate some of its beliefs more openly and systematically. A number of **creeds**, or professions of faith, were composed for use in religious instruction and baptism, to define who Jesus was and his relationship to God, and to provide clear stands against the challenge of various heresies. For example, an important early creed is known as the Old Roman Creed:

The Holy Trinity, depicted in a famous icon by Rublev, is a distinctively Christian view of God. God is One as a communal plurality, an endless circle sharing the love intrinsic to the Godhead, inviting all to be healed and saved by this love.

I believe in God the Father Almighty,
And in Jesus Christ, his only Son, our Lord,
Who was born by the Holy Ghost, of the Virgin Mary, was crucified under
    Pontius Pilate, and was buried.
The third day he rose from the dead,
He ascended into heaven and sits on the right hand of the Father;
From thence he will come to judge the quick and the dead.
And in the Holy Ghost, the Holy Church, the forgiveness of sins, the
    resurrection of the body.

As theological debates continued, phrases were added to affirm the Church's position in contrast to beliefs that were determined to be heresies. For example, there was the heresy that God did not create this physical world, which was seen by Gnostics as hopelessly evil. This heresy was countered in later creeds by the phrase "Maker of heaven and earth" after "God the Father Almighty." The early creeds were developed by global councils of representatives of all area churches. The first of these gatherings for all areas to discuss church matters together was held in 325 CE in Nicaea (in present-day Turkey) as Christianity was just emerging from persecution.

Early monasticism

Alongside the development of doctrine and the consolidation of church structure, another trend was developing. Some Christians were turning away from the world to live in solitary communion with God, as ascetics. There had been a certain amount of asceticism in Paul's writings. He himself was celibate, as he believed that avoiding family entanglements helped one to concentrate on the Lord.

By the fourth century CE, Christian monks were living simply in caves in the Egyptian desert with little regard for the things of the world. They had no central organization but tended to learn from the examples of sincere monks. Avoiding emphasis on the supernatural powers that often accompany the ascetic life, they told stories demonstrating the virtues they valued, such as humility, submission, and the sharing of food. For example, an earnest young man was said to have visited one of the desert fathers and asked how he was faring. The old man sighed and said, "Very badly, my child." Asked why, he said, "I have been here forty years doing nothing other than cursing my own self each day, inasmuch as in the prayers I offer, I say to God, 'Accursed are those who deviate from Your commandments.'"[50] The young seeker was moved by such humility and made it his model.

> *The carefree man, who has tested the sweetness of having no personal possessions, feels that even the cassock which he wears and the jug of water in his cell are a useless burden, because these things, too, sometimes distract his mind.*
>
> *A Desert Father*[51]

The desert monks were left to their own devices at first. In Christian humility, they avoided judging or trying to teach each other and attempted to be, at best,

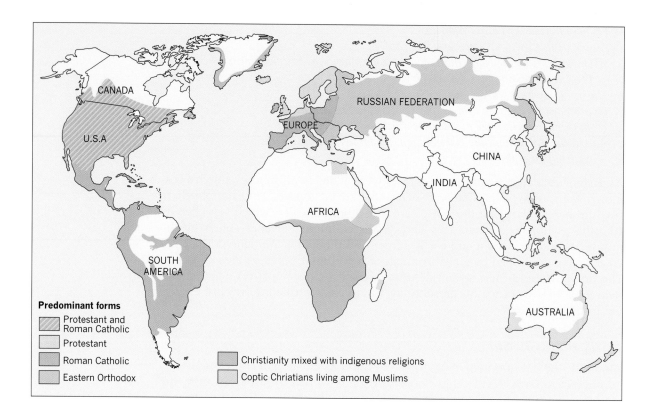

Predominant forms

- Protestant and Roman Catholic
- Protestant
- Roman Catholic
- Eastern Orthodox
- Christianity mixed with indigenous religions
- Coptic Chriatians living among Muslims

Map showing the approximate distribution of Christians in the world today.

harmless. But by the fifth century CE, the monastic life shifted from solitary, unguided practice, to formal spiritual supervision. Group monasteries and structures for encouraging obedience to God through an abbot or abbess were set up, and rules devised to help monks persevere in their calling. The Rule of St. Benedict became a model for all later monastic orders in the West, with its emphasis on poverty, chastity, and obedience to the abbot, and its insistence that each monastery be economically self-sufficient through the labor of the monastics. The Benedictines have been famous over the centuries for their practice of hospitality to pilgrims and travelers, and are today active participants in interreligious monastic dialogue.

The Eastern Orthodox Church

Christianity's history has been marked by internal feuds and divisions. One of the deepest schisms occurred in 1054, when the Roman Catholic Church, whose followers were largely in the West, and the Eastern Orthodox Church split apart.

The history of the Orthodox Church

Late in the third century CE, the Roman Empire had been divided into two: an eastern section and a western section. In the fourth century CE, Constantine established a second imperial seat in the east, in Constantinople (now Istanbul, Turkey). It was considered a "second Rome," especially after the sack of Rome by the Goths in 410. The two halves of the Christian world grew apart from each other, divided by language (Latin in the west, Greek in the east), culture, and religious differences.

In the western half, religious power was becoming more and more centralized in the Roman **pope** and other high officials. The Byzantine east was organized into a number of **sees**. Organizationally, the five major sees were those of Rome, Constantinople, Alexandria, Antioch, and Jerusalem. But this distinction was for organizational purposes; spiritually, all bishops, regardless of the status of the cities with which they are associated, are to today thought to be equal as successors to the original apostles, equally empowered to perform the sacraments, and equal as teachers of the faith. Rome was accorded a "primacy of honor" but not supreme jurisdiction.

The east did not recognize the Roman pope's claim to universal authority in the Church. By the early Middle Ages, there were also doctrinal disagreements. In its version of the Niceno-Constantinopolitan Creed, for example, the Western Church added a *filioque*, a formula professing that the Holy Spirit came from the Father *"and from the Son"*; the Eastern Church retained what is considered the more original text, professing that the Holy Spirit proceeds only from the Father.

In 1054, leaders of the eastern and western factions excommunicated each other over the disagreement about the Holy Spirit, and also over the papal claim, celibacy for priests (not required in the Eastern Church, which requires celibacy for bishops only), and whether the eucharistic bread should be leavened or unleavened. To the Eastern Church, the last straw was its treatment by crusaders.

From 1095 to about 1290, loosely organized waves of Christians poured out of Europe in what were presented as "holy crusades" to recapture the holy land of Palestine from Muslims, to defend the Byzantine Empire against Muslim Turks, and in general to wipe out the enemies of Christianity. It was a tragic and bloody time. One of the many casualties was the already tenuous relationship between the Eastern and Western Churches. When crusaders entered Constantinople in 1204, they tried to intervene in local politics. Rebuffed, they were so furious that they ravaged the city. They destroyed the altar and sacred icons in Hagia Sophia, the awesome Church of the Holy Wisdom (later taken over as a Muslim mosque), and placed prostitutes on the throne reserved for the patriarch of the region. Horrified by such profanity, the Orthodox Church ended its dialogue with Rome and proceeded on its own path, claiming to be the true descendant of the apostolic Church. Despite periodic attempts at reconciliation the Eastern and Western Churches are still separate.

The Russian Orthodox Church

When the Ottoman Turks took Constantinople in the fifteenth century, Russia became more prominent in the Orthodox Church, calling itself the "third Rome." The Orthodox Church had spread throughout the Slavic and eastern Mediterranean countries.

Russian Orthodox Christianity was closely associated with Russian national history since its adoption by Vladimir I in 988. But it was severely repressed by the

RELIGION IN PRACTICE

Russian Orthodox Kenoticism

A great mystical spiritual tradition emerged on Russian soil. The **kenotic** pattern of loving and world-directed monastic work was set by the eleventh-century saint Theodosius, who attempted to imitate the poverty and self-sacrificing humility of Jesus. He ate nothing but dry bread and herbs, spent his nights in prayer and his days in work. He dressed in the rough clothes of a peasant, patiently bore insults, worked with his own hands—chopping wood, spinning thread, baking bread, comforting the sick—and refused to present himself as an authority, even though he became the revered leader of this monastic community.

It is recorded that once, after Theodosius had visited a distant prince, the prince sent his own coach to take the saint home in comfort. The coachman, seeing Theodosius's crude clothing, assumed he was a beggar, and asked him to mount the horse so that the coachman could sleep. The saint humbly did so and thus drove the coach all night, with the coachman sleeping inside. When St. Theodosius became too sleepy to drive, he dismounted and walked; when he became weary of walking, he rode again. As the morning sun rose, the noblemen of his area recognized him, dismounted, and bowed to him, whereupon the saint gently said to the coachman, "My child, it is light. Mount your horse." The coachman was amazed and terrified as he saw the great reverence paid to the saint as they proceeded. Rather than chastizing him, Theodosius led him by the hand to the refectory, ordered that he should be given all the food and drink that he wanted, and paid him for the journey.

In the thirteenth century, Russia suffered from Mongolian invasions. Even though the Mongol khans nominally protected the Christians' freedom of religious practice when they themselves adopted Islam, spiritual and social life were in disarray. Monasticism shifted from urban settlements to the wilderness of the great forests of northern Russia. Hermit monks lived there in silence and solitary prayer until so many of the faithful gathered that thriving communities developed around them.

One of the most celebrated of the forest monks was St. Sergius. As a boy, Sergius retreated to the forest and built a small chapel for his intense devotions. Despite his noble lineage, he dressed like a peasant and did manual work. Even when he was abbot of the community that grew up around him, he was asked by one of his monks to build a cell, for which labor he was given a bit of moldy bread. In his contemplations, Sergius was said to be graced with visions of Mary, Mother of Christ, and of angels, fire, and light. He was nonetheless socially engaged with the national effort to resist foreign rule, and his blessing of the first victorious battle of Russians against the Tartars set the precedent for the future close links between Church and State in Russia. The relics of St. Sergius's body still lie undecayed in the huge and ornate Holy Trinity Lavra near Moscow in Zagorsk where once he had built his simple chapel. Among his followers were seventy famous saints of Russia.

Soviet government during the twentieth century. Lenin saw institutionalized religion as a divisive, backward force in society, an apology for oppression, which should wither away in the socialist state. Following the 1917 Revolution, anti-Church propaganda was broadcast, and many intellectuals who sincerely wanted the good of society left the Church. Lenin proclaimed that all Church property belonged to the State, and Church properties were seized. Thousands of monasteries and churches were taken over during the Revolution, and in the early 1920s thousands of priests, nuns, and lay Christians were killed. During the 1930s more

> **EASTERN ORTHODOX CHURCH**
>
> - Patriarchate of Constantinople
>   (Turkey, Mt. Athos)
> - Patriarchate of Alexandria
>   (Egypt, Africa)
> - Patriarchate of Antioch
>   (Syria, Lebanon)
> - Patriarchate of Jerusalem
>
> - Self-governing local churches
>   (Russia, Serbia, Rumania, Bulgaria,
>   Georgia, Cyprus, Greece, Poland,
>   Albania, Finland, Czech Republic)
> - Plus archbishops or metropolitans
>   in the Americas, Australia, India,
>   and European countries

monasteries were disbanded, multitudes of churches were closed, and great numbers of clergy were imprisoned. Bishops who refused to accept Soviet control issued what is called the Solovky Memorandum, which stated in part:

> *The Church recognizes spiritual principles of existence; communism rejects them. The Church believes in the living God, the Creator of the world, the leader of its life and destinies; communism denies his existence. Such a deep contradiction in the very basis of their Weltanschauungen [world views] precludes any intrinsic approximation or reconciliation between the Church and state, . . . because the very soul of the Church, the condition of her existence and the sense of her being, is that which is categorically denied by communism.[52]*

The bishops were imprisoned in the Solovky labor camp; many were killed there. It is estimated that some 40,000 priests were killed from 1918 to 1940. Out of almost 80,000 churches and chapels in the Russian Empire in 1914, only a few hundred or a thousand remained by the beginning of World War II. Under Khrushchev, a new campaign against religion was unleashed, and perhaps two-thirds of the remaining Orthodox churches were closed.

Nevertheless, the Orthodox Church did not die, for it was deeply rooted in the minds and hearts of the people, and was closely linked to national identity. In the mid-1980s, the Russian Orthodox Church had an estimated 50 million members. Most of those who dared to worship publicly were the *babushkas*—the faithful old women who were apparently not regarded as politically dangerous.

After decades of severe oppression, the Russian Orthodox Church witnessed a great change in government policy in 1988, the celebration of its first millennium in Russia and Ukraine. Mikhail Gorbachev's government approached the Orthodox Church leaders, asking their help in Perestroika and returning some Church buildings, which had been turned into museums or warehouses. Some 1,700 churches were reopened in 1988 and 1989, and each was immediately filled with worshippers again. Seminaries where new clergy are trained report a great increase in enrolment. Late in 1989, Soviet President Mikhail Gorbachev ended seven decades of suppression of religion, pronouncing the right of the Soviet faithful to "satisfy their spiritual needs."[53]

Nevertheless, many people are disillusioned with the contemporary Russian Orthodox Church because of its politics. As in all other institutions in the former Soviet Union, its staff included many KGB agents, and some of these people seem to have remained in their positions after the fall of the Soviet Union. Some church leaders felt that they had to make compromises in order to survive at all

A very visible symbol of the official recognition of the Russian Orthodox Church is the huge reconstructed Christ the Savior Temple, which now looms over the landscape of central Moscow.

as a religion under Soviet rule. Now the Russian Orthodox Church has very powerful influence in government policy and is strongly supported by political leaders from all parties, including communists. Indeed, President Vladimir Putin, a former KGB officer, in 2000 praised the Orthodox Church's contribution to Russia's post-Soviet spiritual rebirth, and stated: "I believe that together (with the Church) we will achieve the spiritual revival of a strong, prospering Russia in the twenty-first century."[54] In the same year, the Orthodox Church declared the last Tsar a martyr and a saint because he was shot by a firing squad of Bolsheviks, described as enemies of the Church. The ceremony canonizing Czar Nicholas and his family was held in the huge new Christ the Savior Temple in Moscow, which had been torn down by Stalin and has been rebuilt on the same site.

Since the early days of the Soviet Union, there have also been Orthodox Christians who refused to collaborate or compromise with the government. At the risk of their jobs and lives, some Christian laypeople and priests began to worship secretly in what became known as catacomb churches, just as the early

Christians had worshipped in underground catacombs to evade persecution. Father Alexey Vlasov, a catacomb priest, explains:

> Members of this catacomb Church were risking their lives by worshipping. They tried to live by the Ten Commandments and live by love within society. It was not their intention to oppose the Orthodox Church but to bring Christ's love into society.[55]

Even today, some Orthodox Christians continue to worship in secret rather than subject their congregations to the registration requirements of the state and disapproval of the official Church. Bishop Feodor, bishop of underground Christians in Moscow, Riga, and the Far East, objects to the assertive power of the Russian Orthodox Church:

> If the Church has pride, it has no holy power. We are all brothers in Adam and in Christ. We are all baptized by God. This is true for each Christian. If you cannot love your brother who is next to you, how can you love one you cannot see, such as Christ, who has not been with us for two thousand years?[56]

The Orthodox world today

There are now fifteen self-governing Orthodox Churches worldwide, each having its own leader, known as patriarch, metropolitan, or archbishop. The majority of Orthodox Christians now live in Russia, the Balkan states, and eastern Europe,

Contemporary Russian Orthodox worship in Zagorsk before an elaborate iconostasis, where St. Sergius of Radonezh once built a small chapel in the forest to worship the Holy Trinity.

in formerly communist countries where the teaching and propagation of Christianity had been severely restricted. Autocephalous (independent) churches there include the large Church of Russia, which is dominated by the Patriarchate of Moscow, plus the Churches of Serbia, Bulgaria, Romania, Albania, Poland, and the Czech Republic. The original and still central Patriarchate of Constantinople is based within Turkey, as a small minority within a Muslim country, which now has no Orthodox seminaries. This Patriarchate also includes islands in the Aegean and the precipitous Mount Athos peninsula. The latter was historically a great center of Orthodox monasticism, but its population of monks declined considerably in the twentieth century when emigration of monks was prohibited by communist regimes. Now women are agitating to be allowed to enter Mount Athos, where even the presence of female animals is banned. Traditionalists maintain that Mount Athos is the only truly monastic community left in the world and should continue its antique ways unchanged and undistracted; women counter that the ban on women is degrading, a "sexist, anti-democratic decision taken by men, not by God."[57]

The Patriarchate of Alexandria is based in Egypt and includes all of Africa, where Orthodoxy arose independently in Uganda and has been embraced with considerable enthusiasm. The Patriarchate of Antioch consists mostly of Orthodox Christian Arabs in Syria and Lebanon. The Patriarchate of Jerusalem is charged with guarding the Holy Places of Christianity.

The Greek Orthodox Church dominates religious life in Greece and is assisting in the revival of interest in the classical books and arts of Orthodox spirituality. In the Church of Cyprus, the archbishop is also traditionally the political leader of the people. The Church of Sinai consists of only one monastery.

Most icon painters, such as this monk at Mt. Athos, Greece, use the ancient Byzantine style in creating sacred icons, which represent Christian stories and open windows to the divine.

Extensive emigration, particularly from Russia during the first few years of communist rule, has also created large Orthodox populations in Western countries. Some retain direct ties to their home patriarchate, such as the New York-based Archdiocese of the Greek Orthodox Church in North and South America. Alongside that, the Orthodox Church in America was granted its independence in 1970, and now claims over four million members in a country where Protestantism and Roman Catholicism are the predominant forms of Christianity. Missionary activity by the Russian Orthodox Church also established Orthodoxy in China, Korea, and Japan.

Distinctive features of Orthodox spirituality

Over the centuries, the individual Orthodox Churches have probably changed less than have the many descendants of the early Western Church. There is a strong conservative tradition, attempting to preserve the pattern of early Christianity. Even though the religious leaders can make local adaptations suited to their region and people, they are united in doctrine and sacramental observances. Any change that will affect all churches is decided by a **synod**—a council of officials trying to reach common agreements, as did the early Church. Although women are important in local church affairs, they cannot be ordained as priests or serve in hierarchical capacities.

In addition to the Bible, Orthodox Christians honor the writings of the saints of the Church. Particularly important is a collection called the *Philokalia*. It consists of texts written by Orthodox masters between the fourth and fifteenth centuries. "Philokalia" means love of the exalted, excellent, and beautiful, in other words, the transcendent divine source of life and truth.

The *Philokalia* is essentially a Christian guide to the contemplative life for monks, but it is also for laypeople. A central practice is called "unceasing prayer": the continual remembrance of Jesus or God, often through repetition of a verbal formula that gradually impresses itself on the heart. The most common petition is the "Jesus prayer": "Lord Jesus Christ, Son of God, have mercy on me, a sinner." The repetition of the name of Jesus brings purification of heart and singularity of desire. To call upon Jesus is to experience his presence in oneself and in all things.

The Orthodox Church has affirmed that humans can approach God directly. Some may even see the light of God and be utterly transformed by it:

> *He who participates in the divine energy, himself becomes, to some extent, light: he is united to the light, and by that light he sees in full awareness all that remains hidden to those who have not this grace; ... for the pure in heart see God ... who, being Light, dwells in them and reveals Himself to those who love Him, to His beloved.*[58]

Another distinctive feature of Orthodox Christianity is its veneration of **icons**. These are stylized paintings of Jesus, his mother Mary, and the saints. They are created by artists who prepare for their work by prayer and ascetical training. There is no attempt at earthly realism, for icons are representations of the reality of the divine world. They are beloved as windows to the eternal. In addition to

Christians light candles around a Christmas tree in Bucharest, Romania, December 25, 1989, as communism collapsed.

their devotional and instructional functions, some icons are reported to have great spiritual powers, heal illnesses, and transmit the holy presence. Believers enter into the grace of this power by kissing the icon reverently and praying before it.

Some of the major icons in an Orthodox church are placed on an iconostasis, a screen separating the floor area for the congregation from the Holy of Holies, the sanctuary that can be entered only by the clergy. On either side of the opening to the altar are icons of Jesus and the Virgin Mary ("Mother of God," often venerated as Protectress and Ruler of Russia).

Orthodox choirs sing the divine liturgy in many-part harmony, producing an ethereal and uplifting effect as the sounds echo and re-echo around each other. Everything strives toward that beauty to which the *Philokalia* refers. Archimandrite Nathaniel of the Russian Othodox Pskova-Pechorsky Monastery, which has been a place of uninterrupted prayer for almost six hundred years despite eight hundred attacks on its walls and numerous sieges, speaks of the ideal of beauty in Orthodox Christianity:

> *The understanding of God is the understanding of beauty. Beauty is at the heart of our monastic life. The life of prayer is a constant well of beauty. We have the beauty of music in the Holy Liturgy. The great beauty of monastic life is communal life in Christ. Living together in love, living without enmity, as peaceful with each other as one dead body is peaceful with another dead body, we are dead to enmity.*[59]

Medieval Roman Catholicism

In the West, from the sixth to tenth centuries CE, the old Roman Empire gradually fell to non-Christian invaders. Islam also made spectacular advances in areas

The young Catherine of Siena, "mother of thousands of souls," had a vision in which Christ, in the company of the Virgin Mary and other saints, gave her a wedding ring, the sign of the mystical marriage.

previously converted to Christianity. Arabs took Palestine, Syria, Mesopotamia, Egypt, North Africa, and part of Spain. However, the Angle and Saxon invaders of England were new converts to Christianity, with whole tribes joining the faith at the behest of their chiefs. By the fourteenth century, most of central and western Europe was claimed for Christianity, and missionaries spread the faith to isolated areas of Asia.

The Holy Roman Empire became politically decentralized into feudal kingdoms, with the Christian Church the major force uniting Europe. The chief factors sustaining Christianity through these chaotic centuries were its centralized organization and the periodic refreshing of its spiritual wellsprings through monasticism and mysticism.

Papal power

During the late first and early second centuries CE, some men and women had followed a charismatic Christian life, leaving home to preach, baptize, prophesy, and perhaps die as martyrs; others had moved toward an institutionalized patriarchal

Church. By the beginning of the second century CE, a consolidation of spiritual power had begun with the designation of specific people to serve as clergy and bishops (superintendents) to administer the church affairs of each city or region. While some women served as deacons ministering to women, the clergy and bishops had to be male, with wife and children. The bishops of the chief cities of the Roman Empire had the greatest responsibilities and authority, with the greatest prestige being held by the Bishop of Rome, eventually known as the pope. By the fifth century CE, Pope Leo I argued that all popes were apostolic successors to Peter, the "rock" on which Jesus in Matthew's gospel said he would found his Church. The Roman emperor passed an edict that all Christians were to recognize the authority of the Bishop of Rome, the successor to Peter.

The strongest of Church administrators during these early centuries was Gregory I ("the Great"), who died in 604 CE. Wealthy by birth but ascetic by choice, he devoted his personal fortune to founding monasteries and feeding the poor. Suffering from health problems and longing for the quiet life of a monk, he was reluctantly convinced to be pope at a time of pestilence, floods, and military invasions. Even in this setting, he managed to provide for the physical needs of the poor, promote the discipline of the clergy (including the Western

Although the Roman Catholic pope wields enormous power, he is also expected to carry out a rite of humility dating from the 7th century or earlier: lovingly washing the feet of the less powerful, as Jesus did for his disciples.

ideal that priests should be celibate), revamp the liturgy (Gregorian chanting is named after him), and to re-establish the Church as a decent, just institution carrying high spiritual values.

The papacy began to wield tremendous secular power. Beginning in the eighth century, the approval of the papacy was sought as conferring divine sanction on feudal kings. In the ninth century the Church produced documents old and new establishing the hierarchical authority of the papacy over the Church, and the Church over society, as the proper means of transmitting inspiration from the divine to humanity. Those who disagreed could be threatened with **excommunication**. This exclusion from participation in the sacraments was a dread ban, cutting a person off from the redemption of the Church (blocking one's entrance to heaven in the afterlife), as well as from the benefits of the Church's secular power. Crusades were launched under the auspices of the Church, with war used ostensibly in defense of the faith, with no humane restraints on the treatment of the "infidel."

Late in the eleventh century, Pope Gregory VII set forth unprecedented claims for the papacy. The pope, he asserted, was divinely appointed and therefore could be ruled by no human. The pope had the right to depose emperors; the princes of the world should kiss his feet.

This centralization of power became a major unifying element in Europe of the Middle Ages. Kingdoms broke up between 800 and 1100 as Vikings invaded from the north and Magyars from the east. For the sake of military protection, peasants gave up their freedom to feudal lords. The feudal lords in turn began to war among themselves. In the midst of the ensuing chaos, people looked to the pope as an orderly wielder of power.

Church and states were at times locked in a mutual struggle for dominance, with popes alternately supporting, dominating, and being deposed by secular rulers. The power of the papacy was also somewhat limited by the requirement that the pope be elected by a council of cardinals. The position could not become hereditary. But it was nonetheless open to intrigue, scandal, and power-mongering.

The thirteenth century saw the power of the papacy placed behind the **Inquisition**, an ecclesiastical court set up in 1229 to investigate and suppress heresy. This instrument of terror was based on Augustine's concept that heretics should be controlled for the sake of their own eternal salvation, out of love for their souls. But whereas Augustine saw fines and imprisonment as reasonable coercion to help people change their minds, in some cases the medieval Inquisitors had them tortured and burned to deter others from dangerous views. For example, in northern Italy and southern France a sect arose that was later called Cathari ("the pure"), for its members lived ascetically, emphasizing poverty and mutual aid. Though similar to Christianity in organization and worship, the movement denied that Jesus was the incarnation of God, and saw spirit as good but matter as bad. Such beliefs were proclaimed heretical by the papacy; the Cathari sect, attacked by the Inquisition, disappeared.

Though strong, the papacy was often embroiled in its own political strife. During the fourteenth century, the popes left their traditional seat in turbulent Rome for the more peaceful climate of Avignon, France. There they built up an elaborate administrative structure, increasingly involved in worldly affairs. After the papacy was persuaded to return to Rome, a would-be reformer, Pope Urban

IV, turned to terror tactics to get his way. At one point he had five cardinals tortured and killed. Many people refused to follow him; for a while they followed an "anti-pope" they established in Avignon.

Intellectual revival and monasticism

Although the papacy was subject to abuses, mirrored on a lesser scale by the clergy, Christian spirituality was vigorously revived in other quarters of medieval society. During the twelfth and thirteenth centuries great universities developed in Europe, often from cathedral schools. Theology was considered the greatest of the sciences, with Church ideals permeating the study of all areas of life. Soaring Gothic cathedrals were built to uplift the soul to heavenly heights, for God was perceived as being enthroned in the heavens, far above the workaday world.

The yearning for spiritual purity was particularly pronounced in monasticism. It was largely through monks and nuns that Christian spirituality survived and spread. Monasteries also became bulwarks of Western civilization. In Ireland, particularly, they were the centers of larger communities of laypeople and places of learning within illiterate societies.

During the twelfth century many new monastic orders appeared in the midst of a massive popular re-invigoration of spiritual activity. A major influence was a community in Cluny, France. Its monks specialized in liturgical elaborations and prayer, leaving agricultural work to serfs. An alternative direction was taken by the Cistercians, Gregorians, and Carthusians. They returned to St. Benedict's Rule of combining manual work and prayer; "to labor is to pray," said the monks. The Carthusians lived cloistered lives as hermits, meeting each other only for worship and business matters. Despite such austere practices, people of all classes flocked to monastic life as a pious refuge from decadent society.

> *It is not only prayer that gives God glory but work. . . . He is so great that all things give Him glory if you mean they should.*
>
> *Gerard Manley Hopkins*[60]

In contrast to monks and nuns living cloistered lives, mendicant friars, or brothers, worked among the people. In 1215, the Dominican Order was instituted primarily to teach and refute heresies. A famous Dominican scholar, Thomas Aquinas, created a monumental work, *Summa Theologiae*, in which rational sciences and spiritual revelations were joined in an immense, consistent theological system. Aquinas was much influenced by the recovery of classical writings of Muslims.

Franciscans, following the lead of the beloved St. Francis of Assisi (see below), wandered about without personal property or established buildings, telling people about God's love and accepting charity for their meager needs. The mendicant Dominicans and Franciscans, still noted as missionaries today, became one of the major features of medieval Christianity.

In addition to organized orders of nuns, there was a grassroots movement among thirteenth-century German and Flemish women to take private vows of chastity and voluntary simplicity. These women, who were called "beguines," lived frugally by their own work. Because they were not organized into a religious order, they chose their own lifestyles, with their chief intention being simply to live "religiously." At times persecuted because it did not fit into any traditionally sanctioned pattern, the movement persisted, drawing tens of thousands of women. Eventually they built small convents for themselves; by the end of the fourteenth century, there were 169 beguine convents in Cologne, the heart of the movement.

Medieval mysticism

Mysticism also flowered during the Middle Ages, renewing the spiritual heart of the Church. Especially in cloistered settings, monks and nuns sat in contemplation of the meanings of the scriptures for the soul. Biblical stories of battles between heroes and their enemies were, for instance, interpreted as the struggle between the soul and one's baser desires. Beyond this rational thought, some engaged in quiet non-conceptual prayer, simply resting receptively in the presence of God.

In thirteenth-century Italy, there was the endearing figure of St. Francis of Assisi (1182–1226). The carefree, dashing son of a merchant, he underwent a radical spiritual transformation. He traded his fine clothes for simple garb and "left the world"[61] for a life of total poverty, caring for lepers and rebuilding dilapidated churches, since in a vision Jesus spoke to him from the cross, saying: "Repair my Church." Eventually Francis understood that his real mission was to rebuild the Church by re-emphasizing the gospel and its commands of love and poverty. A band of brothers and then of sisters, led by the saintly Clare, gathered around him. The friars preached, worked, begged, tended lepers, and lived a simple life of penance and prayer while wandering from town to town. This ascetic life was permeated with mystical joy, one of St. Francis's hallmarks. He was also known for his rapport with wild animals and is often pictured with birds resting lovingly on his shoulders. Two years before his death, Francis received the "stigmata," replicas on his own body of the Crucifixion wounds of Jesus. This miracle was interpreted as a sign of the saint's union with Christ by suffering, prayer, holiness, and love.

The flowering of English mysticism during the fourteenth century was exemplified by Julian of Norwich (1342–c. 1416). As a girl, she had prayed that when she reached the age of thirty (the age at which Jesus began his public mission) she would have an illness that would bring her an understanding of his Passion (the sufferings of his final days). As requested, she did indeed become so ill when she was thirty that she almost died. During this crisis, she had visions and conversations with Christ, which revealed the boundless love with which he continually offers himself for humanity. Her writings delve into the perennial problem of reconciling the existence of evil with the experience of a loving God, whom she sometimes referred to as "God our Mother."

An anonymous fourteenth-century English writer contributed a volume entitled *The Cloud of Unknowing*. Christianity then and now largely follows what is called the affirmative way, with art, liturgy, scriptures, and imagery to aid devotion. But the author of *The Cloud* spoke to those who were prepared to undertake

Statues of St. Francis often show birds perched on him, representing his kinship with the natural world.

the negative way of abiding in sheer love for God, with no thoughts. God cannot be known through ideas or physical images; "a naked intent toward God, a desire for him alone, is enough."[62] In the silence of wordless prayer, the light of God may pierce the cloud of human unknowing that obscures the divine from the seeker.

Fourteenth-century Italy witnessed a period of unprecedented degradation among the clergy, while the papacy occupied itself with organizational matters in Avignon. In this spiritual vacuum, laypeople gathered around saintly individuals to imbibe their atmosphere of genuine devotion. One of the most celebrated of these was the young Catherine of Siena. In her persistent efforts to restore spiritual purity and religious discipline to the Church, she gained the ear of Pope Gregory XI, helping to convince him to return to Rome. She was called "mother of thousands of souls," and people were said to be converted just by seeing her face.

The Protestant Reformation

Despite the genuine piety of individuals within the Catholic Church, some who clashed with its authority claimed that those in power seemed often to have lost touch with their own spiritual tradition. With the rise of literacy and printing in the late fifteenth century, many Christians were rediscovering early Christianity and comparing it unfavorably with what the Roman Catholic Church had made of it. Roman Catholic fund-raising or church-building financial activities were particularly criticized. These included **indulgences** (remission of the punishment for sin by the clergy in return for services or payments), the sale of relics, purchases of masses for the dead, spiritual pilgrimages, and the earning of spiritual "merit" by donating to the Church.

Salient among the reformists was Martin Luther (1483–1546). Luther was a monk and priest who lectured at the University of Wittenberg. He struggled personally with the question of how one's sins could ever be totally atoned for by one's own actions. The Roman Catholic Church's position was that to be forgiven of post-baptismal sins, people should repent and then confess their sins to a priest and be pardoned. In addition, the punishment after death due to sins could be

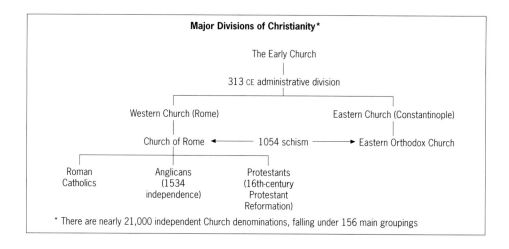

Major Divisions of Christianity*

The Early Church

313 CE administrative division

Western Church (Rome)   Eastern Church (Constantinople)

Church of Rome ◄─── 1054 schism ───► Eastern Orthodox Church

Roman   Anglicans   Protestants
Catholics   (1534   (16th-century
                   independence)   Protestant
                                        Reformation)

* There are nearly 21,000 independent Church denominations, falling under 156 main groupings remitted either for the performance of prescribed penances or through the granting of an indulgence. Indulgences could even be procured to make sure that the souls of those who had died repentant were freed from **Purgatory** (the intermediate place of purifying suffering for those who died in a state of repentance and grace but who were not yet sufficiently stainless to enter heaven). The Castle Church at Wittenberg housed an immense collection of relics, including hairs from the Virgin Mary and a thorn from the "crown" of thorns placed on Jesus's head before he was crucified. This relic collection was deemed so powerful that those who viewed them on the proper day and contributed sufficiently to the Church could receive indulgences from the pope freeing themselves or their loved ones from almost two million years in Purgatory.

By intense study of the Bible, Luther began to emphasize a different approach. Both Paul and Augustine could be interpreted as saying that God, through Jesus, offered salvation to sinners in spite of their sins. This salvation was offered by God's grace alone and received solely by repentant faith. The good works and created graces prescribed by Catholics to earn merit in heaven were not part of original Christianity, Luther argued. Salvation from sin comes from faith in God, which itself comes from God, by grace. This gift of faith brings justification (being found righteous in God's sight) and then flowers as unselfish good works, which characterize the true Christian:

> From faith flows love and joy in the Lord, and from love a joyful, willing and free mind that serves one's neighbor willingly and takes no account of gratitude or ingratitude, of praise or blame, of gain or loss. ... As our heavenly father has in Christ freely come to our help, we also ought freely to help our neighbor through our body and its works, and each should become as it were a Christ to the other.[63]

Martin Luther's political influence and prolific writings led to a deep split in the Western Church, severing Protestant reformers from the Roman Catholic Church. (Lucas Cranach the Elder, Martin Luther, 1533.)

In 1517 Luther invited the university community to debate this issue with him, by the established custom of nailing his theses to the door of the church. He apparently had no intention of splitting with the Church. But a papal bull (decree) of June 15, 1520 excommunicated him.

Cut off from Rome, Luther sought support from the secular princes of Germany. For reasons sometimes more political than spiritual, many came over to his side and helped to enforce his ideas. Although there were some attempts at compromise by followers of both Luther and Rome, conciliatory efforts collapsed.

Luther's evolving theology took him farther and farther from the institutions of the Roman Catholic Church. He did not think that the Bible supported the Roman Catholic tradition that pope, bishops, priests, and monks should have spiritual authority over laypeople; instead, he asserted that there is "a priesthood of all believers." He also felt that the sacred rites, or **sacraments**, of the Church were ways of nourishing faith instituted by Jesus and included **baptism** and the **eucharist**.

Another major reformer who eventually broke with Rome was the Swiss priest Ulrich Zwingli (1484–1531). He rejected practices not mentioned in the Bible, such as abstaining from meat during Lent, veneration of relics and saints, religious pilgrimages, and celibacy for monks and priests. Zwingli asserted that the Lord's Supper, or **mass**, should be celebrated only as a memorial of Jesus's sacrifice; he did not believe in the myserious presence of Jesus's blood and body in the consecrated wine and bread. He even questioned the spiritual efficacy of rituals such as masses for the dead and confession of one's sins to a priest:

Intense emotional intimacy with Jesus is displayed during a service at Mount Vernon Baptist Church in Indianapolis.

It is God alone who remits sins and puts the heart at rest, so to Him alone ought we to ascribe the healing of our wounds, to Him alone display them to be healed.[64]

The ideals of these reformists were adopted by many Christians. The freedom of scriptural interpretation that they opened turned out to be a Pandora's box. Protestantism, as the new branch of Christianity came to be called, was never as monolithic as the Roman Catholic Church had been. Reform movements branched out in many directions.

A major seat of Protestantism developed in Geneva, under John Calvin (1509–1564). He shared the reform principles of salvation by faith alone, the exclusive authority of the Bible, and "the priesthood of all believers." But Calvin carried the doctrine of salvation by faith to a new conclusion. To him, the appropriate response to God is a zealous piety and awe-struck reverence in which one "dreads to offend him more than to die."[65] Human actions are of no eternal significance because God has already decided the destiny of each person. By grace, some are to be saved; for God's own reasons, others are predestined to be damned eternally. Although there was therefore nothing that people could do about it, their behavior would reveal which fate awaited them.

Although only God absolutely knew who was saved, there are three signs which humans could recognize: profession of faith, an upright life, and participation in the sacraments. Calvin felt that the Church has the right to chastize and, in some extreme situations, excommunicate those who seemed to violate the sanctity of the Church. Calvin envisioned a holy commonwealth in which the Church, government, and citizens all cooperate to create a society dedicated to the glory and mission of God.

Calvin's version of Christianity made its followers feel that they should fear no one except God. Convinced that they were predestined to do God's will, they were impervious to worldly obstacles to the spread of their faith. Calvinism became the state religion of Scotland and also had a following in England.

Concurrently, the Church of England separated from the Church of Rome when Henry VIII declared the English Church's independence from the Church of Rome. His daughter Elizabeth I finalized the breach with Rome in the Elizabethan Settlement of 1559. Now called Anglicanism, this form of Christianity is in communion with Old Catholics and also shares some similarities with the Protestant churches. One of its thirty-seven autonomous Churches is the Protestant Episcopal Church in the United States, a name referring to its being a Church with bishops.

As this Protestant Reformation progressed, political entities in Europe chose specific forms of Christianity as their official religions. Spain, France, and Italy remained largely Roman Catholic. Northern Germany was largely Lutheran. Ireland split between Catholicism and Protestantism, leading to wars that continue today. The Calvinist Church of Scotland called itself Presbyterian, a reference to its form of organization. Some Polish and Hungarian communities adopted a form of Unitarianism, which rejected the ideas of original sin, the Trinity, and Jesus's divinity in favor of a simple theism and imitation of Jesus.

These ideas later found a home in America, as some Protestant groups that were outlawed by the Church of England emigrated to new colonies in North America. These offshoots included such **denominations** (organized groups of congregations) as Baptists, Congregationalists, Quakers, and Methodists. One of the largest of these groups is the Baptists, a denomination in which people are baptized as conscious adult believers rather than as infants. Congregationalists emphasize the independence of each local church and the "priesthood" of all members. Quakers (formally known as the Religious Society of Friends) worship without any liturgy or minister, in the hope that as they sit in worshipful silence, God will speak through any one of their members (although most American Quakers now worship in a more programmed service). Methodists are followers of the evangelist John Wesley, who traveled an average of 8,000 miles (12,874 km) a year by horseback to promote "vital practical religion and by the grace of the life of God to beget, preserve, and increase the life of God in the souls of men."[66]

During the nineteenth century, yet more Protestant churches sprang up in the United States. Evangelical churches—those emphasizing salvation by personal faith in Jesus, personal conversion, the importance of the Bible, and preaching instead of ritual—have proliferated in North America. Seventh Day Adventists believe that the Second Coming of Christ will soon occur, and they regard the Bible as an absolute guide to faith and spiritual practice in anticipation of the return of Jesus. Jehovah's Witnesses criticize other Christian Churches as having developed false doctrines from the second century onward, and they urge people to leave these "false religions" and prepare for a coming time when all who do not hold true belief will be destroyed. Fundamentalist evangelical sects are also gaining strongholds in South America, which had been largely Roman Catholic since the Spanish conquests of these countries. Protestant missionaries have also carried the gospel to Asia, Africa, and eastern Europe.

Despite the great diversity among Protestant denominations, most share

A Quaker ("Society of Friends") meeting, in York, England, in which worshippers sit silently, awaiting direct experience of the inner light of God.

several characteristics that distinguish them somewhat from Orthodoxy and Roman Catholicism, though the Catholic Church's positions are now much closer to those of Protestants as a result of the profound changes introduced in 1962 by the Second Vatican Council. First, Protestants place their emphasis on the Bible rather than on the authority of the Church, though they differ in how the Bible should be interpreted. Second, they emphasize individual relationship to Jesus and God rather than the mediation of God's grace through the Church. The Quakers have gone even farther in rejecting human spiritual authority. They follow the example of George Fox (1624–1691), who experienced in the inner light the certainty of the divine; these "Children of the Light" utterly rejected any outer religious forms and instead simply sit in the silence, surrendered to God.

The Roman Catholic Reformation

As the Protestant reformers were defining their positions, so was the Roman Catholic Church. Because reform pressures were underway in Catholicism before Luther, Catholics refer to the movement as the Catholic Reformation, rather than the "Counter-Reformation," as Protestants call it. However, the Protestant phenomena provoked the Roman Catholic Church to clarify its own position through councils of bishops, especially the Council of Trent (1545–1563). It attempted to legislate moral reform among the clergy, to tighten the church administration, and to recognize officially the absolute authority of the pope as the earthly vicar of God and Jesus Christ. The Council also took historic stands on a number of issues, emphasizing that its positions were **dogmas**, or authoritative truths. For example, one of the fundamental doctrines of the Roman Catholic

Church is the dogma of **original sin**. All humans are said to be morally defective, or "fallen," having inherited a sinful nature from the first human ancestors. They can be saved from this condition only by the grace of God, as mediated through the death and resurrection of Jesus.

The Council of Trent ruled that salvation requires "good works" as well as faith. These works include acts of mercy, veneration of the saints, relics, and sacred images, and participation in the sacraments. In the sacrament of the eucharist, the Council reiterated the doctrine of **transubstantiation**: what appear to be ordinary bread and wine are mysteriously transformed into the body and blood of Christ.

In addition to the actions of the Council of Trent, the Roman Catholic Church gradually chose more virtuous popes than some in the past, and several new monastic orders grew out of the desires for reform. The Jesuits offered themselves as an army for God at the service of the pope. The Society of Jesus, as the order was formally called, was begun by Ignatius Loyola (1491–1556) in the sixteenth century. His *Spiritual Exercises* is still regarded as an excellent guide to meditation and spiritual discernment. However, it was as activists and educators in the everyday world that Jesuits were highly influential in the Reformation, and they were among the first to carry Roman Catholicism to Asia.

Roman Catholicism was also carried to the western hemisphere and the Philippines by Spanish conquistadores. At home, Spain was host to a number of outstanding mystics during the sixteenth and seventeenth centuries. St. Teresa of Avila (1515–1582), a Carmelite nun, became at mid-life a dynamo of spiritual activity, in an order of ascetic Reformed (or Discalced) Carmelite nuns and monks. Discalced Carmelites usually pray much, and eat and sleep little. Despite her organizational activity, St. Teresa was able to maintain a calm sense of deep inner communion with God. In her masterpiece entitled *The Interior Castle*, she described the state of "spiritual marriage":

> *Here it is like rain falling from the heavens into a river or a spring; there is nothing but water there and it is impossible to divide or separate the water belonging to the river from that which fell from the heavens.*[67]

St. Teresa's great influence fell onto a young friend, now known as St. John of the Cross. He became a member of one of the Carmelite houses for men; when imprisoned by other Carmelites who opposed the reforms, he experienced visions and wrote profound spiritual poetry. For John, the most important step for the soul longing to be filled with God is to surrender all vestiges of the self. This state he called the "dark night of the soul," a relinquishing of human reasoning into a state of not-knowing into which the pure light of God may enter without resistance. St. John of the Cross is still considered one of the great masters of the spiritual life.

The impact of the Enlightenment

Major potential threats to Christianity arose during the eighteenth-century Enlightenment in Europe. Intellectual circles exalted human reason and on this basis rejected faith in biblical miracles and revelations. Some people felt that nineteenth-century scientific advances undermined the biblical story of the creation of the world. However, many nineteenth-century scientists were devout Christians who viewed the truth of science as supporting the truth of faith. There emerged two opposing trends: a liberal one, trying to join faith with modern knowledge, and a conservative one, emphasizing the conflict between faith and science. Both views spread rapidly, dividing between them much of Christendom, especially Protestantism. In 1911, "fundamentalists" in the United States published as their uncompromising tenets the total inerrancy of the Bible, and Christ's literal virgin birth, substitutionary atonement, bodily resurrection, and anticipated second coming in final glory. Meanwhile, "modernist" theologians were interpreting such concepts in symbolic terms, with an aversion to dogmatism. Individuals were encouraged to judge religious beliefs by their own experience.

Undaunted, and in some cases invigorated, by these challenges to traditional faith, Protestantism developed a strong missionary spirit, joining Roman Catholic efforts to spread Christianity to every country, along with colonialism. John Wesley, the founder of Methodism, explained:

> I looked upon all the world as my parish; . . . that in whatever part of it I am, I judge it meet, right, and my bounden duty to declare unto all that are willing to hear, the glad tidings of salvation.[68]

The "social gospel" movement brought Protestant churches to the forefront of efforts at social and moral reform. Women, long excluded from important positions in the Church, played major roles in Church-related missionary and reform efforts, such as the abolition of slavery; they cited certain biblical passages as supporting equality of the sexes. When Sarah Grimke (1792–1873) and other women were criticized by their Congregational church for speaking publicly against slavery, Grimke asserted, "All I ask of my brethren is that they will take their feet from off our necks and permit us to stand upright on that ground which God has designed us to occupy."[69]

Liberal trends in Protestant theology led to biblical criticism—that is, to efforts to analyze the Bible as literature. What, for instance, were the earliest texts? Who wrote them? How did they relate to each other? Such questions, unthinkable in earlier generations, continue to enliven Christian theological debate.

The Second Vatican Council

In the meantime, the Roman Catholic and Eastern Orthodox Churches had continued to defend tradition against the changes of modern life. A general council of the Roman Catholic hierarchs was held in 1869–1870. It found itself embroiled chiefly in the question of papal infallibility, a doctrine it ultimately upheld. The pope, proclaimed the bishops of the council, can never err when he speaks from the seat of his authority (*ex cathedra*), on matters of faith and morals.

In 1962, Pope John XXIII, known for his holiness and friendliness, convened the Second Vatican Council for the express purposes of updating and energizing the Church and making it serve the people better as a living force in the modern world rather than being an old, embattled citadel. When questioned about his

The large and august Second Vatican Council convened by Pope John XXIII in 1962 came to historic conclusions. Their recommendations turned Catholicism in a new direction, bringing the hierarchy closer to the common people in a compassionate partnership.

intentions, he demonstrated by opening a window to let in fresh air. With progressives and traditionalists often at odds, the majority nevertheless voted for major shifts in the Church's mission.

Many of the changes involved the liturgy of the mass, or the eucharist. Rather than celebrate it in Latin, which most people did not understand, the liturgy was to be translated into the local languages. Rites were to be simplified. Greater use of sacred music was encouraged, and not just formal, traditional organ and choir offerings.

For the first time the laity were to be invited to participate actively. After Vatican II thus unleashed creativity and simplicity in public worship, entirely new forms appeared, such as informal folk masses—with spiritual folk songs sung to guitar accompaniment.

Another major change was the new emphasis on **ecumenism**, in the sense of rapprochement among all branches of Christianity. The Roman Catholic Church acknowledged that the Holy Spirit is active in all Christian churches, including Protestant denominations and the Eastern Orthodox churches. It pressed for a restoration of unity among all Christians, proclaiming that each could preserve its traditions intact. It also extended the concept of revelation, increasing the hope of dialogue with Jews, with whom Christians share "spiritual patrimony"[70] and with Muslims, upon whom the Church "looks with esteem," for they "adore one God" and honor Jesus as a prophet.

Appreciative mention was also made of other world religions as ways of approaching the same One whom Christians call God. Specifically described were Hinduism ("through which men contemplate the divine mystery") and Buddhism ("which acknowledges the radical insufficiency of this shifting world").[71]

Vatican II clearly marked major new directions in Catholicism. Its relatively liberal, pacificistic characteristics are still meeting with some opposition within the Church decades later. In the late twentieth century, conservative elements in the Vatican began to reverse the direction taken by Vatican II to some extent, to the dismay of liberal Catholics. In the final section of this chapter, concerning current trends in Christianity, we will note several ways in which the renewed conservatism in the Vatican is being expressed.

Central beliefs in contemporary Christianity

The history of Christianity is characterized more by divisions than by uniformity among Christian groups. The Church is vast and culturally diverse, and Christian theologies are complex and intricate. Nevertheless, there are a few basic motifs on which the majority of people who are faithful Christians would probably agree today.

A central belief is the divine Sonship of Jesus—the assertion that Jesus is the incarnation of God. According to the Gospel of John, before Jesus's death he told his disciples that he would be going to "my Father's house . . . to prepare a place for you." When they asked how they would find the way to that place, Jesus reportedly said:

I am the way, I am the truth and I am life. No one comes to the Father except by me. . . . Anyone who has seen me has seen the Father. . . . It is the Father who dwells in me doing his own work.[72]

Throughout most of Christian history, there has been the feeling that Jesus was the only incarnation of God. Interestingly, Thomas Aquinas argued that although God could become incarnate in multiple incarnations (as in Hindu belief), in fact he chose to do so only once, in Christ. Theologian Paul Knitter is one of the contemporary voices calling for a less exclusive approach that still honors the unique contribution of Jesus:

What Christians do know, on the basis of their praxis of following Jesus, is that his message is *a sure means for bringing about liberation from injustice and oppression, that it* is *an effective, hope-filled, universally meaningful way of realizing* Soteria *[human welfare and liberation of the poor and oppressed] and promoting God's kingdom. . . . Not those who proclaim "only Lord, only Lord," but those who* do *the will of the Father will enter the kingdom (Matthew 7:21–23).*[73]

For Christians, Jesus is the Savior of the world, the one whom God sent to redeem people from their sins and reconcile them with God. Matthew reports that Jesus said he "did not come to be served, but to serve, and to give up his life as a ransom for many."[74] His own suffering and death are regarded as a substitute sacrifice on behalf of all those who follow and place their faith in him. According to the Gospel of John,

God loved the world so much that he gave his only Son, that everyone who has
faith in him may not die but have eternal life. It was not to judge the world that
God sent his Son into the world, but that through him the world might be saved.[75]

According to Christian belief, humanity has a sinful character, illustrated
metaphorically in the Old Testament by the fall of Adam and Eve. We have lost
our original purity. Given free will by God, we have chosen disobedience rather
than surrender to the will of God. We cannot save ourselves from our fallen condition; we can only be forgiven by the compassion of a loving God.

Through fully surrendered faith in Jesus, Christians hope to be washed of their
egotistical sinfulness, regenerated, made righteous, adopted by God, sanctified,
and glorified in the life to come. These are the blessings of salvation, which
Christians feel Jesus won for them by his sacrifice.

Although Christians worship Jesus as Savior, as the incarnation of a merciful
God, they also see him as a human being showing fellow human beings the way to
God. His own life is seen as the perfect model for human behavior. Archbishop
Desmond Tutu of South Africa emphasizes Jesus's identification with the human
condition:

God does not occupy an Olympian fastness, remote from us. He has this deep, deep
solidarity with us. God became a human being, a baby. God was hungry. God was
tired, God suffered and died. God is there with us.[76]

This is the central mystery of Christianity: that God became human in order to
lead people back to God.

The human virtue most often associated with Jesus is love. Many Christians
say they experience Jesus's love even though he is no longer walking the earth
in human form. And in turn, they have deep love for Jesus. Those who are experiencing problems in life are comforted to feel that Jesus is a living presence in
their lives, standing with them spiritually, supporting them, loving them even in
the darkest of times. Reverend Larry Howard, the African–American pastor of
Hopps Memorial Christian Methodist Episcopal Church in Syracuse, New York,
declares:

We found a Jesus. A Jesus who came in the midnight hour. A Jesus that was able
to rock babies to sleep. A Jesus that stood in the midst and walked the miles when
the freedom train rode through the South all the way through Syracuse. Jesus
brought us through the mighty trials and tribulations. Why did Jesus do that?
Jesus loved us and through that love and because of that love we stand here today.
Not because the world has been so good to us. Not because we have been treated
fair. Not because we have been able to realize the dream that God has given every
man, woman, and child. But we stand here because we love Jesus. We love him
more and more and more each day.[77]

The basic thrust of Jesus's message is to invite us into divine union, which is the
sole remedy for the human predicament.

Father Thomas Keating[78]

Mother Teresa's Missionaries of Charity

The love of which Christ spoke is not an intellectual abstraction. According to the diminutive nun who was known around the world as Mother Teresa, love must be put into action.

Mother Teresa (1910–1997) was born in Albania, to a wealthy family that lost all its money when her father died. She entered a convent of the Loreto Sisters when she was eighteen, but she felt called to India, where she initially taught at a girls' school in Calcutta. Then came an even more difficult inner calling "to be God's love in action to the poorest of the poor." At a time when India was in turmoil after the shooting of Gandhi and the separation into Hindu and Muslim states, Calcutta was crowded with refugees. With no resources, Mother Teresa simply walked through the streets, with only loving care to give to those who had been abandoned by society, beggars, lepers, the dying. She wanted to live and serve the poor like Jesus, claiming nothing for herself, not even the security of knowing where she would sleep. She says, "There is but one person in the poor—Jesus. To be able to love him with undivided love we take a vow of poverty which frees us from all material possessions. We bind ourselves to be one of [the poor], to depend solely on divine providence, to have nothing, yet possess all things in possessing Christ."[79]

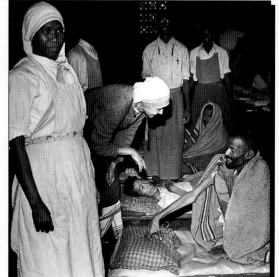

To assist in this work, Mother Teresa eventually received permission to found a new order, the Missionaries of Charity. The sisters wore simple white saris with blue stripes, the colors of the Virgin Mary and the garment of Indian women; they lived in poverty, without possessions or grand institutions, to help them understand the poor. In training them to work without the assurance of financial backing or physical safety, Mother Teresa emphasized that the most important thing is to pray and pray and pray; divine providence will always give what is needed.

As her work expanded around the globe to 230 houses on all continents, the results of her faith have been demonstrated again and again. There is no plan, no fundraising organization (although the Missionaries of Charity do accept individual donations). Wherever the sisters go, they try to help the poorest of the poor in whatever ways are needed. In each person they care for, they see the face of Jesus. In Calcutta, the Missionaries have picked up tens of thousands of sick, starving, and dying people from the streets and given them tender personal care, hand-feeding them a special formula made from soybeans. In New York City, they feed the homeless, shop and clean for the elderly poor, and care for those with AIDS.

During a period of intense mortar-bombing between Christian and Muslim militia in Beirut, Mother Teresa learned that a home for sixty spastic children had been stranded without caretakers on the Muslim side of the battle lines. When she insisted on crossing the lines to get them, the local clergy assured her that it was impossible. With utter faith, she said that she had asked the Virgin to arrange a ceasefire, which did indeed happen the next day, giving her time to rescue the terrified, helpless children. Within a day, the children were smiling. Mother Teresa said: "The Missionaries do small things with great love. It is not how much we do, but how much love we put into doing it. To God there is nothing small. The moment we have given it to God, it becomes infinite."

In addition to being the paragon of love, Jesus also provides a model of sin-lessness. To become like God, humans must constantly be purified of their lower tendencies. This belief has led some Christians to extremes of penance, such as the monks who flogged themselves and wore hairshirts so that their conscience might always be pricked. In a milder form, confession of one's sinfulness is a sig-nificant part of Christian tradition. There is an emphasis on self-discipline to guard against temptations, on examination of one's own faults, and on rituals, such as baptism, that help to remove the contamination that is innate in human-ity. Although one must make these efforts at purification, most Christians believe that it is only through the grace of God—as mediated by the saving sacrifice of Jesus—that one can be delivered from sin and rise above ordinary human nature toward a divine state of sinlessness.

Sacred practices

Imitation of the model set by Jesus in his own life is the primary practice of Christians. In the widely read fourteenth-century book, *The Imitation of Christ*, people are encouraged to aspire to Jesus's own example as well as his teachings:

> *O how powerful is the pure love of Jesus, which is mixed with no self-interest, nor self-love! ... Where shall one be found who is willing to serve God for naught?*[80]

In addition to the inner attempt to become more and more like Jesus, Christians have developed a variety of spiritual practices. Although forms and understandings of the practices vary among the branches of Christendom, they may include public worship services with sermons and offering of the sacraments, celebrations of the liturgical year, private contemplation and prayer, and devo-tions to Mary and the saints.

Worship services and sacraments

Christian worship typically takes place in a church building, which may be revered as a sacred space. The late nineteenth-century Russian Orthodox saint Ioann Kronshtadtsky (d. 1908) explained:

> *Entering the church you enter some special realm which is not like the visible one. In the world you hear and see everything earthly, transient, fragile, liable to decay, sinful. In the church you see and hear the heavenly, the non-transient, the eternal, the holy. A temple is the threshold of heaven. It is like the heaven itself, because here is God's throne, the service of angels, the frequent descent of the Holy Spirit. ... Here everything from icons to censer and the priests' robes fills you with veneration and prayer; everything tells you that you are in God's shrine, face to face with God himself.*[81]

The word sacrament can be translated as "mystery." In Christianity, the sacra-ments are the sacred rites that are thought capable of transmitting the mystery of Christ to worshippers. Roman Catholic and Eastern Orthodox Churches observe

The sacrament of the eucharist, celebrated here in the Philippines, engages believers in a communal mystical encounter with the presence of Christ.

seven sacraments: baptism (initiation and symbolic purification from sin by water), confirmation (of membership in the Church), eucharist (the ritual meal described below), penance (confession and absolution of sins), extreme unction (anointing of the sick with oil, especially before death), holy orders (consecration as a deacon, priest, or bishop), and matrimony. In general, Protestant Churches recognize only baptism and the eucharist as sacraments.

The ritual of public worship, or liturgy, usually follows a set pattern, though in some Churches the actions of the Holy Spirit are thought to inspire spontaneous expressions of faith.

In most forms of Christianity, the central sacrament is the Holy Eucharist (also called Holy Communion). It is a mystery through which the invisible Christ is thought to grant communion with himself. Believers are given a bit of bread to eat, which is received as the body of Christ, and a sip of wine or grape juice, understood as his blood. The priest or minister may consecrate the bread and wine in ritual fashion and share them among the people. In Roman Catholic or Orthodox masses, the cup of wine and the bread are thought to be mystically transformed by the Holy Spirit into the blood and body of Christ. They are treated with profound reverence. In sharing the communion "meal" together, the people are united with each other as well as with Christ. The traditional ideal was to take communion every day and certainly every Sunday (the day set aside as the Sabbath).

Jesus is pictured in the Bible as having set the pattern for this sacrament at what is called the Last Supper, the meal he shared with his inner circle before his capture by the authorities in Jerusalem. The body and blood of Christ are seen as the spiritual nourishment of the faithful, that which gives them eternal life in the midst of earthly life.

Mother Julia Gatta, an Anglican priest, describes this sacred experience from the point of view of the clergy who preside at the liturgy:

> To be the celebrant of Eucharist is, I think, the most wonderful experience on earth. In a sense, you experience the energy flowing both ways. . . . One experiences the Spirit in them offering their prayer through Christ to the Father. But at the same time, you experience God's love flowing back into them. When I give communion to people, I am aware that I am caught in that circle of love.[82]

The partaking of sacred bread and wine is the climax of a longer liturgy of Holy Communion. The communion service, often called a mass in Catholicism, begins with liturgical prayers, praise, and confession of sinfulness. A group confession chanted by some Lutheran congregations enumerates these flaws:

> Most merciful God, we have sinned against you in thought, word, and deed, by what we have done and by what we have left undone. We have not loved you with our whole heart; we have not loved our neighbors as ourselves.[83]

Catholics were traditionally encouraged to confess their sins privately to a priest before taking communion, in the sacrament of **penance**, or "reconciliation." After hearing the confession, the priest pronounces forgiveness and blessing over the penitent, or perhaps prescribes a penance. Orthodox Christians were also traditionally expected to spend several days in contrition and fasting before receiving communion. The reason for the emphasis on purification is that during the service the church itself is perceived as the Kingdom of God, in which everything is holy. In Orthodox services, the clergy walk around the church, swinging an incense censer to set apart the area as a sacred space and to lift the prayers of the congregants to God.

In all Christian churches, passages from the Old and New Testaments may be read and the congregation may sing several hymns, songs of praise or thanksgiving to God. The congregation may be asked to recite a credal statement of Christian beliefs, and to make money offerings. There may be an address by the priest or minister (called a sermon or a homily) on the readings for the day. These parts of the liturgy constitute the Liturgy of the Word, in which Christ is thought to be present as the living Word, addressing the people through scripture and preaching. In Protestant churches, the Liturgy of the Word is often offered by itself, without the communion service.

In both Protestantism and Roman Catholicism, there are now attempts at updating the liturgy to make it more meaningful and personally relevant for contemporary Christians. One innovation that seems to have taken hold everywhere is the "sharing of the peace." Partway through the worship service, congregants turn to everyone around them to hug or shake hands and say, "The Peace of Christ be with you"—"and also with you."

In addition to regular liturgies and the sacrament of the mass or communion, there are special events treated in sacred ways. The first to be administered is the sacrament of baptism. Externally, it involves either immersing the person in water or, more commonly, pouring sanctified water (representing purification) on the candidate's head, while invoking the Holy Trinity. In a recent ecumenical document, the World Council of Churches defined the general meaning of the practice:

> By baptism, Christians are immersed in the liberating death of Christ where their sins are buried, where the "old Adam" is crucified with Christ, and where the power of sin is broken ... They are raised here and now to a new life in the power of the resurrection of Jesus Christ.[84]

Aside from adult converts to Christianity, the rite is usually performed on infants, with parents taking vows on their behalf. There are arguments that infant baptism has little basis in the Bible and that a baby cannot make the conscious repentance of sin and "conversion of heart" implied in the ceremony. Baptists and several other Protestant groups therefore reserve baptism for adults.

A second ceremony—**confirmation**—is often offered in early adolescence in Roman Catholicism and Protestantism. After a period of religious instruction, a group of young people are allowed to make a conscious and personal commitment to the Christian life.

Some Christians observe special days of fasting. Russian Orthodox Old Believer priest Father Appolinari explains fasting as a way of *soprichiastna*, of becoming part of something very large, the spiritual aura of the Lord. He says,

> More and more ordinary people are seeking a comfortable life. More and more we leave spirituality. We try to fill this vacuum with material things. I told my students that there was a fast coming up. They groaned, "Why?" I said that we fast for spiritual reasons. The rule is that you should fast not with a spirit of suffering but with such elevated spirit that your soul sings.
>
> When we limit our physicality, as in limiting our food intake, then we grow in our spirituality. I advise my students to notice whether their brain works better when their stomach is full or when it is almost empty. Monks refuse physical things in order to get spiritual benefits. We look at them and see their lives as dark, but for them, it is light.[85]

The liturgical year

Just as Christians repeatedly enact their union with Christ through participation in the eucharist sacrament, the Church every year celebrates a cycle of festivals, leading the worshipper through the life of Jesus and the gift of the Spirit. As the faithful repeat this cycle year after year, they hope to enter more deeply into the mystery of God in Christ, and the whole body of believers in Christ theoretically grows toward the kingdom of God.

CHRISTMAS AND EPIPHANY There are three major events in the church calendar, each associated with a series of preparatory celebrations. The first is the season of light: Christmas and **Epiphany**. Christmas is the celebration of Jesus's birth on earth. Epiphany means "manifestation" or "showing forth." It celebrates the recognition of Jesus's spiritual kingship by the three Magi (in the Western Church), his acknowledgement as the Messiah and the beloved Son of God when he is baptized by John the Baptist, and his first recognized miracle, the turning of water into wine at the wedding in Cana.

In early Christianity, Epiphany was more important than the celebration of Jesus's birth. The actual birth date is unknown, but the setting of the date near the winter solstice allowed Christianity to take over the older "pagan" rites celebrating the return of longer periods of daylight at the darkest time of year. In the Gospel of John, Jesus is "the true light that enlightens every man,"[86] the light of the divine appearing amid the darkness of human ignorance.

Advent, the month preceding Christmas, is supposed to be a time of joyous anticipation. But in industrialized countries, it is more likely a time of frenzied marketing and buying of gifts, symbolizing God's gift to the world in the person of Jesus.

In some countries churches stage pageants re-enacting the birth story, with people taking the parts of Mary, Joseph, the innkeeper who has no room, the shepherds, and the three Magi. Since the nineteenth century, it has been traditional to cut or buy an evergreen tree (a symbol of eternal life, perhaps borrowed from indigenous ceremonies) and erect it in one's house, decorated with lights and ornaments. On Christmas Eve some Christians gather for a candlelit

Young children re-enact the Christmas story, adoring Jesus as a baby.

"watch-night" service, welcoming the turn from midnight to a new day in which Christ has come into the world. On Christmas Day, Catholic and Protestant children are sometimes told that presents have been magically brought by St. Nicholas, a fourth-century bishop noted for his great generosity. The exchange of gifts may be followed by a great feast.

EASTER In terms of religious significance, the most important event of the Christian liturgical year is Easter. This is the commemoration of Jesus's death (on "Good Friday") and resurrection (on Easter Sunday, which falls in the spring but is celebrated at different times by the Eastern and Western Churches). Like Christmas, Easter is a continuation of earlier rites—those associated with the vernal (spring) equinox, celebrating the regeneration of plant life and the return of warm weather after the cold death of winter. It is also related to Pesach, the Hebrew Passover, the Jewish spring feast of deliverance.

Liturgically, Easter is preceded by a forty-day period of repentance and fasting, called Lent. Many Christians perform acts of asceticism, prayer, and charity, to join in Jesus's greater sacrifice. In the Orthodox Church, the last Sunday before Lent is dedicated to asking forgiveness. People request forgiveness from each other, bowing deeply. In the West, Lent begins with Ash Wednesday, when many Christians have ash smudges placed on their foreheads by a priest who says, "Remember, man, thou art dust and unto dust thou shalt return." On the Sunday before Easter, Jesus's triumphal entry into Jerusalem is honored by the waving of palm or willow branches in churches and the proclaiming of Hosannas. His death is mourned on "Good Friday." The mourning is jubilantly ended on Easter Sunday, with shouts of "Christ is risen!"

In Russia, the Great Vigil welcoming Easter morning lasts from midnight until dawn, with the people standing the entire time. Jim Forest describes such a service in a church in Kiev, with 2,000 people crowding into the building and as many more standing outside:

> *The dean went out the royal doors into the congregation and sang out, "Christos Voskresye!" [Christ is risen!] Everyone responded in one voice, "Veyeastino voskresye!" [Truly he is risen!] It is impossible to put on paper how this sounds in the dead of night in a church overheated by crowds of people and hundreds of candles. It is like a shudder in the earth, the cracking open of the tomb. Then there was an explosion of ringing bells.*[87]

PENTECOST Fifty days after the Jewish Passover (which Jesus is thought to have been celebrating at the Last Supper with his disciples) comes the Jewish celebration Shavuot (which commemorates the giving of the Torah to Moses, as well as the first fruits of the harvest). Jews nicknamed it Pentecost, which is Greek for "fiftieth." Christians took over the holiday season but gave it an entirely different meaning.

In Christianity, Pentecost commemorates the occasion described in Acts when the Holy Spirit descended upon the disciples after Jesus's death and resurrection, filling them with the Spirit's own life and power and enabling them to speak in foreign tongues they had not known. In early Christianity, Pentecost was an occasion for baptisms of those who had been preparing for admission to the Church.

The Christian monk Thomas Merton and the Tibetan Buddhist Dalai Lama, two great ecumenical figures of the 20th century, met shortly before Merton died in 1968 during his trip to visit the monks of the Eastern traditions.

THE TRANSFIGURATION AND ASSUMPTION Some Christian Churches also emphasize two other special feast days. On August 6, people honor the Transfiguration of Jesus on the mountain, revealing his supernatural radiance. On August 15, they celebrate the Assumption of Mary, known as "The Falling Asleep of the Mother of God." These feasts are prominent in the Eastern Church, which generally places more emphasis on the ability of humanity to break out of its earthly bonds and rise into the light, than on the heaviness and darkness of sin.

Contemplative prayer

The contemplative tradition within Christianity is beginning to re-emerge. The hectic pace and rapid change of modern life make periods of quietness essential, if only for stress relief. Many Christians, not aware of a contemplative way within their own Church, have turned to Eastern religions for instruction in meditation.

One of the most influential twentieth-century Christian contemplatives was the late Thomas Merton (1915–1968). He was a Trappist monk who received a special dispensation to live as a hermit in the woods near his abbey in Kentucky. Merton lived simply in nature, finding joy in the commonplace, experienced attentively in silence. He studied and tried to practice the great contemplative traditions of earlier Christianity and reintroduced them to a contemporary audience through his writings. In meditative "prayer of the heart," or "contemplative prayer," he wrote:

We seek first of all the deepest ground of our identity in God. We do not reason about dogmas of faith, or "the mysteries." We seek rather to gain a direct existential grasp, a personal experience of the deepest truths of life and faith, finding ourselves in God's truths. . . . Prayer then means yearning for the simple presence of God, for a personal understanding of his word, for knowledge of his will and for capacity to hear and obey him.[88]

Before he became a Christian monk, Merton had studied Eastern mysticism, assuming that Christianity had no mystical tradition. He became friends with a Hindu monk who advised him to read St. Augustine's *Confessions* and *The Imitation of Christ*. These classic works led Merton toward a deep appreciation of the potential of the Christian inner life, aligned with a continuing openness to learn from Eastern monasticism. He died in an accident while in Asia visiting Buddhist and Hindu monastics.

Spiritual renewal through inner silence has become an important part of some Christians' practice of their faith. Syrian Orthodox Bishop Paulos Mar Gregorios of India, past-President of the World Council of Churches, concluded from the Bible evidence that Jesus himself was a contemplative:

Christ spent seventy percent of his whole life in meditation. He would sleep rarely. All day he gave himself to healing the sick. At night he would pray, sometimes all night. He was not seeking his own self-realization. His meditation and prayer were not for himself but for the world—for every human being. He held the world in his consciousness through prayer, not with attachment but with compassion. He groaned and he suffered with humanity. To follow Jesus in the way of the cross means to say, "I lay aside all personal ambition and dedicate myself to God: 'Here I am, God. I belong to you. I have no idea where to go. It matters not what I am, so long as You lead me.'"[89]

A form of Christian meditation that was instituted by the Franciscan monks and is still practiced in many Catholic and Anglican churches is following the Stations of the Cross. These are fourteen plaques or paintings placed on the walls of the church depicting scenes from the death of Jesus. As one sees him taking up the cross, falling three times under its weight, being stripped of his clothes and being nailed to the cross, one becomes painfully and humbly aware of the suffering that God's Son experienced in manifesting as a human redeemer.

Contemplation of the humanness of Jesus is used to help believers identify with him and thence to aspire to his divine model. Theology professor and spiritual director Kathleen Dugan says that when she teaches devotions on the deep humanity of Jesus:

my students have difficulty assimilating it. "You mean to say that he felt sorrow like I do?" "Yes." "That he cried?" "Yes." "That he felt joy?" "Yes." The Gospel examples show that he wept before Lazarus's tomb. He wept at the sorrow of Martha and Mary over their brother. He rejoiced with the couple that were being married at the wedding of Cana. He felt terrible isolation; so many things in the Gospels speak of that. He said on the cross, "My God, my God, why have you forsaken me?" There is no human emotion that he did not experience. He did suffer. Crucifixion was a long, lingering death, with great agony. Jesus is our brother, our spouse, our son. When students think about these things, it is often transforming.

*Here is a living, breathing image of what it means to be
God. We are called to imitate the saints, but primarily we are
called to imitate Jesus.*[90]

In Orthodoxy, the central contemplative practice is repetition of the Jesus Prayer: "Lord Jesus Christ, have mercy
on me" (and some add, "a sinner"). Eventually its meaning
imbeds itself in the heart and one lives in a state of unceasing prayer. An unknown nineteenth-century Russian
peasant who lived with continual repetition of the Jesus
Prayer described its results:

*The sweetness of the heart, warmth and light, unspeakable
rapture, joy, ease, profound peace, blessedness, and love of life
are all the result of prayer of the heart.*[91]

*The Virgin of
Guadalupe, who
reportedly appeared in
the 16th century to an
indigenous convert to
Catholicism, speaking
the native language
Nahuatl, has been
embraced as patron
saint of the Americas.*

Devotion to Mary

Thus far in this chapter, little has been said about Mary, the
mother of Jesus, for she has not been in the forefront of
historical theological disputes. Veneration of Mary has
come as much from the grassroots as from the top.
Drawings of her were found in the catacombs in which the early Christians met;
explicit devotion to her was well developed by the third or fourth century CE.
Despite the absence of detailed historical information, she serves as a potent and
much-loved spiritual symbol. She is particularly venerated by Roman Catholics,
Eastern Orthodoxy, and Anglicans.

Some researchers feel that devotion to Mary is derived from earlier worship of
the Mother Goddess. They see her as representing the feminine aspect of the
Godhead. She is associated with the crescent moon, representing the receptive
willingness to be filled with the Spirit. In the story of the **Annunciation**—the
appearance of an angel who told her she would have a child conceived by the
Holy Spirit—her reported response was "Behold, I am the handmaid of the Lord;
let it be to me according to your word."[92] This receptivity is not seen as utter
powerlessness, however. Mary, like Christ, embodies the basic Christian paradox:
that power is found in "weakness."

Whether or not devotion to Mary is linked to earlier Mother Goddess worship,
oral Christian traditions have given her new symbolic roles. One links her with
Israel, which is referred to as the daughter of Zion or daughter of Jerusalem in
Old Testament passages. God comes to her as the overshadowing of the Holy
Spirit, and from this love between YHWH and Israel, Jesus is born to save the
people of Israel.

Mary is also called the New Eve. The legendary first Eve disobeyed God and
was cast out of the Garden of Eden; Mary's willing submission to God allows birth
of the new creation, in which Christ is in all.

In the Orthodox and Catholic traditions, she is referred to as the Mother of God.
In Russia, she is also revered as the protectress of all humanity, and especially of
the Russian people. Before he died on the cross, Jesus is said to have told John,

the beloved disciple, that thenceforth Mary was to be his Mother. The story is interpreted as meaning that thenceforth all humanity was adopted by Mary.

Another symbolic role ascribed to Mary is that of the immaculate virgin. According to the gospels of Matthew and Luke, she conceived Jesus by heavenly intervention rather than human biology. Roman Catholicism asserts that at the Immaculate Conception, she herself was conceived without any of the "original sin" exhibited by the rest of humanity. Even in giving birth to Jesus, she remained a virgin. Orthodoxy does not insist on these doctrines, nor on the Catholic dogma that Mary ascended bodily to heaven after her physical death. The emphasis on virginity is a spiritual sign of being dedicated to God alone, rather than to any temporal attachments.

According to the faithful, Mary is not just a symbol but a living presence, like Christ. She is appealed to in prayer and is honored in countless paintings, statues, shrines, and churches dedicated to her name. Catholics are enjoined to repeat the "Hail Mary" prayer:

Hail, Mary, full of grace, the Lord is with thee. Blessed art thou among women, and blessed is the fruit of thy womb, Jesus. Holy Mary, Mother of God, pray for us sinners, now and at the hour of our death.

Theologians are careful to point out, however, that veneration of Mary is really directed toward God; Mary is not worshipped in herself but as the mother of Christ, reflecting his glory. If this were not so, Christians could be accused of idolatry.

Be this as it may, Mary has been said to appear to believers in many places around the world. At Lourdes, in France, it is claimed that she appeared repeatedly to a young peasant girl named Bernadette in the nineteenth century. A spring found where she indicated has been the source of hundreds of medically authenticated healings from seemingly incurable diseases. In 1531, in Guadalupe (within what is now Mexico City), Mary appeared to a converted Aztec, Juan Diego. She asked him to have the bishop build a church on the spot. To convince the skeptical bishop, Juan filled his cloak with the out-of-season roses to which she directed him. When he opened the cloak before the bishop, the petals fell away to reveal a large and vivid image of Mary, with Indian features. The picture is now enshrined in a large new church with moving walkways to handle the crowds who come to see it, and the Virgin of Guadalupe has been declared Celestial Patroness of the New World.

Sightings of Mary continue around the world. What are perceived as her ethereal images have drawn crowds to worship before a large office window in Florida, before a closed church in eastern Europe, and at a site where she reportedly appeared two decades ago in Vietnam. In Mexico, her image is said to be seen frequently, miraculously manifesting in everything from dented car fenders and stovetops to garlic and fruits. In 1997, crowds worshipping what appeared to be the apparition of Mary on the floor of a Mexico City metro station became so thick that the authorities had to remove that section of the floor and place it outside in a shrine. Surrounded by blue tiles, the image—which skeptical officials refer to as a stain from a leaking pipe beneath the floor—was ceremonially blessed by a priest and draws queues of people who reverently touch and pray before it. Such is the perennial appeal of the holy mother.

Veneration of saints and angels

Roman Catholics and Orthodox Christians honor their spiritual heroes as saints. These are men and women who are recognized as so holy that the divine life of Christ is particularly evident in them. After their death, they are carefully judged by the Church for proofs of exalted Christian virtue, such as tolerance under extreme provocation, and of miraculous power. Those who are canonized by this process are subject to great veneration.

> *Each saint is a unique event, a victory over the force of evil. So many blessings can pour from God into the world through one life.*
>
> Father Germann, Vladimir, Russia[93]

Orthodox Christians are given the name of a saint when they are baptized. Each keeps an icon of this patron saint in his or her room and prays to the saint daily. Icons of many saints fill an Orthodox church, helping to make them familiar presences rather than names in history books. Saints are often known as having special areas of concern and power. For instance, St. Anthony of Padua is invoked for help in finding lost things. **Relics**, usually parts of the body or clothes of saints, are felt to radiate the holiness of the saints' communion with God. They are treasured and displayed for veneration in Catholic and Orthodox churches. It is said that saints' physical bodies were so transformed by divine light that they do not decay after death, and that they continue to emit a sweet fragrance.

Roman Catholics and Orthodox Christians also pray to the **angels** for protection. Angels are understood as spiritual beings who serve as messengers from and adoring servants of God. They are usually pictured as humans with wings. In popular piety, each person is thought to have a guardian angel for individual protection and spiritual help.

Contemporary trends

The year 2000 was the subject of major celebrations around the world, as the beginning of the third millennium since the birth of Jesus. At this time, Christianity is gaining membership and enthusiastic participation in some quarters and losing ground in others. In Egypt, Orthodox Coptic Christians, heirs to the ancient tradition of the Desert Fathers, have long been submerged under Muslim rule, but the monasteries have begun to flourish again. The 16 million Coptic Christians have their own pope.

Roman Catholicism is experiencing divisions between conservatives and liberals. After the liberal tendencies of Vatican II, Pope John Paul II reaffirmed certain traditional stands and strengthened the position of the right wing of the Church. In a 1995 encyclical, he emphatically insisted upon what he called the fundamental right to human life as opposed to the "culture of death," condemning abortion and euthanasia as "crimes which no human law can claim to legitimize" and condemning the death penalty.[94] In 2000, Cardinal Joseph Ratzinger, head of the

Vatican's highly conservative Congregation for the Doctrine of the Faith, delivered *"Dominus Jesu,"* a thirty-six-page document proclaiming, "There exists a single Church of Christ, which subsists in the Catholic Church," which has been entrusted with "the fullness of grace and truth." Other Christian communities "are not churches in the proper sense" and non-Christians are in a "gravely deficient situation" with regard to salvation.[95]

Despite his conservative stances, Pope John Paul II uses the latest technologies, including a major Internet website, to spread his messages. He also travels extensively, urging a return to traditional family values. In 1998 the world was stunned to see his tremendous welcome to Cuba, which had been officially atheist for two decades and then neutrally secular since 1991. The Young Communist League encouraged its half a million members to see the pope in Havana, in order to "hear the message of a man of great talent and culture who is concerned about the most pressing problems of modern humanity."[96]

On a special "Day of Forgiveness" held during the Lenten season in the millennial year of 2000, Pope John Paul II delivered a statement asking forgiveness for the past sins of the Roman Catholic Church, incuding its treatment of Jews, other Christians, other religions, women, ethnic groups, indigenous peoples, and heretics. "For the role that each of us has had, with his behaviour, in these evils, contributing to a disfigurement of the face of the Church, we humbly ask forgiveness," he said.

Televised evangelism on Memorial Day, from the Crystal Cathedral, California.

In spite of the public attention paid to the pope as a person, the priesthood is

dwindling considerably in most Western countries, partly because of the requirement that priests be celibate. There is increased interest in participation by
women (who are not allowed by the Vatican to be priests), and widespread
disregard of papal prohibitions on effective birth control, abortion, test-tube
conception, surrogate motherhood, genetic experimentation, divorce, and homo-
sexuality.

While cautioning against a recreational view of sexuality, Sean McDonagh SSC
emphasizes that the environmental and social consequences of unlimited population growth require a rethinking of traditional Catholic proscriptions on birth
control:

> *The pro-life argument needs to be seen within the widest context of the fragility of
> the living world. Is it really pro-life to ignore the warnings of demographers and
> ecologists who predict that unbridled population growth will lead to severe hardship
> and an increase in the infant mortality rate for succeeding generations? Is it pro-life
> to allow the extinction of hundreds of thousands of living species which will
> ultimately affect the well-being of all future generations on the planet?*[97]

The Vatican has responded to these trends by insisting on the value of tradition
and authority. But many American Catholic leaders are concerned that, in the
words of Father Frank McNulty of Newark, New Jersey, "people often do not perceive the church as proclaiming integral truth and divine mercy, but rather as
sounding harsh, demanding."[98] Acting as a group, Roman Catholic bishops in the
United States have issued statements deploring sexism as a "sin" (recommending
that spiritual positions of responsibility and authority be opened to women and
that non-sexist language be used in liturgy), supporting peace efforts, and insisting on the morality of economic social justice.

In Protestantism, traditional denominations in Europe and the United States
are declining in membership. According to a Gallup poll, only a minority of the
"unchurched" actually disagree with their denomination's teachings. They are
more likely to drop away because of apathy, a lack of services, or a lack of welcome on the part of the minister. Dr. George Carey, the former Archbishop of
Canterbury, bemoans his impression that Christians are not taking the Church's
teachings into consideration in making personal moral choices, and feels that in
England God is "being banished to the realm of the private hobby."[99]

Although many traditional Christian churches are losing members, other
groups and trends are taking vigorous root. These include evangelical and charismatic groups, non-Western Christian churches, liberation theology, feminist theology, creation-centered Christianity, and the ecumenical movement.

Evangelicalism

To evangelize is to preach the Christian gospel and convert people to Christianity.
Evangelical theology, with its emphasis on experiencing the grace of God, has
been important throughout the history of American Protestantism. The current
evangelical movement has its roots in the fundamentalist–modernist controversy
of the early twentieth century.

The fundamentalists were reacting against the liberal or modern movement in
Christianity that sought to reconcile science and religion and to use historical and

archaeological data to understand the Bible. This movement had an optimistic view of human nature and stressed reason, free will, and self-determination. In response, a group of Christians called for a return to the "fundamentals" which they identified as (1) the inspiration and authority of scripture (and sometimes its inerrancy); (2) an emphasis on the virgin birth of Christ and other miracles; (3) the deity of Christ and the bodily resurrection as a literal historical event; (4) Christ's atoning and substitutionary death; and (5) an emphasis on the literal and imminent second coming of Christ. The controversy between these two groups received its most famous public expression in the Scopes trial in 1925 when John Thomas Scopes, a high school teacher in Tennessee, challenged a state law forbidding the teaching of evolution in schools.

Beginning in the 1930s and with waves of enthusiasm in the 1950s and late twentieth century, heirs of this movement, who can broadly be called "evangelicals," have become a vigorous movement in many Protestant denominations. Evangelicals study the Bible together and value being "born again" in Christ. They vary from conservative to liberal on other theological and ethical issues (such as the literal interpretation of the Bible and involvement in social issues such as peace movements and the alleviation of poverty).

Evangelicals' messages now enjoy widespread visibility through international electronic media. Television programs relayed around the world by communication satellites and Internet websites offer enthusiastic preaching, videotapes,

The Pentecostalist-charismatic movement has brought spontaneous spiritual expressiveness into previously restrained cultures, such as this congregation in Kent, England.

audiotapes, CDs, and books, prayers for those in need, and the inevitable appeals for financial contributions to support these huge organizations, each centered on a charismatic speaker.

On the ground, evangelicalism is also making great strides in South America, in areas that were largely Roman Catholic as a result of colonization by Spain centuries ago. In the early 1990s, an average of five evangelical churches were being established each week in Rio de Janeiro, most of them in the slum areas, in an attempt to offer food, job training, day care, and perhaps conversion to the very poor.

Charismatics

Overlapping somewhat with the evangelical surge, there is a rising emphasis on charismatic experience—that is, divinely inspired powers—among Christians of all classes and nations. While Christian fundamentalists stress the historical Jesus, charismatics feel they have also been touched by the "third person" of the Trinity, the Holy Spirit. These include members of Protestant Pentecostal churches but also Roman Catholics, members of mainline Protestant denominations, and Orthodox churches who are caught up in a widespread contemporary spiritual renewal that harkens back to the biblical descent of the Holy Spirit upon the disciples of Jesus, firing them with spiritual powers and faith.

Mainstream Christian churches, which have often rejected emotional spiritual experience in favor of a more orderly piety, are gradually becoming more tolerant of it. Among Roman Catholics the movement is often called "Charismatic Renewal," for it claims to bring true life in the Spirit back to Christianity. By broad definition, up to one-fourth of all Christians today could be considered members of this Pentecostal-charismatic movement.[100]

Under the alleged influence of the Spirit, Pentecostalist-charismatics stand and gesture as they lovingly sing praises of Jesus and God, speak in tongues, pray and utter praises, spontaneously heal by the laying on of hands and prayer, and bear witness to spiritual miracles. Spontaneous spiritual gestures are especially prevalent at large renewal sites. A reporter witnessing the gathering of 5,300 people at the Toronto Airport Christian Fellowship described the following scene:

The ballroom carpets were littered with fallen bodies, bodies of seemingly straightlaced men and women who felt themselves moved by the phenomenon they say is the Holy Spirit. So moved, they howled with joy or the release of some buried pain. They collapsed, some rigid as corpses, some convulsed in hysterical laughter. From room to room come barnyard cries, calls heard only in the wild, grunts so deep women recalled the sounds of childbirth, while some men and women adopted the very position of childbirth. Men did chicken walks. Women jabbed their fingers as if afflicted with nervous disorders. And around these scenes of bedlam, were loving arms to catch the falling, smiling faces, whispered prayers of encouragement, instructions to release, to let go.[101]

Speaking of the descent of the Holy Spirit, Roman Bilas, Moscow head of the Union of Pentecostal Christians of Evangelical Faith, says passionately,

This moment when you really feel God's power in yourself brings so much peace and joy within you. It transforms you and society. There comes a sense of total

forgiveness for your sins, and the ability in you to forgive others. At that moment, you start to speak in different languages, maybe such that no one can understand.

We may also receive the gift of prophecy. . . . We check to see if the message is consistent with the Bible. If it is, then we will listen. Otherwise, the person is told not to speak publicly because he would create confusion in the Church.

The main thing is that the person should be filled with God's Power. A nice-looking car will not move unless it is fueled. God's Power will only fill those who are pure. That is why in the early Church people went into the wilderness to fast and repent. Then God could fill them with His Power. Each sermon should have this Power of God; then the people will really listen and repent of their sins.[102]

Cultural broadening

Although contemporary Christianity was largely shaped in Europe and its North American colonies, a large percentage of the Christian Church lies outside these areas. It has great numerical strength and vigor in Africa, Latin America, and parts of Asia.

As missionaries spread Christianity to these regions, they often assumed that European ways were culturally superior to indigenous ways and peoples. But some of these newer Christians have come to different conclusions. Theologians of the African Independent Churches, for instance, reject the historical missionary efforts to divorce them from their traditions of honoring their ancestors. This effort tore apart their social structure, they feel, with no scriptural justification:

As we became more acquainted with the Bible, we began to realise that there was nothing at all in the Bible about the European customs and Western traditions that

Roman Catholic procession of the eucharist, including veneration of Mary, mother of Jesus, in a Kunama village, Eritrea, Africa.

we had been taught. What, then was so holy and sacred about this culture and this so-called civilisation that had been imposed upon us and was now destroying us? Why could we not maintain our African customs and be perfectly good Christians at the same time? . . .

We have learnt to make a very clear distinction between culture and religion. . . . [For instance], the natural customs of any particular nation or race must never be confused with the grace of Jesus Christ our Saviour, Redeemer and Liberator.[103]

Contemporary perceptions of Jesus have been deeply enriched by those from the inhabitants of poor Third World countries who have brought personal understanding of Jesus's ministry to the outcasts and downtrodden. In Asia, where Christians are usually in the minority, there is an emphasis on a Christ who is present in the whole cosmos and who calls all people to sit at a common table to partake of his generous love. In Latin America, Jesus is viewed as the liberator of the people from political and social oppression, from dehumanization, and from sin. In Africa, the African Independent Churches have brought indigenous traditions of drumming, dancing, and singing into community worship of a Jesus who is seen as functioning as the greatest of ancestors—a mediator carrying prayers and offerings between humans and the divine, and watchful caretaker of the people.

Liberation theology

Although many Christians make a distinction between the sacred and the secular, some have involved themselves deeply with social issues as an expression of their Christian faith. For instance, the Baptist preacher, Martin Luther King, Jr. (1929–1968), became a great civil rights leader, declaring: "It was Jesus of Nazareth that stirred the Negroes to protest with the creative weapon of love."[104] This trend is now called **liberation theology**, a faith that stresses the need for concrete political action to help the poor. Beginning in the 1960s with Vatican II and the conference of Latin American bishops in Colombia in 1968, Roman Catholic priests and nuns serving in Latin America began to make conscious, voluntary efforts to understand and side with the poor in their struggles for social justice. A biblical basis for this approach is found in the Acts of the Apostles:

The group of believers was one in mind and heart. No one said that any of his belongings was his own, but they all shared with one another everything they had. . . . There was no one in the group who was in need. Those who owned fields or houses would sell them, bring the money received from the sale and turn it over to the apostles; and the money was distributed to each one according to his need.[105]

The Peruvian theologian Gustavo Gutierrez (b. 1928), who coined the expression "theology of liberation," explains the choice of voluntary poverty as:

a commitment of solidarity with the poor, with those who suffer misery and injustice. . . . It is not a question of idealizing poverty, but rather of taking it on as it is—an evil—to protest against it and to struggle to abolish it.[106]

RELIGION IN PUBLIC LIFE

Archbishop Desmond M. Tutu

During the years of struggle against apartheid in South Africa, one voice that refused to be silenced was that of the Anglican Archbishop of Cape Town, Desmond Mpilo Tutu (b. 1931). Afterward, he served his country as Chairperson of the Truth and Reconciliation Commission, "looking a beast in the eye" to investigate abuses from all sides that were perpetrated during the apartheid era. In this capacity, he still refused to mute his criticisms of those wielding power, no matter what their race and stature. In 1995 he proclaimed,

> The so-called ordinary people, God's favourites, are sick and tired of corruption, repression, injustice, poverty, disease and the violation of their human rights. They are crying out "enough is enough!" It is exhilarating when you are able to say to dictators everywhere: You have had it! You have had it! This is God's world and you will bite the dust! They think it will not happen but it does, and they bite the dust comprehensively and ignominiously.
> 'We will want to continue to be the voice of the voiceless. It is the role of the church to be the conscience of society.[107]

The "Arch's" fearless stance on behalf of truth and justice for the oppressed earned him the Nobel Peace Prize in 1984. He confronted not only those in power but also those who sought change through violence and those in the Church who witnessed the horrors of apartheid but kept silent. He explains, "Our task is to be agents of the Kingdom of God, and this sometimes requires us to say unpopular things."[108]

The former archbishop feels that faith requires one to be actively engaged in politics because government affects the people, but at the same time to remain independent of political factionalism in order to freely stand for truth. He says of the link between religion and politics:

> Faith is a highly political thing. At the centre of all that we believe as Christians is the incarnation— the participation of God in the affairs of this world.

> As followers of that God we too must be politically engaged. We need inner resources, however, in order to face the political demands of our time.[109]

How has Archbishop Tutu developed his inner resources? Through meditation, prayer, and fasting. He observes the traditional daily devotions of the Anglican Church, always starts meetings with prayer, and annually takes a long spiritual retreat. He regularly prays for others, and many are also praying for him; he asserts that intercessory prayer has practical effects. His spiritual confessor, Francis Cull, describes Archbishop Tutu's inner life as rooted in the Benedictine monastic discipline that underlies Anglican spirituality. He explains:

> As I ponder on the prayer life of Desmond Tutu I see the three fundamental Benedictine demands that there shall be: rest, prayer, and work and in that order. It is a remarkable fact, and it is one reason at least why he has been able to sustain the burdens he has carried, that he has within him a stillness and a need for quiet solitude. ... The "rest" of which St. Benedict speaks is not a mere switching off; it is a positive attempt to fulfill the age-old command to rest in God. ... The pattern of Jesus which he follows here: "Come apart and rest awhile," is an urgent need for all those who are caught up in the busyness of church and world.[110]

Desmond Tutu himself insists that spiritual practice is essential in order to know and follow the will of God:

> God's will has to do with what is right, just, decent and healing of the wounds of society. To know what this means we need to cleanse ourselves of ourselves—of our fears, greed, ambitions and personal desires. ... We must be vigilant in ensuring that the good that is within all people triumphs over the evil that is also there. ... We must commit ourselves to tell the truth. We must identify evil wherever we see it.[111]

For liberation theologians, the message of the gospel often entails down-to-earth physical help to the poor. Maryknoll lay sisters Norma Jejia, Julia Mamani, and Delia Gamboa are here lending a hand to the families of a Peruvian barrio.

For their sympathetic siding with those who are oppressed, Catholic clergy have been murdered by political authorities in countries such as Guatemala. They have also been strongly criticized by conservatives within the Vatican. Cardinal Ratzinger, who heads the Congregation for the Doctrine of the Faith, has decried liberation theology. He says that it inappropriately emphasizes liberation from material poverty rather than liberation from sin. The movement has nevertheless spread to all areas where there is social injustice. Bakole Wa Ilunga, Archbishop of Kananga, the Democratic Republic of Congo (formerly Zaire), reminds Christians that Jesus warned the rich and powerful that it would be very difficult for them to enter the kingdom of heaven. By contrast, writes Ilunga:

Jesus liberates the poor from the feeling that they are somehow less than fully human; he makes them aware of their dignity and gives them motives for struggling against their lot and for taking control of their own lives.[112]

Taking control is not easy for those who are oppressed minorities. In the United States, the church offers the large African-American community of Christians a way of developing an alternative reality in the midst of poverty, urban violence, and discrimination. As theologian Dwight Hopkins observes,

The black community has a long tradition of practicing faith as a total way of life. … Within worship, especially, the church is noted for its uplifting preaching, singing, shouting, dancing, and recognition of individual achievements and pain. … The rituals of individual healing and celebration serve to recharge the worshipers' energy to deal with the rigors and racism of a 'cruel, cruel world' from Monday through Saturday. … In addition, the church has functioned as the practical organizing center of all major aspects of group life. … Truly, black faith is public talk about God and the human struggle for a holistic salvation, liberation, and the practice of freedom.[113]

The practical activities of the Black Church range from building shelters and arranging jobs to treatment for addiction, campaigns against police brutality, voter registration drives, and leadership training. Even without social empowerment, people often feel inwardly empowered and cherished by the presence of Jesus in their lives.

Despite the vibrancy of the liberation theology movement, racism has not been eradicated in Christianity. Pioneering Black theologian James H. Cone proclaims that it is time to end the silence over this issue. Rather, he claims, "The challenge for Black theology in the twenty-first century is to develop an enduring race critique that is so comprehensively woven into Christian understanding that no one will be able to forget the horrible crimes of white supremacy in the modern world."[114]

Feminist theology

The issue of taking control of one's life and defining one's identity has also been taken up by feminists within the Christian Church. The Church institution has historically been dominated by men, although there is strong evidence that Jesus had active women disciples and that there were women leaders in the early churches. Reconstructing their history in the early Christian movement and the effects of patriarchical domination is a task being addressed by considerable in-depth scholarship at present. The effect of the apostle Paul in shaping attitudes toward women as he guided the developing Christian communities is one area of particular concern. Some of the statements attributed to him in the biblical Epistles seem oppressive to women; some seem egalitarian. He argues, for

In Bristol, England, newly ordained priest Reverend Susan Shipp blesses the sacramental offerings of bread and wine during her first service.

example, that men should pray or prophesy with their head uncovered but that women should either wear a veil or have their hair cut off:

> *For a man ought not to have his head veiled, since he is the image and reflection of God; but woman is the reflection of man. Indeed, man was not made from woman, but woman from man. Neither was man created for the sake of woman, but woman for the sake of man. . . . Nevertheless, in the Lord woman is not independent of man or man independent of woman. For just as woman came from man, so man comes through woman; but all things come from God.*[115]

Many contemporary scholars are trying to sort out the cultural and historical as well as the theological contexts of such statements. Elisabeth Schüssler Fiorenza, for example, explains:

> *I argue that women were not marginal in the earliest beginnings of Christianity; rather, biblical texts and historical sources produce the marginality of women. Hence texts must be interrogated not only as to* what they say *about women but also* how they construct what they say *or do not say.*[116]

Another area of feminist theological scholarship is the role models for women offered by the Bible. A central female figure in the New Testament is Mary, mother of Jesus. Ivone Gebara and Maria Clara Bingemer of Brazil look at Mary from the perspective of "the great masses of Latin America, the overwhelming majority of whom are poor, enjoy no adequate quality of life, and lack respect, bread, love, and justice." While acknowledging that the dogmas developed by the Catholic Church about Mary may be inflated, they nonetheless reveal a well-spring of hope for women and other oppressed humans:

> *The exaltation that understandably comes out in dogma cannot . . . hide what is essential in God's salvation, that is, making God's glory shine on what is regarded as insignificant, degrading or marginal. . . . In exalting her they exalt precisely her poverty, her dispossession, and her simplicity. This is the only key for understanding the mystery of God's incarnation in human history, of which Jesus and Mary are the protagonists. This is, moreover, the only key for understanding the mystery of the church as a community of salvation, holy and sinful, striving amid the most diverse kinds of limitations and problems to be a sign of the Kingdom in the midst of the world.*[117]

A third major area of Christian feminist theology is the concept of God. The Divine is commonly referred to as "He" or "Father," but scholarship reveals that this patriarchal usage is not absolute; there also existed other models of God as Mother, as Divine Wisdom, as Justice, as Friend, as Lover. Sally McFague points out that to envision God as Mother, for instance, totally changes our understanding of our relationship to the Divine:

> *What the father-God gives us is redemption from sins; what the mother-God gives is life itself, . . . not primarily judging individuals but calling us back, wanting to be more fully united with us. . . . All of us, female and male, have the womb as our first home, all of us are born from the bodies of our mothers, all of us are fed by our mothers. What better imagery could there be for expressing the most basic reality of existence: that we live and move and have our being in God?*[118]

Creation-centered Christianity

Another current trend in Christianity is an attempt to develop and deepen its respect for nature. In the Judeo-Christian tradition, humans are thought to have been given dominion over all the things of the earth. Sometimes this "dominion" was interpreted as the right to exploit, rather than the duty to care for, the earth. This view contrasts with indigenous beliefs that the divine resides everywhere, that everything is sacred, and that humans are only part of the great circle of life. Some Christians now feel that the notion of having a God-given right to control has allowed humans to nearly destroy the planet. In some cases, they are turning to indigenous spiritual leaders for help in extricating the planet from ecological destruction. Historian and passionate earth-advocate Father Thomas Berry feels that "we need to put the Bible on the shelf for twenty years until we learn to read the scripture of life."[119]

A Christianity that would accord greater honor to the created world would also tend to emphasize the miracle that is creation, thus helping to unite science and religion. Creation-centered Christians—such as the late Jesuit priest and paleontologist Teilhard de Chardin—see the mind of God in the perfect, intricate balances of chemistry, biology, and physics that allow life as we know it to exist. Jyoti Sahi, an Indian Roman Catholic who grew up in a natural mountainous environment and spent years in reflection at Christian ashrams, notes that by its earth-dominating strategy the modern world has lost touch with natural processes such as the turn of the seasons. This in turn has affected our spirituality:

> We notice that this loss of the seasons has entered into the very pattern of our inner prayer life, as the demands of a culture that is no longer part of the rhythm of nature eats away at all those natural periods of rest and prayerfulness that characterized the life of even the busiest farmer. . . .
>
> Prayer helps us to create a kind of cosmology whereby our immediate world of physical experience is recreated as a microcosm of a whole universe of inner experience. In this way work, as physical or manual effort, becomes a spiritual discipline that opens the way for an inner vision.[120]

Ecumenical movement

The restoration of religious freedom to multitudes of Christians in formerly communist countries increases the great diversity of Christian ways of worshipping. Another contemporary trend is the attempt to unify all Christians around some point of agreement or at least fellowship with each other.

Vatican II asserted that the Roman Catholic Church is the one Church of Christ, but opened the way to dialogue with other branches of Christianity by declaring that the Holy Spirit was active in them as well. The Orthodox Church likewise believes that it is the "one, holy, Catholic, and Apostolic Church." Although it desires reunion of all Christians and denies any greed for organizational power, it insists on uniformity in matters of faith. Orthodox and Roman Catholic Churches therefore do not share Holy Communion with those outside their respective disciplines. Some Protestant denominations have branches that also refuse to acknowledge each other's validity.

There are, however, attempts to restore some bonds among all Christian Churches. There are dozens of official ecumenical dialogues going on. The World Council of Churches, centered in Geneva, was founded in 1948 as an organizational body allowing Christian Churches to cooperate on service projects even in the midst of their theological disagreements. Its Faith and Order Commission links three hundred culturally, linguistically, and politically, not to mention theologically, different Christian Churches in working out the problems of Christian unity.

As Christians around the world struggled to find an appropriate Christian response to the September 11, 2001 terrorist attacks on the United States, the World Council of Churches announced a "Decade to Overcome Violence." They proposed that the members would be using this decade as:

- *an opportunity to discover afresh the meaning of sharing a common humanity, to confirm our commitment to the unity of all God's people and to the ministry of reconciliation*
- *a call to repent for our own complicity in violence, and explore, from within our faith traditions, ways to overcome the spirit, logic and practice of violence*
- *a forum in which to work together for a world of peace with local communities, secular movements, and people of other faiths*
- *a time to analyse and expose different forms of violence and their interconnection, and to act in solidarity with those who struggle for justice and the integrity of creation.*[121]

Suggested reading

Abbott, Walter M., ed., *The Documents of Vatican II*, New York: The America Press, 1966. Landmark conclusions of the Council Fathers, with special emphasis on the poor, religious unity, and social justice.

Borg, Marcus, J., *Meeting Jesus Again for the First Time: The Historical Jesus and the Heart of Contemporary Faith*, San Francisco: HarperSanFrancisco, 1994. An accessible and appreciative discussion of the Jesus of history, as opposed to the Jesus of faith, by a leading figure in the Jesus Seminar.

Bainton, Roland Herbert, *Christianity*, New York: Houghton Mifflin, 2000. A contemporary survey of Christian history.

Braybrooke, Marcus, *The Explorer's Guide to Christianity*, London: Hodder & Stoughton, 1998. With the sensitivity of a global interfaith leader, Rev. Braybrooke offers a succinct introduction to Christianity for people of every faith and country.

Dawes, Gregory W., ed., *The Historical Jesus Quest: A Foundational Anthology*, Westminster John Knox Press, 2000. A collection of scholarly investigations into the life of Jesus.

Dillenberger, John and Welch, Claude, *Protestant Christianity Interpreted through its Development*, New York: Charles Scribner's Sons, 1954. The classic history and interpretation of Protestantism.

Fernando, Antony, *Christianity Made Intelligible*, Eldeniya, Kadawata, Sri Lanka: Intercultural Book Promoters, 1990. A usefully concise and yet sensitive portrayal of Christianity for both Christians and people of other faiths.

Fosdick, Harry Emerson, ed., *Great Voices of the Reformation*, New York: Random House, 1952. Extensive quotations, with commentary, from major early Protestant leaders.

Hopkins, Dwight N., ed., *Black Faith and Public Talk*, Maryknoll, New York: Orbis Books, 1999. Taking off from James H. Cone's influential *Black Theology and Black Power*, these essays probe how people of color relate Christian understanding to economic, social, and religious situations and ideals in today's world.

King, Ursula, ed., *Feminist Theology from the Third World: A Reader*, Maryknoll, New York: Orbis Books, 1994. Excellent compendium of the voices of marginalized peoples, which give a special poignance and depth of meaning to efforts to give women a voice in shaping and interpreting Christianity.

Pope-Levison, Priscilla and Levison, John R., *Jesus in Global Contexts*, Louisville, Kentucky: Westminster/John Knox Press, 1992. Examinations of the question "Who is Jesus?" from poor cultures and feminist perspectives.

Price, James L., *Interpreting the New Testament*, second edition, New York: Holt, Rinehart and Winston, 1971. An excellent survey of the literature and interpretation of the New Testament.

Robinson, James M., ed., *The Nag Hammadi Library*, San Francisco: Harper & Row, 1977. A fascinating collection of early scriptures that are not included in the Christian canon.

Schüssler Fiorenza, Elisabeth, *In Memory of Her: A Feminist Theological Reconstruction of Christian Origins*, New York: Crossroad, 1983, 1994. Extensive scholarship about the role of women in early Christianity.

Theissen, Gerd, *The Religion of the Earliest Churches: Creating a Symbolic World*, Minneapolis, Minnesota: Fortress Press, 1999. An excellent survey of the emergence of Christian religion that emphasizes the development and diversity of early Christian myth, ethics, and ritual in their socio-historical contexts.

Tugwell, Simon, *Ways of Imperfection*, London: Darton, Longman and Todd, 1984, and Springfield, Illinois: Templegate Publishers, 1985. Spirituality as a whole vision of life, as seen by a series of great Christian practitioners.

Walker, Williston, Norris, Richard A., Lotz, David W., and Handy, Robert T., *A History of the Christian Church*, fourth edition, New York: Charles Scribner's Sons, 1985, and Edinburgh: T&T Clark, 1986. A classic history of Christianity.

Ware, Timothy, *The Orthodox Church*, Middlesex, England and Baltimore, Maryland: Penguin Books, 1984, 1993. An excellent overview of the history, beliefs, and practices of the Eastern Church.

CHAPTER 5
ISLAM
"There is no god but God"

In about 570 CE, a new prophet was born. This man, Muhammad, is considered by Muslims to be the last of a continuing chain of prophets who have come to restore the true religion. They regard the way revealed to him, Islam, not as a new religion but as the original path of monotheism, which also developed into Judaism and Christianity.

After carrying the torch of civilization in the West while Europe was in its Dark Ages, in the twentieth century Islam began a great resurgence. It is now the religion of nearly one-fifth of the world's people. Its monotheistic creed is simple: "There is no god but God, and Muhammad is his Messenger." Its requirements of the faithful are straightforward, if demanding. But beneath them lie profundities and subtleties of which non-Muslims are largely unaware. Glimmers of appreciation for the faith are just beginning to appear outside Islam, partly as sincere Muslims attempt to counteract negative media portrayals of their religion.

The Prophet Muhammad

Islam, like Christianity and Judaism, traces its ancestry to the patriarch Abraham. Isma'il (Ishmael) was said to be the son of Abraham and an Egyptian slave, Hagar. When Abraham's wife, Sarah, also bore him a son (Isaac), Abraham took Isma'il and Hagar to the desert valley of Becca (Mecca) in Arabia to spare them Sarah's jealousy.

The sacred book of Islam, the Holy Qur'an, received as a series of revelations to Muhammad, relates that Abraham and Ishmael together built the holiest sanctuary in Islam, the Ka'bah. It was thought to be the site of Adam's original place of worship; part of the cubic stone building is a venerated black meteorite. According to the Qur'an, God told Abraham that the Ka'bah should be a place of pilgrimage. It was regarded as a holy place by the Arabian tribes.

According to Islamic tradition, the region sank into historical oblivion as it turned away from Abraham's monotheism. For many centuries, the events of the rest of the world passed it by, aside from contact through trading caravans. Then into a poor clan of the most powerful of the tribes in the area was born a child named Muhammad ("the praised one"). His father died before he was born, and after the death of his mother and then his grandfather, Muhammad became the ward of his uncle, who put him to work as a shepherd.

Allah (God) is *the* focus in Islam, the sole authority, not Muhammad. But

The Ka'bah in Mecca is Islam's holiest place of worship.

Muhammad allegedly undertook spiritual retreats in this cave on Mount Hira outside Mecca. It was here that he received the first revelations of the Qur'an.

ISLAM

CE	
500	
	c.570 Birth of Prophet Muhammad
600	c.610 Revelation of the Qur'an to Prophet Muhammad begins 622 The *hijrah* (migration) from Mecca to Medina 630 Prophet Muhammad's triumphant return to Mecca 632 Death of Prophet Muhammad; election of Abu Bakr as first caliph 650 Written text of the Qur'an established 661–750 Umayyad dynasty 680 Karbala massacre of Husayn, grandson of the Prophet, and his relatives
700	732 European advance of Islam stopped at Battle of Tours 750–1258 Islam reaches its cultural peak under Abbasid caliphs
800	
900	922 al-Hallaj killed
1000	
1100	1058–111 Life of al-Ghazali
1200	1187 Salah-al-Din recaptures Jerusalem from Crusaders
1300	
1400	
1500	1453 Turks conquer Constantinople, renaming it Istanbul 1478–1834 Spanish Inquisition 1492 Surrender of Grenada, last foothold of Islam in Spain 1556 Akbar becomes Mogul emperor in India
1600	
1700	
1800	1800s–1900s Muslim areas fall under European domination
1900	1947 Partition of Muslim Pakistan from Hindu India 1970s Oil-rich Muslim states join OPEC and Muslim resurgence begins
2000	2001 Muslim terrorists fly aircraft into US buildings; Muslims face counter-attacks

Muhammad's life story is important to Muslims, for his character is considered a model of the teachings in the Qur'an. The stories of Muhammad's life and his sayings are preserved in a vast, not fully authenticated literature called the **Hadith**, which reports on the Prophet's **Sunnah** (sayings and actions). When he was a teenager, on a trip to Syria with his uncle, Muhammad was noticed by a Christian monk who identified marks on his body indicating his status as a prophet. As a young man, Muhammad managed caravans for a beautiful, intelligent, and wealthy woman named Khadijah. When she was forty and Muhammad was twenty-five, she offered to marry him. Khadijah became Muhammad's strongest supporter during the difficult and discouraging years of his early mission.

With Khadijah's understanding of his spiritual propensities, Muhammad began to spend periods of time in solitary retreat. These retreats were not uncommon in his lineage. They were opportunities for contemplation, away from the world.

When Muhammad was forty years old, he made a spiritual retreat during the month called Ramadan. An angel in human-like form, Gabriel, reportedly came to him and insisted that he recite. Three times Muhammad demurred that he could not, for he was unlettered, and three times the angel forcefully commanded him. In desperation, Muhammad at last cried out, "What shall I recite?" and the angel began dictating the first words of what became the Qur'an:

Proclaim! (or Recite!)
In the name
Of thy Lord and Cherisher,
Who created—
Created man, out of
A (mere) clot
Of congealed blood:
Proclaim! And thy Lord
Is Most Bountiful,—
He Who taught
(The use of) the Pen,—
Taught man that
Which he knew not.[1]

Muhammad returned home, deeply shaken. Khadijah comforted him and encouraged him to overcome his fear of the responsibilities and ridicule of prophethood. The revelations continued intermittently, asserting the theme that it was the One God who spoke and who called people to Islam (which means complete, trusting surrender to God). According to tradition, Muhammad described the form of these revelations thus:

Revelation sometimes comes like the sound of a bell; that is the most painful way.
When it ceases I have remembered what was said. Sometimes it is an angel who
talks to me like a human, and I remember what he says.[2]

The Prophet shared these revelations with the few people who believed him: his wife, Khadijah; his young cousin, 'Ali; his friend, the trader Abu Bakr; and the freed slave, Zayd.

After three years, Muhammad was instructed by the revelations to preach publicly. He was ridiculed and stoned by the Qurayshites, the aristocrats of his tribe who operated the Ka'bah as a pilgrimage center and organized profitable trading caravans through Mecca. While Muhammad was somewhat protected by the influence of his uncle, his followers were subject to persecution. A dark-skinned Abyssinian slave named Bilal, who was among the first converts, was imprisoned and brought out daily under the hot sun, pinned to the ground with a heavy stone on his chest, and ordered to deny the Prophet and worship the old gods. He staunchly refused, saying, "One, one." Once bought by the Prophet's friend Abu Bakr, Bilal became the first **muezzin** (one who calls the people to prayer from a high place), illustrating the Prophet's discarding of racial and social class distinctions. Finally, according to some accounts, Muhammad and his followers were banished for three years to a desolate place where they struggled to survive by eating wild foods such as tree leaves.

The band of Muslims was asked to return to Mecca, but the persecution by the Qurayshites continued. Muhammad's fiftieth year, the "Year of Sorrows," was the worst of all: he lost his beloved wife Khadijah and his protective uncle. With his strongest backers gone, persecution of the Prophet increased.

According to tradition, at the height of his trials, Muhammad experienced the Night of Ascension. He is said to have ascended through the seven heavens to the far limits of the cosmos, and thence into the Divine Proximity. There he met former prophets and teachers from Adam to Jesus, saw paradise and hell, and received the great blessings of the Divine Presence.

Pilgrims to Mecca from Yathrib, an oasis to the north, recognized Muhammad as a prophet. They invited him to come to their city to help solve its social and political problems. Still despised in Mecca as a potential threat by the Qurayshites, Muhammad and his followers left Mecca secretly. Their move to Yathrib, later called al-Medina ("The City [of the Prophet]"), was not easy. The Prophet left last,

Faithful Muslims pray five times a day, no matter where they are. The prayer rug provides a sacred precinct from which one can turn toward Mecca, the center of the faith.

accompanied (according to some traditions) by his old friend Abu Bakr. To hide from the pursuing Meccans, it is said that they took refuge in a cave, where the Prophet taught his friend the secret practice of the silent remembrance of God.

This **hijrah** (migration) of Muslims from Mecca to Medina took place in 622 CE. The Muslim era is calculated from the beginning of the year in which this event took place, for it marked the change from persecution to appreciation of the Prophet's message.

In Medina, Muhammad drew up a constitution for the city of Yuthrib/Medina that later served as a model for Islamic social administration. The departure of Muslims from Mecca was viewed with hostility and suspicion by the leaders of Mecca. Their assumption was that Medina had become a rallying point for ene-mies of the Meccans who, under Muhammad's leadership, would eventually attack and destroy Mecca. To forestall this, Mecca declared war on Medina, and a period of open conflict between the two cities followed.

Although representations of humans, including himself, were forbidden by the Prophet to avoid idolatry, Persian artists later gave imaginative expression to Muslim stories, such as the Miraj, *or Ascension, of the Prophet. (*Ascent of the Prophet Muhammad to Heaven, *by Aqa Mirak, 16th century, Persia.)*

Muhammad himself directed the first raid against a Meccan caravan on its return journey. The battle between Muslim emigrants and Meccans took place at Badr near Medina; the small group of Muslims was victorious.

According to the Qur'anic revelations, God had sent thousands of angels to help Muhammad. Furthermore, Muhammad threw a handful of pebbles at the Meccans and this turned the tide, for it was God who threw, and "He will surely weaken the designs of the unbelievers."[3] Enraged by the Islamic victory, Mecca made a surprise attack against Medina and routed the Muslims, injuring Muhammad and scattering the Islamic forces. Within two years, Mecca had mounted a much larger force, including cavalry and numerous archers, for a siege intended to subdue Medina permanently. Warned by spies, the Muslims defended Medina with a large trench encircling the city. Unable to press their attack, the Meccans were forced to retreat. Rather than continue hostilities, Muhammad negotiated a truce between the two warring cities.

The Qur'anic revelations to Muhammad emphasize the basic religious unity of Jews, Christians, and Muslims, members of the same monotheistic tradition of Abraham. But most of the Jews of Medina refused to accept Islam, because it recognized Jesus and claimed to complete the Torah. In addition, they were politically allied to those who opposed the Prophet. Eventually, their farms were appropriated by increasing numbers of Muslim converts, and some Jews were killed as political opponents. The Qur'an taught that the Jews and Christians had distorted the pure monotheism of Abraham; Muhammad had been sent to restore and supplement the teachings of the apostles and prophets. He was instructed to have the people face Mecca rather than Jerusalem during their prayers.

In 630 CE the Prophet returned triumphant to Mecca with such a large band of followers that the Meccans did not resist. The Ka'bah was purged of its idols, and from that time to the present it has been the center of Muslim piety. Acquiescing to Muhammad's political power and the Qur'anic warnings about the dire fate of those who tried to thwart God's prophets, many Meccans converted to Islam. Muhammad declared a general amnesty, and his former opponents were reportedly treated leniently.

The Prophet then returned to Medina, which he kept as the spiritual and political center of Islam. From there, campaigns were undertaken to spread the faith. In addition to northern Africa, the Persian states of Yemen, Oman, and Bahrain came into the fold. As the multi-cultural, multi-racial embrace of Islam evolved, the Prophet declared that the community of the faithful was more important than the older tribal identities that had divided people. The new ideal was a global family, under God. In his "Farewell Sermon," Muhammad stated, "You must know that a Muslim is the brother of a Muslim and the Muslims are one brotherhood."[4]

In the eleventh year of the Muslim era, Muhammad made a final pilgrimage to the Ka'bah to demonstrate the rites that were to be followed thenceforth. After his return to Medina, he became very ill. As he recognized that the end was near, he gave final instructions to his followers, promising to meet them at "the Fountain" in Paradise. Muhammad died in 632 CE. He left no clear instructions as to who should succeed him. In the circumstances that followed Muhammad's death, his steadfast friend Abu Bakr was elected the first **caliph** (successor to the Prophet). Another possible successor was the trustworthy and courageous 'Ali, the Prophet's cousin and husband of his favorite daughter, Fatima. Tradition has

TEACHING STORY

The Humility of the Prophet

The Prophet Muhammad's followers had such reverence for him that they caught the very water dripping from his arms when he did his ablutions, in order to rub it on themselves as a blessing. But he himself was so humble that he asked for God's forgiveness at least seventy times a day.

Once the Prophet asked his companions to prepare goat's meat for the group as they were traveling. One said he would kill the goat; another said he would skin it; another volunteered to cook it. The Prophet said he would gather the wood for the fire. His companions immediately protested: "You are God's Messenger. We will do everything." "I know you would," said the Prophet, "but that would be discrimination. God does not want His servants to behave as if they were superior to their companions."

When the Prophet was the recognized head of Medina, he borrowed some money from Zaid ibn Sana'a. Several days before the repayment of the loan, Zaid came to the Prophet, grabbed his clothes, and roughly demanded his money, saying, "Your relatives are always late in paying their debts." Umar, the Prophet's supporter, voiced his outrage and prepared to manhandle the moneylender. The Prophet merely said to Zaid, "Three days remain for the fulfillment of my obligation." He reserved his strong words for Umar: "You should have treated us both better. You should have told me to be better at repaying my debts, and you should have told him to be better at demanding payment. Pay him the amount due and give him 40 kilograms extra of dates as compensation for the alarm that you have caused him."

it that the Prophet Muhammad actually transferred his spiritual light to Fatima before his death, but that in the midst of funeral arrangements, neither she nor 'Ali participated in the selection of the first caliph. The Shi'ite faction would later claim 'Ali as the legitimate heir.

Muhammad's own life has continued to be very precious to Muslims, and it is his qualities that a good Muslim tries to emulate. He always denied having any superhuman powers, and the Qur'an called him "a human being like you," just "a servant to whom revelation has come," and "a warner."[5] The only miracle he ever claimed was that, though unlettered, he had received the Qur'anic revelations in extraordinarily eloquent and pure Arabic. He did not even claim to be a teacher—"God guides those whom He will,"[6] he was instructed to say—although Muslims consider the Prophet the greatest of teachers.

Nevertheless, all who saw the Prophet remarked on his touching physical beauty, his nobility of character, the fragrance of his presence, his humility, and his kindness. In his devotion to God, he quietly endured poverty so extreme that he tied a stone over his stomach to suppress the pangs of hunger. He explained, "I eat as a slave eats, and sit as a slave sits, for I am a slave (of God)." Although the Qur'an says that the Prophet is the perfect model for humanity, the purest vehicle for God's message, he himself perpetually prayed for God's forgiveness. When he was asked how best to practice Islam, he said, "The best Islam is that you feed the hungry and spread peace among people you know and those you do not know."[7]

Muhammad's mystical experiences of the divine had not led him to forsake the world as a contemplative. Rather, according to the Qur'an, the mission of Islam is to reform society, to actively combat oppression and corruption, "inviting to all that is good, enjoining what is right, and forbidding all that is wrong."[8] The Prophet's task—which Muslims feel was also undertaken by such earlier prophets as Moses and Abraham—is not only to call people back to faith but also to create a just moral order in the world as the embodiment of God's commandments.

The Qur'an

The heart of Islam is not the Prophet but the revelations he received. Collectively they are called the Qur'an ("reading" or "reciting"). He received the messages over a period of twenty-three years, with some later messages replacing earlier ones. At first they were striking affirmations of the unity of God and the woe of those who did not heed God's message. Later messages also addressed the organizational needs and social lives of the Muslim community.

After the *hijrah*, Muhammad heard the revelations and dictated them to a scribe; many of his companions then memorized them. They are said to have been carefully safeguarded against changes and omissions. Recited, the passages have a lyrical beauty and power that Muslims believe to be unsurpassed; these qualities cannot be translated. The recitation is to be rendered in what is sometimes described as a sad, subdued tone, because the messages concern God's sadness at the waywardness of the people. Muhammad said, "Weep, therefore, when you recite it."[9]

Reading the Qur'an in Java.

Recitation of the Qur'an is thought to have a healing, soothing effect, but can also bring protection, guidance, and knowledge, according to Islamic tradition. It is critical that one recite the Qur'an only in a purified state, for the words are so powerful that the one who recites it takes on a great responsibility. Ideally, one learns the Qur'an as a child, when memorization is easiest and when the power of the words will help to shape one's life.

During the life of the Prophet, his followers attempted to preserve the oral tradition in writing as an additional way of safeguarding it from loss. The early caliphs continued this effort until a council was convened by the third caliph around 650 CE to establish a single authoritative written text. This is the one still used. It is divided into 114 *suras* (chapters). The first is the **Fatiha**, the opening sura, which reveals the essence of the Qur'an:

In the name of God, Most Gracious, Most Merciful.
Praise be to God,
The Lord of the Worlds;
Most Gracious, Most Merciful;
Master of the Day of Judgment.
Thee do we worship,
And Thine aid we seek.
Show us the straight way,
The way of those on whom
Thou has bestowed Thy Grace
Those whose portion
Is not wrath,
And, who go not astray.

The verses of the Qur'an are terse, but are thought to have multiple levels of meaning. Translator and commentator Abdullah Yusuf Ali notes that in the mystical early passages there are often three layers: (1) a reference to a particular person or situation; (2) a spiritual lesson; and (3) a deeper mystical significance. He offers interpretation of these three levels in the first two verses of Sura 74 ("O thou wrapped up / [In a mantle]! / Arise and deliver thy warning!"):

As to 1, the Prophet was now past the stage of personal contemplation, lying down or sitting in his mantle; he was now to go forth boldly to deliver his Message and publicly proclaim the Lord ... As to 2, similar stages arise in a minor degree in the life of every good man, for which the Prophet's life is to be a universal pattern. As to 3, the Sufis understand, by the mantle and outward wrappings, the circumstances of our phenomenal existence, which are necessary to our physical comfort up to a certain stage; but we soon outgrow them, and our inner nature should then boldly proclaim itself.[10]

The Qur'an makes frequent mention of figures and stories from Jewish and Christian sacred history, all of which is considered part of the fabric of Islam by Muslims. Islam is the original religion, according to the Qur'an. Submission has existed as long as there have been humans willing to submit. Adam was the first prophet. Abraham was not exclusively a Jew nor a Christian; he was a monotheistic, upright person who had surrendered to Allah. Jesus was a very great prophet.

Muslims believe that the Jewish prophets and Jesus all brought the same messages from God. However, the Qur'an teaches that God's original messages have been added to and distorted by humans. For instance, Muslims do not accept the idea developed historically in Christianity that Jesus has the authority to pardon or atone for our sins. The belief that this power lies with anyone except God is considered a blasphemous human interpolation into what Muslims understand as the basic and true teachings of all prophets of the Judeo-Christian-Islamic tradition: belief in one God and in our personal moral accountability before God on the Day of Judgment. In the Muslim view, the Qur'an was sent as a final corrective in the continuing monotheistic tradition. Muslims, citing John 14:16, 26 from the Christian New Testament, believe that Jesus prophesied the coming of Muhammad when he promised that the **Paraclete** (advocate) would come to assist humanity after him.

The Qur'an revealed to Muhammad is understood as a final and complete reminder of the prophets' teachings, which all refer to the same God. For example, in Sura 42, Muhammad is told:

> Say: "I believe in whatever Book Allah has sent down; and I am commanded to judge justly between you. Allah is our Lord and your Lord! For us is the responsibility for our deeds, and for you for your deeds. There is no contention between us and you. Allah will bring us together, and to Him is our final goal."[11]

The central teachings

On the surface, Islam is a very straightforward religion. Its teachings can be summed up very simply, as in this statement by the Islamic Society of North America:

> Islam is an Arabic word which means peace, purity, acceptance and commitment. As a religion, Islam calls for complete acceptance of the teachings and guidance of God.
>
> A Muslim is one who freely and willingly accepts the supreme power of God and strives to organize his life in total accord with the teachings of God. He also works for building social institutions which reflect the guidance of God.[12]

This brief statement can be broken down into a number of articles of faith.

The Oneness of God and of humanity

The first sentence chanted in the ear of a traditional Muslim infant is the **Shahadah**—"La ilaha ill-Allah Muhammad-un Rasulu-llah" ("There is no god but God, and Muhammad is the Messenger of God"). Exoterically, the Shahadah supports absolute monotheism. As the Qur'an reveals in Sura 2:163,

> Your God is One God:
> There is no god but He,
> Most Gracious, Most Merciful.

Esoterically, the Shahadah means that ultimately there is only one Absolute Reality; the underlying essence of life is eternal unity rather than the apparent

Muslims express their belief in the Oneness of the divine by saying the Shahadah ("There is no god but God, and Muhammad is the Messenger of God"), the sentence emblazoned on this Turkish plaque.

separateness of things in the physical world. Muslims think that the Oneness of God is the primordial religion taught by all prophets of all faiths. Muhammad merely reminded people of it.

It has been estimated that over ninety percent of Muslim theology deals with the implications of Unity. God, while One, is referred to by ninety-nine names. These are each considered attributes of the One Being, such as *al-Ali* ("The Most High") and *ar-Raqib* ("The Watchful"). Allah is the name of God that encompasses all the attributes. Each of the names refers to the totality, the One Being.

Unity applies not only to the conceptualization of Allah, but also to every aspect of life. In the life of the individual, every thought and action should spring from a heart and mind intimately integrated with the divine. Islam theoretically rejects any divisions within itself; all Muslims around the globe are supposed to embrace as one family. All humans, for that matter, are a global family; there is no one "chosen people," for all are invited into a direct relationship with God. Science, art, and politics are not separate from religion in Islam. Individuals should never forget Allah; the Oneness should permeate their thoughts and actions. Abu Hashim Madani, an Indian Sufi sage, is said to have taught: "There is only one thing to be gained in life, and that is to remember God with each breath; and there is only one loss in life, and that is the breath drawn without the remembrance of God."[13]

> "The 'remembrance of God' is like breathing deeply in the solitude of high mountains: here the morning air, filled with purity of the eternal snows, dilates the breast; it becomes space and heaven enters our heart."
>
> *Frithjof Schuon*[14]

Prophethood and the compass of Islam

Devout Muslims feel that Islam encompasses all religions. Islam honors all prophets as messengers from the one God:

> *Say ye: We believe*
> *In God, and the revelation*
> *Given to us, and to Abraham,*
> *Isma'il, Isaac, Jacob,*
> *And the Tribes, and that given*
> *To Moses and Jesus, and that given*
> *To (all) Prophets from their Lord:*
> *We make no difference*
> *Between one and another of them:*
> *And we bow to God in surrender.*[15]

Muslims believe that the original religion was monotheism, but that God sent prophets from time to time as religions decayed into polytheism. Each prophet came to renew the message, in a way specifically designed for his culture and time. Muhammad, however, received messages meant for all people, all times. The Qur'anic revelations declared him to be the "Seal of the Prophets," the last

Farid Esack

Although Farid Esack is known as one of the world's most brilliant young Muslim scholars, his life has not been spent only in poring through books and speaking to intellectuals. On the contrary, he grew up as a victim of apartheid in South Africa and was active in the resistance that has led to the liberation of South Africa's oppressed peoples. Farid remembers running to school in bare feet to avoid frostbite, for often he had no shoes. His family was so poor that they had to beg for food and search through gutters for bits of food. Farid observes:

When you live in poverty and isolation, one of the things you hold on to is religion for your sanity, to keep you going. When you hear people crying in suffering and pain, instead of asking, "Where is God?", this is God crying out to you, "Why are you allowing this?"[16]

Thus it was not only poverty that drove Farid to risk his life again and again to build resistance to apartheid policies. It was also his deep commitment to Islam. He understands his religion as a mandate for struggling against injustice in society. He explains:

I was strangely and deeply religious as a child, with a deep concern for the suffering which I experienced and witnessed all around me. I dealt with these two impulses by holding on to an indomitable belief that for God to be God, God had to be just and on the side of the marginalized. More curious was a logic, based on a text in the Qur'an, "If you assist Allah then He will assist you and make your feet firm" (47:7). For me this meant that I had to participate in a struggle for freedom and justice and, if I wanted God's help in this, then I had to assist Him.[17]

Muslims constituted only 1.32 percent of the population of South Africa, and yet in 1984 Farid and three friends founded the Call of Islam as an affiliate of the United Democratic Front, the major liberation movement. The Call of Islam was very active in organizing resistance to apartheid, gender inequality, environmental destruction, and tensions between religions. At last, after years fraught with danger, Farid found himself in a queue of the rural poor, armed with a ballot and a pencil to cast his vote for a freely elected government. He mused:

I thought of the pain our country had endured in its long march to freedom, the loneliness of exile, of detention without trial, the political murders, the dispossession, the sighs of the tired and the exploited factory and farm workers, the months of living on the run like a fugitive, the attacks by police dogs, the clandestine pamphleteering . . . all for a single mark with a cheap little lead pencil![18]

Earlier, he had said at public meetings,

"Can you imagine that we are the generation responsible for the death of apartheid; that we are going to slay the monster of racial arrogance; that we are going to be the first South Africans in 350 years who are going to live in a non-racial, non-sexist and democratic homeland?" Difficult as it was to sustain this belief at times, we did it.[19]

Farid embodies and wrestles with the tensions between having full faith in one's own religion and keeping one's heart open to people of other faiths. During the freedom struggle and later in other struggles against "the madness of humankind in our day and age,"[20] Farid has often found himself working side by side with people of different religions. He is trying to show through intense Muslim scholarship that if a person of another religion is righteous, just, and God-fearing, he or she should be accepted by Muslims as a *mu'min* (believer), not a *kafir* (non-believer). In this context, he cites the Qur'anic Sura 8:2–4:

Indeed, the mu'minun [believers] are those whose hearts tremble with awe whenever God is mentioned; and whose iman [faith, belief] is strengthened whenever His ayat [signs] are conveyed unto them; and who place their trust in their Sustainer. Those who are constant in prayer and spend on others out of what We provide for them as sustenance. It is they who are truly the mu'minun.

Having served as a member of South Africa's Gender Equality Commission, Farid concludes:

In the Last Judgment, I will not be asked whether I succeeded or not. It is not our task to solve the problems of the world. We will only be asked what we did with the gifts He gave us. In Islam and in the Christian Gospels, it is said that God will ask you on the Day of Judgment, "When I was hungry, why did you not feed Me?"[21]

and ultimate authority in the continuing prophetic tradition. The prophets are mere humans; none of them is divine, for there is only one Divinity.

Islam is thought to be the universal religion in its pure form. All scriptures of all traditions are also honored, but only the Qur'an is considered fully authentic, because it is the direct, unchanged, untranslated word of God. Whatever exists in other religions that agrees with the Qur'an is divine truth.

Human relationship to the divine

> *We are nearer to [a person] than his jugular vein.*
>
> *The Holy Qur'an, Sura 50:16*

In Muslim belief, God is all-knowing and has intelligently created everything for a divine purpose, governed by fixed laws that assure the harmonious and wondrous working of all creation. Humans will find peace only if they know these laws and live by them. They have been revealed by the prophets, but the people often have not believed. To believe is to surrender totally to Allah. As the Qur'an states,

> *None believes in Our revelations save those who, when reminded of them, prostrate themselves in adoration and give glory to their Lord in all humility; who forsake their beds to pray to their Lord in fear and hope; who give in charity of that which We have bestowed on them. No mortal knows what bliss is in store for these as a reward for their labors.*[22]

The Qur'an indicates that human history provides many "signs" of the hand of God at work bestowing mercy and protection on believers. Signs such as the great flood, which was thought to have occurred at the time of Noah, illustrate that non-believers and evil-doers ultimately experience great misfortune in this life or the afterlife. None is punished without first being warned by a messenger of God to mend his or her ways. Creation itself is a sign of God's compassion, as well as of God's omnipotent will.

According to Islam, the two major human sins involve one's relationship to God. One is **shirk** (associating anything else with divinity except the one God). The Qur'an instructs,

> *Say: "Oh People of the book!*
> *Come to common terms as between us and you:*
> *That we worship none but Allah;*
> *That we associate no partners with Him;*
> *That we erect not from among ourselves*
> *Lords and patrons other than Allah."*[23]

In other words, in Islam's pure monotheism one is enjoined not to worship anything but God—not natural forces, or mountains, or stones, or incarnations of God, or lesser deities, or human rulers. Idol-worship is vigorously denounced, as is worship of natural phenomena: "Adore not the sun nor the moon, but adore Allah Who created them."[24]

The other major sin is **kufr** (ungratefulness to God, unbelief, atheism).

Furthermore, a major human problem is forgetfulness of God. God has mercifully sent us revelations as reminders. The veils that separate us from God come from us, not from God; Muslims feel that it is ours to remove the veils by seeking God and acknowledging the omnipresence, omniscience, and omnipotence of the Divine. For the orthodox, the appropriate stance is a combination of love and fear of God. Aware that God knows everything and is all-powerful, one wants to do everything one can to please God, out of both love and fear. This paradox was given dramatic expression by the Caliph 'Umar ibn al-Khattab:

> If God declared on the Day of Judgment that all people would go to paradise except one unfortunate person, out of His fear I would think that I am that person. And if God declared that all people would go to hell except one fortunate person, out of my hope in His Mercy I would think that I am that fortunate person.[25]

The unseen life

Muslims believe that our senses do not reveal all of reality. In particular, they believe in the angels of God. These are non-physical beings of light who serve and praise God day and night. They are numerous, and each has a specific responsibility. For instance, certain angels are always with each of us, recording our good and bad deeds. The Qur'an also mentions archangels, including Gabriel, highest of the angelic beings, whose main responsibility is to bring revelations to the prophets from God. But neither he nor any other angel is to be worshipped, according to strict monotheistic interpretation of Islam, for the angels are simply utterly submissive servants of God. By contrast, according to Islamic belief, there is a non-submissive being called Satan. He was originally one of the **jinn**—immaterial beings of fire, whose nature is between that of humans and angels. He proudly refused to bow before Adam and was therefore cursed to live by tempting Adam's descendants—all of humanity, in other words—to follow him rather than God. According to the Qur'an, those who fall prey to Satan's devices will ultimately go to hell.

Popular Muslim piety also developed a cult of saints. The tombs of mystics known to have had special spiritual powers have become places of pilgrimage. Many people visit them out of devotion and desire for the blessings of the spirit, which is thought to remain in the area. This practice is frowned upon by some reformers, who assert that Muslim tradition clearly forbids worship of any being other than God.

The Last Judgment

In the polytheistic religion practiced by Arabs before Muhammad, the afterlife was only a shadow, without rewards or punishments. People had little religious incentive to be morally accountable. By contrast, the Qur'an emphasizes that after a period of repose in the grave, all humans will be bodily resurrected and assembled for a final accounting of their deeds. At that unknown time of the Final Judgment, the world will end cataclysmically: "The earth will shake and the mountains crumble into heaps of shifting sand" (Sura 73:14). Then comes the terrible confrontation with one's own life:

According to Muslim belief, angels are everywhere; they come to our help in every thought and action. A group of angels is here shown helping the 8th-century Sufi ascetic, Ibrahim ibn Adham.

The works of each person We have bound about his neck. On the Day of Resurrection, We shall confront him with a book spread wide open, saying, "Read your book."[26]

Hell is the grievous destiny of unrepentant non-believers—those who have rejected faith in and obedience to Allah and His Messenger, who are unjust and who do not forbid evil. Hell also awaits the hypocrites who even after making a covenant with Allah have turned away from their promise to give in charity and to pray regularly:

It is a flaming Fire. It drags them down by their scalps; and it shall call him who turned his back and amassed riches and covetously hoarded them.[27]

Muslim piety is ever informed by this belief in God's impartial judgment of one's actions, and of one's responsibility to remind others of the fate that may await them.

Basically, Islam says that what we experience in the afterlife is a revealing of our tendencies in this life. Our thoughts, actions, and moral qualities are turned into our outer reality. We awaken to our true nature, for it is displayed before us. For the just and merciful, the state after death is a Garden of Bliss. Those who say, "Our Lord is God ... shall have all that your souls shall desire. ... A hospitable gift from One Oft-Forgiving, Most Merciful!" (Sura 41:30–32). The desire of the purified souls will be for closeness to God, and their spirits will live in different levels of this closeness. For them, there will be castles, couches, fruits, sweet-meats, honey, houris (beautiful virgin women), and immortal youths serving from goblets and golden platters. Such delights promised by the Qur'an are inter-preted metaphorically to mean that human nature will be transformed in the next life to such an extent that the disturbing factors of this physical existence will no longer have any effect.

> *People are asleep, but when they die, they wake up.*
> *Hadith of the Prophet Muhammad*

By contrast, sinners and non-believers will experience the torments of hell, fire fueled by humans, boiling water, pus, chains, searing winds, food that chokes, and so forth. It is they who condemn themselves; their very bodies turn against them "on the Day when their tongues, their hands, and their feet will bear witness against them as to their actions" (Sura 24:24). The great medieval mystic al-Ghazali speaks of spiritual torments of the soul as well: the agony of being separated from worldly desires, burning shame at seeing one's life projected, and terrible regret at being barred from the vision of God. Muslims do not believe that hell can last forever for any believer, though. Only the non-believers will be left there; the others will eventually be lifted to paradise, for God is far more merciful than wrathful.

The Sunni–Shi'a split

The preceding pages describe beliefs of all Muslims, although varying interpret-ations of these beliefs have always existed. Groups within Islam differ somewhat on other issues. After Muhammad's death, resentments over the issue of his suc-cession began to divide the unity of the Muslim community into factions. The two main opposing groups have come to be known as the **Sunni**, who now comprise about eighty percent of all Muslims worldwide, and the **Shi'a** (adj. Shi'ite).

As discussed earlier, a caliph was elected to lead the Muslim community after Muhammad's death. The office of caliph became a lifetime appointment. The first three caliphs, Abu Bakr, Umar, and Uthman, were elected from among the Prophet's closest companions. The fourth caliph was 'Ali, the Prophet's cousin and son-in-law. He was reportedly known for his holy and chivalrous qualities, but the dynasty of Umayyads never accepted him as their leader, and he was assassinated by a fanatic who was a former member of his own party. 'Ali's son Husayn, grandson of the Prophet, challenged the legitimacy of the fifth caliph, the Umayyad Mu'awiyya. When Mu'awiyya designated his son Yazid as his successor, Husayn rebelled and was massacred in 680 by Yazid's troops in the desert of Karbala along with many of his relatives, who were also members of the Prophet's own family. This martyrdom unified Shi'ite opposition to the elected successors and they broke away, claiming their own legitimate line of succession through the direct descendants of the Prophet, beginning with 'Ali. The two groups are still separate.

Sunnis

Those who follow the elected caliphs are "the people of the Sunnah" (the sayings and practices of the Prophet, as collected under the Sunni caliphs). They consider themselves traditionalists, and they emphasize the authority of the Qur'an and the Hadith and Sunnah. They believe that Muhammad died without appointing a successor and left the matter of successors to the **ummah**, the Muslim community. They look to the time of the first four "rightly guided caliphs" (Abu Bakr, Umar, Uthman, and 'Ali) as the golden age of Islam. They regard the caliph as the leader of worship and the administrator of the **Shari'ah**, the sacred law of Islam.

The Shari'ah consists of teachings and practices for everything in Muslim life, from how to conduct a war to how to pray. Like the Torah for Jews, the Shari'ah sets the pattern for all individual actions and theoretically bonds them into a coherent, divinely regulated, peaceful community.

The Shari'ah is based chiefly on the Qur'an and Sunnah of Muhammad, who was the first to apply the generalizations of the Qur'an to specific life situations. Religion is not a thing apart; all of life is to be integrated into the spiritual unity that is the central principle of Islam. For example, the faithful are enjoined to be kind to their parents and kin, children and strangers, to protect orphans and women, to exercise justice and honesty in their relationships and business interactions, to stop killing infants, to manage their wealth carefully, and to avoid adultery and arrogance.

In the second century of Islam, the Abbasid dynasty replaced the Umayyads, who had placed more emphasis on empire-building and administration than on spirituality. At this point, there was a great concern for purifying and regulating social and political life in accord with Islamic spiritual tradition. Mechanisms for establishing the Shari'ah were developed. Since then, Sunnis have felt that as life circumstances change, laws in the Qur'an, Hadith, and Sunnah should be continually interpreted by a consensus of opinion and the wisdom of learned men and jurists. For example, a contemporary Muslim faces new ethical questions not specifically addressed in the Qur'an and Hadith, such as whether or not test-tube fertilization is acceptable (some think yes, on condition that the sperm is the father's and the egg the mother's). Divorce has always been addressed by the Shari'ah, but the conditions under which a wife may petition for divorce have been closely examined in recent years.

Shi'a

The Shi'a feel that 'Ali was the rightful original successor to the Prophet Muhammad. Several weeks before the death of the Prophet Muhammad, the Prophet reportedly took 'Ali's hand and said, "Whoever I protect, 'Ali is also his protector. O God, be a friend to whoever is his friend and an enemy to whoever is his enemy." This is construed by the Shi'a as a veiled way of designating 'Ali as his successor. They feel that spiritual power was passed on to 'Ali, and that the caliphate is based on this spiritual as well as temporal authority. They are ardently devoted to the memory of Muhammad's close relatives: 'Ali, Fatima (the Prophet's beloved daughter), and their sons Hasan and Husayn. The martyrdom of Husayn at Karbala in his protest against the alleged tyranny, oppression, and injustice of the Umayyad caliphs is held up as a symbol of the struggle against human oppression. It is commemorated yearly as 'Ashura, a memorial on the tenth day of the month of Muharram. Participants in mourning processions cry and beat their chests or, in some areas, offer cooling drinks to the populace in memory of the martyred Husayn. Shi'ite piety places great emphasis on the touching stories told of 'Ali and Husayn's dedication to truth and integrity, even if it leads to personal suffering, in contrast to the selfish power politics ascribed to their opponents.

Rather than recognize the Sunni caliphs, the Shi'a pay allegiance to a succession of seven or twelve **Imams** (leaders, guides). The first three were 'Ali, Hasan, and Husayn. According to a saying of the Prophet acknowledged by both Sunni and Shi'a:

> I leave two great and precious things among you: the Book of Allah and my Household. If you keep hold of both of them, you will never go astray after me.[28]

"Twelver" Shi'a believe that there were a total of twelve Imams, legitimate hereditary successors to Muhammad. The twelfth Imam, they believe, was commanded by God to go into an occult hidden state to continue to guide the people and return publicly at the Day of Resurrection as the Mahdi. A minority of the Shi'a, the Isma'ilis and "Seveners," recognize a different person as the seventh and last Imam, and believe that it is he who is hidden and still living. There must always be an Imam.

Unlike the Sunni caliph, the Imam combines political leadership (if possible) with continuing the transmission of Divine Guidance. This esoteric religious knowledge was given by God to Muhammad, from him to 'Ali, and thence from each Imam to the successor he designated from 'Ali's lineage. It includes both the outer and inner meanings of the Qur'an. The Shari'ah is therefore interpreted for each generation by the Imam, for he is closest to the divine knowledge.

Aside from the issue of succession to Muhammad, Sunnis and Shi'a are in general agreement on most issues of faith. The Shi'a follow the same essential practices as Sunnis, but, as discussed in a later section on spiritual practices, add several that express their ardent commitment to re-establishing what they see as the true spirit of Islam in a corrupt, unjust world.

Sufism

In addition to these two main groups within Islam, there is also an esoteric tradition, which is said to date back to the time of the Prophet. He himself was at once a political leader and a contemplative with a deep prayer life. He reportedly said that every verse of the Qur'an has both an outside and an inside. Around him were gathered a group of about seventy people. They lived in his Medina mosque in voluntary poverty, detached from worldly concerns, praying night and day. After the time of the first four caliphs, Muslims of this deep faith and piety, both Sunni and Shi'a, were distressed by the increasingly secular, dynastic, wealth-oriented characteristics of Muhammad's Umayyad successors. The mystical inner tradition of Islam, called **Sufism** (Arabic: *tasawwuf*), also involved resistance to the legalistic, intellectual trends within Islam in its early development.

Sufis have typically understood their way as a corrective supplement to orthodoxy. For their part, some orthodox Sunnis do not consider Sufis to be Muslims. Sufis consider their way a path to God that is motivated by longing for the One. In addition to studying the Qur'an, Sufis feel that the world is a book filled with "signs"—divine symbols and elements of beauty that speak to those who understand. The intense personal journeys of Sufis and the insights that have resulted from their truth-seeking have periodically refreshed Islam from within. Much of the allegorical interpretation of the Qur'an and devotional literature of Islam is derived from Sufism.

The early Sufis turned to asceticism as a way of deepening their piety. The Prophet had said: "If ye had trust in God as ye ought He would feed you even as He feeds the birds."[29] Muhammad himself had lived in poverty, reportedly gladly so. Complete trust in and surrender to God became an essential step in the journey. **Dervishes** (poor mendicant mystics) with no possessions, no attachments in the world, were considered holy people like Hindu *sannyasins*. But Sufi asceticism is based more on inner detachment than on withdrawal from the world; the ideal is to live with feet on the ground, head in the heavens.

Sufi dervishes enter a state of ecstatic unity with the divine by repeating the Shahadah.

To this early asceticism was added fervent, selfless love. Its greatest exponent was Rabi'a (c. 713–801). A famous mystic of Iraq, she scorned a rich man's offer of marriage, saying that she did not want to be distracted for a moment from God. All her attention was placed on her Beloved, which became a favorite Sufi name for God. Rabi'a emphasized disinterested love, with no selfish motives of hope for paradise or fear of hell. "I have served Him only for the love of Him and desire for Him."[30] Any other motivation is a veil between lover and Beloved. When no veils of self exist, the mystic dissolves into the One she loves.

> *The Beloved is all, the lover just a veil.*
> *The Beloved is living, the lover a dead thing.*
>
> *Jalal al-Din Rumi*[31]

In absolute devotion, the lover desires *fana*, total annihilation in the Beloved. This Sufi ideal was articulated in the ninth century CE by the Persian Abu Yazid al-Bistami. He is said to have fainted while saying the Muslim call to prayer. When he awoke, he observed that it is a wonder that some people do not die when saying it, overwhelmed by pronouncing the name Allah with the awe that is due to the One. In his desire to be annihilated in God, al-Bistami so lost himself that he is said to have uttered pronouncements such as "Under my garment there is nothing but God,"[32] and "Glory be to Me! How great is My Majesty!"

The authorities were understandably disturbed by such potentially blasphemous statements. Sufis themselves knew the dangers of egotistical delusions inherent in the mystical path. There was strict insistence on testing and training by a sufficiently trained, tested, and illumined **murshid** (teacher) or **shaykh** (spiritual master). Advanced practices were taught only to higher initiates. It was through the *shaykh* that the **barakah** (blessing, sacred power) was passed down, from the *shaykh* of the *shaykh*, and so on, in a chain reaching back to Muhammad, who is said to have transmitted the barakah to 'Ali.

A number of **tariqas** (esoteric orders) evolved, most of which traced their spiritual lineage back to Junayd of Baghdad (who died in 910 CE). He taught the need for constant purification, a continual serious examination of one's motives and actions. He also knew that it was dangerous to speak openly of one's mystical understandings; the exoteric-minded might find them blasphemous, and those who had not had such experiences would only interpret them literally and thus mistakenly. He counseled veiled speech, and much Sufi literature after his time is couched in metaphors accessible only to mystics.

Despite such warnings, the God-intoxicated cared little for their physical safety and exposed themselves and Sufism to opposition. The most famous case is that of Mansur al-Hallaj (c. 858–922). After undergoing severe ascetic practices, he is said to have visited Junayd. When the master asked, "Who is there?", his disciple answered, *"ana'l-Haqq"* ("I am the Absolute Truth," i.e., "I am God"). After Junayd denounced him, al-Hallaj traveled to India and throughout the Middle East, trying to open hearts to God. He wrote of the greatness of the Prophet Muhammad, and introduced into the poetry of divine love the simile of the moth that flies ecstatic into the flame and, as it is burned up, realizes Reality.

Political maneuverings made a possible spiritual revival a threat to authorities back home, and they imprisoned and finally killed al-Hallaj for his *"ana'l-*

Hajji Waris Ali Shah (1819–1905) of Deva Sharif near Lucknow, India, was a great shaykh revered by people of all religions. Understanding Islam as ideally encompassing every religion, he said, "All are equals in my eyes."

Haqq." Now, however, al-Hallaj is considered by many to be one of the greatest Muslim saints, for it is understood that he was not speaking in his limited person. Like the Prophet, who had reportedly said, "Die before ye die,"[33] al-Hallaj had already died to himself so that nothing remained but the One.

> *What's in your head—toss it away! What's in your hand—give it up! Whatever happens—don't turn away from it. . . . Sufism is the heart standing with God, with nothing in between.*
>
> *Abu Sa'id Abu al-Khayr[34]*

A more moderate Sufism began to make its way into Sunni orthodoxy through Abu Hamid al-Ghazali (1058–1111). He had been a prominent theologian but felt compelled to leave his prestigious position for a life of spiritual devotion. Turning within, he discovered mystical truths, which saved him from his growing skepticism about the validity of religion. Like mystics of all religions, he urged awareness of the certainty of death as an antidote to entanglements in worldly concerns:

Pilgrimage to the tombs of the Sufi saints is a popular form a piety. Women are not allowed to enter this tomb of a Chisti Sufi saint in Delhi, so they tie bits of fabric with their prayers to the grillework outside.

> *You do not normally sell two things for one; how can you give up an endless life for a limited number of days? . . . Suppose that death is near and say to yourself, "I shall endure the hardship today; perhaps I shall die tonight," . . . for death does not come upon us at a specified time or in a specified way or at a specified age; but come upon us he does, and so preparation for death is better than preparation for this world. You know that you remain here for only a brief space—perhaps there remains but a single day in your allotted span, perhaps but a single breath. Imagine this in your heart every day and impose upon yourself patience in obeying God daily.[35]*

Al-Ghazali's persuasive writings combined accepted Muslim theology with the assertion that Sufism is needed to keep the mystical heart alive within the tradition. By the fourteenth century, three sciences of religion were generally accepted by the orthodoxy: jurisprudence, theology, and mysticism.

Over the centuries, other elements have been added to Sufism. Some Sufis have embraced teachings from various religions, emphasizing that the Qur'an clearly states that the same Voice has spoken through all prophets. Shihabuddin Suhrawardi (1153–1191), for instance, combined many currents of Islam with spiritual ideas from the Zoroastrians of ancient Iran and the Hermetic tradition from ancient Egypt. His writings are full of references to the divine light and hierarchies of angels. We humans have descended from the angels and realms of light, he wrote; we are in exile here on earth, longing for our true home, searching for that radiant purity, dimly remembered, in this dark world of matter.

Although Sufi teachings and practices have been somewhat systematized over time, they resist doctrinal, linear specification. They come from the heart of mystical experiences which defy ordinary logic. Paradox, metaphor, the world of creative imagination, of an expanded sense of reality—these characteristics of Sufi thought are better expressed through poetry and stories. A favorite character in Sufi teaching tales is Mulla Nasrudin, the wise fool. An example, as told by Idries Shah:

> One day Nasrudin entered a teahouse and declaimed, "The moon is more useful than the sun." Someone asked him why. "Because at night we need the light more."[36]

These "jokes" boggle the mind, revealing the limitations of ordinary thinking at the same time that they offer flashes of metaphysical illumination for those who ponder their deeper significances.

Poetry has been used by Sufis as a vehicle for expressing the profundities and perplexities of relationship with the divine. The Turkish dervish Jalal al-Din Rumi (c. 1207–1273), by whose inspiration was founded the Mevlevi Dervish Order in Turkey (famous for its "Whirling Dervishes" whose dances lead to transcendent rapture), was a master of mystical poetry. He tells the story of a devotee whose cries of "O Allah!" were finally answered by God:

> Was it not I that summoned thee to service?
> Did not I make thee busy with My name?
> Thy calling "Allah!" was My "Here am I,"
> Thy yearning pain My messenger to thee.
> Of all those tears and cries and supplications
> I was the magnet, and I gave them wings.[37]

The aim of Sufism is to become so purified of self that one is a perfect mirror for the divine attributes. The central practice is called *dhikr*, or "remembrance." It consists of stirring the heart and piercing the solar plexus, seat of the ego, by movements of the head, while continually repeating *"la ilaha illa Allah,"* which Sufis understand in its esoteric sense: "There is nothing except God." Nothing in this ephemeral world is real except the Creator; nothing else will last. As the seventy thousand veils of self—illusion, expectation, attachment, resentment, egocentrism, discontent, arrogance—drop away over the years, this becomes one's truth, and only God is left to experience it.

The Five Pillars and jihad

While Sufism carries the inner practice of Islam, the outer practice is set forth in the Shari'ah, the straight path of the Divine Law. It specifies patterns for worship (known as the Five Pillars of Islam) as well as detailed prescriptions for social conduct, to bring remembrance of God into every aspect of daily life and practical ethics into the fabric of society. These prescriptions include injunctions against drinking intoxicating beverages, eating certain meats (including pork, rodents, predatory animals, certain birds, and improperly slaughtered animals), gambling and vain sports, sexual relations outside of marriage, and sexually provocative dress, talk, or actions. They also include positive measures, commanding justice, kindness, and charity. Women are given many legal rights, including the right to own property, to divorce (according to certain schools of law), to inherit, and to make a will. These rights divinely decreed during the time of the Prophet, fourteen hundred years ago, were not available to women in the West until the nineteenth century. Polygyny is allowed for men who have the means to support several wives, to bring all women under the protection of a husband. Women are allowed to inherit only half as much as men because men have the obligation to support women financially.

The Shari'ah is said to have had a transformative effect on Muhammad's community. Before Muhammad, the people's highest loyalty was to their tribe. Tribes made war on each other with no restraints. Women were possessions like animals. Children were often killed at birth either because of poverty or because they were females in a male-dominated culture. People differed widely in wealth. Drunkenness and gambling were commonplace. Within a short time, Islam made great inroads into these traditions, shaping tribes into a spiritual and political unity with a high sense of ethics.

A Muslim must do his or her best to fulfill the Five Pillars because they are considered God's commandments.

Belief and witness

The first pillar of Islam (the Shahadah) is believing and professing the unity of God and the messengership of Muhammad: "There is no god but God, and Muhammad is the Messenger of God." The Qur'an requires the faithful to tell others of Islam, so that they will have the information they need to make an intelligent choice. However, it rules out the use of coercion in spreading the message:

For one and a half weeks every year, a huge event is held in the Hadhramaut area of Yemen to praise the Prophethood.

AN INTERVIEW WITH KHALED ALY KHALED

Living Islam

Trained as a doctor of pharmacy, Khaled aly Khaled of Egypt did not appreciate his Muslim heritage when he was a child. He explains that his faith grew slowly as he became aware of the scientific accuracy and literary genius of the Qur'an.

"For a very long time in Egypt, we had the idea that it is better for you not to stick to a religion. If you stuck to a religion, people looked at you as just a fool. They thought there is a correlation between the success in the real life and the religion. If you have success in the real world, you didn't have to do these things that were religious. If you pray and fast and talk about Qur'an, the people start to think that you are not having any success.

"Ten years ago I could not even read Qur'an. So I started from the very end, very far from religion, but I am getting back to it. For me, maybe the most important thing is scientific interpretation of the Qur'an. I can just believe what I can see, what I can feel, and just try to make interpretation of what I can collect from data. I started to read about the planets and their movement, from the scientific point of view. It is hard to believe these kind of things come just from blind nature. But a Big Mind behind this system? I could not believe that. That's against the science. But it cannot come as an accident. If you change one part out of one hundred million parts, the whole universe will collapse. So you cannot be accurate unless you have some mind or some knowledge to control the whole thing.

"Now I'm sure that someone is behind the universe, is creating it, is creating me. You cannot feel the miracle of the universe unless you work in science. The human body cannot come from a primary cell reacting to another primary cell to create a creature from two cells and construct the body. It is beyond probability. Some supreme power created everything.

"Some of the statements in the Qur'an had no scientific verification at that time, fourteen hundred years ago, but now they have meaning. For example, 'We have created this universe and we have made it expanding.' 'We have made the earth look like an egg.' Such statements cannot come from just an average person living fourteen hundred years ago. Among ancient Egyptians, ancient Syrians, we cannot find this information. I started to believe that someone was giving the knowledge to Muhammad. I'm not a very good believer—don't ask me to believe just because there is a book. But this information cannot come from any source except One Source.

"As for the language of the Qur'an, scholars who speak Arabic have tried to write just one statement similar to this book in beauty. They could not. One computer scientist did a computer analysis of the Qur'an. He found that the number of chapters, the number of statements, and the number of times each letter is used are all multiples of nineteen (which is the number of angels in the Hellfire). Then he tried to see if he could write a book about any subject, using multiple numbers of any figure. No one could do it. The beauty of the Qur'an is pure, supreme.

"If you compare the speech of Muhammad to the Qur'an, there is a big difference in beauty. He himself cannot make even one statement like that. He cannot write, he doesn't have know-ledge, he just was taking care for the sheep. From this, I started to believe that there is a God."

Let there be [or: There is] no compulsion
In religion: Truth stands out
Clear from Error: whoever
Rejects Evil and believes
In God hath grasped
The most trustworthy
Hand-hold, that never breaks.[38]

The Qur'an insists on respect for all prophets and all revealed scriptures.

Daily prayers

The second pillar is the performance of a continual round of prayers. Five times a day, the faithful are to perform ritual ablutions with water (or sand or dirt if necessary), face Mecca, and recite a series of prayers and passages from the Qur'an, bowing and kneeling. Around the world, this joint facing of Mecca for prayer unites all Muslims into a single world family. When the prayers are recited by a congregation, all stand and bow shoulder to shoulder, with no social distinctions. In a mosque, women and men usually pray in separate groups, with the women in rows behind the men, to avoid sexually distracting the men. There may be an **imam**, or prayer-leader, but no priest stands between the worshipper and Allah. On Friday noon, there is usually a special prayer service in the mosque, but Muslims observe no Sabbath day. Remembrance of God is an everyday obligation; invoking the Name of Allah continually polishes the rust from the heart.

At a Muslim mosque, there are no social distinctions, as all worshippers line up shoulder to shoulder to pray together.

Repeating the prayers is thought to strengthen one's belief in God's existence and goodness and to carry this belief into the depths of the heart and every aspect of external life. Praying thus is also expected to purify the heart, develop the mind and the conscience, comfort the soul, encourage the good and suppress the evil in the person, and awaken in the believer the innate sense of higher morality and higher aspirations. The words of praise and the bowing express continual gratefulness and submission to the One. At the end, one turns to the two guardian angels on one's shoulders to say the traditional Muslim greeting—*"Assalamu Alaykum"* ("Peace be on you")—and another phrase adding the blessing, "and mercy of God."

While mouthing the words and performing the outer actions, one should be concentrating on the inner prayer of the heart. The Prophet reportedly said, "Prayer without the Presence of the Lord in the heart is not prayer at all."[39]

The Prophet's Mosque in Medina has been enlarged to allow room for over one million praying pilgrims.

Zakat

The third pillar is **zakat**, or spiritual tithing and almsgiving. At the end of the year, all Muslims must donate at least two and a half percent of their accumulated wealth to needy Muslims. This provision is designed to help decrease inequalities in wealth and to prevent personal greed. Its literal meaning is "purity," for it purifies the distribution of money, helping to keep it in healthy circulation.

Saudi Arabia devotes fifteen percent of its kingdom's GDP to development and relief projects throughout the world. The Islamic Relief Organization that it funds makes a point of helping people of all religions, without discrimination, where there is great need following disasters. Many stories from the life of the Prophet Muhammad teach that one should help others whether or not they are Muslims. For example, the Prophet's neighbor was Jewish. The Prophet reportedly gave him a gift every day, even though the neighbor daily left garbage at his door. Once the neighbor was sick, and the Prophet visited him. The neighbor asked, "Who are you to help me?" The Prophet replied, "You are my brother. I must help you."

In addition to *zakat*, the Shi'a are obligated to give one-fifth of their disposable income to the Imam. Because the Imam is now hidden, half of this now goes to the deputy of the Imam to be used however he thinks appropriate; the other half goes to descendants of the Prophet to spare them the humiliation of poverty.

Fasting

The fourth pillar is fasting. Frequent fasts are recommended to Muslims, but the only one that is obligatory is the fast during Ramadan, commemorating the first revelations of the Qur'an to Muhammad. For all who are beyond puberty, but not infirm or sick or menstruating or nursing children, a dawn-to-sunset abstention from food, drink, sexual intercourse, and smoking is required for the whole month of Ramadan.

Because Muslims use a lunar calendar of 354 days, the month of Ramadan gradually moves through all the seasons. When it falls in the summer, the period of fasting is much longer than in the shortest days of winter. The hardship of abstaining even from drinking water during these long and hot days is an unselfish surrender to God's commandment and an assertion of control over the lower desires. The knowledge that Muslims all over the world are making these sacrifices at the same time builds a special bond between haves and have-nots, helping the haves to experience what it is to be hungry, to share in the condition of the poor. Those who have are encouraged to be especially generous in their almsgiving during Ramadan.

Fasting is expected to allow the body to burn up impurities and provide one with "a Transparent Soul to transcend, a Clear Mind to think and a Light Body to move and act."[40] Many people feel that they are spiritually more sensitive and physically more healthy during Ramadan fasting, and they look forward eagerly to this period each year. It is believed that control of the body's desires also builds the mastery needed to control the lower emotions, such as anger and jealousy.

Hajj

The fifth pillar is **hajj**, the pilgrimage to Mecca. All Muslims who can possibly do so are expected to make the pilgrimage at least once in their lifetime. It involves a series of symbolic rituals designed to bring the faithful as close as possible to God. Male pilgrims wrap themselves in a special garment of unsewn cloths, rendering them all alike, with no class distinctions. The garment is like a burial shroud, for by dying to their earthly life they can devote all their attention to God. It is a time for *dhikr*, the constant repetition of the Shahadah, the remembrance that there is no god but God.

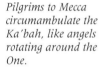

Pilgrims to Mecca circumambulate the Ka'bah, like angels rotating around the One.

1. Pilgrimage begins at the Great Mosque, with seven circumambulations of the Ka'bah

2. Pilgrims stop at Mina

3. They pray from noon to evening in the Arafat valley. The prophet Muhammad gave his last talk here

4. Pilgrims gather 49 stones

5. They throw their stones at three pillars which represent the devil. Three days of ritual sacrifice begin

6. They return to the Great Mosque and again circle the Ka'bah seven times

7. Pilgrims walk seven times between hills near the Great Mosque and then drink from the sacred spring Zum-Zum

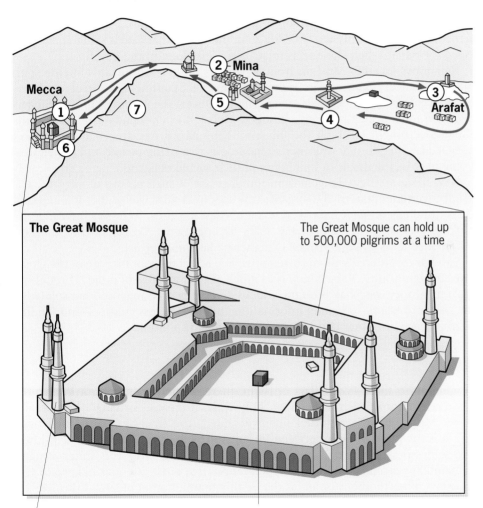

Mecca

Mina

Arafat

The Great Mosque

The Great Mosque can hold up to 500,000 pilgrims at a time

Seven minarets, 90 meters tall

The Ka'bah is a black stone 15 meters high, draped in black silk, engraved with the sacred names of Allah. Pilgrims walk around it seven times until they reach the center and touch the Ka'bah itself

The pilgrimage to Mecca.

Pilgrims walk around the ancient Ka'bah seven times, like the continual rotation around the One by the angels and all of creation, to the seventh heaven. Their hearts should be filled only with remembrance of Allah.

Another sacred site on the pilgrimage is the field of Arafat. It is said to be the place where Adam and Eve were taught that humans are created solely for the worship of God. Here pilgrims pray from noon to sunset to be forgiven of anything that has separated them from the Beloved. In addition, pilgrims carry out other symbolic gestures, such as sacrificing an animal and throwing stones at the devil, represented by pillars. The animal sacrifice reminds the *hajjis* of Abraham's willingness to surrender to God that which was most dear to him, his own son, even though in God's mercy he was allowed to substitute a ram for the sacrifice. Most of the meat is distributed to the needy, a service for which Saudi Arabia has had to develop huge preservation and distribution facilities. *Hajjis* also perform symbolic acts at the holy well of Zam-Zam, the spring that God is said to have provided for Hagar when she and Ishmael were left alone in the desert.

Hajj draws together Muslims from all corners of the earth for this intense spiritual experience. Because Islam is practiced on every continent, it is truly an international gathering. The crowds are enormous. During the month of the pilgrimage, over two million pilgrims converge upon Mecca. To help handle the crowds, the Saudi government has built the immense King Abdul Aziz International Airport near Jedda. The journey was once so hazardous that many people and camels died trying to cross the desert in fulfillment of their sacred obligation.

Now there are new dangers from the presence of such masses of pilgrims. The Saudi government has tried to organize the sites to avoid tragedies, but still in recent years hundreds of *hajjis* have died in stampedes and fires. To lessen the danger of cooking fires, the government has made arrangements for 10,000 fireproof air-conditioned tents and 600 trucks selling sealed fast-food meals.

Though considerably modernized now, *hajj* is still the vibrant core of the global Muslim community. To be a *hajji* is as much as ever a badge of pride. Throughout Muslim history, *hajj* has brought widely diverse people together, consolidating the center of Islam, spreading information and ideas across cultures, and sending pilgrims back into their communities with fresh inspiration.

Jihad

In addition to these Five Pillars of Islam, there is another important injunction: **jihad**. Commonly mistranslated as "holy war," it means "striving". The Greater Jihad, Muhammad is reported to have said, is the struggle against the lower self. It is the internal fight between wrong and right, error and truth, selfishness and selflessness, hardness of heart and all-embracing love. This inner struggle to maintain peaceful equilibrium is then reflected in outer attempts to keep society in a state of harmonious order, as the earthly manifestation of Divine Justice.

On the external level, the Lesser Jihad is exerting effort to protect the Way of God against the forces of evil. This jihad is the safeguarding of one's life, faith, livelihood, honor, and the integrity of the Muslim community. The Prophet Muhammad reportedly said that "the preferred jihad is a truth spoken in the presence of a tyrant."[41]

Jihad is not to be undertaken for personal gain. The Qur'anic revelations that apparently date from the Medina period when the faithful were being attacked by Meccans make it clear that

> To those against whom
> War is made, permission
> Is given (to fight), because
> They are wronged;—and verily,
> God is Most Powerful
> For their aid;
>
> (They are) those who have
> Been expelled from their homes
> In defiance of right,
> (For no cause) except
> That they say, "Our Lord
> Is God."[42]

The Qur'an gives permission to fight back under such circumstances, but also gives detailed limitations on the conduct of war and the treatment of captives, to prevent atrocities.

Muhammad is the prototype of the true **mujahid**, or fighter in the Path of God,

Forbidden to indulge in pictorial representation, Muslim artists lavished great devotion on elaborate calligraphy and decoration for the word of God, revealed in the Holy Qur'an. The illuminations express the luminous flowing outward from the Sacred Word.

one who values the Path of God more than life, wealth, or family. He is thought to have had no desire for worldly power, wealth, or prestige. By fasting and prayer, he continually exerted himself toward the One, in the Greater Jihad. In defending the Medina community of the faithful against the attacking Meccans, he was acting from the purest of motives. It is believed that a true *mujahid* who dies in defense of the faith goes straight to paradise, for he has already fought the Greater Jihad, killing his ego.

The absolute conviction that characterizes jihad derives from the recognition of the vast disparity between evil and the spiritual ideal, both in oneself and in society. Continual exertion is thought necessary in order to maintain a peaceful equilibrium in the midst of changing circumstances. Traditionalists and radicals have differed in how this exertion should be exercised in society.

In terms of the Lesser Jihad, support can be found in the Qur'an both for a pacifist approach and for active opposition to unbelievers. The Qur'an asserts that believers have the responsibility to defend their own faith as well as to remind unbelievers of the truth of God and of the necessity of moral behavior. In some passages, Muslims are enjoined simply to stand firm against aggression. For example, "Fight for the sake of Allah those that fight against you, but do not be aggressive. Allah does not love the aggressors."[43] In other passages, Qur'an suggests active opposition to people who do not believe in the supremacy of the one God:

> *Tumult and oppression are worse than slaughter.*
> *Nor will they cease fighting you*
> *Until they turn you back from your faith*
> *If they can. . . .*
> *Fight them on*
> *Until there is no more tumult or oppression*
> *And there prevail justice and faith in God.*[44]

The ultimate goal and meaning of Islam, and of jihad, is peace through devoted surrender to God. A peaceful society is like paradise. Sri Lankan Sufi Shaykh M. R. Bawa Muhaiyaddeen observes:

> *If one knows the true meaning of Islam, there will be no wars. All that will be heard are the sounds of prayer and the greetings of peace. Only the resonance of God will be heard. That is the ocean of Islam. That is unity. That is our wealth and our true weapon. Not the sword in your hand.*[45]

The spread of Islam

In the time of Muhammad, Islam combined spiritual and secular power under one ruler. This tradition, which helped to unify the warring tribes of the area, was continued under his successors. Islam expanded phenomenally during the centuries after the Prophet's death, contributing to the rise of many great civilizations. The ummah became a community that spread from Africa to Indonesia. Non-Muslims have the impression that it was spread by the sword, but this was not typically the case. The Qur'an forbids coercion in religion, recommending instead that Muslims invite others to the Way by their wisdom, beautiful

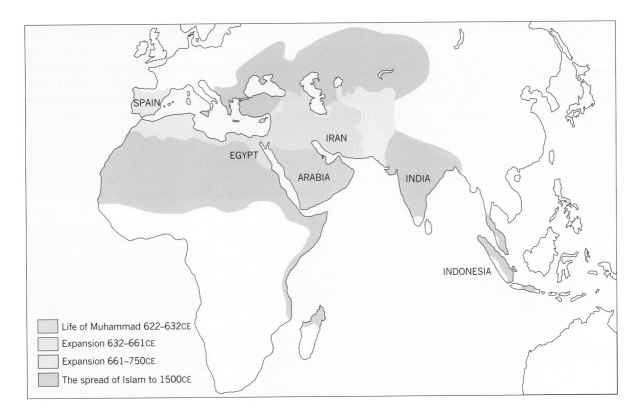

Life of Muhammad 622–632CE

Expansion 632–661CE

Expansion 661–750CE

The spread of Islam to 1500CE

teaching, and personal example. Islam spread mostly by personal contacts: trade, attraction to charismatic Sufi saints, appeals to Muslims from those feeling oppressed by Byzantine and Persian rule, unforced conversions. There were some military battles conducted by Muslims over the centuries, but they were not necessarily for the purpose of spreading Islam, and many Muslims feel that wars of aggression violate Muslim principles. Non-Muslim citizens of newly entered territories were asked to pay a poll tax entitling them to Muslim defense against enemies and exempting them from military service.

Muhammad's non-violent takeover of Mecca occurred only two years before he died. It was under his successors that Islam spread through what is commonly known today as the Middle East and far beyond. Only a year after Muhammad died, a newly converted Qurayshite, Khalid ibn al-Walid (d. 642), commanded a series of campaigns that within seven years had claimed the entire Arabian peninsula and Syria for Islam. Newly Islamic Arab armies quickly swept through the elegant Sassanian Persian Empire, which had stood for twelve centuries. Defeated in battle in 637 CE, the Persian emperor fled, leaving the capital in Arab hands. Within ten years of the Prophet's death, a mere 4,000 horsemen commanded by Amr ibn al-As took the major cities of Egypt, centers of the brilliant Byzantine Empire. Another wave of Islamization soon penetrated into Turkey and Central Asia, North Africa, and north through Spain, to be stopped in 732 CE in France at the battle of Tours. At this point, only a hundred years after Muhammad died, the Muslim *ummah* under the Umayyad caliphs was larger than the Roman Empire had ever been.

Only one hundred years after Muhammad's death, Islam had spread around the Mediterranean. Its diffusion continued for centuries and the numbers of converts are still increasing, making Islam the fastest growing religion today. Of areas previously converted to Islam, all remain Muslim except Spain, Greece and the Mediterranean islands.

Muslims cite the power of the divine will to establish a peaceful, God-conscious society as the reason why this happened. By contrast with their strong convictions, the populations they approached were often demoralized by border fighting among themselves and by grievances against their rulers. Many welcomed them without a fight. For example, the Christians of Damascus expected Muslim rule to be more bearable than Byzantine rule, so they opened the city gates to the Muslim armies. Jerusalem and Egypt accepted the Muslims in similar fashion. Syrian Christians at Shayzar under Byzantine rule reportedly went out to meet the Muslim commander and accompanied him to their city, singing and playing tambourines. In Spain, Visigoth rule and taxation had been oppressive; the persecuted Jews were especially glad to help Islam take over. Both Christians and Jews often converted to Islam.

Some historians cite economic factors as an underlying motive for Arabs' expansion beyond their original territory. Although Islamic civilization did become quite opulent, the central leadership did not always support the far-reaching adventures. The conquered peoples were generally dealt with in the humane ways specified in the Qur'an and modeled by Muhammad in his negotiations with tribes newly subjected to Muslim authority. The terms offered by Khalid to the besieged Damascans were these:

> *In the name of God, the merciful, the compassionate. This is what Khalid would grant the inhabitants of Damascus when he enters it. He shall grant them security for their lives, properties and churches. Their city wall shall not be demolished, neither shall any Moslem be quartered in their homes. Thereunto we give them the pact of God and the protection* (dhimmah) *of His Messenger, upon whom be God's blessing and peace, the caliphs and the Believers. So long as they pay poll-tax nothing but good shall befall them.*[46]

Monotheistic followers of revealed traditions, Christians and Jews, who like Muslims were "people of the book," were treated as **dhimmis**, or protected people. They were allowed to maintain their own faith, but not to try to convert others to it. The Dome of the Rock was built on the site of the old Temple of the Jews in Jerusalem, honoring Abraham as well as Muhammad in the city that is still sacred to three faiths: Judaism, Christianity, and Islam.

The Umayyad caliphs had their hands full administering this huge *ummah* from Damascus, which they had made its capital. They tended to focus more on organizational matters than on the spiritual life. Some were also quite worldly; Walid II, for example, is said to have enjoyed a pool filled with wine so that he could swim and drink at the same time. In 747 CE a rival to the caliphate is said to have invited eighty of the princes of the line to a banquet, where he had them all killed. Three years after "the bloodshedder," a new series of caliphs took over: the Abbasids. They held power until 1258 CE.

Islamic culture

Under the Abbasids, who took over the caliphate in 750 CE, Muslim rule became more Persian and cosmopolitan and Islamic civilization reached its peak. The capital was moved to the new city of Baghdad. No more territories were brought under centralized rule, and merchants, scholars, and artists became the cultural

heroes. A great House of Wisdom was built, with an observatory, a famous library, and an educational institution where Greek and Syriac manuscripts on subjects such as medicine, astronomy, logic, mathematics, and philosophy were translated into Arabic. In Cairo, Muslims built in 972 CE a great university and mosque, Al-Azhar, which still plays an important role in Muslim scholarship.

In its great cities, Islam went through a period of intense intellectual and artistic activity, absorbing, transmitting, and expanding upon the highest traditions of other cultures. For instance, from Persia, which was to become a Shi'ite stronghold, it adopted a thousand-year-old tradition of exquisite art and poetry. To these avid cultural borrowings Islam added its own innovations. The new system of nine Arabic numerals and the zero derived from Indian numbers revolutionized mathematics by liberating it from the clumsiness of Roman numerals. A love of geometry and a spiritual understanding of numbers, from the One to infinite divisions, provided the basis for beautifully elaborated art and architectural forms. Muslim philosophers were highly interested in Aristotelian and Neo-Platonic thought, but in their unique synthesis these intellectual ways were harmonized with revealed religion. Muslim scholars' research into geography, history, astronomy, literature, and medicine lifted these disciplines to unprecedented heights.

The pivotal institution of Islamic society was the **ulama**, whose primacy and

Dome in the Alhambra, Granada, an exquisite example of the heights to which architecture evolved in Muslim Spain.

influence was unchallenged. The *ulama* were not only guardians of the faith but were also the pervasive force holding together Islamic society. They were *qadis* (judges), *muftis* (jurisconsultants), guides and pastors of the artisans' guilds, spiritual leaders, mosque *imams*, the sole teachers of the civil and military schools, state scribes, and market inspectors. The major sources of their economic power and their independence from the state were religious endowments and private endowments, run and controlled by the *ulama*.

Although Baghdad was the capital of the Abbasids, independent caliphates were declared in Spain and Egypt. Muslim Spain was led by successors to the Umayyads and became a great cultural center. Cordoba, the capital, had seven hundred mosques, seventy libraries, three hundred public baths, and paved streets. Europe, by contrast, was in its Dark Ages; Paris and London were only mazes of muddy alleys.

Tunisia and Egypt comprised a third center of Islamic power: the Shi'ite Fatimid imamate (so named because they claimed to be descendants of Muhammad's daughter Fatima). Under the deranged Fatimid caliph, al-Hakim (985–c. 1021), the Fatimids broke with Islamic tradition and persecuted *dhimmis*; they also destroyed the Church of the Holy Sepulcher in Jerusalem, provoking European Christian crusades to try to recapture the Holy Lands.

Crusading Christians fought their way to Jerusalem, which they placed under a month-long siege in 1099. When the small Fatimid garrison surrendered, the crusaders slaughtered the inhabitants of the holy city. Eyewitnesses recount the beheading of seventy thousand captives at the el-Aqsa mosque, near the altar site of the ancient Jewish temple. Severed hands and feet were piled everywhere. Anti-crusading Muslims led by the famous Salah-al-Din (known in the West as Saladin) retook Jerusalem in 1187 and treated its Christian population with the generous leniency of Islam's highest ideals for the conduct of war. But widespread destruction remained in the wake of the crusaders, and a reservoir of ill-will against Christians lingered, to be exacerbated centuries later by European colonialism in Muslim lands.

The Islamic period in Spain was known for its tolerance of Judaism. But during the thirteenth century, Christians took Spain and later instituted the dread

Inquisition against those not practicing Christianity. By the beginning of the sixteenth century, an estimated three million Spanish Muslims had either been killed or had left the country.

Eastward expansion

Its westward advance stopped at Europe, Islam carried its vitality to the north, east, and south. Although Mongol invasions from Central Asia threatened, the Mongols were converted to Islam; so were the Turks. It is noteworthy that while Uzbek Khan, Mongol leader from 1313 to 1340, zealously desired to spread Islam throughout Russia, he nonetheless maintained tolerance toward the Christians in the conquered lands. He granted a charter to the Orthodox Metropolitan concerning the treatment of Christians: "Their laws, their Churches; their monasteries and chapels shall be respected; whoever condemns or blames this religion, shall not be allowed to excuse himself under any pretext but shall be punished with death."[47]

Similar tolerance toward other religions was practiced by the Muslim Turks, but in 1453 the Turks conquered Constantinople, the heart of the old Byzantine Empire, and renamed it Istanbul; Hagia Sophia was turned into a mosque even though it did not face Mecca. At its height, the Turkish Ottoman Empire dominated the eastern Mediterranean as well as the area around the Black Sea.

Farther east, Islam was carried into northern India, where Muslims destroyed many Hindu idols and temples but allowed the Hindu majority a protected *dhimmi* status. The Chishti Sufi saints drew people to Islam by their great love for God. "The heart of a mystic is a blazing furnace of love which burns and destroys everything that comes into it because no fire is stronger than the fire of love," declared Khwaja Muinuddin Chishti.[48]

Southern arch of the Taj Mahal, Agra, India, surrounded by verses from the Qur'an in fine marble inlay. From 1632 to 1654, the finest masons and twenty thousand laborers worked under the Mogul emperor Shah Jahan to create this mausoleum for his beloved wife, Mumtaz Mahal.

Under the Muslim Moguls, the arts and learning flourished in India. In the ecumenical spiritual curiosity of the Emperor Akbar, who rose to the Mogul throne in 1556, representatives from many traditions—Hindu, Zoroastrian, Jain, Christian—were invited to the world's first interfaith dialogues. Eventually Akbar devised a new religion that was a synthesis of Islam and all these other religions, with himself as its supposedly enlightened head, but it died with him, and Muslim orthodoxy returned.

Under British colonization of India, tensions between Hindus and Muslims were inflamed, partly to help Britain divide and rule. India gained its independence under the influence of Mahatma Gandhi, who was unable to end the enmity between the two faiths. In 1947, West and East Pakistan (now the independent nation of Bangladesh) were partitioned off to be Muslim-ruled and predominantly populated by Muslims, while India was to be run by Hindus. Millions lost their lives trying to cross the borders, and the strife between the two faiths continues. In December 1992, militant Hindus set off renewed communal violence by destroying a mosque in Ayodhya, India, in the belief that it had been built by the Moguls on the site of an ancient temple to Lord Rama.

The greatest concentration of Muslims developed even farther east, in Indonesia, where Muslim traders and missionaries may have first landed as early as the tenth century CE. About ninety percent of the people are now Muslim, but despite recent violence between Hindus and Muslims the government refuses to establish Islam as the state religion. In 1989, then-President Suharto stated: "We want each and all religions existing and developing in our country to achieve progress in an atmosphere of unity and mutual respect."[49] China and the former Soviet Union encompass tens of millions of Muslims.

To the south, Islam spread into Africa along lines of trade. In competition with Christianity, Islam sought the hearts of Africans and eventually won in many areas. Many converted to Islam; many others maintained some of their indigenous ways in combination with Islam. The prosperous Mali Empire was headed by a Muslim, who made an awe-inspiring pilgrimage to Mecca with a gold-laden retinue of 8,000 in 1324. As the spread of Islam encompassed an increasing diversity of cultures, *hajj* became important not only for individuals but also for the religion as a whole, holding its center in Mecca in the midst of worldwide variations.

Relationships with the West

Although Islam honors the prophets of all traditions, its own religion and prophet were denounced by medieval Christian Europe. Christianity had considered itself the ultimate religion and had launched its efforts to bring the whole world under its wings. Islam felt the same way about its own mission. In the struggle for souls, the Church depicted Muhammad as an idol-worshipper, an anti-Christ, the Prince of Darkness. Islam was falsely portrayed as a religion of many deities, in which Muhammad himself was worshipped as a god (thus the inaccurate label "Muhammadanism"). Europeans watched in horror as the Holy Lands became Muslim and the "infidel" advanced into Spain. Even though Muslim scholars and artists preserved, shared, and advanced the classic civilizations while Europe was benighted, the wealth of Arabic culture was interpreted in a negative light.

By the nineteenth century, Western scholars began to study the Arabic classics, but the ingrained fear and loathing of Muhammad and Muslims remained. The ignorance about, and negative stereotyping of, Muslims continues today. Western cartoonists, for instance, have inevitably drawn Muslims as wild-eyed radicals dressed in desert robes and brandishing scimitars. Annemarie Schimmel, Professor of Indo-Muslim Culture, Harvard University, explains:

The idea that the Muslims conquered everything with fire and sword was unfortunately deeply ingrained in the medieval mind. All these misconceptions about Islam as a religion and the legends and lies that were told about it are really unbelievable. I have often the feeling that this medieval image of Islam as it was perpetuated in ever so many books and even scholarly works is part of our subconscious. When someone comes and says, "But real Islam is something completely different," people just will not believe it because they have been indoctrinated for almost fourteen hundred years with the image of Islam as something fierce and something immoral. Unfortunately, some of the events of our century have revived this medieval concept of Islam.[50]

Borrow the Beloved's eyes. Look through them and you'll see the Beloved's
   face everywhere. . . .
Let that happen, and things you have hated will become helpers.

                              Jalal al-Din Rumi[51]

Although it had enjoyed great heights of culture and political power, the Muslim world fell into decline. It seems that the Mongol invasions were at least partly responsible, for they eradicated irrigation systems and libraries and killed scholars and scientists, erasing much of the civilization that had been built up over five hundred years. Some Muslims today feel that spiritual laxness was the primary reason that some of the previously glorious civilizations became impoverished Third World countries. Another theory is that Muslim culture was no longer dynamic. As it rigidified and stagnated, it was overwhelmed by cultures both less civilized than itself (the Monguls) and more civilized (the Europeans, who were becoming major world powers on the strength of their industrialization and colonizing navies).

During the late eighteenth and early nineteenth centuries, many Muslim populations fell under European domination. From the mid-twentieth century onward, most gained their independence as states that had adopted certain Western ideals and practices. In many cases, they had let go of some aspects of their Muslim heritage, considering it a relic that prevented them from success in the modern world. Arabic was treated as an unimportant language; Western codes of law had replaced the Shari'ah in social organization. But yet they were not totally Westernized, and they resumed local rule with little training for twentieth-century self-government and participation in a world economy dominated by industrial nations.

Societies that had been structured along traditional lines fragmented from the

Dome of the Rock, Jerusalem. In an area held sacred by Jews, Christians, and Muslims, the dome was completed in 692 as the first major Muslim monument. The rock had been associated with Abraham's sacrifice of his son. Muslim tradition identified it as the place of the Prophet Muhammad's ascension to heaven during his night journey.

mid-nineteenth century onward, as wide-ranging programs of reforms and modernization were unleashed throughout the Muslim world. The local autonomy of the traditional Islamic society was swept away and replaced by centralized regulations of Western origin. Traditional schools, markets, guilds, and courts into which the societies had been organized lost much of their reason for being.

Before the colonial forces moved out, foreign powers led by Britain helped to introduce a Jewish state in the midst of the Middle East. After long and terrible persecution in many countries, Jewish Zionists sought resettlement in what they considered their ancient homeland. But some historians allege that the chief motive of the countries supporting this claim was to protect European interests. Lord Palmerston of Britain suggested that a wealthy Jewish population transplanted to Palestine, and highly motivated to protect itself, would prop up the decaying Ottoman Empire so that it could serve as a bulwark against Russian imperialism; the new Jewish presence in Palestine would also serve as a check against the attempts of Egypt to create a pan-Islamic state encompassing Egypt, Syria, and the Arabian peninsula.

Islam in the United States

Even as Muslims were feeling humiliated by foreign domination elsewhere, they were growing in numbers and self-pride within the United States. Islam is the fastest growing religion in the United States, and may now be the second largest religion in the country. Two-thirds of American Muslims are immigrants; one-third of American Muslims are converts, most of them African–Americans.

Conversion to Islam by African–Americans was encouraged early in the twentieth century as a form of separatism from white oppression. The Christianity espoused by the dominant white population was interpreted as part of the pattern of oppression, and awareness grew that many of the slaves who had been brought from West Africa had been of Muslim faith. A number of movements developed to bring the former slaves back to their suppressed ancestral faith. For instance, in 1913 Noble Drew Ali (1886–1929) began a movement, eventually called the Moorish Science Temple of America, that was designed to begin teaching the elements of the faith to African–Americans and thus give them a strong sense of their own identity.

Members were encouraged to adopt Noble Drew Ali's understanding of Muslim lifestyles, with modest dress, gender separation, traditional family structure, and community solidarity. The Holy Prophet Noble Drew Ali declared that it was his "Divine Mission" to "uplift fallen humanity."

Some other early Muslim communities in the United States were based on missionary efforts, such as that of the Ahmadiyyah Movement from India, which was active in publishing tracts and English translations of the Qur'an and in helping African–American converts learn Arabic. By the end of the twentieth century, the Ahmadiyyah Movement had established branches in thirty-eight cities in the United States as part of its global family of ten million members, complete with social service programs.

Other movements had a strong nation-building character. In particular, under the leadership of Elijah Muhammad, who proclaimed himself a messenger of Allah, tens of thousands of African–Americans became "Black Muslims," calling themselves the Nation of Islam. However, faith in Elijah Muhammad himself was shaken by allegations about his sexual relationships with his secretaries. Some followers—especially the influential leader Malcolm X and Warith Deen Muhammad, son of Elijah Muhammad—developed contacts with mainstream Muslims in other countries and came to the conclusion that Elijah Muhammad's version of Islam was far removed from Muslim orthodoxy. They steered converts toward what they perceived as the true traditions of Islam and alliance with the world Muslim community.

Others of African–American heritage, especially Minister Louis Farrakhan, current leader of the Nation of Islam, maintain Elijah Muhammad's more political focus on unifying against white oppression, despite Islam's strong tradition of

Malcolm X (second from left) visiting the future rector of Egypt's Al-Azhar University during a 1964 journey in which he drew closer to mainstream Islam.

non-racism. However, politicization of Islamic identity is probably not the main aspect of the growth of Islam. Many American Muslims embrace their religion as a bulwark of discipline and faith against the degradations of materialism. The Nation of Islam, for instance, has played a strong role in combating violence and drug abuse in some inner cities, and members are encouraged to observe a disciplined "December Fast" in contrast to the commercial frenzy of the Christmas season.

The homes of African–American Muslims become places of refuge from the surrounding culture, with Qur'anic inscriptions, provisions for prayer spaces, cleanliness and lack of clutter, and windows covered as privacy screens. Soon after birth, children are placed with their mothers on their prayer rugs and gradually learn to recite portions of the Qur'an. They are carefully trained in politeness to elders, modest dress, and proper behavior. The environment these children encounter in public schools is a great contrast to this traditional upbringing. Young Muslim girls are taunted about their head scarves, and sex education classes, which begin at an early age, are offensive to Muslim parents who do not accept dating and extramarital sexuality for their children. Some African–American Muslim parents thus attempt to home-school their children.

Muslim resurgence

The Muslim world had lost its own traditional structure and was also generally helpless against manipulations by foreign nations until it found its power in oil. In the 1970s, oil-rich nations found that by banding together they could control the price and availability of oil. OPEC (the Organization of Petroleum Exporting Countries) brought greatly increased revenues into previously impoverished countries and strengthened their self-image as well as their importance in the global balance of power. Most of the oil-rich nations are predominantly Muslim.

As the wealth suddenly poured in, it further disrupted established living patterns. Analysts feel that some people may have turned back to a more conservative version of Islam in an effort to restore a personal sense of familiarity and stability amid the chaos of changing modern life; the increase in literacy, urbanization, and communications helped to spread revived interest in Islam. There was also the hope that Islam would provide the blueprint for enlightened rule, bringing spiritual values into community and politics as Muhammad had done in Medina. It is thought that the Prophet had intentionally tried to create a united community in which each Muslim is responsible for his fellow human beings, in which no one should be hungry or unfairly treated, and in which the leader of the community is a just and religious person. This social ideal has perhaps never been fully realized anywhere, but it continues to inspire committed Muslims today as the best defense against social decadence and, perhaps, the salvation of the world.

Traditionally, Muslims have seen the world as divided into *dar al-Islam*, "the abode of Islam" (those places where Muslims are a majority and Shari'ah governs worldly life), *dar al-sulh*, "the abode of peace" (where Muslims are a minority but can live in peace and freely practice Islam), and *dar al-harb*, "the abode of conflict" (where Muslims are in the minority, struggling to practice Islam).

As overt colonialism wanes, the world has become divided into autonomous nation-states with strong central governments. In this process, forty-three primarily Islamic nation-states have been created. They differ greatly in culture and in the degree to which each society is ruled by Islamic ethics. But all are now being reconsidered as possible frameworks for *dar al-Islam*, within which the Muslim dream of religion-based social transformation might be accomplished. Those who seek to establish Islamic states in which the sovereignty of God is supreme are often now referred to as **Islamists**.

In the past few centuries, modern industrial societies separated religion from politics. Social, political, and economic issues have been treated without any reference to a higher authority or to the values taught by the prophets; religion has been considered a largely private matter, even within some Muslim majority states such as Turkey. By contrast, a re-emerging ideal among contemporary Muslim social reformers is that, as Professor Muhammad Mashuq ibn Ally explains:

> The human being, the servant, is the trustee of creation under the sovereignty
> of God, capable of transforming it within the framework of the divine will.
> Humankind's obedience to, and fulfillment of, the divine command results in
> happiness and thus unites worldly and cosmic justice. This visionary paradigm
> in the unity of religious and cultural consciousness enables the assembly of a
> formidable force to spearhead a new world order, where the consensus is salam—
> peace.[52]

Tradition and modern life

The resurgence of Islam takes several forms. One is a call for a return to Shari'ah rather than secular law derived from European codes. The feeling of the orthodox is that the world must conform to the divine law, rather than diluting the law to accommodate it to the material world. For example, Egypt has made it illegal for its Muslim citizens to drink alcoholic beverages in public. In Saudi Arabia, morality squads actively enforce the obligatory prayers, and women are not allowed to leave home unless they are accompanied by a close male relative. In Iran, an attempt has been made to shape every aspect of life according to Shari'ah. Fasting during Ramadan is strictly enforced in Saudi Arabia and Iran, and restaurants in many Muslim countries close during the fasting hours. In Muslim-dominated northern Nigeria, despite a national constitution that prohibits the adoption of any religion by the state, a 1999 Shari'ah ruling barred men and women from traveling in the same public vehicles, in an effort to combat immorality and crime.

Private behaviors are also becoming more traditional. In particular, to honor the Qur'anic encouragement of physical modesty to protect women from being molested, many Muslim women have begun covering their bodies except for hands, face, and feet, as they have not done for decades. In Saudi Arabia, where women have been ordered to be "properly covered" outside their homes, some wear not only head-to-toe black cloaks but also full veils over their faces without even slits for their eyes. Some Muslim women assert that they like dressing more modestly so that men will view them as persons, not as sex objects. Others feel that men are simply treating women as slaves.

In November 2001, when Taliban forces were defeated, an Afghan woman bared her face in public for the first time since five years of Taliban law requiring women to wear head-to-toe burqas.

In Afghanistan, veiling of women was part of a larger pattern of extreme oppression. Under five years of Taliban restrictions women had to wear head-to-toe *burqas*. Military removal of the Taliban from the capital of Kabul quickly brought a shedding of *burqas* by hundreds of women, who came out publicly to demand the right to work, education for their daughters, and a voice in politics. The tenacious Revolutionary Association of the Women of Afghanistan has long been fighting against the anti-women regimes of both the Taliban and other ruling factions and has maintained a website detailing the raping, killing, and kidnapping of women by militia members, as well as attacking religious fanaticism and male oppression.

Under less oppressive circumstances in some largely Muslim countries, such as Egypt, it is the possibility of employment that motivates women to adopt ***hijab*** (veiling for the sake of modesty). Women are allowed to join the work force only if they are veiled. In Iran, the replacement of more Westernized customs with Muslim moral codes, including veiling of women, has allowed women from conservative backgrounds to leave their homes and enter public life without antagonizing their families. Now that a great number of Iranian Muslim women have been educated and have entered the workforce and politics, they are a formidable part of reformist efforts to challenge the control of the male clerical elite over social life. Not only in Iran but internationally, concludes Professor Anouar Majid, "the scope of the Islamic feminist movement is so large and thoroughly revolutionary that it may well be one of the best platforms from which to resist the effects of global capitalism and contribute to a rich, egalitarian polycentric world."[53]

Women's rights to divorce and to choose their own marriage partners are among the hotly debated issues in contemporary attempts to define Shari'ah. Shari'ah has been locally adapted to various societies over the centuries; to attempt to restore its original form designed for Muhammad's time or any other form from another period is to deny the usefulness of its flexibility. Some customs thought to be Muslim are actually cultural practices not specified in the basic sources; they are the result of Islamic civilization's assimilation of many cultures in many places. Muhammad worked side-by-side with women, and the Qur'an encourages equal participation of women in religion and in society. Veiling and seclusion were practices absorbed from conquered Persian and Byzantine cultures, particularly the upper classes; peasant women could not carry out their physical work under encumbering veils or in seclusion from public view.

Muslim women scholars are now carefully re-examining the Qur'an and Hadith to determine the historical realities and principles of women's issues that have long been hidden behind an exclusively male interpretation of the traditions. Qur'anic scholar Amina Wadud, for instance, asserts that the Qur'an is potentially a "world-altering force" that offers universal moral guidance for all believers, be they male or female:

> The more research I did into the Qur'an, unfettered by centuries of historical androcentric reading and Arabo-Islamic cultural predilections, the more affirmed I was that in Islam a female person was intended to be primordially, cosmologically, eschatogologically, spiritually, and morally a full human being, equal to all who accepted Allah as Lord, Muhammad as Prophet, and Islam as din [religious way]. . . . In the area of gender, conservative thinkers read explicit Qur'anic reforms of existing historical and cultural practices as the literal and definitive statement on these practices for all times and places. What I am calling for is a reading that regards those reforms as establishing precedent for continual development toward a just social order. A comprehensive just social order not only emphasizes fair treatment of women, but also includes women as agents, responsible for contributing to all matters of relevance to human society.[54]

Another problem with applying Shari'ah as civil law is that some ethical issues that arise today either did not exist in their present form at the time of Muhammad or were not specifically addressed by the Qur'an or Hadith. Artificial birth control methods, for example, were not available then. However, infanticide and abortion were mentioned by the Qur'an: "Do not kill your children for fear of poverty. We will provide for them and for you." Does this mean that all forms of population control should be considered forbidden by Islam, or should the overpopulation of the earth be a major contemporary consideration? According to Islamic legal reasoning, the accepted method for determining such ambiguous issues is to weigh all the benefits and disadvantages that might result from a course of action and then discourage it if the likely disadvantages outweigh the advantages. For those Muslim intellectuals who want to retain their faith within the context of modern life, the process of **ijtihad** (reasoned interpretation, independent judgment by a qualified scholar) is critical.

The global family of Islam is not a political unit; its unity under Arab rule broke up long ago. There is as yet no consensus among Muslim states about how to establish a peaceful, just, modern society based on basic Muslim principles. But there is widespread recognition that there are problems associated with modern Western civilization that should be avoided, such as crime, drug abuse, corruption of values, and unstable family life.

> *Today everyone cries for peace but peace is never achieved, precisely because it is metaphysically absurd to expect a civilization that has forgotten God to possess peace.*
>
> *Seyyed Hossein Nasr*[55]

Outreach and education

Another sign of Muslim resurgence is the increase in outreach, as Muslims become more confident of the value of their faith. Islam is the fastest growing of all world religions, with almost 1,200 million followers. New mosques are going up everywhere, including one thousand new mosques each year in Turkey alone, and a grand Islamic Cultural Center in the heart of Manhattan. Muslims who constitute a minority in their countries are beginning to assert their rights to practice their religion. They no longer feel they have to be secretive about praying five times a day or apologetic about leaving work to attend Friday congregational prayer at noon. Special Islamic satellite channels offer alternatives to Western-oriented programming that Muslims find offensive, and also act as a force for international Muslim unity. The channel Iqra, for instance, is financed by a Saudi Arabian millionaire, offering free broadcasting of what it describes as "entertaining programmes that are devoid of decadence and impropriety and are appropriate for viewing by Muslim families."[56]

A third sign of Muslim resurgence is the increasing attention being given to developing educational systems modeled on Islamic thought. Islam is not anti-scientific or anti-intellectual; on the contrary, it has historically bridged reason and faith and placed a high value on developing both in order to tap into the fullness of human potential. Western education has omitted the spiritual aspects of life, so Muslims consider it incomplete and imbalanced. The 1977 First World Conference on Muslim Education defined the goals of education thus:

> *Education should aim at the balanced growth of the total personality of Man through the training of Man's spirit, intellect, his rational self, feelings and bodily senses. Education should cater therefore for the growth of Man in all its aspects: spiritual, intellectual, imaginative, physical, scientific, linguistic, both individually and collectively and motivate all aspects toward goodness and the attainment of perfection. The ultimate aim of Muslim education lies in the realisation of complete submission to Allah on the level of the individual, the community and humanity at large.*[57]

Islam in politics

In addition to return to Shari'ah, numerical growth, and Muslim-based education, governments are becoming Islamicized. There are more frequent references to Islam and Qur'anic statements by political leaders. Some use it to support the status quo and glorify Islam's past heights. In Arabic countries, others have used Muslim idealism to rally opposition to ruling elites who are perceived as being corrupt or tied to the West. However, in contemporary nationalistic

struggles, Muslims have often been the losers, to such an extent that some eighty percent of the world's huge refugee population is Muslim. There is as yet no political unity among Muslim states, despite appeals from some Muslims that they should unite in order to advance the Islamization of society.

In predominantly Shi'ite Iran, the Pahlavi Shahs had tried to rapidly modernize their country, turning it into a major military and industrial power. In the process, they eroded the authority of the *ulama*, the clerics and expounders of the Shari'ah. A revolutionary leader emerged from this disempowered group, the Ayatollah Khomeini (c. 1900–1989), and swept the Shah from power in 1979. Once in power, however, the ulama had no clear program for reorganizing society according to Muslim principles. Shari'ah has never specified a single political or economic system as best. Khomeini made some drastic changes in interpretation of Islam in order to justify violent revolutionary behavior.

He also attempted to export his revolution to other Muslim countries with Shi'ite populations that could carry on the work. He conducted a war against "atheist" Iraq (where the fifty percent of citizens who are Shi'a are ruled by the forty-five percent who are Sunni), denounced predominantly Sunni Saudi Arabia for its ties to the West, and inspired some Lebanese Shi'a to see their political struggle against Christians and Jews as part of a great world battle between Islam and the satanic forces of Western imperialism and Zionism. He issued a legal opinion that Indian-born British author Salman Rushdie could be sentenced to

Appreciative posters of Ayatollah Khomeini continued to be displayed in Iran after his death in 1989.

Palestinian children participate in a candlelight vigil in front of the United States Consulate in East Jerusalem on September 14, 2001. Hundreds of Muslim and Christian Palestinians gathered to pray together for peace in the region and in the whole world, expressing their support for victims of the terrorist attacks in the United States.

death under Islamic law, because his novel, *The Satanic Verses*, seemed to defame the Prophet and his wives. Many people died in resultant riots over the still-controversial book.

Khomeini's call for governmental change was not heeded, so radicals resorted to sabotage and terrorism as their most powerful weapons. Their surprise attacks on civilians tended to turn world opinion against Islam, rather than promoting its ideals. More moderate leadership is now in power in Iran. Islamist reformers propose that the government should be founded on Islamic law, but that this law should be interpreted in ways that allow a considerable degree of individual freedom and free expression rather than authoritarianism.

Iraq is another Muslim nation that has used Islam as a rallying point for political power. When Saddam Hussein of Iraq tried to annex Kuwait, Islam was cast as a political football by both sides in the Gulf War. Hussein, an Arab nationalist, resorted to Islam as a means of mass mobilization against what he saw as a foreign Western intrusion in the Gulf. Even after the Gulf War, years of economic sanctions by the United Nations against Iraq over continuing suspicion of its military intentions have created such hardships for the populace that the Iraqis refer to the sanctions as a means of genocide.

In the five years of Taliban control over most of Afghanistan, all secular laws were discarded; the Sunni Shari'ah was law. The orthodox Sunni Taliban Islamists claimed to be trying to create what they regarded as a pure Muslim state. In accordance with their interpretation of Shari'ah, the Taliban government organized public spectacles to deter crime by amputating the hands of thieves and whipping adulterers.

The Taliban government provoked an anguished international protest when it destroyed huge ancient cliff-hewn statues of the Buddha on the grounds that they were idolatrous. This protest came from within as well as from outside Islam. Law professor Azizah Y. al-Hibri asserted that this action by the Taliban violated central principles of Islam. For instance:

> While there is no central interpretive authority in Islam, an acceptable
> interpretation must satisfy a minimum number of requirements. For example, the
> interpretation must be based on the Qur'an and Sunnah. It must be based on
> knowledge and motivated by Piety. It must also serve (rather than harm) maslaha,
> the public interest of Muslims in particular and humanity in general. ... The
> Taliban seems to have no such concerns. This is consistent with their rejection of
> other basic Islamic principles, such as shura (consultation with other Muslims) and
> bay-ah (a system of elective non-authoritarian governance). It is also consistent
> with their rejection of the Islamic injunction that the pursuit of education is the
> duty of every Muslim, male and female. Finally, it is consistent with their rejection
> of the overarching Islamic model of harmonious gender, racial, religious, and
> general human relations.
>
> For centuries, Islam has preserved and even maintained all prior cultural
> expressions. ... [To destroy the Bamiyan statues, which have been protected under
> Muslim rule for fourteen centuries] is to consider oneself to be a better Muslim than
> all of one's predecessors. That is truly hubris and is contrary to the fundamental
> Islamic principles of humility, tolerance, freedom of thought, consultative democracy,
> and preservation of public maslaha.[58]

Despite their background in a form of Islamic purism and their success at bringing a certain orderliness into Afghani society, the Taliban—as well as other factions within Afghanistan—have been accused of brutalities that are in direct opposition to the instructions of the Qur'an regarding humane treatment of political opponents even during armed conflict. At training camps in Afghanistan, militants from many Muslim countries were taught to mix religion and politics. The best known of these militant groups, Al Qaeda, under the leadership of Saudi Arabian exile Osama bin Laden, is reportedly responsible for many acts of global terrorism, including the devastating attacks on the World Trade Center and Pentagon in the United States and perhaps also chemical terrorism. Bin Laden's agenda was to strike back at the United States for its support for Israel and its intrusive presence in the Arabian peninsula, which he and others interpreted as non-Muslim control over Muslim lands. He has stirred up strong sentiments, which threaten to divide the world into Muslims and non-Muslims. But there are efforts to avoid reversion to this medieval dichotomy, in which both are calling each other "infidels," and to deal with the underlying situations as political rather than religious. Anwar Ibrahim, for instance, former deputy prime minister of Malaysia, asserts:

> One wonders how, in the 21st century, the Muslim world could have produced a
> Bin Laden. In the centuries when Islam created civilizations, men of wealth created

pious foundations supporting universities and hospitals. Princes competed with one another to patronize scientists, philosophers and men of letters. . . . But Bin Laden uses his personal fortune to sponsor terror and murder, not learning or creativity, and to wreak destruction rather than promote creation. Osama bin Laden and his protégés are the children of desperation; they come from countries where political struggle through peaceful means is futile. . . .

Muslim intellectuals and elites carry the enormous moral responsibility of stamping out terrorism in their midst, unless they want Islam to be demonized everywhere because of the outrageous acts of a small band of misguided faithfuls.[59]

There have indeed been hate crimes against Muslims as a result of a renewed idea among non-Muslims that Islam breeds violence and fanaticism. But, alongside this reaction, there are also attempts at deeper understanding of the complex factors that support terrorism. John Esposito, American Professor of Religion and International Affairs and Director of the Center for Muslim–Christian Understanding, writes:

The fallout has again been a tendency to equate violence with Islam, to fail to distinguish between illegitimate use of religion by individuals and the faith and practice of the majority of the world's Muslims who, like their fellow believers in other religious traditions, believe in a religion of peace. . . .

The specter of attacks by terrorists motivated by ethnic, religious, or ideological beliefs and grievances is real. The challenge today, as in the past, is to avoid the easy answers yielded by stereotyping or the projection of a monolithic threat, to distinguish between the beliefs of the majority (whether they be Hindus, Muslims, and Sikhs, Christians and Jews, Arabs and Israelis, Tamils and Buddhists) and a minority of extremists who justify their aggression and violence in the name of religion, ethnicity, or political ideology. It is equally important to distinguish between the aspirations and demands of legitimate political opposition groups and those of extremist groups.

If we are to understand and respond to the challenge of political Islam, its diverse manifestations must be seen within the multiplicity of intellectual and political contexts in which it occurs. While the threats of extremism and violence must be countered forcefully and effectively, the long-term relations of the West with the Muslim world—like the legitimacy of governments within the Muslim world—will hinge on its response to the emergence of new social and political forces and its respect for their legitimate aspirations for greater political participation, social justice, and human rights.[60]

Islam for the future

An unusual side-effect of the negative publicity about Muslim militancy has been a widespread attempt by moderate Muslims to share positive information about their faith. Interest has grown rapidly: Muslim speakers are now in great demand by non-Muslim communities who want to understand and appreciate Islam, rather than remain ignorant about it. Jews are surprised to discover how closely it parallels their own faith; Christians are gradually undoing centuries of sensationalist misinformation about Islam bred by fear.

At the same time, various contemporary political events and situations such as the rise of Hindu extremism and hate crimes toward Muslims in India, the struggle of Palestinians for political freedom from Israeli control, and the psychologically devastating terrorist attacks on the World Trade Center and Pentagon—intentionally chosen symbols of American power and globalization—have brought new polarization into the religious and political world scene. There is a growing perception of an increasing division between Muslims and non-Muslims, or of a so-called "clash of civilizations"—the Muslim world versus the West. But as we have seen, Islam is in fact part of the evolution of Western monotheism, with close theological and historical links to Judaism and Christianity. There is hope that Islamic values can play a positive role in shaping the future not only in Muslim majority countries but also in the evolving global culture.

Until recently, Muslims tended to point to their glorious past as proof of the value of their tradition. But the newest thought is forward-looking, exploring how Islam can help to shape a new social order in the world. At present, Muslim resistance movements are trying to tear down existing social structures in many parts of the world in order to replace them with something presumably better. Professor Asaf Hussain of the University of Leicester, England, points out that the goal of a just society inspires but still eludes Muslim resistance movements:

> In the Qur'an all Muslims are part of the Ummah (community of Islam) because of their belief in one Allah but the social reality prevailing in the Muslim world divides the Ummah on the basis of class, ethnicity, nationality and even sect. . . . Islamic fundamentalists have been very critical of traditional Islamic thought and theology that created an Iman (faith) bereft of Amal (action), so the strategy of Islamic resistance has been to deconstruct the traditional and colonial structures that dominated Muslim cultures and created pseudo Islamic societies. The instrument of social change is jihad (struggle). . . .
>
> Today many Islamic fundamentalist movements have declared war on their own people and are trying to transform their states on the model of the First Islamic state. But the conditions of the seventh century do not obtain today. A new model of the Islamic state has to be devised. The dominating civilization of the present day is Western and its models control the Third World, including the Muslim world. Islamic movements have revolted against this but their strategies have not been well thought out. They do not have to dominate Western civilization but create a parallel which excels it. This will be a long, arduous task but the struggle has just begun.[61]

Mahmoon-al-Rasheed, Founder of the Comprehensive Rural Educational, Social, Cultural and Economic Center in Bangladesh, maintains that there is violence within and between nations because people have not developed a sense of duty toward each other and have not recognized how inseparably all people of the earth are related to each other. He proposes that Islamic values are not aimed at creating a political state but rather a harmoniously integrated world society, for:

> We cannot begin to realize our full potential until we have achieved a community which knows no limit but that of human society and renders all obedience to a Law common to all.[62]

Dr. Ahmad Kamal Abu'l Majd, an ex-Minister of Culture in Egypt, looks toward the future:

I'm glad and proud I'm a Muslim. I carry on my shoulders a scale of values, a code of ethics that I genuinely believe is good for everybody. . . . I even venture sometimes to say that Islam was not meant to serve the early days of Islam when life was primitive and when social institutions were still stable and working. It was meant to be put in a freezer and to be taken out when it will be really needed. And I believe that time has come. But the challenge is great because not all Muslims are aware of this fact: That the mission of Islam lies not in the past but in the future.[63]

Suggested reading

Ali, Maulana Muhammad, *The Religion of Islam*, sixth edition, Columbus, Ohio: Ahmadiyya Anjuman Isha'at Islam, 1994. A classic reference explaining all aspects of Muslim belief and practice, with extensive scriptural quotations.

Dessouki, Ali E. Hillal, ed., *Islamic Resurgence in the Arab World*, New York: Praeger Publishers, 1982. A scholarly study of the contemporary Islamic resurgence in specific Arab nations.

El Fadl, Khaled Abou, *Speaking in God's Name: Islamic Law, Authority, and Women*, Oxford: Oneworld, 2001. Itself an example of the rationality of Islamic legal processes, this extensively researched volume examines the basis of Islamic law and the injustices that have occurred when it has been interpreted in an authoritarian way.

Esack, Farid, *On Being a Muslim: Finding a Religious Path in the World Today*, Oxford: Oneworld, 1999. A passionate and personal account by a scholar who continually faces the conflict between modernity and traditional faith.

Esack, Farid, *Qur'an, Liberation and Pluralism: An Islamic Perspective of Interreligious Solidarity against Oppression*, Oxford: Oneworld Publications, 1997. A first-person account of the struggle for justice in South Africa from the point of view of a Muslim scholar and activist, exploring Qur'anic principles that lead to inter-religious fraternity.

Esposito, John L., *The Islamic Threat: Myth or Reality?*, third edition, New York: Oxford University Press, 1999. An insighful survey of militant Islamic movements around the world.

Esposito, John L., *Islam: The Straight Path*, New York, Oxford: Oxford University Press, 1988. A scholarly, clear introduction to historical and contemporary Islam.

Hefner, Robert W. and Patricia Horvatich, eds., *Islam in an Era of Nation-states: Politics and Religious Renewal in Muslim Southeast Asia*, Honolulu: University of Hawaii Press, 1997. Detailed analyses of Muslim reformist movements in Southeast Asia with reference to modern governmental structures.

The Holy Qur'an. Although the Qur'an is considered untranslatable, numerous translations from the Arabic have been attempted. Many Muslims' favorite English translation is by Abdullah Yusuf Ali (Durban, South Africa: Islamic Propagation Center International, 1946). The King Fahd Holy Qur'an Printing Complex in Medina has published a very helpful revision based on Yusuf Ali's translation, with extensive thematic index. Thomas Ballantine Irving (Al-Hajj Ta'lim'Ali) has prepared "The First American Version" of the Qur'an (translation and commentary, Brattleboro, Vermont: Amana Books, © 1985).

Lings, Martin, *Muhammad*, London: George Allen & Unwin, and Islamic Text Society, 1983. A highly regarded biography of the Prophet.

Lunde, Paul, *Islam: Faith, Culture, History,* London: DK Publishing, Inc., 2002. Extensively illustrated, sympathetic introduction to Islam, with country-by-country details of the variety of socio-political contexts in which Islam is practiced today.

McCloud, Aminah Beverly, *African American Islam*, New York and London: Routledge, 1995. An accessible inside view of contemporary African–American Muslim communities and issues they face in a contrasting cultural context.

Nasr, Seyyed Hossein, *Ideals and Realities of Islam*, second edition, London: Unwin Hyman Ltd., 1985. Thoughtful presentation of both esoteric and exoteric features of Islam.

Nasr, Seyyed Hossein, ed., *Islamic Spirituality I: Foundations*, New York: Crossroad Publishing Company, 1987 and London: SCM Press, 1989. Excellent chapters on key features of Muslim spirituality, from fasting to angels, with sections on Sunnism, Shi'ism, and Sufism.

Nasr, Seyyed Hossein, *Traditional Islam in the Modern World*, London and New York: Kegan Paul International, 1990. Religiously sensitive discussions of varied topics in attempts to bring forth traditional Muslim values within contemporary social settings.

Nasr, Seyyed Hossein, Dabashi, Hamid, and Nasr, Seyyed Vali Reza, *Shi'ism: Doctrines, Thought, and Spirituality*, Albany, New York: State University of New York Press, 1988. To balance the predominant media attention to Shi'ite politics, a set of thoughtful essays on aspects of Shi'ite spirituality.

Paige, Glenn D., Satha-Anand, Chaiwats, and Gilliatt, Sarah, *Islam and Nonviolence*, Honolulu: University of Hawaii, Center for Global Nonviolence Planning Project, 1993. Strong essays on theories and practice of non-violence stemming from Muslim values.

Pinault, David, *The Shiites: Ritual and Popular Piety in a Muslim Community*, New York: St. Martin's Press, 1992. Sensitive discussions of Shi'ite interpretations of Muslim history and how these inform communal life and action.

Rashid, Ahmed, *Taliban: Militant Islam, Oil and Fundamentalism in Central Asia*, New Haven: Yale University Press, 2000. A Pakistani journalist chronicles the Taliban's rise to power, including global politics and economics as well as religion.

Rumi, Jalal al-Din, *We Are Three,* translations of Rumi poems by Coleman Barks, Athens, Georgia: Maypop Books, 1987. Free contemporary renderings of Rumi's startling, passionate poetry of the love between humans and the divine.

Schimmel, Annemarie, *And Muhammad is His Messenger: The Veneration of the Prophet in Islamic Piety*, Chapel Hill, North Carolina: University of North Carolina Press, 1985. Extensive exploration of Muslims' love for the Prophet.

Schimmel, Annemarie, *My Soul is a Woman: The Feminine in Islam,* New York: Continuum Publishing, 1999. Examination of mystical Islamic traditions in which all seekers long to be like brides of the Beloved.

Schimmel, Annemarie, *Mystical Dimensions of Islam*, Chapel Hill, North Carolina: University of North Carolina Press, 1975. A classic survey of Sufi history, teachings, and saints.

Schuon, Frithjof, *Understanding Islam*, London: George Allen & Unwin, 1963. Profound and lyrical observations about the way of Islam.

Smith, Margaret, *Rabi'a: The Life and Work of Rabi'a and Other Women Mystics in Islam,* Oxford: Oneworld, 1994. Perceptive study of the intense mysticism of Rabi'a and other women who have contributed to the depths of mystical experience in Islam.

Stowasser, Barbara Freyer, *The Islamic Impulse*, Washington, D.C.: Center for Contemporary Arab Studies, Georgetown University, 1987. Sensitive articles exploring the meanings of Islamist movements.

Wadud, Amina, *Qur'an and Woman*, New York/Oxford: Oxford University Press, 1999. Probing hermeneutic analysis of the Qur'an, revealing its principles of social justice, including gender equality.

Walther, Wiebke, *Women in Islam from Medieval to Modern Times*, Princeton: Markus Wiener Publishers, 1981, 1993. Contrary to the stereotype of the veiled, submissive Muslim woman, the author describes women in many historical roles, such as fighters, poets, concubines, and career women.

Webb, Gisela, *Windows of Faith: Muslim Women Scholar-Activists in North America*, Syracuse, New York: Syracuse University Press, 2000. Articles revealing the depth of feminist scholarship within Islam, particularly with reference to the ideal of social justice as seen from the point of view of women of faith.

CHAPTER 6

NEW RELIGIOUS MOVEMENTS

"That yielding of the human mind to the divine"

The history of religions is one of continual change. Each religion changes over time, new religions appear, and some older traditions disappear. Times of rapid social change are particularly likely to spawn new religious movements, for people seek the security of the spiritual amidst worldly chaos. In the period since World War II, thousands of new religious groups have sprung up around the world. In sub-Saharan Africa, there are now over 7,000 different religions; every Nigerian town of several thousand people now has up to fifty or sixty different kinds of religion.[1] In Japan, an estimated thirty percent of the population belongs to one of hundreds of new religious movements. Imported versions of ancient traditions, such as Hinduism and Buddhism, have made many new converts in areas such as North America, Europe, and Russia, where they are seen as "new religions." Internet websites now offer global opportunities for new religious movements to explain themselves and attract new followers.

To move into a new religious movement may be a fleeting experience or it may signal a deep change in one's life. In religion, as in other life commitments such as marriage, there are potential benefits in dedication and obedience. Many religions, including the largest world religions, teach self-denial and surrender as cardinal virtues, which help to vanquish the ego and allow one to approach ultimate reality. The question for a sincere person of faith is where to place one's faith.

Social context of new religious movements

New religious movements are often popularly referred to as **cults** or **sects**. These words have specific, neutral meanings: a cult represents a distinct break from other traditions, while a sect is a splinter group or a subgroup associated with a larger tradition. Both words have sometimes been used imprecisely and pejoratively to distinguish new religions from older ones, each of which already claims to be the best or only way. The word cult has often been used to signify a group temporarily gathered around a charismatic leader whose influence may be dangerous to his or her followers.

The label "new religious movement" seems more neutral at this time and is becoming widely used, particularly in academic circles, to avoid such negative connotations. However, the word "new" is itself imprecise, for many of these groups have a rather lengthy history and have survived long after the death of the original founder.

Professors Rodney Stark and William Sims Bainbridge have attempted to classify new religious movements on the basis of their relationship to their social environment as well as to previous traditions. A mainstream religious tradition typically accepts and accommodates itself to the society in which it operates. A sect, by contrast, rejects its social environment as "worldly" and "unbelieving," i.e., opposed to its beliefs. Sects usually have previous ties to a religious organization but have broken off from it, often in the attempt to return to what they perceive as its pristine original form. Cults are independent religious traditions. But they may also be in conflict with the surrounding society because they are perceived as new and different. They may refer back to some ancient tradition but over a long gap in time, rather than being a direct split from that tradition.

According to Stark and Bainbridge's typology, cults can be further defined by the degree to which they influence their followers' relationship to society. What they call "audience cults" do not require conversion, and allow their followers great flexibility. They may sample many religious movements and attend workshops here and there, making their own choices about what to believe and do. New Age groups tend to fall in this category. "Client cults" offer some kind of service, usually some kind of therapy. Involvement with the organization may become deeper and more socially defining over time. Scientology, which is based on the writings of L. Ron Hubbard (1911–1986), is considered such a group. The initial agenda is therapeutic: "auditing" in order to clear the mind of the negative effects of past experiences. But once this process begins, the client learns of more complex levels of involvement, and other members may become their primary social group. Auditing to clear the mind often leads to membership in the Church of Scientology, which worships the greater spirit that observes and directs the mind.

What Stark and Bainbridge call a "cult movement" is a full-fledged organization that requires conversion and does not allow dual allegiances to other organizations. Some offer a total way of life, with community-based lodging and work as well as group worship. Commitment to this way of life ranges from partial, with people still involved with family and friends outside the movement, to total, in which they are largely cut off from the larger social environment.

In this chapter we will survey some representative examples of the new religious movements that developed in the nineteenth and twentieth centuries. All have some link with previous traditions but are sufficiently different to be studied independently. Previous chapters included groups that are modern versions of older ways with which they are still identified, such as Pentecostalism, whose outer manifestations vary considerably from more staid mainstream versions of Christianity, but which is nonetheless considered part of the worldwide Christian church. The pages that follow provide a sampling of more distinct manifestations of the current burgeoning of spiritual vitality. The headings do not delineate separate categories, but rather common aspects of the new religious movements.

Apocalyptic expectations

As the twenty-first century began, according to Christian dating, speculations abounded that some major change was about to occur in the world. Some people expected better times ahead; some prophesied forthcoming planetary disaster. The disastrous weather patterns in 1997 and 1998 linked with the worst El Niño in history, unstable political and economic conditions around the world, the sudden collapse of the Asian "tiger" economies, and epidemic exposures of government scandals gave many people the impression that we were experiencing a global crisis of supernatural dimensions. After 2000 came and went without any world-shaking events, the 2001 terrorist attacks on the United States and subsequent bombing of Afghanistan reawakened fears of worldwide calamity.

The expectation of major world changes appears in many religions, including Hinduism, Zoroastrianism, Judaism, Christianity, Islam, and some indigenous religions. In Christianity, for instance, the last book in the Bible, Revelation, predicts an **apocalypse**, or dramatic end of the present world. Revelation foretells a world war between the forces of Satan and the forces of God, with great destruction, followed by the **millennium**, a thousand-year period of special holiness in which Christ rules the earth. Hindus anticipate that Kali Yuga, the worst of times, will be followed by the return of Sat Yuga, when *dharma* will again prevail over evil. However, when members of less established new religious movements genuinely anticipate a doomsday or a new world order, they tend to be regarded as eccentrics by the rest of their society. To maintain their faith, they may isolate themselves from mainstream society and try to prepare for the coming changes. This was the strategy of the Branch Davidians, whose devotional community in Waco, Texas, was attacked in 1993 by federal officials on weapons charges (even though Texas has twice as many guns per capita as was apparently the case within the community), with the result that over eighty of the members died in the resulting conflagration. Alternatively, those who anticipate the end of the present world may accept social scorn and try to share their prophecies with others in order to save them from the anticipated coming destruction. Two examples of the latter approach—Rastafarians and Jehovah's Witnesses—demonstrate some ways in which people may try to engage others in their expectations.

Rastafarianism

In Jamaica, millenarian expectations have been expressed as Rastafarianism. In 1895, Alexander Bedward of the Baptist Free Church in Jamaica prophesied a coming holocaust in which all the white people would be killed, leaving the Blacks, "the true people," to celebrate the new world. He sat in his special robes as the predicted date came and went; eventually he was placed in an asylum for the insane. A more generalized hopeful vision was spread by Marcus Garvey (1887–1940), who saw a fundamental change in society that would be led by Blacks. Garvey linked these dreams to the return of Blacks to Africa, from which their ancestors had been taken as slaves; there they would rebuild a great civilization. A prophecy attributed to Garvey—"Look to Africa when a black king

Rastafarian male musicians carry the message of reasserting black spiritual and social rights.

shall be crowned, for the day of deliverance is near"[2]—was thought to have been realized when Ras (Prince) Tafari of Ethiopia was crowned as Haile Selassie, Emperor of Ethiopia.

An elaborate mystique was built up around Haile Selassie as the living God (though neither Selassie nor Garvey shared this view). Hopeful lore was based on interpretations of Selassie's statements and passages from the Old Testament and the New Testament Book of Revelation. Poor Jamaicans (who likened themselves to the Jews in captivity in Babylon) repeatedly prepared to be given free passage back to Africa.

Haile Selassie's reign (until his death in 1974) did nothing to liberate Jamaican Africans, but Blacks in Jamaica nevertheless developed a new religious movement around these ideals. They intend to revive the "Way of the Ancients," their concept of the lost civilization of pre-colonial Africa, and to free people of African extraction from subservience. "Babylon," the oppressor, is the United States, Britain (the former colonial power in Jamaica), the state of Jamaica, and the Christian Church. In protest against Babylon, Rastafarians wear their hair in long uncombed curls, called "dreadlocks," a lion-like mane symbolizing the natural non-industrial life. Some give use of marijuana (ganja) religious significance as a sacrament. A distinctive music, reggae, has evolved as an expression of Black pride, social protest, and Rastafarian millenarian ideals. However, in many areas the movement has developed mostly through men; they consider women incapable of experiencing Rasta awareness except through their husbands.

The Rastafarian movement has spread beyond Jamaica to Blacks and a few whites elsewhere in the Caribbean, North America, Europe, Southern Africa, Australia, and New Zealand. It is a very localized and diverse movement. Rastas insist that the truths they espouse are not just for people of African descent. According to a Rasta website, until a "secret hour known only to a devout few," when "Babylon" will fall and they will return to Ethiopia, "As Rastas they could now await with dignity the Judgment Day, when the last shall be first and the first shall be last."[3]

Jehovah's Witnesses

Those who call themselves Jehovah's Witnesses foresee a new world in which people of all races (including many raised from the dead) will join hands in peace. They believe that this will happen only after the majority of humanity is destroyed for not obeying the Bible. In the understanding of Jehovah's Witnesses, God will not let anyone, including "false Christians," ruin the earth. Those who are of the true religion will be saved from the general destruction, reunited with their dead loved ones in a paradise on earth (except for 144,000 who will live with God in heaven). According to the teachings, in the earthly paradise there will be no pain, no food shortages, no sickness, no death.

The founder of Jehovah's Witnesses, Charles Taze Russell (1852–1916), supported a prediction that 1873 or 1874 would be the date of this apocalypse. When that period passed uneventfully, the date for the "harvest of believers" was changed to 1878, and then 1914, 1925, and 1975. As the dates came and went without any apparent end of the world, Russell developed the idea that Christ had arrived, but was invisibly present. Only the faithful "Jehovah's Witnesses" would recognize his presence. Their mission is to warn the rest of the populace about what is in store. They thus go from door to door, encouraging people to follow their program of studying the Bible as an announcement of the millennium. They encourage people to leave politics and "false religions." The latter include mainstream Christian Churches, which, the Witnesses feel, began to

A Jehovah's Witness shares Bible study lessons.

deviate from Jesus's message in the second and third centuries by developing untrue doctrines: that God is a Trinity, that the soul is resurrected after death, and that the unrepentant wicked endure eternal torment (rather than the utter annihilation that the Witnesses predict for them).

During the 1930s and 1940s in the United States, many Jehovah's Witnesses were persecuted and arrested for their refusal to engage in military activities. Their trials became tests of the preservation of freedom of speech, press, assembly, and worship, and ultimately they won forty-three Supreme Court cases. They have been similarly successful in high courts of other countries. The movement continues to grow, with over 90,000 congregations in 235 countries. Despite their apocalyptic expectations, their website attempts to portray them as normal people, and thus encourage others to talk with their door-to-door canvassers and join their movement:

> In most ways Jehovah's Witnesses are like everyone else. They have their problems—economic, physical, emotional. They make mistakes at times, for they are not perfect, inspired, or infallible. But they try to learn from their experiences and diligently study the Bible to make needed corrections. They have made their dedication to God to do his will, and they apply themselves to fulfil this dedication. In all their activities they seek guidance from God's Word and his holy spirit.
>
> It is of vital importance to them that their beliefs be based on the Bible and not on mere human speculations or religious creeds. . . . They understand that many of the prophecies of the Bible have been fulfilled, others are in the course of fulfilment, and still others await fulfilment.[4]

Unification Movement

Another movement that has gone through many manifestations but is increasingly announcing itself as a harbinger of a renewed earth is now called the Unification Movement. Its founder, Sun Myung Moon, has proclaimed himself and his second wife, Hak Ja Han, to be jointly the Messiah. He was born in 1920 in what is now North Korea into a family of farmers. Christianity was practiced secretly during the Japanese occupation of Korea. Christians met underground, hiding first from the Japanese authorities and then from the communists, who began to suppress religion in North Korea in 1945. Many of the Christian Churches had strong messianic expectations. Moon's parents converted to Christianity, and the young Moon became a Sunday school teacher. He says that in Easter 1935, while he was praying in the mountains, Jesus appeared to him in a vision. Jesus reportedly told him that it had not been God's desire that he be crucified, for his mission on earth was left unfinished. By Moon's account, Jesus asked him to complete the task of establishing God's kingdom on earth.

To this end, Moon developed the "Unification Principle," according to which God created the universe in order to manifest true love. The family is considered the primary institution for the growth of love. Based on spiritual and moral education in the family, people are to live for the sake of others in all situations. However, concludes Moon, humans do not live according to God's design; selfishness prevails in human relationships and in relationships between ethnic groups and nations.

Moon traces this situation to the story of the fall of Adam and Eve. In Moon's unique interpretation, Eve lost her purity through an illicit relationship with Satan, symbolized as a serpent, and she in turn seduced Adam. They never grew to the spiritual maturity whereby they could have manifested true love. Instead, Moon teaches, their son Cain murdered his brother Abel because he inherited a false and selfish kind of love from his parents. According to Moon's theology, false love has thence been passed down from generation to generation, infecting the whole human race.

Moon says that God directed him to teach publicly in North Korea, where communist leaders were seeking to quash religious activity. He was arrested and tortured, and his apparently lifeless body was thrown into a snowdrift. After followers found him and nursed him back to health, he continued preaching in public, was arrested again, and sentenced to five years of hard labor in a concentration camp. Moon was liberated when American forces bombed the prison.

In the 1970s, the Unification Church staged a series of well-publicized rallies in the United States and saw a rapid growth in membership. Middle-class youths put aside their careers, gave up their worldly possessions, broke off from their girlfriends and boyfriends, and devoted themselves to the religious path. They saw their sacrificial and ascetic way of life as a rejection of the materialistic and

Reverend and Mrs. Sun Myung Moon conclude a Blessing Ceremony in Seoul for 30,000 couples from around the world.

Living New Religions

Ursula is German and was matched by the Unification Movement to David McLackland from England; they have three children and live in Bahrain, where Ursula is a Regional Director for the Unification Movement. She explains why Unification appeals to her:

"I was raised in a Protestant church, but I was not interested in religion. I just learned whatever prayers by heart, but I had never any experience. When I was fifteen I followed my elder sister and left the church. I went to the government and officially said, 'I am not a Christian any more.' When I was a student I joined the communist movement at the university. But I soon became disappointed in the difference between theory and practice of the communists.

"Maybe the most motivating experience was when I was in a project trying to help drug addicts overcome their internal spiritual addiction to drugs. I was confronted with them with the question 'What is the purpose of life?' They said, 'I don't care if I die in two years or twenty years, so why?' So then I felt if I want to help drug addicts, I must give them the purpose of life—why they could have hope. I felt if I want to help them, I have to invest the same sincerity as they do. A friend had by that time introduced me to a yoga group. I felt the love among the people, the sacred singing, the meditation was what really drew and completely changed my life. Through the moral principles and starting a disciplined lifestyle, many questions in my life were answered, and I felt my mind got cleared up.

"When I met the Unification Movement, that is the point which really attracted me, because they had a very clear logical explanation about the relationship between man and woman, and they were teaching about the ideal of the family. I could see in their own members that even though they were married, now as a family they were sacrificing for society and for the world, not just an individual living for the sake of the world.

"David and I were matched and then engaged for one and a half years. We got to know each other through writing letters. When I met him after one and a half years, I felt tremendous love from God for my husband. This feeling was really immense. I felt this love is not me for him; it is God's love coming through us.

"[In contrast to criticisms that the 'Moonies' are being exploited as cheap labor by the higher-ups in the movement] I see that the higher people are in the hierarchy, the more loving, the more sacrificial they are. I couldn't live like Reverend Kwak (Reverend Moon's direct assistant) or Reverend Moon. Literally, they sleep just a few hours a day, and all day they are active and busy. They are always loving, they are always there for you, they are always supporting you. I want to become like them because they really show me what is a parent's heart, what is a father's or mother's love.

"For us, of course it's true that we are not looking for job security in that sense of money or savings. I think our members come because all of them are very idealistic, that we look for internal satisfaction. Maybe what is most commonly accused is that our members start with sales to support our projects. But some of my most beautiful and wonderful experiences are doing these sales. When I go out and work hard all day to sell, I can really feel God's love, because I do this to do some good work. This money is not for me, it is to help others. I have such beautiful experiences where I can just feel actually it is God who is selling it. It is not me. Actually I could not sell by myself. I think that is for all of our members who have these experiences: We have the most beautiful and wonderful experiences with God doing this.

"We feel that through this type of experience, for example going door to door, you meet all kinds of people in all levels of society. Normally we would meet maybe people from our background—that's it. As a laborer, you wouldn't meet a manager. As a manager you wouldn't get involved with laborers or academics. But through this we meet all kinds of people, and that is really Reverend Moon's internal motivation: To give members broad experience and to train them to get to know all kinds of people and relate to them and love them and understand them.

"When I met the movement, I felt, 'Wow—here are people who are more sincere than I am, people who are more sacrificial, who are more sincere to live for others.' I felt I want to become like them. I think that is really the motive of our members—we don't want to live for ourselves, we really want to live for others."

hedonistic American lifestyle. However, alarmed parents accused the church of brainwashing their adult children. The church was viewed with suspicion by the established Christian Churches and vilified by the political left because of its anti-communist activities.

Dodging controversy and mockery, the Unification Movement began engaging in large-scale international activities reportedly designed to transform the world. For instance, the Unification-sponsored Inter-Religious Federation for World Peace and the Religious Youth Service have created international inter-religious dialogues among leading scholars of religion, and service projects in many countries. Such expensive projects, including air travel and hotel accommodations for participants in elite conferences, are financially supported by members' door-to-door sales and their establishment of business companies such as industrial-scale fishing ventures.

A unique aspect of the Movement's work is massive wedding ceremonies in which couples matched by the movement or already-wed couples wanting to dedicate themselves to "live for the sake of others" and "create an ideal family which contributes to world peace" are simultaneously "blessed" by Reverend and Mrs. Moon, tens of thousands in a large stadium and many more by satellite links. The goal of thus blessing 360 million couples by the year 2000 was report-edly met, although some who were counted may have been administered Holy Wine and Holy Water or given "holy candy" in public places without knowing the meaning the Unification Movement placed on these acts. With Reverend Moon announcing himself as the "Second Adam," Unificationists view these mass wed-dings as a movement to create one human family, with couples of all races and nationalities being "engrafted" onto "God's lineage of true love."

Reverend and Mrs. Moon also undertake global speaking tours, giving the same prepared speeches in many countries to announce that they are the True Parents of all humankind, come to establish the reign of true love. They are now developing a huge territory in the center of South America as the "New Hope East Garden." Comprising some 7.5 million acres (3 million ha) of land they have bought, some of it deforested, some pristine, it is being promoted as "the zero point for the Kingdom of Heaven on Earth." Agricultural and reclamation projects are begin-ning there, with an emphasis on sustainable development. Families who have been "blessed" are requested to attend a forty-day workshop there as one of the requirements for "registration for Heaven." As we shall see in the next section, there is also a strong spiritualist component to Reverend Moon's attempts to bring about a new world.

Supernatural powers and revelations

Numerous new religious movements operate in the realm of the supernatural—that is, beyond the experiences of the senses and therefore mysterious to most people. Those who are interested in penetrating these mysteries may do so to attain personal power, or they may seek to use their presumed contacts with invisible realities to bring healing to those who are suffering and insights for those who want to understand what they cannot see.

Many founders of these new religions are women with shamanistic gifts. Miki Nakayama, founder of the Tenrikyo movement in 1838, was acting as a trance medium for the healing of her son when she was reportedly possessed by ten *kami* (spirits), including the chief God the Parent. They proclaimed through her, "Miki's mind and body will be accepted by us as a divine shrine, and we desire to save this three-thousand-world through this divine body."[5] It is said that she later spontaneously composed 1711 poems under divine inspiration, and that these became the sacred scriptures of a new religion. One of these begins with this revelation:

> *Looking all over the world and through all ages, I find no one who has understood My heart. No wonder that you know nothing, for so far I have taught nothing to you. This time I, God, revealing Myself to the fore, teach you all the truth in detail.*[6]

Tenrikyo has continued to be popular since Miki's death, and she is revered as the still-living representative of the divine will.

The Mahikari movement was founded in Japan in 1959 by Sukui Nushi Sama, who believes he is the successor to the Buddha and Christ as God's representative on earth. The path he taught has become popular in the Caribbean. Although it does not claim to be a religion in itself, but rather to bring all religions together, it involves certain distinctive practices centering on spiritual "light." Mahikarians are taught to heal by radiating light out of their hands, to send light to disturbed ancestral spirits to help them find peace, and to spread the divine civilization through the world by transmitting light. Inverting the conventional opinion of such practices, Mahikarians are taught that the spiritual realm is the only reality; science and medicine are ignorant superstitions.

Communication with spirits of the dead has surfaced within a Christian context in the United States as Spiritualism. The National Spiritualist Association of Churches defines Spiritualism as "the science, philosophy, and religion of continuous life." Its services resemble Christian worship services, with a sermon and the singing of devotional hymns, but without the focus on Jesus or sinfulness. They include periods of spiritual healing in which trained "healing vehicles" are believed to serve as channels for God's healing power, which is transmitted through their hands to a seated person. Equally important are messages transmitted by a medium who delivers them to members of the congregation from deceased relatives "on the other side." Spiritualist medium Sandra Pfortmiller explains:

> *The gift and faculty of mediumship is to prove that life continues, that our loved ones are only a prayer away, that we do have help, guidance, communication and inspiration from another Plane of existence. It shows that we should not fear death but rather understand that the personality continues, always growing.*[7]

The Unification Movement has developed a strongly spiritualist component, especially in its South Korean headquarters. It is said that Mrs. Moon's deceased mother and Reverend and Mrs. Moon's son, who died in a car crash, are assisting Unificationists from the spirit world, through the help of a medium. Hundreds of thousands of members have participated in workshops designed to free them from evil spirits, who are then said to be given training in the Unification Principle and duly "blessed." People cite miraculous physical healings and visions of spirits leaving their bodies. There are also liberation ceremonies for ancestors and even historical "infamous personages," such as Hitler, Lenin, and Stalin. A Unification spokesman reports: "The same personages were blessed as the representatives of all wicked people, thereby opening the gate for the 'liberation of Hell.' "[8]

Throughout human history, certain people have felt that they are receiving revelations from unseen spiritual powers. Some of them, such as the Prophet Muhammad, have become the founders of major religions as others became convinced of the truth of their revelations. This process continues today with great numbers of people around the world feeling that they are serving as "channels" for divine wisdom.

Offshoots and combinations of older religions

In previous chapters we have looked at contemporary versions of ancient religions . . . as they evolve and adapt to new circumstances. Mixtures of more than one religion also arise in many places. This process is referred to as **syncretism**— the combining of normally differing beliefs.

Indigenous African plus Christian traditions

In the Caribbean and Latin America, many mixtures of African and Catholic traditions have evolved, with a prevailing interest in contacting and cooperating with spirits. **Santeria**, which literally means "the way of the saints," blends some of the deities and beliefs of slaves from Dahome, baKonga, and Yoruban cultures with images of Catholic saints. Since the slaves were prevented from openly practicing their ancestral faiths, they continued to do so in symbolic ways, such as hanging a white cloth from a doorway or tying bananas with red string, and also by worship of the African *orisa* in the form of Catholic saints. For instance, the female *orisa* Oshun is worshipped in Nigeria as the patron of love, marriage, and fertility, and is associated with river water. In Cuba and in areas of the United States with large Cuban populations, devotions to Oshun have merged into reverence of the Virgin Mary as Our Lady of Charity, the patron saint of Cuba. She is said to have appeared to three shipwrecked fishermen at sea. Similarly, **Voodoo**, meaning "spirits," developed in Haiti as a blending of West African and French Catholic teachings. Specialists in these traditions have techniques for "magical" intervention in people's lives to help solve problems that cannot be fixed by ordinary means. The *santeros*, for example, say they are able to clear away negative spiritual influences around people, help them get jobs, heal sickness, attract mates, block their enemies, and get ahead financially. The Yoruba see the world as a mesh of interconnections among all beings, linked by the energy known as *ashe*. Human efforts are required to keep the ashe flowing properly through creation and to nourish the *orisa*. Then, by knowing how to feed and communicate with the **orisa** and understanding the principles of energy, practitioners are thought to be able to wield some control over the environment.

In the syncretism of Santeria, the Yoruba river goddess Oshun is merged with the Christian Our Lady of La Caridad del Cobre, patron saint of Cuba.

Where remnants of slave populations have coalesced, the renewed practice of African traditions has given the people a link with their cultural heritage, a sense of inner integrity, and a means of sheer survival. But these African traditions have been viewed with some suspicion by the dominant societies. For instance, traditional African methods of communicating with the spirits include divination and the consecrated slaughter of animals, in the context of a community meal. The latter practice was outlawed in Hialeah, Florida, as "animal sacrifice," but in a landmark judgment in 1993, the United States Supreme Court overruled the ban as an unconstitutional barrier to religious freedom. According to a majority of the Supreme Court Justices: "Religious beliefs need not be acceptable, logical, consistent, or comprehensible to others in order to merit First Amendment protection."[9] Santeria has become so popular in Latin America and the United States that it has an estimated 100 million practitioners, as well as Internet websites, and there are pilgrimages to Nigeria for people seeking to explore the roots of their religion.

Syncretism has also developed in Africa itself. For example, a number of "new" religions in West Africa combine ritual elements of indigenous and Christian traditions which had been brought by missionaries. The missionaries regarded worship of ancestors as religiously invalid, but communications with ancestors and spirits had been a major aspect of the indigenous religions. The syncretistic new religions take seriously problems with the spirit world, such as retaliations from spirits who have not been treated respectfully, and mix Christian prayers and incense with fetishes, talismans, divining, chanting, and drumming. This syncretistic mixture gives a sense of power against evil spirits and is also applied to contemporary, this-worldly problems. These groups are most popular in urban areas, where they offer a refuge from unpleasant aspects of city life. Those such as the Brotherhood of the Cross and Star are deeply committed to serving the people in areas where the governments have failed them. They therefore operate their own schools, food shops, industries, health care centers, and transportation services. Those who say they once felt like nobodies, alienated within modern impersonal culture, now feel recognized as important individuals within a loving group. The movements revive the traditional African community spirit as a stable support network within a changing society. They may also build a sense of African pride and spiritual destiny. Rev. William Kingsley Opoku of Ghana, International Coordinator of the African Council of Spiritual Churches and member of the Brotherhood of the Cross and Star asserts:

> *African Scriptures confirm that the world peace process will finally be founded in Africa, and the whole world will come and help build it, to signify the unity of mankind under the Government of God on earth.*[10]

Christian Science

Some new religions profess certain aspects of older religions but eschew so many other features of those religions, perhaps also adding new elements of their own, that they may no longer be considered within the mainstream of the earlier tradition. These days there are many groups promoting personal growth, with a basis in Christianity or in Eastern meditation.

Emphasis on self-improvement through positive thinking has burgeoned in the United States into a number of new religious movements. Christian Science, founded by Mary Baker Eddy (1821–1910) in the late nineteenth century, is centered on the Bible and on Jesus. Mrs. Eddy sought to reinstate what she considered "primitive Christianity," and maintained that human sinfulness is what stands between humans and the loving God. When humans live in moral and spiritual sinfulness—including states such as hatred, fear, selfishness, and envy—these qualities obscure the true reality. When one squarely faces these manifestations of mental darkness and surrenders oneself prayerfully to the reality that is God, Christian Scientists affirm that healing naturally takes place as one's true being emerges. Not only are states such as hatred and fears "errors of the mortal mind," so also are organic diseases and physical deformities. Only God is real; the physical body, with its ailments, is not. In their faith, Christian Scientists usually refuse medical treatment, turning instead to prayer. Christian Scientist Tom Johnson explains:

> *This is not positive thinking or psychological training, and it is not beseeching God. Prayer is so much more than that. It is a yielding of heart and being to God, to divine love. It affirms truth. When there is that yielding of the human mind to the divine, the body naturally manifests that reality, and healing takes place, as in the New Testament. Healing is not magical, not just an occasional lightning bolt from on high. Health is the natural and very normal result when one's whole being grasps and is grasped by one's relationship to God.*[11]

Despite its longevity as a new religious movement, Christian Science has been jarred in recent years by legal claims on behalf of children whose parents refuse medical care for them.

Radhasoami

The Radhasoami movement is an outgrowth of Sikhism in India. Its leaders often have Sikh backgrounds, but while orthodox Sikhs believe in a succession of masters that stopped with the Tenth Guru and was transferred to the holy scripture, Radhasoamis believe in a continuing succession of living masters. The first of the Radhasoami gurus was Shiv Dayal Singh. In 1861, he offered to serve as a spiritual savior, carrying devotees into "Radhasoami," the ineffable Godhead. Some 10,000 took initiation under him. After his death, the movement eventually split into what are now over thirty branches, each with its own living master, although there is theoretically only one of these at a time on the earth. The Punjabi branches are known collectively as Sant Mat, or Path of the Masters.

Radhasoami is primarily an esoteric path, without exoteric ceremonies. Initiates are taught a secret yoga practice of concentrating on the third eye with attention to the inner sound and inner light in order to commune with the all-pervading power of God, the "Word" or Nam. The faithful are told that the experience must be both initiated and guided by a perfected being. Sant Mat masters teach respect for all earlier Perfect Masters for they feel they are of the same continuing lineage that includes Buddha, Mahavira, Jesus, Muhammad, Kabir, and the Sikh saints.

The Radhasoami movement now claims an estimated 1.7 million initiates. Those in the Agra area of India have created whole spiritual suburbs who live and

In the Radhasoami tradition, the living master is seen as one's beloved and essential guide to the divine. Master Sant Darshan Singh died in 1989; his position was filled by his son Rajinder Singh, who is standing in the left background in this photograph.

work as well as worship together. Outside of India, devotees gather in *satsangs* (spiritual congregations), who are supposed to support each other in the path. They are required to be vegetarians, to meditate every day, to forego alcohol and, if possible, tobacco, and to be employed.

Sant Rajinder Singh, the contemporary "god–man" in one Sant Mat lineage which is now called the Science of Spirituality, emphasizes universal harmony among people of different religions and different countries. He says his aim is to "take the mystery out of mysticism, to help people put mysticism into action in their own lives. By doing so, they will help themselves as well as those around them attain bliss and universal love."[12]

Nature spirituality

If religion is defined in the broadest sense as that which ties us back to the sacred, one of the strongest trends in our time is that of the religion of nature. Many who are experiencing a reconnection with the natural world do not think of this path as a religion, for it has no clear structure. It is growing spontaneously, from within. Its power as a global "religion" was illustrated by the 1992 UN Earth Summit in Rio de Janeiro, Brazil, to which tens of thousands of people from all religions and all countries flocked to voice and coordinate their mutual concerns for the ways in which we humans are destroying our planetary home. The effects of unchecked industrialization are gruesome. The unique ecosystem of Russia's huge Lake Baikal, for instance, has been highly contaminated by the production of cellulose on its shores and by the discharge into the lake of millions of tons of waste water from industrial and agricultural projects. Some heavily industrialized areas are nearly dead ecologically, with high rates of birth defects and disease among their human inhabitants.

Revival of old models

Some who seek to practice a nature-oriented spirituality look to the past for models. This trend is sometimes called Neo-Paganism, with reference to pre-Christian spiritual ways that are thought to have been practiced in Europe. Some, particularly women, are interested in evidence that the divine was once worshipped as a female power. They feel that by worshipping the Goddess they are reviving an ancient tradition, rejecting what they see as the negative aspects of patriarchal religions. Some call their way Witchcraft or "Wicca." As Starhawk, minister of the Covenant of the Goddess, explains:

> *Modern Witches are thought to be members of a kooky cult, . . . lacking the depth, the dignity and seriousness of purpose of a true religion. But Witchcraft is a religion, perhaps the oldest religion extant in the West . . . and it is very different from all the so-called great religions. The Old Religion, as we call it, is closer in spirit to Native American traditions or to the shamanism of the Arctic. It is not based on dogma or a set of beliefs, nor on scriptures or a sacred book revealed by a great man. Witchcraft takes its teachings from nature, and reads inspiration in the movements of the sun, moon, and stars, the flight of birds, the slow growth of trees, and the cycles of the seasons.[13]*

Fountain International members invoke the Earth spirit at the Merry Maiden's stone circle, Land's End, Cornwall, England.

Some Neo-Pagans honor pantheons such as the Egyptian gods and goddesses, balancing "masculine" and "feminine" qualities. Some try to reproduce some of the sacred ways of earlier European peoples, such as the Celts in the British Isles or the ancient Scandinavians. Reconstructing these ways is difficult, for they were largely oral rather than written traditions. After religions such as Christianity were firmly established, the remaining practitioners of the old ways were often tortured and killed as witches and blamed for social ills such as the plague. They were said to be in league with the devil against God, but the pagan pantheons had no devil—he was introduced by the Judeo-Christian-Muslim traditions.

Teachers from life-affirming religions that were never totally destroyed, such as certain Native American sacred ways, are highly valued as guides to worship for the natural world. From them, contemporary seekers have learned to use traditions, such as vision quests, sweat lodges, and medicine wheels. But the traditions are complex, requiring life-long training, and are interwoven with ways of life that have passed; Neo-Pagans from non-native backgrounds usually cannot experience them in their original fullness. What remains is the intent: to honor and cooperate with the natural forces, to celebrate the circle of life rather than destroy it, as "civilization" has done.

In the absence of sure knowledge of ancient ways of honoring Spirit, Neo-Pagans often make up their own forms of group ritual, attempting to draw on divine inspiration for these new ceremonies. Usually they are held outside, with the trees and rocks and waters, the sun, moon, and stars as the altars of the sacred. Speakers may invoke the pantheistic Spirit within all life or the invisible spirits of the place. At ceremonies dedicated to a phase of the moon or the change of the seasons, worshippers may be reminded of how their lives are interwoven with and affected by the natural rhythms. Prayers and ritual may be offered for the healing of the earth, the creatures, or the people.

Certain spots have traditionally been known as places of high energy, as indicated in Chapter 2, and these are often used for ceremonies and less structured sacred experiences. Ancient ceremonial sites in the British Isles, such as

Stonehenge and Glastonbury Tor, draw a new breed of tour groups wanting to experience the atmosphere of the places.

At the same time, some contemporary Neo-Pagans also conduct "ceremonies" through Internet connections, with computer graphics representing altars, sacred fires, and offerings made by the participants. Neo-Pagan festivals—some sixty each year in the United States alone—are popular gatherings where participants shed their usual identities and perhaps their clothes, create temporary "kinship groups," and enjoy activities such as ritual fires, storytelling, dancing, drumming, and workshops on subjects ranging from astrology to old methods of herbal healing.

Deep ecology

In addition to groups that are looking to replicate or re-invent past ways of earth-centered worship, many people in non-traditional societies are now feeling their way toward new ways of connecting themselves with the cosmos. What is called deep ecology is the experience of oneness with the natural world. By contrast, most Western religions have cast humans as controllers of the natural world, of a different order of being than bears and flowers, mountains and rivers. Australian deep ecologist John Seed refers to this attitude as **anthropocentrism**—"human chauvinism, the idea that humans are the crown of creation, the source of all value, the measure of all things."[14]

> *What is man without the beasts? If all the beasts were gone, men would die from a great loneliness of spirit. For whatever happens to the beasts soon happens to the man. . . . The earth does not belong to man; man belongs to the earth. This we know. All things are connected like the blood which unites one family.*
>
> *Attributed to Chief Seattle*[15]

During the twentieth century, many people came to a new awareness of our planetary home when they first saw it photographed from space. Rather than a globe divided by natural political boundaries, it appeared as a beautiful being, its surface mostly covered by oceans, wreathed in clouds, floating in the darkness of space. Some scientists have taken up this metaphor of the earth as a being and are finding evidence of its scientific plausibility. Biogeochemist James Lovelock (b. 1919) proposed in 1969 that the biosphere ("the entire range of living matter on Earth, from whales to viruses, and from oaks to algae") plus the earth's atmosphere, oceans, and soil can be viewed as "a single living entity, capable of manipulating the Earth's atmosphere to suit its overall needs and endowed with faculties and powers far beyond those of its constituent parts."[16] Lovelock named this complex, self-adjusting entity Gaia, after the Greek name for the Earth Goddess. In more recent elaborations of his Gaia theory, Lovelock emphasizes the "feminine" and divine characteristics of this being:

> *Any living organism a quarter as old as the Universe itself and still full of vigour is as near immortal as we ever need to know. She is of this Universe and, conceivably, a part of God. On Earth she is the source of life everlasting and is alive now; she gave birth to humankind and we are part of her.*[17]

"New Age" planetary consciousness

A corollary to the Gaia hypothesis is the concept that humans are becoming the global brain of the planet, its mode of conscious evolution. In the "body" of Gaia, the tropical rainforests function as the liver and/or lungs, the oceans as the circulatory system, and so on. As the evolving brain of the planet, we are becoming conscious of the dangers our activities pose to these other parts of "our body." Peter Russell, author of *The Global Brain*, warns that we have little time to become fully conscious of our potential destructiveness, our connectedness to everything else, and to take appropriate action to forestall environmental disaster:

> *As a species we are facing our final examination; . . . it is in fact an intelligence test—a test of our true intelligence as a species. In essence we are being asked to let go of our self-centred thinking and egocentric behaviour. We are being asked to become psychologically mature, to free ourselves from the clutches of this limited identity, and express our creativity in ways which benefit us all.[18]*

Russell acknowledges that "the wisdom of the human psyche" is already embodied in many of our religions, philosophies, and psychologies. But he feels that this understanding of our sacred oneness must be re-interpreted in contemporary language and scientific terms if it is to be grasped by enough people to make a difference.

Many believers in planetary consciousness feel that there is some mechanism by which the consciousnesses of all members of our species are interlinked, and if enough of us change our way of thinking, the rest of us will spontaneously change as well. The "Harmonic Convergence," August 16 and 17, 1987, seemingly predicted by the Mayan calendars as a time of major transition in the consciousness of humanity toward less anthropocentric thinking, drew hundreds of thousands of people to gatherings and sacred power spots around the earth. They were attempting to raise their own awareness above self-centeredness to planetary and even cosmic conciousness, in the hope that this mental/spiritual energy would have an impact on the whole globe.

Such thinking is a hallmark of what has been called New Age spirituality. Promoted in popular books and workshops, this amorphous but widespread movement anticipates that a network of personally transformed individuals will eventually lead to the transformation of the planet. Author Marianne Williamson voices this hope:

> *A mass movement is afoot in the world today, spiritual in nature and radical in its implications. After decades of declining influence on the affairs of the world, there is once again a widespread consideration of spiritual principles as an antidote to the pain of our times. Like flowers growing up through pieces of broken cement, signs of hope and faith appear everywhere. These signs reflect the light of a transcendent force at the center of things, present in our lives in a corrective and even miraculous manner, a light we can reach personally through internal work of a devotional nature. We are experiencing now an alteration of collective consciousness, centered not in government or science or religion per se. It is centered nowhere because it is present, at least potentially, everywhere. It is the rising up of our true divine nature, a reassertion of God in the consciousness of modern man.[19]*

This New Age spirituality often blossoms in individual mystical experiences of union with the cosmos. Some people find that if they commune nonverbally in a friendly spirit of oneness, they transcend the cultural boundaries between humanity and the rest of nature. It seems that those who have such experiences have often prepared themselves by spiritual disciplines, such as meditation practices, but the mystical experience itself comes spontaneously. Dorothy Maclean studied with Sufi masters, learning how to receive "inner guidance," before joining with Eileen and Peter Caddy in developing Findhorn, a transformation of desolate dunes on the coast of Scotland into a lush farming community. Dorothy's role was to receive communications from the energies that she called the plant *devas*, after the Hindu term for the invisible "shining ones." Dorothy developed a cooperative relationship with the *devas*, asking for their "advice" on matters such as what nutrients the plants needed.

Those who perceive a oneness of all life are often inspired to take political action to protect other members of the earth's body. Many support "Green" political agendas on behalf of the environment. In Australia and the northwest coast of the United States, people have chained themselves to giant trees to try to keep loggers from cutting them down. Julia Butterfly Hill spent 736 days living high in a thousand-year-old redwood tree to protect it from loggers. She braved winter storms with 90-mile-per-hour (145-kph) winds and harassment by helicopter, refusing to come down until an agreement was negotiated with the logging company to protect the tree and the surrounding 2.9 acres (1.2 ha) of virgin forest. She was sustained by spirituality. As she wrote,

> One day, through my prayers, an overwhelming amount of love started flowing into me, filling up the dark hole that threatened to consume me. I suddenly realized that what I was feeling was the love of the Earth, the love of Creation. Every day we, as a species, do so much to destroy Creation's ability to give us life. But that Creation continues to do everything in its power to give us life anyway. And that's true love.[20]

Similarly, in 1974, the women and children of Reni, a Himalayan village, wrapped themselves around trees to protect them from woodcutters seeking wood for the cities. They knew that the trees' roots were like hands that kept the hillside from washing away, that they provided shade for the plants they used for medicine and homes for the animals and birds. They said, "The trees are our brothers and sisters."[21] Although some view such actions as romantically naive and hopeless, the "Tree Hugging" movement grew to such proportions in northern India that the government banned commercial wood-cutting in Uttar Pradesh.

In contrast to the spiritual earnestness of those who care enough for the life of a tree to protect it with their own bodies, sociologists note that many people who participate in nature rituals and New Age movements are nomads, dabbling here and there without any deep commitment to what Stark and Bainbridge called "audience cults." In countries allowing freedom of religious choice, they may wander through a growing supermarket of spiritual offerings, taking a bit here and there according to their needs of the moment. Sandra Duarte de Souza describes "spiritual nomadism" in contemporary Brazil, where most people remain nominally Christian but many are also attracted to nature-oriented New Age groups. As opposed to a "radical change of life, marking the biography of the converted forever and demanding his faithfulness, . . . the idea of 'religious transit' admits the 'walk through' several religions, does not demand intestinal changes in the way of life of the 'transilient,' and exempts or attenuates the commitment."[22] Of course, the same can be said of established religions—that many people belong to them in a superficial way, without deeply transformational inner commitment.

Universalist religions

At the same time that an amorphous new religious movement toward "Green" spirituality is bringing humans into connection with nature, efforts are being made to harmonize the world's religions. To cite some examples, the Theosophical Society encourages the study of all religions and maintains interfaith libraries. Their books are made available to all who are interested in world religions. Many Protestant ministers are trained at interfaith theological seminaries in the United States. A number of temples are being built to honor all religions. In addition, several groups have religious unity as their major focus.

The inter-religious Dances of Universal Peace ("Sufi dancing") are often used to bring people into harmony with each other and with the divine during Universal Worship services inspired by the Sufi Master, Hazrat Inayat Khan. Rahima Dziubany (left) led the dances at a British community of handicapped adults and said: "I met their hearts in the very first moment, and from that place we danced."

Theosophical Society

One of the pioneering universalist religious movements began in Russia during the nineteenth century, the Theosophical Society. "Theosophy" means "divine wisdom," as revealed to Madame Helena Blavatsky (1831–1891) by unseen

H. P. BLAVATSKY

Madame Blavatsky, mystic and founder of the Theosophical Society.

Ascended Masters. Born into a noble Russian family, she was a fierce character with notable psychic powers. She traveled around the globe studying with masters of esoteric schools and said she had undergone initiations with Tibetan masters. She founded the Theosophical Society with the motto, "There is no religion higher than truth." It was an attempt, she said, "to reconcile all religions, sects and nations under a common system of ethics, based on eternal verities."[23]

The Theosophical Society introduced ancient Eastern ideas to Western seekers, especially Hindu beliefs such as *karma*, reincarnation, and subtle energies. Madame Blavatsky was particularly interested in the secret esoteric teachings of each religion, which collectively she called the "Wisdom Religion" or the "secret doctrine." Madame Blavatsky insisted that:

Theosophy is not a Religion. Theosophy is Religion itself. A Religion in the true and only correct sense, is a bond uniting men together—not a particular set of dogmas and beliefs. Now Religion, per se, in its widest meaning is that which binds not only all MEN, but also all BEINGS and all things in the entire Universe into one grand whole. ... Theosophy is RELIGION, and the Society its one Universal Church; the temple of Solomon's wisdom,—in building which "there was neither hammer, nor axe, nor any tool of iron heard in the house while it was building" (1 Kings, vi.); for this "temple" is made by no human hand, nor built in any

In Pearl of Searching, *the Russian painter Nicholas Roerich depicted a spiritual seeker and his guru in the Himalayas, a magnet for spiritual aspiration.*

locality on earth—but, verily, is raised only in the inner sanctuary of man's heart wherein reigns alone the awakened soul.[24]

The Theosophical Society now has members in seventy countries. The movement has splintered into several factions, which use the same name, and has also spawned other groups, such as the Roerich Society. Nicholas Roerich (1874–1947), a Russian painter, philosopher, and humanitarian, traveled in the Himalayas with his wife, Helena. He painted the spiritual light he perceived in those mountains and placed in his paintings holy figures from many religious traditions. After his death, Helena encouraged students to revere unseen Masters from India as well as Jesus. Now a steady stream of Russian pilgrims visit Roerich's mountain home in Kulu, India, seeking to establish the same connection with Indian spirituality which they see in his paintings.

Baha'i

A major new religion has been developed that attempts to unite all of humanity in the belief that there is only one God, the foundation of all religions. This is the Baha'i faith. It was foreshadowed in Persia in 1844 when a young man called the Bab ("Gate") announced that a new messenger of God to all the peoples of the world would soon appear. Because he proclaimed this message in a Muslim state, where Muhammad was considered the Seal of the Prophets, he was arrested and executed in 1850. Some 22,000 of his followers were reportedly massacred as well. One of his imprisoned followers was Baha'u'llah (1817–1892), a member of an aristocratic Persian family. He was stripped of his worldly goods, tortured, banished to Baghdad, and finally imprisoned for life in Palestine by the Turks. From prison, he revealed himself as the messenger proclaimed by the Bab. He wrote letters to the rulers of all nations, asserting that humanity was becoming unified and that a single global civilization was emerging.

Despite vigorous initial persecution, this new faith has by now spread to over 5 million followers in 233 countries and territories around the world, involving people from a wide variety of racial and ethnic groups. They have no priesthood but they do have their own sacred scriptures, revealed to Baha'u'llah. Baha'is compare this new messenger to previous great prophets, such as Abraham, Moses, Jesus, Muhammad, Krishna, and the Buddha. In fact, they see Baha'u'llah as the fulfillment of the prophecies of all religions. He did not declare himself to be the ultimate messenger, however. Rather, he prophesied that another would follow in a thousand years.

The heart of Baha'u'llah's message appears in the *Kitab-i-Iqan* ("The Book of Certitude"). God, Baha'u'llah says, is unknowable. Mere humans cannot understand God's infinite nature with their limited minds. However, God has become known through divine messengers, the founders of the great world religions. All

Baha'is' efforts are partly devotional and partly worldly, such as the sponsorship of a radio station in Ecuador. Its programs range from information about vaccination of livestock to revitalization of traditional Quechua music.

are manifestations of God, pure channels for helping humanity to understand God's will. The spiritual education of humans has been a process of "progressive revelation," said Baha'u'llah. Humanity has been maturing, like a child growing in the ability to grasp complex ideas as it grows in years and passes through grade school and college. Each time a divine messenger appeared, the message was given at levels appropriate to humanity's degree of maturity. Baha'u'llah proclaimed his own message as the most advanced and the one appropriate for this time. It contains the same eternal truths as the earlier revelations, but with some new features, which humanity is now ready to grasp, such as the oneness of all peoples, prophets, and religions, and a program for universal governance for the sake of world peace and social justice. Contemporary Baha'is are active in trying to develop a just order in the world, creating projects such as schools promoting global awareness, the European Business Forum encouraging business ethics, environmental awareness campaigns, and rural development projects.

Baha'i Houses of Worship, which are open to all, have nine doors and a central dome symbolizing the simultaneous diversity and oneness of humanity. Devotional services include readings from the scriptures of all religions, meditations, unaccompanied singing, and prayers by the Bab, Baha'u'llah, and his successor 'Abdu'l-Baha, his oldest son. 'Abdu'l-Baha describes the unified world that Baha'is envision:

> The world will become the mirror of the Heavenly Kingdom. . . . All nations will become one, all religions will be unified . . . the superstitions caused by races, countries, individuals, languages and politics will disappear; and all men will attain to life eternal under the shadow of the Lord of Hosts. . . . The relations between the countries, the mingling, union and friendship of the people . . . will reach to such a degree that the human race will be like one family. . . . The light of heavenly love will shine, and the darkness of enmity and hatred will be dispelled from the world.[25]

Islam opposes Baha'i as theological heresy, for Baha'i denies that Muhammad is the final prophet. Baha'i also finds theological legitimacy in religions such as Hinduism and Buddhism, which Islam does not consider acceptable God-worshipping traditions of revealed scriptures. Baha'is in Iran have been subjected to persecution since the 1979 Revolution, and one hundred and seventy were reportedly killed in the first five years after the revolution.

Baha'is' attempts to unite the earth in faith extend into the political sphere, where they actively support the United Nations' efforts to unify the planet. Their goal is the building of a unified, peaceful global society. To this end, they work for these principles:

1 The end of prejudice in all forms.
2 Equality for women.
3 Acceptance of the relativity and unity of spiritual truth.
4 Just distribution of wealth.
5 Universal education.
6 The individual responsibility to seek truth.
7 Development of a world federation.
8 Harmony of science and true religion.[26]

RELIGION IN PRACTICE

The Baha'i Model for Governance of the World

One of the most unusual features of the Baha'i faith is its own organization, which it sees as a good model for democratic governance of the whole world. Everywhere that people have converted to Baha'i faith, there is a highly organized framework designed not only to propagate the faith but also to democratize its leadership. Campaigning, electioneering, and nominations are prohibited, thus avoiding the empty promises to voters, corruption, and negative campaigning that tarnish elections in contemporary worldly democracies.

In the Baha'i "administrative order," each local group yearly elects nine or more people to a local Spiritual Assembly. Each local member is asked to pray and meditate and then write down the names of nine adults from the local Baha'i community who seem best qualified to lead the community. The necessary qualities are those of "unquestioned loyalty, of selfless devotion, of a well-trained mind, of recognized ability and mature experience."[27] By this simple and unusual process, Baha'is feel they choose leaders who are mature and humble rather than politically bold and egotistical. By the same process, the Local Spiritual Assemblies elect the National Spiritual Assemblies, and by the same process, the National Spiritual Assemblies choose the nine members of the Universal House of

Justice, seated in Haifa. Baha'is feel that this framework allows both grassroots access to decision-making and a superstructure for efficient international coordination of activities.

Within these elected groups—and also within business, school, and family settings—Baha'is attempt to reach decisions by a non-adversarial process of "consultation." The point of the process is to investigate truth in depth and to build consensus rather than struggle for power. Participants are enjoined to gather information from as many sources as possible and to be at once truthful and courteous to each other. Any idea once proposed is thereafter considered group property; it does not belong to one person or group to cling to, but rather is investigated impartially. As Svetlana Dorzhieva, formerly Executive Secretary of the National Spiritual Assembly of Baha'is of Russia, Georgia, and Armenia, explains: "What is wonderful is that when a person says his opinion, he just forgets that it belonged to him. It is offered and then it is discussed."[28] Attempts are made to reach unanimous consensus, but failing that, a majority vote may be taken. The success of this process is demonstrated in the fact that people from very diverse backgrounds manage to work and worship together.

If the religions are true it is because each time it is God who has spoken, and if they are different it is because God has spoken in different "languages" in conformity with the diversity of the receptacles. Finally, if they are absolute and exclusive, it is because in each of them God has said "I."

Frithjof Schuon[29]

Opposition to new religious movements

Throughout history, new religious movements have met with opposition from previously organized religions, which perceive them as threats to their own strength or brand them as heresies. In Russia, various foreign-based new religious movements are fighting for freedom of worship against a 1997 law passed at the behest of the Russian Orthodox Church and restricting the activities of groups that were newly introduced to Russia. Lawyers defending these groups have had some success in court cases. Some of these legal battles have taken place in Russia with reference to Jehovah's Witnesses and organizations sponsored by the Unification Movement, which are opposed by the Russian Orthodox Church.

With or without prompting by established religions, nations may attempt to suppress new religious movements. China has taken strong measures to stamp out Falun Gong, one of many movements based on traditional Taoist Ch'i-kung energy practices. Untraditionally, Falun Gong has a living charismatic teacher, Li Hongzhi, who now lives in exile in New York City, from where he has spread Falun Gong to thirty countries. He claims to be the only living person who has the authority to specify which practices should be used, and he insists that the simple exercises—which Falun Gong claims can be learned from its books, cassettes, and websites—are of no value and may even be destructive unless they are practiced in combination with "cultivation of the Xinxing." This moral aspect is based on the Buddhist and Confucian virtues of truthfulness, benevolence, and

Falun Gong members doing their meditation practices.

forbearance. In 1999, the Chinese government declared Falun Gong an "evil cult" that has cheated and brainwashed its followers, leading to 1,500 deaths by suicide or failure to seek medical care due to faith in the teachings. Not agreeing with this assessment, 10,000 Falun Gong followers staged a silent protest in Tiananmen Square. Protestors were jailed and beaten, followed by wave upon wave of peaceful protests by daring members who met the same fate. Some are said to have died from torture while in police custody. Nonetheless, members refuse to give up their new religion. Practitioners claim that Falun Gong has brought them physical healing, inner peace, and answers to the central questions of life.

In addition to negative reactions from governments and previously organized religions, new religious movements usually meet with opposition from family members of those who join. There is also concern that new religious movements may cause psychological damage, especially to vulnerable young people. In the United States, the "anti-cult" movement has employed special agents who capture and "deprogram" followers of new religions, at the request of their parents. However, the old Cult Awareness Network went bankrupt in 1996 after one of its deprogramming victims won a multi-million dollar damage suit against it.

Much of the effort to eliminate or control new religious movements has now shifted to Europe, where governments are struggling with issues of religious freedom versus public safety. France is reportedly home to 172 "sects" and eight hundred small new religious groups, some of them rather bizarre, including satanic groups that pull bodies out of graves and turn their crosses upside down, and groups that have committed mass suicide. There is concern that some are using a religious front to carry on illegal businesses or extort money from gullible followers. Some are neo-fascist groups in the guise of medieval cults whose intentions seem to involve the propagation of white supremacy ideas and hatred of immigrants.

Violence in new religious movements

The issue of violence and mass suicide within some new religious movements is causing serious concern. In 1994 and 1995, seventy-four members of the Order of the Solar Temple committed suicide or were killed by the others, in Switzerland, France, and Quebec. The group had claimed to be descendants of the medieval Knights Templars and to be receiving communications from superhuman "Masters of the Temple" through their founder, Joseph di Mambro. When his health worsened, membership declined, and French and Canadian authorities challenged the group, its leaders apparently decided that the apocalypse they awaited was near and that ritual death would transport them safely to another planet.

In 1995, members of the Japanese new religious movement Aum Shinrikyo killed twelve people and injured thousands by releasing sarin gas in the Tokyo subway system. The movement had begun with secret meditation training more or less based on Buddhism but with long night rituals that reportedly include drinking pots of sea water and then vomiting, for purification. Perhaps due to declining membership and attacks in the media, the founder, Shoko Asahara,

Members of Aum Shinrikyo are watched by riot police as they walk through the Aum's complex in Kamikuishiki village in 1995 after the movement was accused of poison gas attacks on the Tokyo subway.

began propagating apocalyptic teachings that justified murder as beneficial to the *karma* of the victims.

In 2000, more than 800 members of the Movement for the Restoration of the Ten Commandments of God died in a fire in their headquarters in Uganda or were found in mass graves elsewhere in the country. It appears that they were expecting the apocalypse and hoped that the Virgin Mary would come to conduct them to heaven. As in the case of the Order of the Solar Temple, it seems that many were "helped" to die by the core members, perhaps as traitors.

Law enforcement agencies are now trying to understand and anticipate what makes some religious movements turn violent and thus pose a threat to themselves or others. One theory is that members are brainwashed by an evil guru. Another theory is that some leaders are simply mad, as are those who follow them. According to another line of thinking, conversion to a new religious movement is a sign of psychopathology—but this argument could be made about commitment to any religion. Another theory is "deviance amplification," as in the case of the Branch Davidians killed at Waco, Texas; there is a widespread feeling that the tragedy might have been avoided if law enforcement agencies had not been so provocative. Dr. Marc Galanter of New York University Medical School had earlier concluded from interviews with thousands of members of new religious movements with charismatic leaders that those most likely to join such a group are already lonely and alienated from the mainstream culture. Those who most feel a sense of belonging within the new group are those who share its distrust of outsiders. The "shared paranoia" that holds the group together may be exacerbated in the case of apocalyptic groups. Dr. Galanter explained:

The only source of information becomes what the leader tells you. They have to rebuff any external reality that would undermine their beliefs. Then, if outsiders actually appear to threaten the group, it bonds them more closely and validates their view that it's better to die together than to submit to evil outside forces.[30]

As indicated in Chapter 1, there are both potential dangers and potential benefits associated with giving power over one's life to any religion, new or old. After members of the Aum Shinrikyo movement were accused of launching a poison gas attack on the Tokyo subway and its leader of murdering a lawyer and his wife and child, Japanese people asked themselves how their intelligent countrymen could have been drawn to the movement. Previously associated with secret meditation training, after the subway attack the movement was described in the media as a doomsday cult making chemical weapons. Japanese observers have looked at their modern society and concluded that it creates a susceptibility to blind obedience. Author Reiko Hatsumi writes:

I think most of my countrymen are honest and hardworking, yet also gullible, with a childlike naivete and a disinclination to think on their own. Japanese education has always encouraged this. Students are taught to absorb knowledge but not to judge or rationalize. . . .

By being childlike, we also demand emotional security, a guiding hand. Unfortunately, we no longer have a family system. Fathers have abdicated their position as head of the family. They are too busy working late and commuting. The mothers spur their children to get into good schools. . . . The children don't have much to look forward to, except a struggle to get ahead in a crowded, competitive society.

So when someone such as Asahara [leader of Aum Shinrikyo] comes along and takes time to listen and to give advice that seems to resolve dilemmas and solve problems, the young hand over their hearts and follow.[31]

In trying to determine the characteristics of a religious movement that might become suicidal, as opposed to the long-standing forbearance of groups such as Jehovah's Witnesses, New Religious Movements specialists Massimo Introvigne and Jean-François Mayer determined that these groups perceived threats from the outside and encouraged members to feel that they were not of this world. When under attack and also shaken by internal defections, these groups may conclude that suicide is their only good option. As expressed in a document prepared by Heaven's Gate, a group that in 1997 committed ritual suicide in anticipation of being transported in UFOs to the Kingdom of Heaven by benevolent extraterrestrials, "There is no place for us to go but up."[32]

With global terrorism increasing, what are known as "world-destroying cults" by Robert Jay Lifton bear careful watching. According to Lifton's assessment, world-destroying cults such as Aum Shinrikyo have these characteristics: (1) "totalized guruism," to the extent that both guru and disciples lose the ability to distinguish between reality and metaphors; (2) "a vision of an apocalyptic event or series of events that would destroy the world in the service of renewal;" (3) an "ideology of killing to heal, of altruistic murder and altruistic world destruction;" (4) "the relentless impulse toward world-rejecting purification;" (5) "the lure of ultimate weapons;" (6) "a shared state of aggressiveness," with no scruples against illegal actions; and (7) "a claim to absolute scientific truth," such as Aum Shinrikyo's use of hallucinogens to transform their disciples by "extreme technocratic manipulation."[33] Some of these characteristics are shared by extremist wings of established religions who are proving their ability to wreak global havoc in the name of their own mission.

Will new religious movements last?

All of the major religions we have examined were once new and were once resisted by more entrenched institutions. Will any of today's new religious movements last more than a few generations? Those who study the sociology of religion are researching the secular factors that seem to predispose a new religious movement to become widespread and longlasting. One of these is a balance between similarities to existing beliefs (making it attractive and nonthreatening to potential converts) and differences compelling enough for people to convert. A second factor is organization, personal commitment, and bonds between members that will survive the death of the prophet and the original followers. Third is the social setting: Times of great social change, places that allow freedom of choice in matters of religion, and societies with fragmented relationships between people are most conducive to the recruitment of new members. Fourth is the status of prevailing religions; if they have become merely institutional with little spiritual life, they are susceptible to being supplanted by more vibrant new faiths. Fifth is the younger generations: Children must be continually born or recruited into the faith, taught its values, and given responsible parts to play in keeping the faith alive.

The spiritual aspects of new religions are also of major importance but they cannot easily be quantified. Among these are the genuine spirituality of the founder or spreader of the message, and the ability of the new teachings and their presentation to capture people's hearts, change their lives, motivate them to act collectively, and give them the courage to face social opposition. Finally, there is the necessity of divine assistance, in the parlance of theistic religions, or alliance with absolute truth, from the point of view of nontheistic religions.

Suggested reading

Barker, Eileen, *New Religious Movements: A Practical Introduction*, London: Her Majesty's Stationery Office, 1989. A sociological study on the effects of new religious movements on people's lives.

Blavatsky, H. P., *The Key to Theosophy*, Los Angeles: The United Lodge of Theosophists, 1920. A wide-ranging survey of esoterica from many of the world's religions.

Bromley, David G. and Hammond, Phillip E., eds., *The Future of New Religious Movements*, Macon, Georgia: Mercer University Press, 1987. Interesting sociological analyses of the likelihood of longrun success of some contemporary movements.

Bryant, M. Darrol and Dayton, Donald W., *The Coming Kingdom*, Essays in American Millennialism and Eschatology, Barrytown, New York: International Religious Foundation, 1983. Studies of Christianity-based movements, such as Jehovah's Witnesses and Mormons, which foretell a dramatic coming of the Kingdom of God on earth.

Ellwood, Robert S. and Partin, Harry B., *Religious and Spiritual Groups in Modern America*, Englewood Cliffs, New Jersey: Prentice Hall, 1988. Useful source of information and appreciation of new religions that have flourished in the United States.

Gaver, Jessyca Russell, *The Baha'i Faith: Dawn of a New Day*, New York: Hawthorn Books, Inc., 1967. The history and beliefs of Baha'is, in appreciative detail.

Hall, John R., Sylvaine Trinh, Philip Schuyler, eds., *Apocalypse Observed: Religious Movements, Social Order and Violence in North America, Europe, and Japan*, Routledge, 2000. Articles analyzing situations within which violent new religious movements have developed.

Melton, J. Gordon, *Encyclopedic Handbook of Cults in America*, New York: Garland Publications, 1992. History and criticism of new religious movements that are considered controversial in North America.

Miller, Timothy, ed., *When Prophets Die: The Postcharismatic Fate of New Religious Movements*, Albany, New York: State University of New York Press, 1991. Contemporary case studies of how the followers of strong founders have or have not succeeded in keeping the faith alive.

Miller, Timothy, *America's Alternative Religions*, Albany: State University of New York Press, 1995. A lengthy survey of the major alternative traditions in America, with chapters written by scholars specializing in specific groups.

Seed, John, Macy, Joanna, Fleming, Pat, Naess, Arne, *Thinking Like a Mountain: Towards a Council of All Beings*, Philadelphia: New Society Publishers, 1988. Some of the leaders of the deep ecology movement offer a collection of thoughts and exercises leading one into the experience of kinship with all life.

Starhawk, *The Spiral Dance: A Rebirth of the Ancient Religion of the Great Goddess*, San Francisco and London: Harper and Row, 1979. A lyrical, experimental introduction to the interweaving of the God and Goddess principles.

Stark, Rodney and William Sims Bainbridge, *The Future of Religion: Secularization, Revival, and Cult Formation*, University of California Press, 1985. Includes a sociological classification of religous groups in relation to their broader environment.

Wessinger, Catherine, *How the Millennium Comes Violently: From Jonestown to Heaven's Gate*, Seven Bridges Press, 2000. Develops the theory that violence is catalyzed by certain types of interactions.

CHAPTER 7

TWENTY-FIRST-CENTURY PLURALISM

As the twenty-first century begins, the global landscape is a patchwork of faiths. A major feature of religious geography is that no single religion dominates the world. Although authorities from many faiths have historically asserted that theirs is the best and only way, in actuality new religions and new versions of older religions continue to spring up and then divide, subdivide, and provoke reform movements.

With migration, missionary activities, and refugee movements, religions have shifted from their country of origin. It is no longer so easy to show a world map in which each country is assigned to a particular religion. In Russia there are not only Russian Orthodox Christians but also Muslims, Catholics, Protestants, Jews, Buddhists, Hindus, shamanists, and members of new religions. At the same time, there are now sizable Russian Orthodox congregations in the United States. Buddhism arose in India but now is most pervasive in East Asia and popular in France, England, and the United States. Islam arose in what is now Saudi Arabia, but there are more Muslims in Indonesia than in any other country. There are large Muslim populations in Central Asia, and growing Muslim populations in the United States, with over fifty mosques in the city of Chicago alone.

Professor Diana Eck, Chairman of the Pluralism Project at Harvard University, describes what she terms the new "geo-religious reality":

> Our religious traditions are not boxes of goods passed intact from generation to generation, but rather rivers of faith—alive, dynamic, ever-changing, diverging, converging, drying up here, and watering new lands there.
> We are all neighbors somewhere, minorities somewhere, majorities somewhere. This is our new geo-religious reality. There are mosques in the Bible Belt in Houston, just as there are Christian churches in Muslim Pakistan. There are Cambodian Buddhists in Boston, Hindus in Moscow, Sikhs in London.[1]

Hardening of religious boundaries

As religions proliferate and interpenetrate geographically, one common response has been the attempt to deny the validity of other religions. In many countries there is tension between the religion that has been most closely linked with national history and identity and other religions that are practiced or have been introduced into the country. Protestant congregations are rushing to offer Bibles and religious tracts to citizens of formerly atheistic communist countries, with the idea that they are introducing Christianity there. But Orthodox Christianity, established more than a thousand years ago in Russia, had continued to exist there despite communist rule, sometimes by collaboration with the oppressive authorities, and sometimes by sheer devotion in the midst of hardship, even though the Church structures were limited and controlled by the State. People from the more established religions seek to find a balance between freedom of religion for all and the threat they perceive to their traditional values, customs, and sense of national identity.

The issue arises of which religions will receive state funding. In Ontario, Canada, for instance, the government has given funding to Roman Catholic schools for a hundred years, yet such funds have been denied to Jewish, Muslim, and Protestant Christian schools. In some countries, there is resistance to offering such public funds to new groups that are organized and well financed from abroad. For example, it was not until 1997 that the British government recognized Islamic schools on a par with the long-established Christian and Jewish academic institutions.

Registration requirements are another means used to help control or at least track the introduction of religions into countries where they did not originate. Another is outright banning of new or minority religions. In 1994, the Russian Orthodox Church warned that any of its followers who promoted the teachings of new religious movements would be excommunicated. It referred to newly introduced religions and new religious movements as predatory wolves in sheep's clothing and claimed that they were destroying "the traditional order of life which grew under the influence of the Orthodox Church, our common spiritual and moral ideal, and threaten the integrity of national self-conscience and cultural identity." Then in 1997, the Russian parliament passed a law prohibiting religions that had not been officially existing in Russia longer than fifteen years from distributing religious materials or newspapers or running schools. The law protects the powerful status of the Russian Orthodox Church and provides "respect" only to other long-established religions—Islam, Buddhism, and Judaism—with some concessions to Protestant and Roman Catholic Christianity.

In some previously communist countries, old animosities between people of different ethnic groups resurfaced with great violence once totalitarian regimes toppled. These intense ethnic and political struggles often pit people of different faiths against each other, as in former Yugoslavia. Where there had been a seemingly peaceful society, horrifying atrocities arose among largely Orthodox Christian Serbs, Roman Catholic Croats, and the Muslims living mainly in Bosnia and Hercegovina. Gyorgy Bulanyi, founder of the Hungarian Bokor Movement, charges that religious leaders were instigators of rather than dissuaders from violence:

Neither the cardinal in Zagreb nor the Patriarch of Belgrade nor the Great Mufti of Sarajevo preaches to his people that Serbians—or Croats or Muslims—are also created by God, and that it is therefore a cardinal sin to kill them. This is not the line we hear from them, but rather another one: "It is a human right and duty to defend one's family and nation against attack."[2]

The twentieth-century rush for materialism and secular values also fanned an increase in "fundamentalism." Reactionaries do not want their values and life patterns to be despoiled by contemporary secular culture, which they see as crude and sacrilegious. They may try to withdraw socially from the secular culture even while surrounded by it. Or they may actively try to change the culture, using political power to shape social laws or lobbying for banning of textbooks that they feel do not include their religious point of view. As described by the Project on Religion and Human Rights,

> *Fundamentalists' basic goal is to fight back—culturally, ideologically, and socially—against the assumptions and patterns of life that are taken for granted in contemporary secular society and culture, refusing to celebrate them or to embrace them fully. They keep their distance and refuse to endorse the legitimacy of any culture that opposes what they perceive as fundamental truths. Secular culture, in their eyes, is base, barbarous, crude, and essentially profane. It produces a society that respects no sacred order and ignores the possibility of redemption.[3]*

Although fundamentalism may be based on religious motives, it has often been politicized and turned to violent means. Political leaders have found the religious loyalty and absolutism of some fundamentalists an expedient way to mobilize political loyalties, and fundamentalists have themselves attempted to control the political arena in order to bring the social changes they prefer. The United States, which had prided itself on being a "melting pot" for all cultures, with full freedom of religion and no right of government to promote any specific religion, has witnessed attempts by Christian fundamentalists to control education and politics, and a simultaneous rise in violence against ethnic and religious minorities. Christians and Muslims are clashing in Indonesia and Nigeria. Violence among different branches of the same religion also rages—Roman Catholic churches in Northern Ireland have been burned by Protestants, and Sunni and Shi'ite Muslims have taken up arms against each other in neighboring Arabic countries. The Internet reveals the sentiments and activities of a troubling number of hate groups promoting intolerance, bigotry, hatred and violence against specific others in the name of religion.

The devastating attacks by terrorists on United States targets in 2001 brought instant polarization along religious and ethnic lines. Hundreds of hate crimes were committed in the United States against Muslims and foreign immigrants who were mistaken for Muslims and were suddenly seen as "outsiders" as some Americans responded in fear and rage. With the subsequent bombing of Afghanistan, the perpetrators of terrorism such as Osama bin Laden incited Muslims to see the world in terms of Muslims versus the infidels, and to join together to drive the United States out of its strategic positions in Muslim lands. Both sides claimed that God was on their side and their cause a holy one.

Interfaith movement

At the same time that boundaries between religions are hardening in many areas, there has been a rapid acceleration of **interfaith dialogue**—the willingness of people of all religions to meet, explore their differences, and appreciate and find enrichment in each other's ways to the divine. This approach has been historically difficult, for many religions have made exclusive claims to being the best or only way. Professor Ewert Cousins, editor of an extensive series of books on the spiritual aspects of major religions, comments: "I think all the religions are overwhelmed by the particular revelation they have been given and are thus blinded to other traditions' riches."[4]

Religions are quite different in their external practices and culturally-influenced behaviors. There are doctrinal differences on basic issues, such as the cause of and remedy for evil and suffering in the world, or the question of whether the divine is singular, plural, or nontheistic. And some religions make apparent claims to superiority which are difficult to reconcile with other religions' claims. The Qur'an, for instance, while acknowledging the validity of earlier prophets as messengers of God, refers to the Prophet Muhammad as the "Seal of the Prophets" (Sura 33:40). This description has been interpreted to mean that prophecy was completed with the Prophet Muhammad. If he is believed to be the last prophet, no spiritual figures after he passed away in c. 632 could be considered prophets, though they might be seen as teachers. Similarly, Christians read in John 14:6 that Jesus said, "I am the way, the truth, and the life; no one comes to the Father but by me." But some Christian scholars now feel that it is inappropriate to take this line out of its context (in which Jesus's disciples were asking how to find their way to him after they died) and to interpret it to mean that the ways of Hindus and Buddhists are invalid. Relationships with other faiths was not the question being answered.

Many people of broad vision have noted that many of the same principles reappear in all traditions. Every religion teaches the importance of setting one's own selfish interests aside, loving others, harkening to the divine, and exercising control over the mind. What is called the "Golden Rule," expressed by the Prophet Muhammad as "None of you truly have faith if you do not desire for your brother that which you desire for yourself," is found in every religion.

The absolute authority of scriptures is being questioned by contemporary scholars who are interpreting them in their historical and cultural context and thus casting some doubt upon their exclusive claims to truth. Some liberal scholars are also proposing that there is an underlying experiential unity among religions. Wilfred Cantwell Smith, for instance, concluded that the revelations of all religions have come from the same divine source. Christian theologian John Hick suggests that religions are culturally different responses to one and the same reality. The Muslim scholar Frithjof Schuon feels that there is a common mystical base underlying all religions, but that only the enlightened will experience and understand it, whereas others will see the superficial differences.

Responses to other faiths

With these contrasting views, there are several different ways in which people of different religions may relate to each other.

Diana Eck, Professor of Comparative Religion and Indian Studies of Harvard Divinity School and Chair of the World Council of Churches committee on interfaith dialogue, observes that there are three responses to contact between religions. One is **exclusivism**: "Ours is the only true way." Eck and others have noted that such a point of view has some value, for deep personal commitment to one's faith is a foundation of religious life and also the first essential step in interfaith dialogue.

Eck sees the second response to interfaith contact as **inclusivism**. This may take the form of trying to create a single world religion. Or it may appear as the belief that our religion is spacious enough to encompass all the others, that it supersedes all previous religions, as Islam said it was the culmination of all monotheistic traditions. In this approach, the inclusivists do not see other ways as a threat. They feel that all diversity is included in a single world view—their own.

The third way Eck discerns is **pluralism**: to hold one's own faith and at the same time ask people of other faiths about their path, about how they want to be understood. As Eck sees it, this is the only point from which true dialogue can take place. And it is a place from which true cooperation, true relationship can happen. Uniformity and agreement are not the goals—the goal is to collaborate, to combine our differing strengths for the common good. For effective pluralistic dialogue, people must have an openness to the possibility of discovering sacred truth in other religions. This is the premise on which this book has been written.

Interfaith initiatives

People of all faiths have begun to put their hearts together. Initially, ecumenical conferences involved pairs of related religions that were trying to agree to disagree, such as Judaism and Christianity. Now a large number of interfaith organizations and interfaith meetings draw people from all religions in a spirit of mutual appreciation.

In 1986, Pope John Paul II invited one hundred and sixty representatives of all religions to Assisi in honor of the humble St. Francis, to pray together for world peace. "If the world is going to continue, and men and women are to survive in it, it cannot do without prayer. This is the permanent lesson of Assisi," declared the pope.[5]

Two years later, the Assisi idea was extended to include governmental leaders, scientists, artists, business leaders, and media specialists as well as spiritual leaders. Some two hundred of them from around the globe met in Oxford, England, in 1988 at the Global Forum of Spiritual and Parliamentary Leaders on Human Survival. They held their plenary sessions beneath an enormous banner with the image of the earth as seen from space. Statements of concern for the environment brought participants to the conclusion that the ecological dangers now threatening the entire human race may be the key that draws us together. But it was spiritual camaraderie rather than shared fear that brought the participants together. Dr. Wangari Maathai, leader of the Green Belt movement in Kenya, observed:

All religions meditate on the Source. And yet, strangely, religion is one of our greatest divides. If the Source be the same, as indeed it must be, all of us and all religions meditate on the same Source.[6]

In 1990, a great assembly of spiritual leaders of all faiths with scientists and parliamentarians took place in what, until a few years before, would have been the most unlikely place in the world for such a gathering—Moscow, capital of the previously officially atheistic Soviet Union. The final speaker was Mikhail Gorbachev, who called for a merging of scientific and spiritual values in the effort to save the planet.

Throughout 1993, special interfaith meetings were held around the world to celebrate the one hundredth anniversary of the 1893 Parliament of the World's Religions in Chicago. In 1893, the figure who most captured world attention was Swami Vivekananda (1863–1902). He brought appreciation of Eastern religions to the West, and made these concluding remarks:

> If the Parliament of Religions has shown anything to the world it is this: It has proved to the world that holiness, purity, and charity are not the exclusive possessions of any church in the world, and that every system has produced men and women of the most exalted character. In the face of this evidence, if anybody dreams of the exclusive survival of his own religion and the destruction of others, I pity him from the bottom of my heart.[7]

The largest 1993 centenary celebration of the Parliament of the World's Religions was again held in Chicago. It gathered hundreds of well-known teachers from all faiths and thousands of participants to consider the critical issues facing humanity. It included an attempt to define and then use as a global standard for behavior the central ethical principles common to all religions. The provisional conference document signed by many of the leaders, "The Declaration Toward a Global Ethic", included agreement on what has been called the Golden Rule:

> There is a principle which is found and has persisted in many religious and ethical traditions of humankind for thousands of years: What you do not wish done to yourself, do not do to others. Or in positive terms: What you wish done to yourself, do to others! This should be the irrevocable, unconditional norm for all areas of life, for families and communities, for races, nations, and religions.[8]

The effort to draw up an interfaith global standard for ethical national behavior has been taken up by the United Nations, in a project involving religious representatives, philosophers, and political leaders from many cultures.

Many people have also had the vision that the United Nations could be home to representatives or leaders from all faiths, jointly advising the United Nations on international policy from a religious perspective. This dream has taken many forms, including the United Religions Initiative, the dream of Episcopal bishop William Swing of California. His aim is to:

> bring religions and spiritual traditions to a common table, where, respecting each other's distinctness, they may seek the common ground necessary to make peace among themselves and to work together, in dialogue with local, national, and international organizations, to create a sustainable future for all people on the earth.[9]

Questions arise in such an effort, in addition to the necessity for substantial funding. Which religions should be represented? Major religions have many offshoots and branches that do not fully recognize each other's authority. And should any of the myriad new religious movements be included? Should indigenous religions be included? If so, could one representative speak for all the varied traditions? Would such an organization reflect the bureaucratic patriarchal structures of existing religions, or would it include women, the poor, and enlightened people rather than managers? If the members of the body were not elected by their respective organizations, but were rather simply interested individuals, what authority would they have? Such organizational questions surfaced in the Millennium World Peace Summit of Religious and Spiritual Leaders, held in 2000 in New York. Women and young people were not well represented among the one thousand 800 invited participants, and despite the efforts to invite people of all faiths, there were complaints that speeches were necessarily too short to provide any in-depth dialogue, and that some speakers did not truly represent the essence of their religions.

The Internet carries the efforts of many organizations to provide accurate information about a variety of religions to help overcome ignorance and intolerance. The Ontario Consultants on Religious Practice, for instance, sponsor www.religioustolerance.org, a rich offering of articles and resources on a long list of religions plus essays on interfaith themes. Non-governmental organizations, such as the Council for Global Education in Washington, D.C., are attempting to develop curricula for teaching children about the world's religions in classrooms.

A common response in the United States to the September 2001 terrorist attacks was interfaith prayer meetings, from local communities to the National Cathedral. Many leaders broadcast appeals against confusing Islam with terrorism. To help prevent hate attacks on their Muslim sisters, non-Muslim women in the United States, Britain, and Australia donned head scarves in the "Scarves for Solidarity" campaign. They explained:

To protect Muslim women who have been afraid to leave their houses because of ignorant hatred, we will dress piously. The hijab is worn outwardly to show the inner hijab of compassion, honesty, and love, which is carried in the hearts and souls of Islamic men and women alike. It is not meant to be a political symbol in any way, just a symbol of love.[10]

Inter-religious groups and projects are quite active in Britain, with its increasingly multi-cultural population. The Leicester Council of Faiths, for instance, includes representatives from Christianity, Hinduism, Islam, Sikhism, Judaism, Jainism, Buddhism, and the Baha'i faith. Their efforts include developing a multi-faith Welcome Centre, ensuring that there is balanced representation of all faiths at civic events, providing multi-faith counseling and a multi-faith chaplaincy service in some healthcare institutions, informing the various faiths about political matters that affect them, and working with the National Health Service on care that is sensitive to people's specific faiths.

> *"Spirituality is not merely tolerance. . . . It is the absolute recognition of the other's faith in God as one's own."*
>
> Sri Chinmoy

Whatever the organizational strategy, Gordon Kaufman, Harvard professor and Mennonite Christian minister, sees interfaith dialogue as crucial in solving the problems of the planet:

The problems with which modernity confronts us—extending even to the possibility that we may obliterate mankind completely in a nuclear holocaust—demand that we bring together all the wisdom, devotion, and insight that humanity has accumulated in its long history. ... We simply cannot afford not to enter into conversation with representatives of other traditions, making available to each other whatever resources each of our traditions has to offer, and learning from each other whatever we can.[11]

Suggested reading

Barney, Gerald O. and others, *Threshold 2000: Critical Issues and Spiritual Values for a Global Age*, Ada, Michigan: CoNexus Press, 2000. Projections of environmental and social crises in the twenty-first century, with multi-faith spiritual perspectives that may offer solutions.

Beversluis, Joel V., ed., *A Sourcebook for Earth's Community of Religions*, second edition, Grand Rapids, Michigan: 1995. Essays on contemporary issues, reflections on how religious people might come together in harmony, and resources guides for religious education, first prepared for the 1993 Chicago Parliament of the World's Religions.

Braybrooke, Marcus, *Faith and Interfaith in a Global Age*, Grand Rapids, Michigan: CoNexus Press and Oxford: Braybrooke Press, 1998. One of the world's central interfaith coordinators surveys the interfaith movement at the turn of the century.

Forward, Martin, *Ultimate Visions: Reflections on the Religions we Choose*, Oxford: Oneworld Publications, 1995. Interesting personal essays by scholars and leaders of many religions, reflecting upon why they like their religion and how it can contribute to a future of harmony among all religions.

Khan, Hazrat Inayat, *The Unity of Religious Ideals*, New Lebanon, New York: Sufi Order Publications, 1927, 1979. A master of Sufi mysticism explores the underlying themes in the religious quest that are common to all religions.

Swidler, Leonard, ed., *Toward a Universal Theology of Religion*, Maryknoll, New York: Orbis Books, 1988. Leaders in the evolving interfaith dialogue grapple with the issues of transcending differences.

Tobias, Michael, Morrison, Jane, and Gray, Bettina, eds., *A Parliament of Souls: In Search of Global Spirituality*, Ada, Michigan: CoNexus Press, 1994. Interviews with twenty-eight spiritual leaders from the 1993 Parliament of the World's Religions, plus supplementary material.

World Scripture: A Comparative Anthology of Sacred Texts, New York: Paragon House/International Religious Foundation, 1991. A thematic compendium of appealing excerpts from the scriptures and oral traditions of many religions, in excellent translations selected by major scholars.

NOTES

CHAPTER ONE
THE RELIGIOUS RESPONSE

1 Karl Marx, from "Contribution to the Critique of Hegel's Philosophy of Right," 1884, *Karl Marx, Early Writings*, translated and edited by T. B. Bottomore, London: C. A. Watts and Co., 1963, pp. 43–44; Capital, vol. 1, 1867, translated by Samuel Moore and Edward Aveling, F. Engels, ed., London: Lawrence & Wishart, 1961, p. 79; "The Communism of the Paper 'Rheinischer Beobachter'," *On Religion*, London: Lawrence & Wishart, undated, pp. 83–84.

2 Karl Marx, "Religion as the Opium of the People," in Karl Marx and Friedrich Engels, *On Religions*, Moscow: Foreign Language Publishing House, 1955, p. 42.

3 Emile Durkheim, *The Elementary Forms of Religious Life*, New York: Free Press, 1915, p. 62.

4 Mata Amritanandamayi, *Awaken Children!* vol. IV, Amritapuri, Kerala, India: Mata Amritanandamayi Mission Trust, 1992, pp. 103–104.

5 Jiddu Krishnamurti, *The Awakening of Intelligence*, New York: Harper & Row, 1973, p. 90.

6 Buddha, *The Dhammapada*, translated by P. Lal, 162/92 Lake Gardens, Calcutta, 700045 India. (Originally published by Farrar, Straus & Giroux, 1967, p. 97.) Reprinted by permission of P. Lal.

7 Mahatma Gandhi, quoted in Eknath Easwaran, *Gandhi the Man*, Petaluma, California: Nilgiri Press, 1978, p. 121.

8 *The Bhagavad-Gita*, portions of Chapter 2, translated by Eknath Easwaran, quoted in Easwaran, op. cit., pp. 121–122.

9 Excerpted from Agnes Collard, in "The Face of God," *Life*, December 1990, p. 49.

10 Philippians 4:7, *The Holy Bible*, King James Version.

11 *Brihadaranyaka Upanishad*, Fourth Adhyaya, Fourth Brahmana, 20, 13, translated by F. Max Müller, *Sacred Books of the East*, vol. 15, Oxford: Oxford University Press, 1884, pp. 178–179.

12 William James, *The Varieties of Religious Experience*, New York: New American Library, 1958, p. 49.

13 From *The Kabir Book* by Robert Bly, copyright 1971, 1977 by Robert Bly, copyright 1977 by Seventies Press. Reprinted by permission of Beacon Press.

14 William Wordsworth, "Ode on Intimations of Immortality from Recollections of Early Childhood."

15 Pierre Teilhard de Chardin, *The Heart of Matter*, translated by Rene Hague, New York and London: Harcourt Brace Jovanovich, 1978, pp. 66–67.

16 AE (George William Russell), *The Candle of Vision*, Wheaton, Illinois: The Theosophical Publishing House, 1974, pp. 8–9.

17 Rudolf Otto, *The Idea of the Holy*, translated by John W. Harvey, New York: Oxford University Press, 1958, p. 1.

18 Wilfred Cantwell Smith, *The Meaning and End of Religion*, London: SPCK, 1978, pp. 128, 130.

19 John White, "An Interview with Nona Coxhead: The Science of Mysticism—Transcendental Bliss in Everyday Life," *Science of Mind*, September 1986, pp. 14, 70.

20 Martin Luther, as quoted in Gordon Rupp, "Luther and the Reformation," in Joel Hurstfield, ed., *The Reformation Crisis*, New York: Harper & Row, 1966, p. 23.

21 William James, op. cit., p. 298.

22 Abu Yazid, as quoted in R. C. Zaehner, *Hindu and Muslim Mysticism*, London: University of London, The Athalone Press, 1960, p. 105.

23 Sallie McFague, *Models of God: Theology for an Ecological, Nuclear Age*, Philadelphia: Fortress Press, 1987, p. 133.

24 *Marx and Engels on Religion*, Introduction by Reinhold Niebuhr, New York: Schocken Books, 1964, pp. viii–ix.

25 As quoted by Huston Smith, "The Future of God in Human Experience," *Dialogue and Alliance*, vol. 5, no. 2, Summer 1991, p. 11.

26 Maimonides, "Guide for the Perplexed," 1, 59, as quoted in Louis Jacobs, *Jewish Ethics, Philosophy, and Mysticism*, New York: Behrman House, 1969, p. 80.

27 Guru Gobind Singh, *Jaap Sahib*, English translation by Surendra Nath, New Delhi: Gobind Sadan, 1992, verses 7, 29–31.

28 Bede Griffiths, *Return to the Center*, Springfield, Illinois: Templegate, 1977, p. 71.

29 Pir Vilayat Inayat Khan, "The Significance of Religion to Human Issues in the Light of the Universal Norms of Mystical Experience," *The World Religions Speak on the Relevance of Religion in the Modern World*, Finley P. Ounne, Jr., ed., The Hague: Junk, 1970, p. 145.

30 Antony Fernando, "Outlining the Characteristics of the Ideal Individual," paper for the Inter-Religious Federation for World Peace conference, Seoul, Korea, August 20–27, 1995, p. 9.

31 Joseph Campbell, *The Hero with a Thousand Faces*; second edition, Princeton, New Jersey: Princeton University Press, 1972, p. 29.

32 Rev. Valson Thampu, "Religious Fundamentalisms in India Today," *Indian Currents*, November 2, 1995, p. 3.

33 Quoted in John Gliedman, "Mind and Matter," *Science Digest*, March 1983, p. 72.

34 Ilya Prigogine, abstract for "The Quest for Certainty," Conference on a New Space for Culture and Society, New Ideas in Science and Art, November 19–23, 1996.

35 Murray Gell-Mann, in Kitty Ferguson, *Stephen Hawking: Quest for a Theory of Everything*, London: Bantam Press, 1992, p. 30.

36 Albert Einstein, *The World As I See It*, New York: Wisdom Library, 1979; *Ideas and Opinions*, translated by Sonja Bargmann, New York: Crown Publishers, 1954.

37 Kenneth R. Miller, "Finding Darwin's God: The New Battle over Evolution," Keynote Address at Science Teaching and the Search for Origins, April 14–15, 2000, The University of Kansas, p. 10 on www.aaas.org/spp/dser/evolution/science/kennethmiller.

38 Francis Collins, in "Science and God: A Warming Trend?" *Science*, vol. 277, August 15, 1997, p. 892.

39 Fred Hoyle, quoted in Patrick Glynn, *God, the Evidence,* Rocklin, California: Prima Publishing, 1997.

40 Stephen Hawking, *A Brief History of Time: From the Big Bang to Black Holes*, London: Bantam Press, 1988.

41 Quoted in Merlin Stone, *When God was a Woman*, San Diego, California: Harcourt Brace Jovanovich, 1976, p. x.

42 Rosemary Radford Ruether, *Woman-Church: Theology and Practice of Feminist Liturgical Communities*, San Francisco: Harper & Row, 1985, p. 3.

43 Jonathan Edwards, sermon in Enfield, Connecticut, July 8, 1741. Reproduced in Charles Hurd, *A Treasury of Great American Speeches*, New York: Hawthorn Books, 1959, pp. 19–20.

44 John Welwood, "Principles of Inner Work: Psychological and Spiritual," *The Journal of Transpersonal Psychology*, 1984, vol. 16, no. 1, pp. 64–65.

45 Declaration of The World Conference of Religions on Religious and Human Solidarity, Kochi, Kerala, India, October 1–6, 1991.

46 Dr. Syed Z. Abedin, "Let There be Light," *Saudi Gazette*, Jeddah, June 1992, reprinted in Council for a Parliament of the World's Religions Newsletter, vol. 4, no. 2, August 1992, p. 2.

CHAPTER TWO
INDIGENOUS SACRED WAYS

1 Vine Deloria, Jr., *God is Red*, New York: Grosset & Dunlap, 1973, p. 267.

2 Quoted by Bob Masla, "The Healing Art of the Huichol Indians," *Many Hands: Resources for Personal and Social Transformation*," Fall 1988, p. 30.

3 John (Fire) Lame Deer and Richard Erdoes, *Lame Deer: Seeker of Visions*, New York: Pocket Books, 1972, p. 100.

4 Knud Rasmussen, *Across Arctic America*, New York: G. P. Putnam's Sons, 1927, p. 386.

5 Clyde Ford, *The Hero with an African Face: Mythical Wisdom of Traditional Africa*, New York: Bantam Books, 2000, p. 146.

6 Jo Agguisho/Oren R. Lyons, spokesman for the Traditional Elders Circle, Wolf Clan, Onondaga Nation, Haudenosaunee, Six Nations Iroquois Confederacy, from the speech to the Fourth World Wilderness Conference, September 11, 1987, p. 2.

7 Jaime de Angulo, "Indians in Overalls," *Hudson Review*, II, 1950, p. 372.

8 Kahu Kawai'i, interviewed by Mark Bochrach in *The Source*, as quoted in *Hinduism Today*, December 1988, p. 18.

9 Quoted in Matthew Fox, "Native teachings: Spirituality with power," *Creation*, January/February 1987, vol. 2, no. 6.

10 John (Fire) Lame Deer and Richard Erdoes, op. cit., p. 116.

11 Tlakaelel, talk at Interface, Watertown, Massachusetts, April 15, 1988.

12 Leonard Crow Dog and Richard Erdoes, *The Eye of the Heart*, unpublished manuscript, quoted by Joan Halifax, *Shamanic Voices: A Survey of Visionary Narratives*, New York: E. P. Dutton, 1979, p. 77.

13 Quoted in John Neihardt, *Black Elk Speaks 1932*, Lincoln, Nebraska: University of Nebraska Press, 1961, pp. 208–209.

14 John (Fire) Lame Deer with Richard Erdoes, op. cit., pp. 145–146.

15 Dhyani Ywahoo, *Voices of our Ancestors*, Boston: Shambhala Publications, 1987, p. 89.

16 Tlakaelel, op. cit.

17 Winona LaDuke, *Last Standing Woman*, Stillwater, Minnesota: Voyageur Press, 1997, p. 17.

18 Winona LaDuke, as quoted by Jamie Marks, "A campaignless campaign," *Becker County Record*, September 8, 1996, p. 1A.

19 Winona LaDuke, as quoted by Willmar Thorkelson, "Indians ask for help in regaining land," *Post-Bulletin*, Rochester, Minnesota.

20 Winona LaDuke, *Last Standing Woman*, op. cit., p. 299.

21 Rigoberta Menchú, quoted in Art Davidson, *Endangered Peoples*, San Francisco: Sierra Club Books, 1994, p. ix.

CHAPTER THREE
JUDAISM

1 Genesis 1:1. *Tanakh—The Holy Scriptures*: The New JPS Translation According to the Traditional Hebrew Text, Philadelphia: The Jewish Publication Society, 1985. This translation is used throughout this chapter.

2 Genesis 1:28.

3 Genesis 6:17.

4 Genesis 9:17.

5 Genesis 22:12.

6 Personal communication, March 24, 1989.

7 Deuteronomy 7:7.

8 Exodus 3:5.

9 Exodus 3:10.

10 Exodus 3:12, 14–15.

11 I Samuel 17:32–54, and the Ten Commandments on p. 224, Exodus 20:2–17, *New English Bible*, © Oxford University Press and Cambridge University Press, 1961, 1970.

12 Exodus 34:13.

13 I Kings 9:3.

14 Daniel 7:13–14.

15 From the Talmud and Midrash, quoted in *The Judaic Tradition*, Nahum N. Glatzer, ed., Boston: Beacon Press, 1969, p. 197.

16 The Mishnah, 4.5, 5.5, translated by Jacob Neusner, New Haven: Yale University Press, 1988, p. 388.

17 Jacob Neusner, *Recovering Judaism*, Minneapolis: Fortress Press, 2001, p. 25.

18 Jerusalem Talmud, Demai 22a, in C. G. Montefiore and H. Lowe, eds., *A Rabbinic Anthology*, New York: Schocken Books, 1974.

19 Maimonides, *The Guide of the Perplexed*.

20 Quoted in S. A. Horodezky, *Leaders of Hasidism*, London: Ha-Sefer Agency for Literature, 1928, p. 11.

21 Elie Wiesel, *Night*, New York: Bantam Books, 1960, 1982, p. 64.

22 Elie Wiesel, speech for the UConn Convocation, September 7, 1988, University of Connecticut, Storrs, Connecticut.

23 Emil Fackenheim, *God's Presence in History* (1970), quoted in Francine Klagsbrun, *Voices of Wisdom*, New York: Jonathan David Publishers, p. 435.

24 Aviezer Ravitzky, *Messianism, Zionism, and Jewish Religious*

Radicalism, Chicago: The University of Chicago Press, 1993, p. 1.

25 Michael Lerner, "Israel's War Against the Palestinians," *Tikkun,* http://tikkun.org/magazine/index/ctm/action/tikkun/issue/tik0109/article/010903.html

26 Ravitzky, op. cit.

27 Maimonides' "First Principles of Faith," as quoted in Louis Jacobs, *Principles of Jewish Faith,* Northvale, New Jersey: Jason Aronson, 1988, p. 33.

28 Ibn Gabirol, *Keter Malkhut,* quoted in Abraham J. Heschel, "One God," in *Between God and Man: An Interpretation of Judaism, from the Writings of Abraham J. Heschel,* Fritz A. Rothschild, ed., New York: Free Press, 1959, p. 106.

29 Abraham Joshua Heschel, *Man is not Alone,* New York: Farrar, Straus & Giroux, 1951, 1976, p. 112.

30 Abraham J. Heschel, "One God," op. cit., p. 104.

31 Martin Buber, in *The Way of Response: Martin Buber – Selections from His Writings,* Nahum N. Glatzer, ed., New York: Schocken Books, 1968, p. 53.

32 Isaiah 65:25, JPS Tanakh.

33 Ismar Schorsch, "Learning to Live with Less: A Jewish Perspective," in Steven C. Rockefeller and John E. Elder, *Spirit and Nature: Why the Environment is a Religious Issue,* Boston: Beacon Press, 1992, p. 35.

34 Translated from the Hebrew by Rabbi Sidney Greenberg, *Likrat Shabbat,* Bridgeport, Connecticut: Media Judaica/The Prayer Book Press, 1981, p. 61.

35 Job 1:20–21.

36 The Jewish Prayer Book, as quoted by Jocelyn Hellig, "A South African Jewish Perspective," in Martin Forward, ed., *Ultimate Visions,* Oxford: Oneworld Publications, 1995, p. 136.

37 Leviticus 11:45.

38 Talmud Berakhoth 11a, in *Ha-Suddur Ha-Shalem,* translated by Philip Birnbaum, New York: Hebrew Publishing Company, 1977, p. 14.

39 Excerpted from Ruth Gan Kagan, "The Sabbath: Judaism's Discipline for Inner Peace," paper presented at the Assembly of the World's Religions, Seoul, Korea, August 24–31, 1992, pp. 3, 7.

40 Sanhedrin 22a, quoted in *The Second Jewish Catalog,* Sharon Strassfeld and Michael Strassfeld, eds., Philadelphia: The Jewish Publication Society, 1976.

41 Rabbi Yochanan ben Nuri, Rosh Hashanah prayer quoted by Arthur Waskow, *Seasons of Our Joy,* New York: Bantam Books, 1982, p. 11.

42 Isaiah 55:6–7.

43 Michael Lerner, *Jewish Renewal: A Path to Healing and Transformation,* New York: HarperCollins, 1994, p. 365.

44 Prayer quoted by Arthur Waskow, op. cit., p. 175.

45 Mordecai M. Kaplan, "The Way I Have Come," in *Mordecai M. Kaplan: An Evaluation,* I. Eisenstein and E. Kohn, eds. , New York: Jewish Reconstructionist Foundation, 1952, p. 293.

46 Joseph I. Lieberman with Michael D'Orso, *In Praise of Public Life: The Honor and Purpose of Political Service,* New York: Simon & Schuster/Touchstone, 2000, pp. 24–25.

47 Ibid., pp. 26–27.

48 Ibid., p. 34

49 Ibid., pp. 100–101.

50 Genesis 1:26 from *The Torah,* Philadelphia: The Jewish Publication Society, 1962.

51 *The Gates of Repentance,* New York: Central Conference of American Rabbis, p. 197.

52 Susannah Heschel, "The Feminist Confrontation with Judaism," in Alan L. Berger, ed., *Judaism in the Modern World,* New York: New York University Press, 1994, p. 276.

53 Judith Plaskow, *Standing Again at Sinai,* San Francisco: HarperCollins, 1991, p. 120.

54 "Declaration of the ELCA to the Jewish Community," as quoted in Joel Beversluis, *A Sourcebook for Earth's Community of Religions,* revised edition, Grand Rapids, Michigan: CoNexus Press-Sourcebook Project, 1995, p. 170.

55 Rabbi Dovid Karpov, interviewed October 24, 1994.

56 Michael Lerner, op. cit., pp. xvii, xxviii.

CHAPTER FOUR
CHRISTIANITY

1 Publishing Department of Moscow Patriarchate, *The Russian Orthodox Church,* Moscow, 1980, p. 239 in English translation by Doris Bradbury, Moscow: Progress Publishers, 1982.

2 *The Gospel According to Thomas,* Coptic text established and translated by Guilloaumont et al., Leiden: E. J. Brill; New York: Harper & Row, 1959, verse 77.

3 Luke 2:47, 49. Most biblical quotations in this chapter are from the Revised Standard Version of the Bible, copyright 1946, 1952, 1971 by The Division of Christian Education of the National Council of the Churches of Christ in the USA. Used by permission.

4 Mark 1:10–11.

5 Dietrich Bonhoeffer, *The Cost of Discipleship,* New York: Simon & Schuster, 1959, 1995, p. 90.

6 Matthew 6:25–27.

7 Matthew 7:7.

8 Luke 9:17.

9 John 6:48.

10 William, quoted in *The Gospel in Art by the Peasants of Solentiname,* Philip and Sally Scharper, eds., Maryknoll, New York: Orbis Books, 1984, p. 42.

11 Matthew 5:21–22.

12 Matthew 5:44–45.

13 Mark 10:27.

14 Matthew 22:39.

15 Matthew 25:37–40.

16 Luke 10:25–37, The New English Bible.

17 Matthew 5:3.

18 Matthew 13:47–50, The New English Bible, Cambridge, England: Cambridge University Press, corrected impression, 1972.

19 Mark 1:15.

20 Luke 4:43.

21 Matthew 6:10.

22 Matthew 24:29–31.

23 Isaiah 29:13, The New English Bible.

24 Matthew 15:1–20, The New English Bible.

25 Matthew 23:1–3, 27–28, The New English Bible.

26 Isaiah 56:7.

27 Jeremiah 7:11.

28 Mark 11:15–18, The New English Bible.

29 Mark 8:29–30.

30 John 11:27.

31 Matthew 17:2–5.

32 John 7:16, 8:12, 23, 58.

33 Matthew 26:28.

34 Mark 11:10.

35 Mark 14:36.

36 Joachim Jeremias, *New Testament Theology: The Proclamation of Jesus*, translated by John Bowden, New York: Charles Scribner's Sons, 1971, p. 40.

37 Mark 14:41.

38 Matthew 26:64.

39 Matthew 27:11.

40 Matthew 27:46.

41 Matthew 28:18–20.

42 Elisabeth Schüssler Fiorenza, *In Memory of Her*, New York: Crossroad, 1983, 1994, p. xliv.

43 Acts 2:36.

44 Acts 26:18.

45 Philippians 3:8–10.

46 Acts 17:28.

47 *The Gospel According to Thomas*, op. cit., 82.

48 *Confessions of St. Augustine*, translated by Edward Bouverie Pusey, Chicago: Encyclopedia Britannica, vol. 18 of Great Books of the Western World, 1952, p. 64.

49 Rowan Williams, *Resurrection*, New York: The Pilgrim Press, 1984, p. 46 with quotations from John 14:19.

50 Archimandrite Chrysostomos, *The Ancient Fathers of the Desert*, Brookline, Massachusetts: Hellenic College Press, 1980, p. 78.

51 Ibid., p. 80.

52 The Solovky Memorandum, as quoted in Barbara von der Heydt, *Candles Behind the Wall*, Grand Rapids, Michigan: William B. Eerdmans Publishing Company, 1993, p. 46.

53 Mikhail S. Gorbachev, quoted in Michael Dobbs, "Soviets, Vatican to Establish Ties," *The Hartford Courant*, December 2, 1989, p. 1.

54 Vladimir Putin, quoted in Elizabeth Piper, "Putin backs Orthodox 'spiritual revival,'" *Asian Age*, May 1, 2000, p. 5.

55 Father Alexey Vlasov, interviewed October 26, 1994.

56 Father Feodor, interviewed October 29, 1994.

57 Fotini Pipili, in Iina Kyriakidou, "Greek women poised to take on all-male monastic community," *Asian Age*, October 14, 1997, p. 7.

58 St. Gregory Palamas, "Homily on the Presentation of the Holy Virgin in the Temple," in Sophocles, *22 Homilies of St. Gr. Palamas*, Athens, 1861, pp. 175–177, quoted in Vladimir Lossky, *The Mystical Theology of the Eastern Church*, New York: St. Vladimir's Seminary Press, 1976, p. 224.

59 Jim Forest, *Pilgrim to the Russian Church*, New York: Crossroad Publishing Company, 1988, p. 50.

60 From *A Hopkins Reader*, John Pick, ed., New York: Oxford University Press, 1953, quoted in D. M. Dooling, ed., *A Way of Working*, New York: Anchor Press/Doubleday, 1979, p. 6.

61 St. Francis, *Testament*, April 1226, p. 3, quoted in Jean Leclerc, Francois Vandenbroucke, and Louis Bouyer, eds., *The Spirituality of the Middle Ages*, vol. 2 of *A History of Christian Spirituality*, New York: Seabury Press, 1982, p. 289.

62 *The Cloud of Unknowing and The Book of Privy Counseling*, Garden City, New York: Image Books, 1973 edition, p. 56.

63 Martin Luther, *A Treatise on Christian Liberty*, quoted in John Oillenberger and Claude Welch, *Protestant Christianity*, New York: Charles Scribner's Sons, 1954, p. 36.

64 Ulrich Zwingli, "On True and False Religion," quoted in Harry Emerson Fosdick, ed., *Great Voices of the Reformation*, New York: Random House, 1952, p. 169.

65 John Calvin, "Instruction in Faith," quoted in Fosdick, op. cit., p. 216.

66 John Wesley, as quoted in F. L. Cross and E. A. Livingstone, eds., *The Oxford Dictionary of the Christian Church*, Oxford: Oxford University Press, 1983, p. 1467.

67 St. Teresa of Avila, *The Interior Castle*, translated by E. Allison Peers from the critical edition of P. Silverior de Santa Teresa, Garden City, New York: Image Books, 1961, p. 214.

68 John Wesley, as quoted in John Dillenberger and Claude Welch, *Protestant Christianity*, New York: Charles Scribner's Sons, 1954, p. 134.

69 Sarah Grimke, "Letters on the Equality of the Sexes and the Condition of Women" (1836–37), in *Feminism: The Essential Historical Writings*, M. Schneir, ed., New York: Vintage, 1972, p. 38.

70 The Documents of Vatican II, Walter M. Abbott, ed., New York: Guild Press, 1966, p. 665.

71 Ibid., pp. 661–662.

72 John 14:2–10, The New English Bible.

73 Paul Knitter, in John Hick and Paul F. Knitter, eds., *The Myth of Christian Uniqueness: Toward a Pluralistic Theology of Religions*, Maryknoll, New York: Orbis Books, 1987, pp. 192–193.

74 Matthew 20:28.

75 John 3:16–17, The New English Bible.

76 Archbishop Desmond Tutu, "The Face of God," *Life*, December 1990, pp. 49–50.

77 From Mother Teresa, as quoted in Malcolm Muggeridge, *A Gift for God*, London: Collins, 1975, pp. 37–38.

78 Rev. Larry Howard, interfaith service, Syracuse, New York, October 25, 1992.

79 Thomas Keating, *The Mystery of Christ: The Liturgy as Spiritual Experience*, Amity, New York: Amity House, 1987, p. 5.

80 (Thomas a Kempis), *The Imitation of Christ*, p. 139.

81 F. Ioann Kronstadtsky, as quoted in F. Veniamin Fedchenkov, *Heaven on Earth*, Moscow: Palmnik, 1994, p. 70.

82 Julia Gatta, personal communication, July 22, 1987.

83 "Brief Order for Confession and Forgiveness," *Lutheran Book of Worship*, prepared by the churches participating in the Inter-Lutheran Commission on Worship, Minneapolis, Minnesota: Augsburg Publishing House, 1978, p. 56.

84 World Council of Churches, *Baptism, Eucharist and Ministry*, Faith and Order Paper No. 111, Geneva, 1982, p. 2.

85 Father Appolinari, interviewed October 28, 1994.

86 John 1:9.

87 Jim Forest, *Pilgrim to the Russian Church*, op. cit., p. 72.

88 Thomas Merton, *Contemplative Prayer*, Garden City, New York: Image Books, 1969, p. 67.

89 Bishop Paulos Mar Gregorios, World Congress of Spiritual Concord, Rishikesh, India, December 11, 1993.

90 Interview with Professor Kathleen Dugan, February 4, 1993.

91 *The Way of a Pilgrim and The Pilgrim Continues His Way*, translated by Helen Bacovcin, New York/London: Doubleday, 1978, 1992, p. 160.

92 Luke 1:38.

93 Quoted in Jim Forest, *Pilgrim to the Russian Church*, New York: Crossroad Publishing Company, 1988, p. 63.

94   *New York Times*, as reprinted in "The Gospel of Life," Indian Currents, April 8, 1995, p. 1.

95   Associated Press, Vatican City: "Only Catholicism 'proper': Vatican," *The Globe and Mail*, September 6, 2000, A14; Philip Pullella (Reuters), "Vatican says no religion equals Roman Catholicism," *Asian Age*, September 6, 2000, p. 5.

96   Young Communist League, as quoted by Gerardo Tena, "Catholic imagery for papal visit transforms Havana," *Asian Age*, January 20, 1998, p. 6.

97   Sean McDonagh, *The Greening of the Church*, Maryknoll, New York: Orbis Books, p. 65.

98   Quoted in Don A. Schanche and Russell Chandler, Los Angeles Times, "Tensions confront pope in U.S.," *The Hartford Courant*, September 11, 1987, p. 1.

99   "Archbishop says religion reduced to a hobby in UK," *Asian Age*, July 6, 1996, p. 10.

100 Harvey Cox, *Fire from Heaven: The Rise of Pentecostal Spirituality and the Reshaping of Religion in the Twenty-first Century*, Reading, Massachusetts: Addison-Wesley, 1995.

101 Leslie Scrivener, in *Toronto Star*, October 8, 1995, as quoted in Margaret M. Poloma, "Mysticism and Identity Formation in Social Context: The Case of the Pentecostal-Charismatic Movement," The Seventh International Congress of Professors World Peace Academy, Washington, D.C., November 1997, p. 5.

102 Roman I. Bilas, interviewed October 25, 1994.

103 Members of African Independent Churches Report on their Pilot Study of the History and Theology of their Churches, "Speaking for Ourselves," Braamfontein, South Africa: Institute for Contextural Theology, 1985, pp. 23–24.

104 Martin Luther King, Jr., "An Experiment in Love," in *A Testament of Hope: The Essential Writings of Martin Luther King, Jr.*, James Melvin Washington, ed., San Francisco: Harper & Row, 1986, p. 16.

105 Acts 4:32–35.

106 Gustavo Gutierrez, quoted in Phillip Berryman, *Liberation Theology*, New York: Pantheon Books, 1987, p. 33.

107 Desmond Tutu, quoted in Charles Vila-Vicencio, "Tough and Compassionate: Desmond Mpilo Tutu," in Leonard Hulley, Louise Kretzschmar, and Luke Lungile Pato, eds., *Archbishop Tutu: Prophetic Witness in South Africa*, Cape Town: Human and Rousseau, 1996, pp. 41–42.

108 Ibid., p. 37.

109 Ibid., p. 38.

110 Francis Cull, "Desmond Tutu: Man of Prayer," in Hulley et al., op. cit., pp. 31–32.

111 Desmond Tutu, in Vila-Vicencio, op. cit., pp. 44–45.

112 Bakole Wa Ilunga, *Paths of Liberation: A Third World Spirituality*, Maryknoll, New York: Orbis Books, 1984, p. 92.

113 Dwight N. Hopkins, ed., *Black Faith and Public Talk*, Maryknoll, New York: Orbis Books, 1999, pp. 1–2.

114 James H. Cone, "Looking Back, Going Forward," in Hopkins, op. cit., p. 257.

115 1 Corinthians 11:7–12.

116 Fiorenza, op. cit., p. xx.

117 Ivone Gebara and Maria Clara Bingemer, *Mary, Mother of God, Mother of the Poor*, Maryknoll, New York: Orbis Books, 1989, as excerpted in Ursula King, ed., *Feminist Theology from the Third World*, Maryknoll, New York, Orbis Books, 1994, pp. 277, 280–281.

118 Sally McFague, *Models of God: Theology for an Ecological, Nuclear Age*, Philadelphia: Fortress Press, 1987, pp. 101, 106.

119 Thomas Berry, remarks at "Seeking the True Meaning of Peace" conference in San Jose, Costa Rica, June 27, 1989.

120 Jyoti Sahi, "The Ultimate Vision of the Living Seed," in Martin Forward, ed., *Ultimate Visions*, Oxford: Oneworld Publications, 1995, pp. 241–242.

121 "Decade to Overcome Violence," World Council of Church website, www.wcc-coe.org, October 1, 2001.

CHAPTER FIVE
ISLAM

1   *The Holy Qur'an*, XCVI:1–5, English translation by Abdullah Yusuf Ali, Durban, R.S.A.: Islamic Propagation Center International, 1946. This translation is used throughout this chapter, by permission. Note that despite the layout of this translation, the Qur'an is not a work of poetry.

2   Abu Abdallah Muhammad Bukhari, *Kitab jami as-sahih*, translated by M. M. Khan as *Sahih al-Bukhari*, Lahore: Ashraf, 1978–80, quoted in Annemarie Schimmel, *And Muhammad is His Messenger*, Chapel Hill, North Carolina: University of North Carolina Press, 1985, p. 11.

3   Sura 8:18.

4   Maulana M. Ubaidul Akbar, *The Orations of Muhammad*, Lahore: M. Ashraf, 1954, p. 78.

5   Sura 41:6.

6   Sura 28:56.

7   Hadith quoted by Annemarie Schimmel, *And Muhammad is His Messenger*, Chapel Hill, North Carolina: University of North Carolina Press, 1985, pp. 48 and 55.

8   *The Holy Qur'an*, III:104.

9   Quoted by Mahmoud Ayoub, *The Qur'an and its Interpreters*, Albany: State University of New York Press, 1984, vol. 1, p. 14.

10 Footnote 5778, Sura 74:1, p. 1640.

11 Sura 42:15.

12 Islamic Society of North America, "Islam at a Glance," Plainfield, Indiana: Islamic Teaching Center.

13 Abu Hashim Madani, quoted in Samuel L. Lewis, *In the Garden*, New York: Harmony Books/Lama Foundation, 1975, p. 136.

14 Frithjof Schuon, *Understanding Islam*, translated by D. M. Matheson, London: George Allen & Unwin, 1963, p. 59.

15 Sura 2:136.

16 Farid Esack, personal communication, March 29, 1998.

17 Farid Esack, Qur'an, *Liberation and Pluralism: An Islamic Perspective of Interreligious Solidarity against Oppression*, Oxford: Oneworld Publications, 1997, p. 4.

18 Ibid., p. 223.

19 Ibid., p. 222.

20 Ibid., p. 259.

21 Farid Esack, personal communication, March 29, 1998.

22 Sura 32:16–17.

23 Sura 3:63.

24 Sura 41:37.

25 Quoted by Abdur-Rahman Ibrahim Doi, "Sunnism," *Islamic Spirituality: Foundations*, Seyyed Hossein Nasr, ed., New York: Crossroad, 1987, p. 158.

26 Sura 17:13–14.

27 Sura 70:16–18.

28 Quoted by Muhammad Rida al-Muzaffar, *The Faith of Shi'a Islam*, London: The Muhammadi Trust, 1982, p. 35.

29 Hadith #535 cited in Badi'uz-Zaman Furuzanfar, *Ahadith-i Mathnawi*, Tehran, 1334 sh./1955, in Persian, quoted in Annemarie Schimmel, *Mystical Dimensions of Islam*, Chapel Hill: University of North Carolina Press, 1975, p. 118.

30 Rabi'a al-'Adawiyya al-Qaysiyya, quoted in Abu Talib, *Qut al-Qulub*, II, Cairo, A. H. 1310, p. 57, as quoted in Margaret Smith, *Rabi'a the Mystic and her Fellow-Saints in Islam*, Cambridge: Cambridge University Press, 1928, 1984, p. 102.

31 Jalal al-Din Rumi, opening lines of the *Mathnawi*, as translated by Edmund Helminski, *The Ruins of the Heart: Selected Lyric Poetry of Jelaluddin Rumi*, Putney, Vermont: Threshold Books, 1981, p. 20.

32 Jalal al-Din Rumi, *Mathnawi-i ma'nawi*, ed. and translated by Reynold A. Nicholson, London, 1925–40, vol. 4, line 2102.

33 Hadith of the Prophet, #352 in Zaman Furuzanfar, *Ahadith-i Mathnawi*, op. cit.

34 Quoted in Javad Nurbakhsh, *Sufism: Meaning, Knowledge, and Unity*, New York: Khaniqahi-Nimatullahi Publications, 1981, pp. 19, 21.

35 Al-Ghazali, in *The Faith and Practice of Al-Ghazali*, translated by William Montgomery Watt, Oxford: Oneworld Publications, 1953, 1994, pp. 77, 130.

36 Idries Shah, *The Sufis*, London: Jonathan Cape, 1964, p. 76.

37 Jalal al-Din Rumi, *Mathnawi*, VI, 3220–3246, as translated by Coleman Barks in *Rumi: We Are Three*, Athens, Georgia: Maypop Books, 1987, pp. 54–55.

38 Sura 2:256.

39 Hadith quoted by Syed Ali Ashraf, "The Inner Meaning of the Islamic Rites: Prayer, Pilgrimage, Fasting, Jihad," in *Islamic Spirituality: Foundations*, op. cit., p. 114.

40 Hammudah Abdalati, *Islam in Focus*, Indianapolis, Indiana: American Trust Publications, 1975, p. 88.

41 Hadith of the Prophet, as quoted in Fakhr al-Din Al-Razi, *Tafsir al-Fakhr al-Razi*, 21 vols., Mecca: al-Kaktabah al-Tijariyyah, 1990, vol. 7, p. 232.

42 Sura 22:39–40.

43 Sura 2:190.

44 Sura 2:217, 192.

45 M. R. Bawa Muhaiyaddeen, "Islam's Hidden Beauty: The Sufi Teachings of M. R. Bawa Muhaiyaddeen," tape from New Dimensions Foundation, San Francisco, 1989, side 1.

46 Treaty cited in Philip K. Hitti, *Islam and the West*, Princeton, New Jersey: D. Van Nostrand, 1962, p. 112.

47 Uzbek Khan, 1313 charter granted to Metropolitan Peter, as quoted in *Al Risala*, June 1994, p. 12.

48 Dalil-ul-Arifin, p. 37, as quoted in W. D. Begg, *The Holy Biography of Hazrat Khwaja Muinuddin Chishti*, Botswana, Africa: G. N. Khan, 1979, p. 41.

49 Indonesian President Suharto, quoted in *Hinduism Today*, July 1989, p. 20.

50 Annemarie Schimmel, speaking in "Islam's Hidden Beauty," tape from New Dimensions Foundation, San Francisco, 1989, side 1.

51 Jalal al-Din Rumi, *Mathnawi*, IV, in *Rumi: We Are Three*: op. cit., Barks, p. 52.

52 Muhammad Mashuq ibn Ally, "Theology of Islamic Liberation," in Dan Cohn-Sherbok, ed., *World Religions and Human Liberation*, Maryknoll, New York: Orbis Books, 1992, p. 47.

53 Anouar Majid, *Unveiling Traditions: Postcolonial Islam in a Polycentric World*, Durham/London: Duke University Press, 2000, p. 131.

54 Amina Wadud, *Qur'an and Woman*, New York: Oxford University Press, 1999, pp. ix–x, xiii, xx (italics added); Amina Wadud, "Alternative Qur'anic Interpretation and the Statues of Muslim Women," in Gisela Webb, ed., *Windows of Faith: Muslim Women Scholar-Activists in North America*, Syracuse: Syracuse University Press, 2000, p. 11.

55 Seyyed Hossein Nasr, "The Pertinence of Islam to the Modern World," *The World Religions Speak on the Relevance of Religion in the Modern World*, Finley P. Dunne Jr., ed., The Hague: Junk, 1970, p. 133.

56 "Islamic TV channel to counter the West," *Asian Age*, October 20, 1998, p. 1.

57 The First World Conference on Muslim Education, quoted in Syed Ali Ashraf, *New Horizon in Muslim Education*, Cambridge, England: Hodder & Stoughton/The Islamic Academy, 1985, p. 4.

58 Azizah Y. al-Hibri, "The Taliban and Islamic Teaching," in *Sightings*, an e-mail journal published by the Martin Marty Center at the University of Chicago Divinity School, March 14, 2001.

59 Anwar Ibrahim, "Democracy is missing in terror and tyranny," *International Herald Tribune*, reprinted in *Asian Age*, October 15, 2001, p. 12.

60 John L. Esposito, *The Islamic Threat: Myth or Reality?*, New York: Oxford University Press, 1993, pp. ix–x.

61 Asaf Hussain, "Fundamentalism—An Islamic Perspective," *International Interfaith Center News*, December 2000, p. 7.

62 Mahmoon-al-Rasheed, "Islam, Nonviolence, and Social Transformation," Glenn D. Paige, Chaiwat Satha-Anand, and Sarah Gilliatt, eds., Honolulu: University of Hawaii, Center for Global Nonviolence Planning Project, 1993, p. 70.

63 Dr. A. K. Abu'l Majd, quoted in the video "Islam," Smithsonian World series, Smithsonian Institution and WETA, Washington, D.C., originally broadcast July 22, 1987, transcript pp. 6, 17.

CHAPTER SIX
NEW RELIGIOUS MOVEMENTS

1 Friday M. Mbon, "The Social Impact of Nigeria's New Religious Movements," in James A. Beckford, ed., *New Religious Movements and Rapid Social Change*, Paris and London: Unesco/Sage Publications, 1986, p. 177.

2 Quoted in Ernest Cashmore, *Rastaman*, London: Unwin Paperbacks, 1983, p. 22.

3 www.bobmarley.com/life/rastafari/beliefs.html

4 www.watchtower.org

5 *Tenri kyoso den* ("Life of the Founder of the Tenri-kyo Sect") compiled by the Tenri-kyo doshi-kai, Tenri, 1913, quoted in Ichiro Hori, *Folk Religion in Japan*, Chicago: University of Chicago Press, 1968, p. 237.

6 Miki Nakayama, *Ofudesaki: The Tip of the Divine Writing Brush*, Tenri City, Japan: The Headquarters of the Tenrikyo Church, 1971, verses 1–3.

7 Sandra Pfortmiller, "Messages," *The National Spiritualist Summit*, January 1989, p. 31.

8 Andrew Wilson, "Visions of the Spirit World: Sang Hun Lee's 'Life in the Spirit World and on Earth' Compared with Other Spiritualist Accounts," *Journal of Unification Studies 2*, 1998, p. 123.

9 Justice Anthony M. Kennedy, United States Supreme

Court majority opinion summation in *The Church of the Lucumi vs. The City of Hialeah*, June 11, 1993.

10 Rev. William Kingsley Opoku, personal communication, February 6, 1993.

11 Tom Johnson, personal communication, February 19, 1990.

12 "A Brief Biography of Rajinder Singh," Delhi: Sawan Kirpal Publications Spiritual Society, p. 11.

13 Starhawk, *The Spiral Dance: A Rebirth of the Ancient Religion of the Great Goddess*, San Francisco: Harper & Row, 1979, pp. 2–3.

14 John Seed, "Anthropocentrism," *Awakening in the Nuclear Age*, Issue #14 (Summer/Fall 1986), p. 11.

15 Chief Seattle, "Chief Seattle's Message," quoted in *Thinking Like a Mountain: Toward a Council of All Beings*, John Seed, Joanna Macy, Pat Fleming, and Arne Naess, eds., Santa Cruz, California: New Society Publishers, 1988, p. 71.

15 J. E. Lovelock, *Gaia: A new look at life on Earth*, Oxford: Oxford University Press, pp. 9, 11.

17 James Lovelock, *The Ages of Gaia*, New York: Bantam Books, 1990, p. 206.

18 Peter Russell, "Endangered Earth: Psychological roots of the environmental crisis," *Link Up*, Issue #38 (Spring 1989), pp. 7–8.

19 Marianne Williamson, *Illuminata*, New York: Riverhead Books, 1994, p. xvii.

20 Julia Butterfly Hill, circleoflifefoundation.org./review4.html

21 David Albert, "A Children's Story: Gaura Devi Saves the Trees," *Awakening in the Nuclear Age*, op. cit., p. 15.

22 Sandra Duarte de Souza, "Religious Transit and Ecological Spirituality in Brazil," paper presented at "The Spiritual Supermarket: Religious Pluralism in the 21st Century," April 19–22, 2001, London School of Economics, sponsored by the Center for Studies on New Religions, Italy, p. 4.

23 H. P. Blavatsky, *The Key to Theosophy*, Los Angeles: The United Lodge of Theosophists, 1920, p. 3.

24 H. P. Blavatsky, "Is Theosophy a Religion," [to follow].

27 "The Baha'is: A Profile of the Baha'i Faith and its Worldwide Community," Leicestershire, UK: Baha'i Publishing Trust, p. 42.

28 Svetlana Dorzhieva, interviewed October 26, 1994.

25 'Abdu'l-Baha', as quoted in "One World, One Faith," New Delhi: National Spiritual Assemblies of the Baha'is of India, 1979, p. 3.

26 Adapted from "The Baha'i Faith," New York: Baha'i International Community (unpaginated).

29 Frithjof Schuon, *Understanding Islam*, London: George Allen & Unwin Ltd., translated from French, 1963, p. 41.

30 Dr. Marc Galanter, in Daniel Coleman, "A Cultist's Mind," *New York Times*, April 21, 1993, p. A21.

31 Reiko Hatsumi, "In a spiritual vacuum anything can flourish, even destruction," *Asian Age*, May 28, 1995, p. 9.

32 Massimo Introvigne, "'There is no place for us to go but up': New Religious Movements and Violence," Center for Studies on New Religions, www.cesnur.org, 2001, p. 5.

33 Robert Jay Lifton, *Destroying the World to Save It: Aum Shinrikyo, Apocalyptic Violence and the New Global Terrorism*, New York: Metropolitan Books/Henry Holt and Company, 1999, pp. 202–213.

CHAPTER SEVEN
TWENTY-FIRST-CENTURY PLURALISM

1 Diana Eck, "A New Geo-Religious Reality," paper presented at the World Conference on Religion and Peace Sixth World Assembly, Riva del Garda, Italy, November 1994, p. 1.

2 Gyorgy Bulanyi, "Church and Peace: Vision and Reality," address at Overcoming Violence, a Church and Peace Conference in Pecel, Hungary, April 1995, as printed in *Church and Peace*, Spring 1995, p. 4.

3 Charles Strozier et al., "Religious Militancy or 'Fundamentalism,'" *Religion and Human Rights*, New York: The Project on Religion and Human Rights, 1994, p. 19.

4 Ewert Cousins, Speech at North American Interfaith Conference, Buffalo, New York, May 1991.

5 Pope John Paul II, quoted in Richard N. Ostling, "A Summit for Peace in Assisi," *Time*, November 10, 1986, p. 78.

6 Wangari Maathai, speaking at the Oxford Global Survival Conference, quoted in *The Temple of Understanding Newsletter*, Fall 1988, p. 2.

7 Swami Vivekananda, speech for the Parliament of the World's Religions, Chicago, 1893.

8 "Towards a Global Ethic," Assembly of Religious and Spiritual Leaders, at the Parliament of World Religions, Chicago, 1993.

9 The Right Rev. William E. Swing, "United Religions Initiative 2000: An Invitation to Share the Vision, an Invitation to Change the World," July 1996 pamphlet.

10 www.religioustolerance.org/news-01oct.html

11 Gordon Kaufman, *The Myth of Christian Uniqueness*, Maryknoll, New York: Orbis Books, 1987.

GLOSSARY

In the glossary, most words are accompanied by a guide to pronunciation. This guide gives an accepted pronunciation as simply as possible. Syllables are separated by a space and those that are stressed are underlined. Letters are pronounced in the usual manner for English unless they are clarified in the following list.

a *as in*	flat		ow	now
aa	father		u	but
aw	saw		ă, ĕ, ŏ, ŭ,	about (unaccented vowels represented by "ə" in some phonetic alphabets)
ay	pay			
ai	there		er, ur, ir	fern, fur, fir
ee	see			
e	let		ch	church
i	pity		j	jet
ī	high		ng	sing
o	not		sh	shine
ŏŏ	book		wh	where
oo	food		y	yes
oy	boy		kh	guttural aspiration (ch in Welsh and German)
ō	no			

absolutist Someone who holds rigid, literal, exclusive belief in the doctrines of their religion.

agnosticism (ag <u>nos</u> ti siz ĕm) The belief that if there is anything beyond this life, it is impossible for humans to know it.

Allah (<u>aa</u> lă) The one God, in Islam.

angel In the Zoroastrian, Jewish, Christian, and Islamic traditions, an invisible servant of God.

Annunciation (ă <u>nun</u> see ay shun) In Christianity, the appearance of an angel to the Virgin Mary to tell her that she would bear Jesus, conceived by the Holy Spirit.

anthropocentrism (<u>an</u> thro po <u>sen</u> triz ĕm) The assumption that the whole universe revolves around the human species.

apocalypse (ă <u>paw</u> kă lips) In Judaism and Christianity, the dramatic end of the present age.

Ark of the Covenant In Judaism, the shrine containing God's commandments to Moses.

atheism (<u>ay</u> thee is em) Belief that there is no deity.

baptism A Christian sacrament by which God cleanses all sin and makes one a sharer in the divine life, and a member of Christ's body, the Church.

barakah (bă <u>raa</u> ka) In Islamic mysticism, the spiritual wisdom and blessing transmitted from master to pupil.

Bar Mitzvah (baar <u>mitz</u> vă) The coming-of-age ceremony for a Jewish boy.

Bat Mitzvah (bat <u>mitz</u> vă) The coming-of-age ceremony for a Jewish girl in some modern congregations.

Beatitudes (bee <u>at</u> ĕ toods) Short statements by Jesus about those who are most blessed.

Bhagavad-Gita (<u>ba</u> gă văd <u>gee</u> tă) A portion of the Hindu epic *Mahabharata* in which Lord Krishna specifies ways of spiritual progress.

Brahman (<u>braa</u> măn) The impersonal Ultimate Principle in Hinduism.

caliph (<u>kay</u> lif) In Sunni Islam, the successor to the Prophet.

catholic Universal, all-inclusive. Christian churches referring to themselves as Catholic claim to be the representatives of the ancient undivided Christian church.

charisma (kă <u>riz</u> mă) A rare personal magnetism, often ascribed to a founder of a religion.

Common Era Years after the traditional date used for the birth of Jesus, previously referred to in exclusively Christian terms as AD and now abbreviated to CE as opposed to BCE ("before Common Era").

communion *see* eucharist.

confirmation A Christian sacrament by which awareness of the Holy Spirit is enhanced.

cosmogony (kos <u>mog</u> ŏn ee) A model of the evolution of the universe.

creed A formal statement of the beliefs of a particular religion.

cult Any religion that focuses on worship of a particular person or deity.

davening (daa věn ing) In Hasidic Judaism, prayer.

denomination (di nom ě nay shun) One of the Protestant branches of Christianity.

dervish (der vish) A Sufi ascetic, in the Muslim tradition.

dhimmi (dě hem ee) A person of a non-Muslim religion whose right to practice that religion is protected within an Islamic society.

diaspora (dī ass po ra) Collectively, the practitioners of a faith living beyond their traditional homeland. When spelled with a capital "D", the dispersal of the Jews after the Babylonian exile.

dogma (dog mǎ) A system of beliefs declared to be true by a religion.

ecumenism (ek yoo mě niz ěm) Rapprochement between branches of Christianity or among all faiths.

Epiphany (ee pi fǎni) "Manifestation"; in Christianity the recognition of Jesus's spiritual kingship by the three Magi.

eschatology (es kǎ tol ǒ ji) Beliefs about the end of the world and of humanity.

Essenes (es eenz) Monastic Jews who were living communally, apart from the world, about the time of Jesus.

eucharist (yoo kǎ rist) The Christian sacrament by which believers are renewed in the mystical body of Christ by partaking of bread and wine, understood as his body and blood.

evangelism (i van jě liz ěm) Ardent preaching of the Christian gospel.

exclusivism The idea that one's own religion is the only valid way.

excommunication Exclusion from participation in the Christian sacraments (applied particularly to Roman Catholicism), which is a bar to gaining access to heaven.

exegesis (ex a gee sis) Critical examination of a religious text.

Fatiha (fat haa) The first *sura* of the Qur'an.

fundamentalism (fun dǎ men tǎl iz ěm) Insistence on what people perceive as the historical form of their religion, in contrast to more contemporary influences. This ideal sometimes takes extreme, rigidly exclusive, or violent forms.

Gentile (jen tīl) Any person who is not of Jewish faith or origin.

Geonim In Judaism, the administrators of the two great rabbinic academies in medieval Babylon.

ghetto An urban area occupied by those rejected by a society, such as quarters for Jews in some European cities.

gnosis (nō sis) Intuitive knowledge of spiritual realities.

Gnosticism (nos ti siz ěm) Mystical perception of spiritual knowledge.

gospel In Christianity, the "good news" that God has raised Jesus from the dead and in so doing has begun the transformation of the world.

Hadith (haad ith) In Islam, a traditional report about a reputed saying or action of the Prophet Muhammad.

haggadah (hǎ gaa dǎ) The non-legal part of the Talmud and Midrash.

hajj (haaj) The holy pilgrimage to Mecca, for Muslims.

halakhah (haa laa khaa) Jewish legal decision and the parts of the Talmud dealing with laws.

Hasidism (has īd iz ěm) Ecstatic Jewish piety, dating from eighteenth-century Poland.

heretic (hair i tik) A member of an established religion whose views are unacceptable to the orthodoxy.

heyoka (hay yō kǎ) "Contrary" wisdom or a person who embodies it, in some Native American spiritual traditions.

hijab (hay jab) The veiling of women for the sake of modesty in Islam.

hijrah (hij rǎ) Muhammad's migration from Mecca to Medina.

Holocaust (haw lō cawst) The genocidal killing of six million Jews by the Nazis during World War II.

icon (ī kon) A sacred image, a term used especially for the paintings of Jesus, Mary, and the saints of the Eastern Orthodox Christian Church.

ijtihad (ij ti haad) In Islam, reasoned interpretation of sacred law by a qualified scholar.

Imam (i maam) In Shi'ism, the title for the person carrying the initiatic tradition of the Prophetic Light.

imam (i maam) A leader of Muslim prayer.

immanent Present in Creation.

incarnation Physical embodiment of the divine.

inclusivism The idea that all religions can be accommodated within one religion.

indigenous (in dij ě něs) Native to an area.

indulgence In Roman Catholic Christianity, granting of a remission of sins.

infidel (in fid ěl) The Muslim and Christian term for

"nonbeliever," which each tradition often applies to the other.

Inquisition (in kwi <u>zi</u> shun) The use of force and terror to eliminate heresies and nonbelievers in the Christian Church starting in the thirteenth century.

interfaith dialogue Appreciative communication between people of different religions.

Islamist A person seeking to establish Islamic states in which the rule of God is supreme.

jihad (<u>ji</u> had) The Muslim's struggle against the inner forces that prevent God-realization and the outer barriers to establishment of the divine order.

jinn (jin) In Islam, an invisible being of fire.

justified In Christianity, having been absolved of sin in the eyes of God.

Kabbalah (kă <u>baa</u> lă) The Jewish mystical tradition.

kenotic (ki <u>not</u> ik) In Russian Orthodox Christianity, belief in the monastic pattern of ascetic poverty combined with service in the world.

kensho (ken shō) Sudden enlightenment, in Zen Buddhism.

kosher (<u>kō</u> sher) Ritually acceptable, applied to foods in Jewish Orthodoxy.

kufr (<u>koŏ</u> fer) In Islam, the sin of atheism, of ingratitude to God.

liberal Flexible in approach to religious tradition; inclined to see tradition as metaphorical rather than literal truth.

liberation theology Christianity expressed as solidarity with the poor.

liturgy (<u>lit</u> ĕr jee) In Christianity and Judaism, the rites of public worship.

mass The Roman Catholic term for the Christian eucharist.

materialism The tendency to consider material possessions and comforts more important than spiritual matters, or the philosophical position that nothing exists except matter and that there are no supernatural dimensions to life.

medicine Spiritual power, in some indigenous traditions.

Messiah The "anointed," the expected king and deliverer of the Jews; a term later applied by Christians to Jesus.

Midrash (<u>mid</u> rash) The literature of delving into the Jewish Torah.

mikva (<u>mik</u> vă) A deep bath for ritual cleansing in Judaism.

millennium One thousand years, a term used in Christianity and certain newer religions for a hoped-for period of a thousand years of holiness and happiness, with Christ ruling the earth, as prophesied in the Book of Revelation.

minyan (<u>min</u> yăn) The quorum of ten adult males required for Jewish communal worship.

Mishnah In Judaism, the systematic summation of the legal teachings of the oral tradition of the Torah.

mitzvah (<u>mitz</u> vă) (plural: *mitzvot*) In Judaism, a divine commandment or sacred deed in fulfillment of a commandment.

moksha (<u>mōk</u> shă) In Hinduism, liberation of the soul from illusion and suffering.

monistic (<u>mon</u> iz tik) Believing in the concept of life as a unified whole, without a separate "spiritual" realm.

monotheistic (mon ō <u>thee</u> iz tik) Believing in a single God.

muezzin (moo <u>ez</u> in) In Islam, one who calls the people to prayer from a high place.

mujahid (moo jă hid) In Islam, a selfless fighter in the path of Allah.

muni (<u>moo</u> nee) A Jain monk.

murshid (<u>moor</u> shid) A spiritual teacher, in esoteric Islam.

mystic One who values inner spiritual experience in preference to external authorities and scriptures.

mysticism The intuitive perception of spiritual truths beyond the limits of reason.

myth A symbolic story expressing ideas about reality or spiritual history.

nontheistic Perceiving spiritual reality without a personal deity or deities.

original sin The Christian belief that all human beings are bound together in prideful egocentricity. In the Bible, this is described mythically as an act of disobedience on the part of Adam and Eve.

orisa The Yoruba term for a deity, often used in speaking of West African religions in general.

orthodox Adhering to the established tradition of a religion.

parable (<u>par</u> ă bŭl) An allegorical story.

Paraclete (<u>par</u> ă kleet) The entity that Jesus said would come after his death to help the people.

penance An act of self-punishment to atone for wrongdoings.

Pentateuch (pen tă took) The five books of Moses at the beginning of the Hebrew Bible.

Pentecost (pen tĕ kost) The occasion when the Holy Spirit descended upon the disciples of Jesus after his death.

Pharisees (fair ĕ seez) In Roman-ruled Judaea, liberals who tried to practice Torah in their lives.

phenomenology An approach to the study of religions that involves appreciative investigation of religious phenomena to comprehend their meaning for their practitioners.

pluralism An appreciation of the diversity of religions.

pogrom An attack against Jews.

polytheistic (pol ĕ thee iz ĕm) Believing in many deities.

pope The Bishop of Rome and head of the Roman Catholic Church.

profane Worldly, secular, as opposed to sacred.

Purgatory (pur gă tor ee) In some branches of Christianity, an intermediate after-death state in which souls are purified from sin.

rabbi (rab ī) Historically, a Jewish teacher; at present, the ordained spiritual leader of a Jewish congregation.

relic In some forms of Christianity, part of the body or clothing of a saint.

ritual A repeated, patterned religious act.

Sabbath (sab ăth) The day of the week set aside for rest and worship in Judaism and Christianity.

sacrament Outward and visible signs of inward and spiritual grace in Christianity. Almost all churches recognize baptism and the eucharist as sacraments; some churches recognize five others as well.

sacred The realm of the extraordinary, beyond everyday perceptions, the supernatural, holy.

Sadducees (saj ŭ seez) In Roman-ruled Judaea, wealthy and priestly Jews.

Santeria The combination of African and Christian practices which developed in Cuba.

sect A sub-group within a larger tradition.

Seder Ceremonial Jewish meal in remembrance of the Passover.

see An area under the authority of a Christian bishop or archbishop.

Semite (sem ite) A Jew, Arab, or other, of eastern Mediterranean origin.

Shahadah (shă haa dă) The central Muslim expression of faith: "There is no god but God," and Muhammad is the messenger of God.

shaman (shaa măn) A "medicine person," a man or woman who has undergone spiritual ordeals and can communicate with the spirit world to help the people in indigenous traditions.

Shari'ah (shă ree ă) The divine law, in Islam.

shaykh (shaik) A spiritual master, in the esoteric Muslim tradition.

Shekhinah (she kī nă) God's presence in the world, in Judaism.

Shi'a, (shee īt) (adj. Shi'ite) The minority branch of Islam, which feels that Muhammad's legitimate successors were 'Ali and a series of Imams; a follower of this branch.

shirk (shirk) The sin of believing in any divinity except the one God, in Islam.

Sufism (soo fis ĕm) The mystical path in Islam.

Sunnah (soo nă) The behavior of the Prophet Muhammad, used as a model in Islamic law.

Sunni (soo nee) A follower of the majority branch of Islam, which feels that successors to Muhammad are to be chosen by the Muslim community.

sura (soŏ ră) A chapter of the Qur'an.

symbol Visible representation of an invisible reality or concept.

synagogue (sin ă gog) A meeting place for Jewish study and worship.

syncretism (sing kri tis ĕm) A form of religion in which otherwise differing traditions are blended.

synod In Christianity, a council of church officials called to reach agreement on doctrines and administration.

synoptic (sin op tik) Referring to three similar books of the Christian Bible: Matthew, Mark, and Luke.

talit (ta lit) A shawl traditionally worn by Jewish men during prayers.

Talmud (tal moŏd) Jewish law and lore, as finally compiled in the sixth century CE.

Tanakh (ta nakh) The Jewish scriptures.

tariqa (ta ree ka) In Islam, an esoteric Sufi order.

t'fillin (tĕ fil in) A small leather box with verses about God's covenant with the Jewish people, bound to the forehead and arm.

theistic (thee is tik) Believing in a God or gods.

Torah (tō raa) The Pentateuch; also, the whole body of Jewish teaching and law.

transcendent Existing outside the material universe.

transpersonal Referring to an eternal, infinite reality, in contrast to the finite material world.

transubstantiation (tran sŭb stan shee ay shun) In some branches of Christianity, the idea that wine and bread are mystically transformed into the blood and body of Christ during the eucharist sacrament.

Trinity The Christian doctrine that in the One God are three divine persons: the Father, the Son, and the Holy Spirit.

tzaddik (<u>tzaa</u> dik) An enlightened Jewish mystic.

ulama (oo lă <u>maa</u>) The influential leaders in traditional Muslim society, including spiritual leaders, *imams*, teachers, state scribes, market inspectors, and judges.

ummah (o <u>maa</u>) The Muslim community.

Upanishads (oo <u>pan</u> i shăds) The philosophical part of the Vedas in Hinduism, intended only for serious seekers.

vision quest In indigenous traditions, a solitary ordeal undertaken to seek spiritual guidance about one's mission in life.

Voodoo (<u>voo</u> doo) Latin American and Caribbean ways of working with the spirit world, a blend of West African and Catholic Christian teachings.

zakat (zak at) Spiritual tithing in Islam.

Zealots Jewish resistance fighters who fought the Romans and were defeated in the siege of Jerusalem.

CREDITS

INDEX

Page numbers in *italic* relate to topics mentioned in illustration captions.